w/D

THE POISON SKY

J. Ruskin (se ipsum)
del.

John Ruskin. Self-portrait, c. 1873. Pencil. Courtesy of the Education Trust, Brantwood, Coniston.

The
Poison Sky

Myth and Apocalypse

in Ruskin

RAYMOND E. FITCH

OHIO UNIVERSITY PRESS
Athens, London

Library of Congress Cataloging in Publication Data
Fitch, Raymond E   1930–
    The poison sky.
    Bibliography: p.
    Includes index.
    1.   Ruskin, John, 1891–1900—Criticism and interpreta-
tion. I.   Title. II.   Title: Myth and apocalypse in
Ruskin.
PR5264.F5   828'.809   70-122097
ISBN 0-8214-0090-8
ISBN 0-8214-0642-6 pbk.

For Pat and Matt

CONTENTS

Acknowledgments

My expressions of them here cannot begin to fit the debts I feel, and to name those colleagues and friends who have assisted me in this study may be to associate them with its shortcomings and thereby magnify the debt. Yet I wish to recall with gratitude the encouragement and advice so generously given by Morse Peckham, fifteen years ago, when I was at work on the dissertation on which this book is based. I am particularly grateful also to my former colleague Roma A. King, Jr., for reading my manuscript at a later stage and offering valued suggestions. In a less personal but no less essential way, I am indebted to those whose contribution to this book lies in their having made Ruskin's writings, public and private, more readily available to those who admire them. I am thankful in this regard, as any student of Ruskin must be, especially for the labors of E. T. Cook, Joan Evans, J. H. Whitehouse, Helen Gill Viljoen, John L. Bradley, and Van Akin Burd. The weight of my obligations to these scholars is evident in my notes, as is my debt to the studies of Derrick Leon, Francis Townsend, John D. Rosenberg, George P. Landow, Patricia Ball, and James Clark Sherburne. In this connection I wish to thank Oxford University Press for permission to quote from *The Diaries of John Ruskin*, Yale University Press for permission to quote from *The Brantwood Diary of John Ruskin*, Routledge & Kegan Paul Ltd. and the Estate of the late Derrick Leon for permission to quote from letters first published in *Ruskin: The Great Victorian*, and George Allen & Unwin for permission to quote from Greville MacDonald's *Reminiscences of a Specialist*.

I am also particularly grateful for various kinds of practical assistance I have received in preparing the text of this study. I want to thank the

Baker Fund Committee of Ohio University for a grant of leave in the hour of need. I owe much to my typist, Anne Rioux, for her patience and care with my nearly illegible hand. I am indebted to Elizabeth Coccio for giving my manuscript what it had in the way of textual consistency. In selecting and obtaining illustrations I have benefited from the patience and expertise of J. S. Dearden, Anne Braxton, and Helen Gawthrop. To the Ohio University Press, particularly to Holly Panich, managing editor, I am grateful for the kinds of encouragement and technical assistance that make the ends of publisher and scholar meet.

ILLUSTRATIONS

I have often had the fancy that there is some one Myth for every man, which, if we but knew it, would make us understand all he did and thought.

—W.B. Yeats,
Ideas of Good and Evil

THE POISON SKY

Introduction

> The physical result of that mental vileness is a total carelessness of the beauty of sky, or the cleanness of streams, or the life of animals and flowers: and I believe that the powers of Nature are depressed or perverted, together with the Spirit of Man; and therefore that conditions of storm and of physical darkness, such as never were before in Christian times, are developing themselves, in connection also with forms of loathesome insanity, multiplying through the whole genesis of modern brains.
>
> Ruskin, *Fors Clavigera*, Letter 66

THE MONSTER CLOUD

Before all other things John Ruskin was the great Victorian prophet of what we would now call the apparent deterioration of life. Stylist, aesthete, economist, moralist, glaciologist, naturalist, or nympholept he may also have been, but the compulsive current of his many works is his rising nausea at the prospect of a global slum, a depleted planet. He may be, as one critic has recently observed, "the major Romantic myth-maker of the Victorian era."[1] However, his myth-making does not envision, in Romantic fashion, the ultimate marriage of mind and nature; it intimates some conclusive struggle of grass with goods, life with greed, or form with force.

"I do believe," he told his father in an early letter, "that I shall live to see the ruin of everything good and great in the world, and have nothing left to hope for but the fires of the judgment to shrivel up the cursed idiocy of mankind."[2] The remark is at least predictive of his final message. At the end, he articulated something close to our own recurrent sense that chaos is coming again, that our culture has been blighted, that the world's body has been infected by its mind. He reached these conclusions in becoming the major Victorian prophet and apocalyptist of life's struggle with wealth. "Continue to make that forbidden deity your principal one," he warned in 1864, "and soon no more art, no more science, no more pleasure will be possible. Catastrophe will come; or, worse than catastrophe, slow mouldering and withering into Hades."[3]

The blight came. In 1884, nearing the end of his long agony of lost causes and impossible loyalties, Ruskin went before audiences in London to announce signs of the Last Days of advancing industrial society. In a pair of enigmatic lectures entitled *The Storm-Cloud of the Nineteenth Century* he described in polysemous terms the symptoms of a miasmatic, progressive, and apparently final infection of the sky, the onset of which he had been studying much of his life. Although the visible emblem of this Last Judgment is ordinary smoke, "the sacred fume of modern devotion" polluting the living air, the coming of this "plague-cloud" to blight the biosphere is merely the outward sign of an inward and spiritual pollution. As the symbol of a power opposed to the cohesive and vital energy he invoked in his many uses of the term "purity," Ruskin's "plague-wind" is a meaning analogous to the "asphixied soul" announced by Carlyle in *Past and Present* or the "period of abstractions" in Camus' *The Plague*.

Of course I am short-circuiting Ruskin's ambiguities in asserting this much. He did not present his "storm-cloud" and "plague-wind" as deliberate studies in the symbolism of evil. His meteorological observations point to the onset of adverse phenomena that were as real to him as the Swiss foehn, the French mistral, or the Mediterranean sirocco. Yet the Lear-like "extremities of skies" that shadow his diaries as early as the mid-sixties and the public writings after 1871 are gradually burdened with psycho-mythic implications; this symbolism becomes central to the prophetic process in his writing after 1870, a drive that reaches its most extreme statement in the *Storm-Cloud*. In *The Symbolism of Evil* Paul Ricoeur traces the historical moments of interiorization of that symbolism from archaic symbols, in which defilement is perceived as an objective condition in nature, to the symbolism of sin, in which the language of material defilement or stain is given an ethical dimension (man has broken his covenant with God), to the symbolism of guilt, in which the terms of defilement are applied to the burden of the individual consciousness, the self-infection of the will. To show, by an integrative reading of his works and diaries, how a poison sky became for Ruskin the climactic and inevitable mythopoeic expression of impurity as he struggled with it, an expression that necessarily participates in each of these moments of the symbolism of evil (defilement, sin, guilt), is the main thrust of this study. I must begin it, however, by looking toward my destination; and this means pointing to some of the implicit meaning, some of the resonance, Ruskin set working in these two eschatological lectures. By the resonance of these lectures I mean his way of transcending, in the self-reflexiveness and allusiveness of his discourse, anything like neutral observations of storm phenomena.

This resonance is evident even in the ironic disclaimers of it with which Ruskin opens the *Storm-Cloud* materials. These materials exist in three parts: a preface added for publication, "Lecture 1" and "Lecture 2." "Lecture 2" is printed simply as a series of notes to "Lecture 1" that show Ruskin broadening the allusions and digressions of that first lecture at its second reading. This itself becomes a device for creating resonance. He begins "Lecture 1" ironically by warning his audience not to look for any underlying meaning in his chosen title, *The Storm-Cloud of the Nineteenth Century*. He will simply bring to their attention "a series of cloud phenomena . . . peculiar to our own times . . . which have not hitherto received any notice or description from meteorologists." But within a few sentences these "cloud phenomena" have become "the storm-cloud—or more accurately plague-cloud, for it is not always stormy," a cloud which "never was seen but by now living, or *lately* living eyes. It is not yet twenty years that this—I may well call it, wonderful—cloud has been, in its essence, recognizable."[4]

Then, as if simply to prove the novelty of these phenomena, Ruskin sets off on an allusive reconnaissance of sky symbolism in literary history. No such clouds, he affirms, are to be found in Homer or Aristophanes or Dante or Milton, nor, among moderns, in Scott, Wordsworth, or Byron. But while in one dimension he is asserting the novelty of his cloud, in another dimension he is saying something more by creating a symbolic or archetypal perspective for his own "plague-cloud." No such clouds to be found in Dante, he declares in "Lecture 1"; but "Lecture 2" adds an ironic qualifier: "The vapour over the pool of Anger in the *Inferno*, the clogging stench which rises from Caina, and the fog of the circle of Anger in the *Purgatorio* resemble, indeed, the cloud of the Plague-wind very closely,—but are conceived only as supernatural." However, the word "supernatural" is itself qualified in the same note as Ruskin goes on to explain that, although to most minds we live in a universe in which "diptheria is held to be as natural as song, and cholera as digestion," he is himself accustomed to seeing the earth as a prepared abode ruled by "*agencies* of health and disease, of which the first may be aided by his industry, prudence, and piety; while the destroying laws are allowed to prevail against him, in the degree in which he allows himself in idleness, folly, and vice."[5]

Again, no such plague clouds are to be found in Byron, he declares in the first lecture; yet a moment later he treats his audience to an apocalyptic solar image from Byron's *Sardanapalus*. I quote from this in part, with Ruskin's emphases.

> How red he glares amongst those deepening clouds,
> Like the blood he predicts. . . .
> . . . .
>   . . . Yon disk
> To the star-read Chaldean, bears upon
> Its everlasting page the end of what
> Seem'd everlasting; but oh! thou TRUE sun!
> *The burning oracle of all that live,*
> *As fountain of all life,* and *symbol of*
> *Him who bestows it,* wherefore dost thou limit
> Thy lore unto calamity?[6]

At the lecture's second delivery, in his notes to himself, Ruskin proceeds to give resonance by involved commentary on "deepening clouds," "the blood he predicts" (significantly compared to the encrimsoned skies of J. M. W. Turner), "burning oracle," "fountain of all life," and "thy lore unto calamity"—the whole meant to invoke a tradition in which the sun is "a symbol so perfect and beautiful that it may also be thought of as partly an apocalypse."[7] This involvement with the solar archetype, illustrated also in note 3, is so central to Ruskin's work (as it was to Turner's) that it will be a recurrent topic in this study. For the moment, however, we note merely that Ruskin carefully reminds his audience of the sacramental view of the phenomena he is about to present while at the same time ironically disclaiming such a view. Thus his meteorology becomes, as Erich Auerbach observed of the Old Testament, "fraught with background." In believing times, he is saying, the phenomena I am about to describe would have been read as God-written signs, but by you they can only be received as facts.

The preface he wrote for the published lectures takes a similar tone, but the resonance is personal. Reviewers, he notes, had scouted his observations as "imaginary" or "insane." His reply is appropriately double-edged: "I am indeed, every day of my yet spared life, more and more grateful that my mind is capable of imaginative vision, and liable to the noble dangers of delusion which separate the speculative intellect of humanity from the dreamless instinct of the brutes." But he has always been, he continues, perfectly capable of using or refusing his imaginative power, and in the case of these lectures there is no single *fact* in them which he has not verified "with a chemist's analysis, and a geometer's precision."[8] The indignant ambiguity is what is vital here and throughout the two lectures.

In one sense at least Ruskin had earned the right to insist on the veracity of his data. He had, in fact, kept up an empathic skywatch throughout his life. In youth he had traveled with his own "cyanometer" to measure its blueness daily. His visits to the sunset, his father once declared, were as regular as a soldier's to his evening parade. Sky studies, like verbal Turners, are prominent among the most ecstatic moments of his prose; in his diaries sky effects (even spates of barometric readings) are recorded almost daily as correlatives of his mental states, and they darken together. "I am ashamed," he confided prognostically to an early diary, "to find myself so much at the mercy of a dark sky."[9] This may partly explain why he would later quote, with implicit approval, Turner's supposed deathbed affirmation: "The Sun is God." Ruskin regarded clouds as special problems in the mystery of form. He wrote recurrently and at length on their physics, iconology, and mythology. There is about them, he wrote in his first book, "a spirit-like feeling, a capricious mocking imagery of passion and life, totally different from any effects of inanimate form that the earth can show."[10] The cloud becomes the controlling life-symbol in that justly famous and central homily "The Mystery of Life and Its Arts" (1868); and his "myth-book," *The Queen of the Air* (1869), is subtitled *Greek Myths of Cloud and Storm*.

It is very likely also true, as his editors suggest, that Ruskin had studied with his own eyes the pall of pollutants building up over the industrial centers of Europe, as if the sky were dying. And surely in this particular sense no Victorian projection has come more dangerously into its own. But the language of *The Storm-Cloud of the Nineteenth Century* is loaded with implications more ominous than that of pollution. I do not propose to undo its knots of digression and allusion, but a sampling of descriptive phrases from the two lectures will show how far we are from that dispassionate language of the chemist or geometer.

The new cloud is first described as prismatic (diffracting rather than reflecting light), palpitating, ragged, icy, with "threads, and meshes, and tresses, and tapestries, flying, failing, melting, reappearing; spinning and unspinning themselves, coiling and uncoiling, winding and unwinding, faster than eye or thought can follow."[11] The diary entry from which this passage is adapted describes two ominous ranks of such clouds observed at Brantwood on 6 August 1880, one "with long locks and tresses, as of hair at its edge—and both overlying the range of hills, exactly like the Hesperides dragon—ending northward in a clear sky, against a black monster cloud. . . . I believe these swift and mocking clouds and colours are only between storms. They are assuredly new in

Heaven—so far as my life reaches. I never saw a single example of them till after 1870."[12] Later, quoting from his *Fors Clavigera* (1872–84), he describes the cloud in the language he had used when he first announced it in 1871: "not rain-cloud, but a dry black veil, which no ray of sunshine can pierce. . . . And everywhere the leaves of the trees are shaking fitfully, as they do before a thunderstorm; only not violently, but enough to show the passing to and fro of a strange, bitter, blighting wind. . . . It looks partly as if it were made of poisonous smoke. . . . But mere smoke would not blow to and fro in that wild way. It looks to me as if it were made of dead men's souls."[13] Finally, as their most significant sign, we learn that these malignant clouds produce no roseate suns, as common fogs will, but merely blanch the sun.

The ill wind itself, "the plague-wind of the eighth decade in the nineteenth century," is described somewhat more explicitly as being "a wind of darkness" that cannot coexist with sunlight, "a malignant *quality* of wind," blowing indifferently from any quarter but tending to favor the southwest.[14] It blows *"tremulously,"* setting the trees aquiver as if in "expression of anger as well as of fear and distress." By comparison with known storm winds, "plague-wind is more panic-struck, and feverish; and its sound is a hiss instead of a wail." The effect of it reminds Ruskin of some scenes in a rustic production of *Faust* he had attended at Avallon (in the south of France, where the *Bise*, or "grey wind," is familiar) two years before,

> —a strange ghastliness being obtained in some of the witch scenes merely by fine management of gesture and drapery; and in the phantom scenes, by the half-palsied, half-furious, faltering or fluttering past of phantoms stumbling as into graves; as if not only soulless, but senseless, Dead, moving with the very action, the rage, the decrepitude, and the trembling of the plague-wind.

Not only is the plague wind tremulous, but it is unnaturally "intermittent," a feature anemometers cannot measure, Ruskin reasons, for they cannot measure the frequency of gusts. But then, he queries, "what's the use of telling you whether the wind's strong or not, when I can't tell you whether it's a strong medicine, or a strong poison?"[15] The malignant effects are clear: "Blanched Sun,—blighted grass,—blinded man"; however, modern one-dimensional awareness will not permit him to assign a meaning to these symptoms; he can only remind his hearers that every seer of old predicted physical gloom as a consequence of moral gloom.[16]

Finally, we must notice two details from the second storm lecture that connect obscurely with other aspects of Ruskin's symbolism. One detail relates the wind to his mythography of Medusa, as do the icy and serpentine features of the cloud: "The darkness of the plague-wind, unless in electric states of the air, is always accompanied by deadly chill."[17] Another allusion links the plague sky more specifically to his own earlier studies in mythic symbolism. The effects of this "morbific" weather upon his thoughts and work have been, he concludes, "precisely that which would have resulted from the visible phantom of an evil spirit, *the absolute opponent of the Queen of the Air,*—Typhon against Athena,—in a sense of which I had neither the experience nor the conception when I wrote the illustrations of the myth of Perseus in *Modern Painters.*"[18]

These passages are intended to give a fair indication of the connotative range of Ruskin's storm-cloud and plague-wind imagery. But there are other important features of meaning in the lectures which these quotations do not properly convey. Science, for instance, is always there, consistently interfused and constantly attacked. Ruskin's own observations are laced with digressions into the details of contemporary investigations into glaciology, meteorology, and physics, which he generally satirizes as the blasphemous antitype of his own vision. That is, he belabors science for what Blake called "single vision" or Whitehead the "fallacy of misplaced concreteness." For instance, in a digression on the meaning of light—a meaning as vital to Ruskin's work as to Turner's—we are given Plato's definition, " 'The power that through the eye manifests colour,' " followed by this dictum: "On that definition, you will find, alike by Plato and all great subsequent thinkers, a *moral* Science of Light founded, far and away more important to you than all the physical laws ever learned by vitreous revelation."[19] Through this weft of ironic commentary on modern investigators *The Storm-Cloud* comes to be as much about "the *deliberate* blasphemy of science" as about signs in the skies, and of course the connection of the two is its essential message. As he does elsewhere in his work, Ruskin selects John Tyndall as his special antagonist among scientists. Tyndall's *Glaciers of The Alps, Forms of Water* (matters relating to cloud vapor), and *Heat as a Mode of Motion* are all belittled along the way for the large questions they fail to answer. But other investigations are mentioned; for instance Ruskin takes Balfour Stewart's *The Conservation of Energy* to task for the deadliness of its concept of energy: "Had Mr. Stewart been a better scholar, he would have felt, even if he had not known, that the Greek word 'energy' could only be applied to the living—and of living, with perfect propriety only to the *mental,* action of animals, and that it could no more be applied as

John Ruskin. "A Sunset at Abbeville, 1868." An illustration to *The Storm-Cloud of the Nineteenth Century* reproduced here from *Works* (Library Edition), vol. 34. The diagram was meant to show the effects of ordinary storm clouds, particularly in reflecting sunset light. "There is no local reason assignable for the presence of the cirri above, or of the thundercloud below. There is no conceivable cause either in the geology, or the moral character, of the two sides of the town of Abbeville, to explain why there should be decorative fresco on the sky over the southern suburb, and a muttering heap of gloom and danger over the northern. The electric cloud is as calm in motion as the harmless one: it changes its form, indeed, but imperceptibly; and, so far as can be discerned, only at its own will is exalted, and with its own consent abased." (*Works*, 34:56)

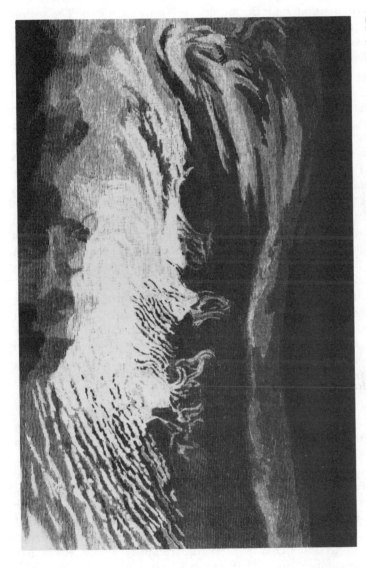

John Ruskin. "An August Sky at Brantwood, 1880." An illustration to *The Storm-Cloud of the Nineteenth Century* reproduced here from *Works* (Library Edition), vol. 34. Ruskin wished to illustrate the coiling, palpitating, light-diffracting qualities of the new cloud, as well as its responsiveness to local conditions. "*In my second diagram are shown forms of vapour sustaining at every instant all kinds of varying local influences; beneath, fastened down by mountain attraction, above, flung afar by distracting winds; here, spread abroad into blanched sheets beneath the sunshine, and presently gathered into strands of coiled cordage in the shade. Their total existence is in metamorphosis, and their every aspect is a surprise, or a deceit.*" (*Works*, 34:56)

a 'scientific garb,' to the flight of a rifle ball, than to the fall of a dead body."[20] The significance to Ruskin of such etymological offences will become apparent later; for the moment it is only the idea of *The Storm-Cloud* as a gathering of meanings that is of interest here.

It is possible also that among these meanings there are such touches of rose symbolism as to intimate to the biographical critic that the plague wind may have arisen first as a kind of "correspondent breeze" to the blighting of his hopes during the period from 1871 to 1875 for union with that fatal girl, Rose La Touche. "Her entire soul and being have been paralysed by the poisoned air,"[21] he wrote, three years before her death. In reading *The Storm-Cloud* one notices, for instance, that Ruskin is particularly offended by the spiritless weather observations made by Professor Tyndall during a solitary ascent of Monte Rosa. The plague-blanched sun, of course, also forbids those sunset revelations in rose light for which Ruskin had always yearned. And one notices such nuances of plague-work as these: "Diabolic clouds over everything: and looking over my kitchen garden yesterday, I found it one miserable mass of weeds gone to seed, the roses in the higher garden putrefied into brown sponges, feeling like dead snails; and the half-ripe strawberries all rotten at the stalks."[22]

But within all these details of meaning there is one controlling current in *The Storm-Cloud*. It is what Frank Kermode, speaking mainly of apocalyptic fiction, has called "the sense of an ending." Obviously Ruskin's real interest in the work is more nearly eschatology than meteorology. The lectures are, as John D. Rosenberg observes, apocalyptic.[23] Indeed, the plague cloud is more to be compared with Yeats's visionary "antithetical multiform influx" than with any specific feature of the skies. These two lectures interconnect with the *Fors Clavigera* letters (in which the plague is first announced) and many other segments of his work after 1870 to form a kind of Ruskinian wasteland myth in which the joint ecological and spiritual perversions of the age are on the brink of appropriate punishment. A report of the first lecture in the *Daily News* accused Ruskin of a "skillful 'hedge' " by which he did not so much declare that the plague cloud was a divine visitation but that it would have been thought so in believing times. Of course as early as Letter 61 (1876) of *Fors Clavigera* he had warned explicitly of "terrible signs of supernatural calamity" evidenced "no less in grievous changes and deterioration of climate, than in forms of mental disease."[24] Therefore in the second lecture he replied to the accusation of hedging by drawing some of his meanings together into a concluding malediction on the broken "harmony" of the life-world:

"fragments, indeed, of what existed still exist, and hours of what is past still return; but month by month darkness gains upon the day, and the ashes of the Antipodes glare through the night."[25]

Apocalypse, as a literary genre, depends heavily upon interpretive continuity with earlier prophecy and mythology. The Jewish apocalyptists interpreted the Old Testament prophecies in order to place the End Time, the moment of God's catastrophic intervention into history to end the fallen world and establish his kingdom, in or nearer to their own time. Thus they encouraged the faithful and issued a fervid commentary on the ripeness of the evils that beset them. In composing their visionary scenarios of cosmic devastation the apocalyptists borrowed liberally, not only from the figurative language of the Old Testament, but also from pagan mythical cosmology and demonology. Similarly, the Christian apocalyptists, typified by John of Patmos, reworked the traditional materials of the genre to re-envision the climax of universal history in Christian terms.

D. H. Lawrence regarded John's Apocalypse, the biblical Revelation, as no one book but a kind of "section through time": an old pagan book, perhaps describing an initiation ritual, was interpreted and adapted by an early Jewish apocalyptist and again re-written by a Jewish-Christian apocalyptist before receiving the distinctive fervor and political bias of John. Although John's Apocalypse suffered further revision by Christians after his time in the effort to efface its pagan elements, the work, in Lawrence's view, still retains the animistic power of its pagan kernel. In his own *Apocalypse* Lawrence becomes a post-Freudian apocalyptist in his effort to invoke the power of the Apocalypse's mythic core and to reveal its latent content of resisted desire. This notion of apocalypse as being, at least in its catastrophic phase, the rhetoric of resisted desire could be suggestive to the biographical reader of Ruskin; however, the point for us here is that apocalyptic writers authenticate their personal visions by drawing upon resonant materials already traditional in the culture as prophecy and myth; their individual visions therefore appear as confirmations of the truth of an eternal design.

Romantic "natural supernaturalism" depends, in a similar way, upon the correlation of subjective experiences in nature with the deeper cultural traditions of scripture and myth. M. H. Abrams observes that the term "apocalypse" in modern criticism has come to be "applied loosely to signify any sudden and visionary revelation—or even anything which is very drastic." He restricts the term "to the sense used in the Biblical commentary, where it signifies a vision in which the old world is replaced by a new and better world."[26] The problem in this definition for us is that while Wordsworth and the earlier Romantics concentrate, in their poetic apocalyptics, on the *consummation* of the biblical Apocalypse (Rev. 21:1-4), Ruskin's primary interest appears to be in those earlier chapters that speak of the coming of the red dragon, the worship of the Beast, and the pouring out of God's wrath upon the earth. Further, since Ruskin's revelations invoke other mythic symbols or schemes (the three "Forses" of *Fors Clavigera*, for instance) we must liberalize the term apocalypse here to include not only literary revelations relating to the biblical Apocalypse, but also any personal revelation confirming the truth of myth or of providential intentions in natural phenomena.

This is not the place to attempt to clarify the relationship between apocalypse and myth, yet it does appear that apocalyptic feeling involves mythic awareness. I refer not merely to the descent of most literary apocalypses from biblical or sibylline models but to some deeper connection. Whether we take apocalypse to mean simply a moment of revelation (as critics do when, for instance, they speak of Wordsworth's "nature apocalypse" at Simplon) or more explicitly as a revelation concerning the imminence of the End, the experience, though it may grow out of a very private sense of immersion of personal anxiety in the infinite will, cannot be communicated as literature without the use of symbols having pre-established mythic or archetypal resonance, such as the plague-cloud or the red dragon. (Their reception, of course, will depend upon the *zeitgeist*, upon the quantity of apocalyptic feeling abroad, and the special relevance of the symbol. Ruskin's plague-cloud was ahead of its time.) In sum, then, apocalypse depends upon myth; an apocalyptic writer will be in some sense a mythic writer. Blake, Yeats, and Lawrence illustrate this; so does Ruskin.

When critics speak of myth or myth-making in a writer they are likely to use this vexed term in one or more of three primary, interconnected senses: the writer communicates visionary or numinous experiences, participates in something like a primitive mythical awareness of things; the writer makes use, especially in a reverent tone, of symbols or structures which are derived from ethnic mythologies; or the writer's work is a recurrence or system of controlling symbols, archetypal or not, which seems to organize and universalize not only his own experience but that of the people for whom he writes. In this last case we speak of "his" myths; however, the fact that the writer generally recognizes the mythic materials he uses *as* mythic makes his use of them to some extent ironic or deconstructive. There is also a fourth, more mundane, sense of myth in a writer; for, even though he may not actually use or "make" myths, his writings may indicate a purely theoretical interest in particular myths or in the nature of myth. I propose to explore Ruskin's involvement with myth in each of these senses while showing how his experience and his message drove him into apocalyptic and mythic expression. This approach means interpreting his works, not as discrete objects but as moments of a process, a continuous signifying intention in which the private and the public writings appear to be dominated by the same archetypal symbols.

It may be possible to experience literature simply as literature, but such experience is ineffable. Criticism and interpretation involve referring the literary experience to a reality that is itself already an interpretation, for, as E. H. Gombrich observes, "there is no reality without interpretation."[27] Therefore any critical procedure suffers the limitations of the reality construct to which it refers. Myth criticism has been charged with at least two such primary limitations. One objection is that the myth critic tends to beg the question of literary value in his claim, explicit or implicit, that a writer's work, because it rests on myth, thereby embodies primordial and otherwise inexpressible truths. But, though Ruskin makes such claims in his own myth criticism, I wish to avoid the claim that his use of mythic symbols in itself confers any special access to truth. His art confers value on the myths he employs by the way he employs them. The second major objection is that the myth critic tends to ignore the immediate phenomenon of the literary work in favor of the search for archetypal patterns, making the artist "the mere occasion for the continued manifestation of that universal agent."[28] This objection may be justified when myth criticism tends to dispense with the author and treat myth as a kind of enabling convention in his work. However, Ruskin's involvement with myth in the four senses mentioned in the preceding paragraph drew myth more and more into his life and thought, as well as into the figurative language of his works; he is the speaker in his work, interpreting mythic symbols for his use. But the mythic figures he elaborates sometimes appear in the dreams he records or return to guide his life. Therefore, while we cannot regard Ruskin the writer as the "mere occasion" for his myths, we must respect, as he did, the view that myths are the quintessential language of the spirit; nor can we ignore the more modern translation of this: that myth is the language by which the unconscious, collective or personal, communicates with the conscious and with the imagination.

Ruskin drew upon myth to replenish earlier spiritual losses. The failure of his Evangelical-Wordsworthian world view, with its thirst for numinous experiences of nature, led, by way of a matured appreciation of the mythic in Turner, to a search for true symbolic apprehension of the world, seen now as the struggle of vital and lethal forces. This expressive necessity drove him, against earlier inclinations, to a serious interest in Greek art and myth, and then to the use of myth as the necessary vehicle for his own message. This movement toward myth is the structuring principle of the body of his work taken as a whole. But it is the movement of his life as well. The myths of his life and work converge in an autobiographical tendency. The "worlds" of both become dominated by the same archetypes; the force of Fors operates in each. Myth criticism, at least, allows us to consider the symbols that are common to the life and the work, at and beneath the level of conscious intention. The writings of C. G. Jung should be brought to bear, if briefly, on this subject because they seem to shed light on the relation between archetypal symbol and individual psychic development.

In Jung, the self is the psychic predisposition to, or archetype of, wholeness, which cannot be distinguished from a God-image; to know the one is to know the other. The self is, therefore, the goal of a mythic quest of the psyche for integration or individuation. In Blake's terms this wholeness of the self requires the reconciliation of contraries in the psyche, marrying Heaven and Hell; for Jung, as for Blake, these contraries have been represented as mythic images: "all deities reside in the human breast." The mythologized processes of nature are not mere allegories but symbolic expressions of the psychic quest for wholeness mirrored on nature by projection. Thus it makes Jungian sense to say that in the process of individuation a person discovers his myth. There would be no particular relevance to Ruskin here were it not for the fact that he also relates mythic personalities or symbols to his own psychic development. His interest in them is by no means purely theoretical or expository; he makes them expressions of his quest for self.

In Jungian theory, psychic wholeness, self, depends upon the reconciliation of consciousness not only with the personal unconscious but with the innate predispositions of the racial or collective unconscious as well. The unconscious articulates itself in the form of archetypes, which Jung spoke of as either primordial images or the psychic aptitudes for such images. The archetypes are known to us objectively through their symbolic expression in myths, folktales, dreams, visions, works of art, etc. Though their projections take innumerable forms, the archetypes themselves, in the sense of unconscious predispositions, are relatively few and specific in Jung, and they are the real basis of his analysis. If psychic wholeness, individuation, is to occur, the projections of these archetypes must be recognized as such and assimilated by consciousness; for they tend to acquire autonomy and can therefore alter, sometimes dangerously, the self's world. (Jung spoke in terms of literal dialogues with his projections.) Projections can be dangerous because they emanate from the unknown or denied side of the psyche; however, projections are, for Jung, the basis of all numinous experience of the world. "Projections," he wrote, "change the world into a replica of one's own unknown face."[29] Contents of the individual or collective unconscious are projected, mirrored externally, in persons, things, or events; therefore the bearers of projection may derive a seemingly autonomous power of attraction or repulsion from the unknown side of the individual's own psyche. As we will see, Ruskin himself approached the subject of projections when he discussed "pathetic fallacy" in terms of the degree of literal belief in them a poet's personifications of nature seemed to involve. Here, however, we must notice two modes of projection, two archetypes described by Jung, that are particularly useful in comprehending the relationship between Ruskin's life and the mythic figures that interested him; these projections Jung called "the shadow" and the "anima" or soul-figure.

The renegade or unacceptable part of the personal unconscious is projected or personified as the shadow, a sinister accompanying presence that the individual can, with considerable moral effort, recognize as an emanation of his own psyche. However, even when the psyche has achieved that selfhood which Jung associates with the God-image, there is still the shadow, for even the deity must reckon with his shadow, as he does in the Apocalypse. It seems reasonable to suggest that Ruskin's storm-cloud, as diabolic weather, is to be read, biographically, as his climactic shadow-struggle projected as apocalyptic myth. It would therefore be a continuation of the diabolic encounters he recorded during his mental illnesses. Since it is the unconscious that does the projecting, Jung reminds us, projections appear to be encountered rather than made. Again, this is not to say that Ruskin was describing entirely imaginary weather in 1884; industrial smog, even the ash-cloud of Krakatoa (to which he alludes), were producing real meteorological effects; it is the causes and portents he assigns to these that are projective and mythic.

"Between the conception/ And the creation/ Between the emotion/ And the response/ Falls the Shadow. . . ." Eliot's familiar evocation of the shadow seems to fit the increasing influence of that archetypal projection over the last three decades of Ruskin's long life. However, there are other relations of Ruskin's psyche to his myth-making that are, perhaps, more clearly illuminated in terms of the Jungian concept of the anima. The projection-making power that mediates between the personal and the collective unconscious is called the anima in man, the animus in woman. As the hidden, erotic, creative, and by nature feminine "soul" in man, this "She-who-must-be-obeyed" is neither good nor evil. She is simply an archetype, the projective tendency of the male eros; therefore projections of the anima are not always angelic. The man projects this archetype on various feminine figures (or objects) in his life, beginning with his mother. If unassimilated by consciousness, anima-projections become increasingly autonomous; the self-world relation of a man beset by an anima-projection is liable, we are told, to strange disturbances: moods, dreams, visions, fateful occurrences. Therefore the "magic poison" of the anima, if her projections are not integrated, becomes dangerous to the psyche; she is, Jung wrote, "the serpent in the paradise of the harmless man."[30]

She is, nonetheless, the object of the chief heroic quest of the male psyche; through assimilation of the anima's projections by consciousness the integrated self discovers the will to love its world. It is the function of the anima to lead the male consciousness from his mother, or whatever functions as a mother, to the world through progressive integration of soul-figures into the unified self. For Jung, integration of the anima depends upon a satisfactory relationship with a real female partner. The anima leads to a person who is her bearer and who becomes the way to the integrated self's more inclusive and creative love of the world, a love like God's. However, there is much to be overcome before this integration can be accomplished; individuation is heroic work. Often, as apparently in Ruskin's case, assimilation of the anima's projections does not occur, and consciousness remains their captive.

In Jungian theory the quest of the hero (particularly the solar hero, with which Ruskin identified) is frequently read as a paradigm of the individuation process. In these symbolic representations the hero-knight must overcome a dragon or chthonic monster who guards his "lady-soul" and/or some other treasure. In the non-psychoanalytic sense the dragon may represent, as Ruskin's do, greed or materialistic grasp of the earth—all the impurities of earth and air that the hero must combat with light. In Jungian readings the dragon represents those dark but vital forces of the unconscious that must be brought to light—recognized and assimilated—if life-process of individuation is to move on, the anima or lady-soul to be attained. As one theorist puts it, "the central content of the numerous myths in which a dragon or some other monster is dismembered is the acquisition of an independent ego-personality, for which purpose the 'devouring, terrible mother' must be overcome."[31] The links of the dragon with greed, earth, and "the mother" are obscure: the mother is interpreted vaguely as the dark womb of the unconscious and, more specifically, as the passive, auto-erotic tendencies of the man who lives in a world still watched over by his mother. Jung speaks of the "secret conspiracy between mother and son" by which "each helps the other to betray life."

In a sense, then, the guardian dragon of the anima is a symbol of the psychic tensions that must arise and the drives to be recognized if a man is to escape the enveloping, embracing, devouring protectiveness of the mother. He must free himself from the grasp of this mothered world if he is to obtain its treasure, which is the will to love the real woman who can now become the bearer of his anima; only through her can the anima be realized and assimilated by consciousness. Failing to escape his bondage to mother, the man remains, figuratively or literally, impotent; but he continues to be obsessed by anima-figures which become increasingly remote projections of denied desire, images of his fate. Finally, since these projections are colored by hostility—by animosity—in a subject who has not freed himself from the mother, they may take on demonic qualities derived from the same source as the dragon itself; the anima becomes Medusa, as it were. Therefore, through the anima as through the shadow, the world may become a turbid mirror for the subject's unknown face.

Of course we do not need such Jungian concepts as the shadow or the anima, nor any other idea of myth as the language of the unconscious, if we are to consider simply Ruskin's public writings—books, essays, lectures—as autonomous critical projects or problems in the adaptation of prose style. But once we begin to relate the public statement to the private experience, zones that Ruskin himself had increasing difficulty keeping separate, we have a Ruskin who becomes a long dialogue of consciousness and projection, of self and its world. His interest in myth, we have noted, does not stop with a theoretical position on the subject, or with illustrative interpretations of particular myths, or with the use of mythic symbols to convey his own message; he makes some of them "his" myths, relates them to his own psychic or spiritual condition.

When, for example, in his diaries of the late seventies and the eighties, Ruskin speaks of daily acts of guidance by "Fors" or of things done "by Fors' order," this is not simply a stylistic tic or a habitual personification of chance. He asserts his belief in personal, guiding feminine powers—daimons or guardian angels. We may speculate that "Fors" is something like a bivalent projection of his anima: sometimes she is the benevolent intermediary with his lady-soul, Rose La Touche; sometimes the

"Forses" take on forbidding qualities of the "terrible mother." Whatever the psychic condition they symbolize, that Ruskin came to believe in such projections as quasi-mythic guiding powers is evident from the fact that he wrote to himself about them as well as to others. In *Fors Clavigera*, Letter 75 (1877), he replied to some of his " 'most intelligent readers,' " who were unable to understand his account (given in the previous letter) of St. Ursula's personal messages to him, by asserting the spiritual continuity and necessity of tutelary deities and guardian angels: "Whatever spiritual powers are in true personality appointed to go to and fro in the earth, to trouble the waters of healing, or bear the salutations of peace, can only be revealed in their reality, by the gradual confirmation in the matured soul of what were at first only its instinctive desires, and figurative perceptions."[32] He had found, as history has, that angels and demons are psychologically inescapable.

The personal instance that Ruskin is defending in this passage is his communication with St. Ursula. After Rose's death she became interfused in his mind with the saint and her myth. We will explore their relation to the rest of Ruskin's myth-making as we proceed. For the moment, however, we should notice that in the introduction to his edition of Rose's diaries Van Akin Burd has recently given a detailed account of Ruskin's "spiritualization" of the departed Rose into a guiding angel like a "Fors." "In his mind," Burd observes, "Rose had achieved a kind of apotheosis, a tutelary force with the same revelatory power as the myth of St. Ursula."[33] Ruskin's consciousness, the Jungian might say, had been unable to assimilate the anima projection, the personification of his denied eros, that Rose had borne for fifteen years; so after her death the projection acquired an autonomous, mythic power out of the sense of incompleteness he felt. He looked for guiding signs from this projected "soul." Ruskin's famous drawing of Rose in 1862 and Carpaccio's painting of *St. Ursula's Dream*, which he studied and copied with obsessive care in 1876, represent girls who have, if any ever did, the look of remoteness or inwardness that might help one to imagine a soul-figure.

But there had been, one might argue, other bearers of Ruskin's anima: the remote mystery of rose-lit, snow-clad peaks; the Effie Gray who is the, largely imaginary, subject of his pre-nuptial letters; the sculptured repose of Ilaria di Caretto on her tomb at Lucca; those domesticated angels, the "Lilies" of *Sesame and Lilies*; Athena, his Greek goddess of the pure air and rosy dawn. But the idea of the anima serves, if only in this way, to remind us of Ruskin's particular interest in other symbolic figures related to the psycho-mythic theme of the hero's quest. He identifies with monster-slayers: Apollo, Hercules, Perseus, Saints Theodore and George; he studies the serpent-demons they oppose, connecting these creatures with greed or materialism in the mind and malignant skies in nature. They are destroyers of the lived-world. The dragon, we have noted, has been linked, in Jungian interpretations, to the mother, the dependent and auto-erotic tendencies of the libido that stand, threatening impotence, between the hero and his projected anima. This figure itself may take on hostile features which are the projection of denied desire. Perhaps the Jungian reading of these symbols, seen in relation to the tenacious dominance of Ruskin's mother, explains something of his interest in those withering women of Greek myth: Medusa, Persephone, the Fates. In this respect Athena, his central mythic figure, had a bivalent significance for him. In her benevolent aspect she is the vital power of the clear air; in her hostility she takes on the aspect of Medusa, signified by the Gorgoneum of her aegis, and becomes a malevolent storm-power. It is her presence that Ruskin detects in the hissing, chilling qualities of his storm-plague phenomena. Therefore, in the Jungian reading, Ruskin's Storm-Cloud might be seen, not only as a projection of his psychic shadow, but also as his anima, projecting her hostile face, the rage of impotent desire, upon the world. In this sense his poison sky is, like Blake's poison tree, an emanation of unacknowledged hostility. Ruskin once challenged a friend who accused his work of being "transparent" by asking: "Who could find [in the works] the roots of my personal angers? or see the dark sprays of them in the sky?"[34] In this challenge he seems to have been giving a clue.

I do not intend to attempt a detailed Jungian analysis in this study; my interest is primarily in Ruskin's deliberate and public uses of myth. However, these archetypal references may serve to suggest the biographical depth and complexity of the Storm-Cloud theme as it looms up through Ruskin's work and may convey the sense in which it can be spoken of as a personal myth. For, as I have already indicated, the Storm (or Plague) is by no means confined to the pair of lectures delivered in 1884. This apocalyptic symbol wreathes its way into the labyrinthine digressions of most of his later works; into *The Queen of the Air* and the *Fors Clavigera* letters; into the series of Oxford lectures on art and taste; into *The Eagle's Nest*, his lectures on relational as opposed to scientific knowing; into his phenomenological and often mythic reclassifications of natural forms: *Proserpina, Love's Meinie,* and *Deucalion*; it even coils its way into *Fiction, Fair and Foul*, his essay on degeneracy in the novel.

But the roots of those "dark sprays" of anger that troubled the skies of his later works can be traced much deeper in his private writing. The Storm-Cloud begins to form in the diaries of the forties and fifties as the delectable Eden-world of his innocence becomes shadowed by experience. Dark weathers gradually become, over the next three decades, the sign of a malefic and vindictive presence he felt in nature. One day in August 1847, for instance, he recorded "a strange deadly shadow over everything. . . . I expected to be touched by it," he wrote, "which I was not, but then came a horror of great darkness—not distress, but cold fear and gloom."[35] The diary entry for 17 June 1849 finds him "abstracting the book of Revelations . . . . especially struck with the general appellation of the System of the world as the Mystery of God"; he moves on to a cataclysmic description of the ice-flow at the source of the Arveron. From this giddying image of power he can lift his eyes to "the great cataract itself," thundering down "like a large avalanche"; finally, above all, he sees "a fearful storm coming up by the Breven, its grisly clouds warping up, as it seemed, against the river and the cataract."[36] One day, a month later, his spirits were again entangled with a dark weather: "I could not write—the sky was lifeless and grey . . . awful scene of grisly cloud foaming in darkness among the crests of the Aiguilles Rouges above the Flégère."[37]

It is impossible, of course, to demonstrate at this point how these nuances of shadow deepen, become more common, and drift toward mythic and apocalyptic intensity in the later diaries. But here are quotations from a series of entries from the diaries of 1874, three years after his first manic attack but a decade before *The Storm-Cloud*. 15 February: "Things better for me, and much good for me; but I heartless because of false Bible and dark skies. No power of religion left—or a shadow only—less, like my life blood." 23 February: Walking through Miss Beever's wood, in the old aredly anger against Mr. L[a Touche]. Sky fearfully dark. After a fierce struggle to conquer the anger, an unexpected piece of light and blue came in sky." 25 February: "The most horrible black-fog all day long, nearly as bad this morning, and a nearly sleepless night, leave me shivery; not beaten, however, but wonder-struck at the cruelty of all things." 29 February: "No fog, but intense black diabolical plague wind, and I generally down." 5 March: "The weather tormenting me as if I were Job." 12 March: "Black, bleak, messy, frightful thaw, the lake literally describable as 'blasted ink'—ink traversed by fierce squalls like black stains on grey. . . . Find invaluable passage of Voltaire on Lucifer and Liberty. . . . The devil being called Lucifer is such a prophetic intimation of Science!" Here, to conclude, is a group of suggestive passages from the entries for 1875. 31 August: "The Furies, however, are not Improving persons; not *Governesses*. Cholera and Plague are sent of Heaven, but in a different sense from health and joy. They are Avengers. Punishment is primarily Vindictive, secondarily educative." 16 September: "An exquisite morning sky, all fretted with sweet white cloud, seen only here and there through miserable rack of the foul storm smoke. Why does—how *can*—God do it, and spoil His own work so wretchedly? At the moment, whistling wind, calm luminous sky, and the black Devil cloud, all contending for mastery." 1 November: "I am always checked in my natural history by the sense of failure or hostility. 'An enemy hath done this.' . . . The world seems dreadful. But how far do we cast ourselves out of Eden by our own disobedience every day?. . . . But I can live, because I know I am gathering corn not chaff. If God chooses to have it ate up like this Rose leaf, that is His business, not mine. Ghastly cloud-spirits of evil." 9 November: "Gloomy light, gaining a little on fog. Him that hath the power of Death, that is the Devil. Apocalypse to music. Hell followed with him. Milton. Prophecy of *this* book. Papias *Daimonia*. 149, of Life *in* Christ."[38]

Notice that the *Storm-Cloud* lectures are still a decade away, that the diarist must yet wrestle with a dozen years of demon-shadow before a final attack of madness silences him in 1889. But whether Ruskin was at *this* time on the threshold of dementia or of prophecy cannot be of primary concern to the student of his writing, for these are not, strictly speaking, properties of literature. What interests us is the way in which, through his style, Ruskin projects his personal anxiety into nature so that it becomes not his crisis only but ours also. And concerning this imaginative process the language of Jung seems especially concise; hence I wish to turn to it again for a moment. I began with his observation that by projection we transform the world into the image of our unknown faces. Deific and demonic powers, in Jung's view, are archetypal (racial) projections of our unconscious impulses, our "gods" in fact. "To call them by this name is to give them that central position in the scale of psychological values which has always been theirs, whether consciously acknowledged or not, for their power grows in proportion to the degree that they remain unconscious."[39]

Apparently even apocalyptic expectation would, in this view, be an unconscious projection. "All in all," Jung continues, "it is not only more advantageous but more 'correct' psychologically to explain as the 'will of God' the natural forces that appear in us as impulses."[40] Projections, especially shadow projections it appears, arise as the ideal interior world of innocence becomes unattainable in reality. "The resultant *sentiment d'incomplétude* and the still worse feeling of sterility are in their turn explained by projection as the malevolence of the environment, and by means of this vicious circle the isolation is intensified. The more projections interpose themselves between the subject and the environment, the harder it becomes for the ego to see through its illusions."[41] The shadow, apparently, can be confronted and exorcized by the subject himself so long as it has not assumed archetypal form in his personal unconscious: "With a little self-criticism one can see through the shadow—so far as its nature is personal. But when it appears as an archetype, one encounters the same difficulties as with anima and animus. In other words, it is quite within the bounds of possibility for a man to recognize the relative evil of his nature, but it is a rare and shattering experience for him to gaze into the face of absolute evil."[42]

It appears that Ruskin came to gaze transfixed, sometime in the 1870s, upon that face of evil absolute in "ancient, inescapable recognition"; and in a sense all his utterances thereafter dwindled into the one which Conrad gave to Mr. Kurtz: "The horror! The horror!" Its symbolic form became the monster-cloud; its conscious meanings were smoke, science, sensuality, and exploitation; but some might also say that his poisoned skies were a projection of something—rage, lust perhaps—that he attempted to repress. As Blake declared, "He who desires but acts not, breeds pestilence." But such a point, of course, is largely speculation. What I do wish to show here is how, in the last lecture of the series entitled *The Art of England*, delivered at Oxford in the year preceding his storm lectures, Ruskin actually attempted to present the cloud and the monster at once with a deliberately apocalyptic shock. The context of its presentation was such as to suggest both the cloud's richness as a symbol and the depth of its involvement with both his private experience and primary message.

He has been saying, as his lecture draws towards its peroration, that Nature's truths must be taken as *she* gives them up to wise passivity, not taken by assault as in bad art or loose science. Then follows a piece of prophecy that is central to Ruskin: "If pursued in that insolence, or in that concupicence, the phenomena of all the universe become first gloomy, and then spectral; the sunset becomes demoniac fire to you, and the clouds of heaven as the smoke of Acheron."[43] Of the actual onset of this chastizing pollution, he who interpreted the truths of "The Open Sky" forty years before in *Modern Painters*, volume 1, has been the unheeded witness. "But it has been my fate," he continues, "to live and work in antagonism to the instincts, and yet more to the interests, of the age; since I wrote that chapter on the pure traceries of the vault of morning, the fury of useless traffic has shut the sight, whether of morning or evening, from more than the third part of England; and the foulness of sensual fantasy has infected the bright beneficence of the life-giving sky with the dull horrors of disease, and the feeble falsehoods of insanity."[44] But, since his immediate subject in these lectures is the condition of modern art, he will let the medium illustrate his message. He has with him a little French book, intended as a child's introduction to physical science, from which his assistant has prepared an enlarged engraving that will illustrate the modern mind's image of cumulous clouds: bad art, bad science, and their symbol. But first, for contrast, he offers a beneficent cloud image by quoting a gilded apocalypse of heaven from Wordsworth's *The Excursion.*[45] Then against this rapturous cloud vision he places the Devil-cloud of the modern "Plutocracy of Knowledge." It was, the *Pall Mall Gazette* reported, a sketch of clouds arranged to represent a mocking fiendish face. Finally, the report of the lecture gives this additional detail: when his assistant went to turn the sketch over Ruskin insisted it be left where it was, a reminder "of the loathsome and lying spirit of defamation which studies men only in the skeleton and nature in ashes."[46]

THE VOICE OF THE BIRDLESS LAKE

Henry James declared that the "great question" to be asked about any vigorous literary career would simply be what is that writer's "total view" of the existence he has had for so long under observation.[47] A writer's "total view," however, could never be fully apprehended in a conceptual statement; this global meaning of his work is, like the meaning of his concrete existence to him, always there animating his acts and works but never fully given. In modern criticism this problem of the "total view" has been approached most consistently by the "consciousness" critics of the Geneva School and by the closely related group of critics who, following Jean Paul Sartre, adopt existential psychoanalysis as their method. The Geneva critics examine the collective body of a writer's work in order to discern, with biographical help, the latent and unique system of experiential patterns or primary self-world relationships which constitutes the embodied and controlling consciousness in his work. For existential psychoanalytic critics like Sartre or, more recently, Serge Doubrovsky,[48] a writer's individual works can only be fully understood in relation to the fundamental impulse of his existence, his life's "forward throw" or *projet*. The task of the interpretive critic is to make himself one with the writer's primary project.

This project, however, like the immanent intentionality discerned by the Geneva critics, lies beneath the writer's recurrent themes or deliberate "intentions"; it belongs to his pre-reflexive and affective apprehensions of the world—to what Edmund Husserl called the *lebenswelt*.

For these critics, literature and biography coincide in their depths (a point of interest with respect to Ruskin, whose public and autobiographical writings converge). That is, the true coincidence is not at the level of biographical facts and discursive statements but, most meaningfully, in the deep conjunction of symbols in the life and the work. Concrete existence, the existential critic tells us, is always incomplete, a "detotalized totality," in Sartre's phrase; it projects toward an imagined existence, representing symbolically before itself the objects of its desire. The meaning of the life would be, in this view, the significance of that completeness of being which the concrete existence continually lacks. However, this completeness can only be conveyed in symbols; it has no objective reality. Since the truths of a concrete life are revealed (and concealed) in its symbols, the project of a writer's life is, therefore, as these critics see it, a dynamic effort to realize an imaginary symbolic scheme in which his works are moments of synthesis. Because there is no analytic language that can express this signifying totality it appears as a system of symbols, something on the order of a personal myth. The reference to myth seems appropriate here since psychoanalysts have long referred to the latent content of the writer's work, as also to the patient's narrative, in mythic terms; symbols, as Paul Ricoeur has reminded us, are "overdetermined" in meaning and partake of the oneric, aesthetic, and mythopoeic modes of the imagination.

In saying this much about modern equivalents of James' "great question" concerning the writer's "total view" I am not proposing a critical procedure by which we must seek the embodied consciousness or the fundamental project in Ruskin's work. Yet I believe several suggestive points of approach can be drawn from the preceding discussion. First, given the vast, diffuse, uneven, and largely neglected mass of Ruskin's work, there is an urgent need for the kind of integrative view these critics aspire to, especially one that links the public and the private writings. Second, there is the reasonable possibility that the core of such a global view is not to be found in Ruskin's discursive statements but in his symbolic and mythological obsessions. Further, Ruskin's writing itself seems to move increasingly, even within its topical fragmentation, toward symbolic and mythic integration, as if he were himself attempting to draw the obsessional, the poetic, and the mythopoeic into the confines of discursive prose. In this therapeutic effort *The Storm-Cloud* achieves a measure of success; however, the Brantwood diary entries for the preceding five years reveal how completely Ruskin's mind could succumb to the tangle of symbolic values it had projected over the years. Finally, whether or not every man's ultimate project is, as Sartre said, "the desire to be God," the self-conscious agent in the becoming of things, this impulse is close to the surface in any apocalyptic utterance, and it is evident in *The Storm-Cloud.*

Of course these lectures need not be read as the climactic expression of an existential project or the frustration of it. The lectures do, however, have deep determinants in Ruskin's life and work. This can be shown most clearly if we assume that the question concerning a writer's "total view" simply asks about the archetypal patterns to which he gave himself. What "myth" has he made or continued? *The Storm-Cloud*, as I have suggested, cannot be dismissed as a demented diatribe against smoke; it is Ruskin's central image for the deterioration of life. It is a mythic sky, "fraught with background," as are the skies of the Old Testament, *King Lear*, Wordsworth's *The Excursion*, Turner's *Slavers Throwing Overboard the Dead and Dying—Typhon Coming On* or Camus' *The Plague*. In his accounts of the onset of storm-cloud and plague-wind after 1870 Ruskin was making a myth of crisis for his age and for ours. But this storm is the embittered climax of an apocalyptic yearning—a thirst for intimations of a forming power in particular forms, of the numinous in the phenomenal—that is at once the controlling dynamic in his work and its primary link with the Romantic awareness.

There is an often-quoted passage in *Praeterita* that neatly illustrates the kind of moment of revelation or cosmic participation Ruskin yearned for. Rambling at Fontainebleau one day in 1842, oppressed by his "savage dislike of palaces and straight gravel walks," he stretched out on the bank of a cart road and languidly began to sketch a small aspen outlined against the sky. As he sketched his perception submitted to the internal necessity of the form, and the languor left him. "The beautiful lines insisted on being traced,—without weariness. More and more beautiful they became, as each rose out of the rest, and took its place in the air. With wonder increasing every instant, I saw that they 'composed' themselves by finer laws than any known of men. At last the tree was there, and everything else that I had thought before about trees, nowhere." But it was not simply the mystery of silvan forms that had been penetrated in that moment: "I then saw," he continues, "in their beauty, the same laws which guided the clouds, divided the light, and balanced the wave." Finally, he asserts that this relational event itself was a manifestation to him of "the bond between the human mind and all visible things."[49]

Ruskin chose to recall this experience in the form of an epiphany, an experience of meaning that altered his self-world relationship in a fundamental way. Whatever the event may actually have been in 1842, he cited it in 1886 as having been a moment of perceptual initiation into the mysterious "laws" of natural form. He offered it in *Praeterita* as a paradigm of his early vision as artist and critic. The revelation is at once aesthetic, religious, and to some extent phenomenological. The "laws" disclosed determine the beauty of all natural forms; they are, of course, not human laws; however, they define the relation of perception to its world. Ruskin says that the experience enabled him to understand that "He hath made everything beautiful, in his time"[50] refers to the ordained "bond" of form linking, mutually implicating, perception and the natural object. Natural form and consciousness are there *for* each other. Further, the composing "laws" are the laws of life because they are unifying; they are the laws of cohesiveness in the world of unmediated perception. Ruskin is, as Whitehead said of Wordsworth and Shelley, "witness to a prehensive unification as constituting the very being of nature."[51] The "laws" are mysterious, not only because they are "finer laws than any known of men," but also because they are revealed only in moments of pure, submissive seeing. These formative "laws" are the vital mystery of being; obedience to them, it follows, is the sign of life in any art or society, but witness to their action or their failure is only granted to the innocent eye. Not in the operations of fancy, or analysis, or dissection, Ruskin is continually telling us, but only in faithful and passionate attention to the immediate object, natural or artistic, are the laws of cohesiveness, which are its life, or the interruption of those laws, which is its death, revealed. Whether he had travelled this far in 1842 is uncertain, but Ruskin does tell us in *Praeterita* that he walked back along the wood-road that day at Fontainebleau with the conviction that it had led him very far, "farther than ever fancy had reached, or theodolite measured."[52]

But this Fontainebleau account is atypical of its author in two important respects, perhaps because it is the deliberate portrayal of an early innocence of eye. First, the later Ruskin was more inclined, not simply to commune with forms, but to read through forms to intentions. Patrick Conner has recently called attention to Ruskin's interest in facial expressions in art; he reminds us that by 1846, under the influence of Alexis-Francois Rio, Ruskin was beginning to read the characters of artists from the expression in their figures, and that he would soon be reading architectural form as an index of the moral condition of the builders.[53] In his later criticism Ruskin generally referred the vital lines of expression in an object to an individual, social, or mythic subjectivity—that is, to the creative life of a particular artist or society, or, in natural objects, to the evident intentions of the Deity or the Devil. A reviewer for the *Athenaeum* was correct, if somewhat contemptuous, in noting that Ruskin "discovers the Apocalypse in a daisy."[54] However, he also discovers it, less sentimentally, in a cigar butt. For Ruskin came to see the Judgment in every transfer of lives, landscapes, and resources into goods—in every social choice. The Ruskin of *Fors Clavigera* would have applauded Camus' assertion in *The Fall* that the Last Judgment takes place daily. He insisted that Being is revealed, as it is concealed, in being. "Through the glass, darkly. But, except through the glass, in no wise."[55]

The second element, then, of Ruskin's mature vision not evident in the early Fontainbleau revelation is something we have noticed in *The Storm-Cloud*: the sense of conflict or crisis in the organicity, the vital mystery, of the world. As Ruskin aged the glass of being lost more and more of the purity it had had for him in his youth; it became shadowed as his childhood faiths, Evangelical and Wordsworthian, were challenged by dangerous knowledge—of sensuality in art, of social distress, of science, and of self. By mid-life the controlling project of his work, I mean its characteristic way of assimilating objects and experiences, was to separate the "laws" of life from those of death as he saw them at work in the primary, interconnected, areas of human activity: in the techniques of the arts, in what was then called "political economy," and in our efforts to comprehend and utilize nature. Ruskin came to read every aspect of existence he studied, whether morning sky or manufactured object or handful of North Country dust or fading fresco by Giorgione, as the adumbration of a conflict of vital with lethal forces. The need was urgent because, as he said in "The Mystery of Life and Its Arts," "We are in the midst of judgment."[56]

Broadly speaking, Ruskin saw vital laws at work whenever "infinity" or mystery was portrayed or venerated: in Turner's skies as opposed to Michelangelo's torsos; in art or architecture that shows the infinity of living organism or of the craftsman's touch rather than the rigidities of formalized or mechanical techniques; in life-oriented as opposed to wealth-oriented economics; in nature perceived as intimating in its forms the intentions of what he came to call the "forming power," nature the "God-written Apocalypse," in Carlyle's phrase, as opposed to nature merely used as an expressionless "there." Diffused light was, for Ruskin, an index of purity and the commonest sign of the operation of the vital laws in nature or in art. This lust for pure, bright infinities of form is perhaps most evident in his adoration of Turner and detestation of Rembrandt, whose work, for Ruskin, epitomized the operation of deadly laws in art.

Antagonistic, lethal laws proceed from all consciousness that jams the vital mystery of being and seeing: consciousness in which perception is blocked by explanation, art in which infinity and clarity succumb to the deceits of formalism or tenebrism. The operations of these laws are manifested, for Ruskin, in neutralized nature with which he can no longer imagine a solidarity, in the sordidness of industrial landscapes, in man considered as an economic biped, in art that evades the mysteries of perception either by deliberate deception of the eye or by taking refuge in shadow. His pervasive images for the presence of destroying laws are the forms of darkness and the worm: dark weather, chilling and hissing wind, blighted landscapes; specious shadow or glitter in painting; archetypal serpents, coils of smoke. Ruskin's storm-plague meteorology is simply his symbolism for what he felt was a crisis in the vital mystery of his *lebenswelt*; its numinous organicity and beauty seemed threatened by antithetical modes of thought and use he represented by a diabolic presence in the skies. *The Storm-Cloud* is his myth of the End: "diabolic" mentality (*dia-bollein*, "to tear apart") is displacing the symbolic (*sym-bollein*, "to throw together") and will be its own punishment, for the world requires some "privileged" perception of its unity.

Ruskin bore witness to a crisis in that dimension of awareness the Romantics called imagination or vision. This crisis results from the repudiation of the organic conception of being and of the kind of revelation that appears (as in Ruskin's Fontainebleau experience) to be a penetration of, or seeing into, the unity of being—into what Carlyle, following Goethe, called "the open secret" of divine oneness. Ruskin, like other Romantics, tested all perception against this ultimate mode of awareness which communes with the vital mystery of its object—the lines, laws, or powers of integration it discloses. Of course Romantic imagination remains a vexed topic. Yet we may appeal, though we have no *positive* evidence that Ruskin did so, to Coleridge, its preeminent theorist, and note simply that in his thought imagination is a theory of the coalescence of consciousness and nature. It is a projective and penetrative experience. Imagination half creates and half perceives, in this view, and thus it animates what it envisions with passion, life, and the same self-integrative power that is characteristic of organic forms in nature. It therefore mediates between man and nature. It values the prehensive principle, the mutual implication of parts, in all forms. It detests the fragment and the mechanical juxtaposition of parts. Imagination is thus a vitalizing power: "it is essentially *vital*, even as all objects (*as* objects) are essentially fixed and dead."[57]

In Ruskin's theory, the imagination is not, or is not understood to be, a projective power; as in the early Wordsworth, it is a seeing into the life of things. He argues that in its highest function imagination is a "Penetrative, possession-taking faculty" that "drinks the very vital sap of that it deals with."[58] In his three-part discussion of the subject in the second volume of *Modern Painters*, Ruskin's overriding concern is to stress the idea that imagination is seeing, a visionary or apocalyptic power that can convey what it sees with the immediacy and truth of prophecy. "There is no reasoning in it," he insists; it does not analyze or make subject-object distinctions; it penetrates to truth in an instant and lays that bare. He does not explicitly share the Romantic view, taken by Coleridge in "Dejection," that imagination may involve the projection of emotional states upon an otherwise inert nature; however, he is much concerned about the effect of mental disorder upon imagination. He tries to avoid the problem of impressionism by relating imagination to vision in both the ocular and prophetic senses and by connecting this imaginative seeing with self-annihilating penetration of, or participation in, the object. "This power of prophecy," he asserts in 1845, "is the very essence of the whole matter"; and in a note of 1883 he cuts through to his meaning by insisting that imagination is, "primarily, the power of seeing anything we describe as if it were real."[59]

This power of vision enters each of the three modes Ruskin assigns to the imagination. His "associative" imagination is an integrative capacity, a "prophetic action of the mind" that can see at an instant, in an infinity of things, the essential rightness of certain things for each other. It is an organic or participatory power; this faculty of the imaginative mind does not integrate things by rational "laws" of composition. The laws of nature are "his own nature"; all others he defies; "he sees his end over the waste from the first, and goes straight at it; never losing sight of it, nor throwing away a step."[60] The "penetrative" imagination sees through crusts and surfaces to the "vital sap" of truth. This "penetrating, possession-taking faculty" is, Ruskin holds, "the highest intellectual power of man."[61] It is visionary in its power to realize spiritual presences. "The whispers at men's ears it lifts into visible angels."[62] It goes, in effect, to the vital mystery beneath the dead, material fact of the world. Ruskin speaks of the third imaginative mode, the "contemplative," as a symbolizing or abstracting power; yet he insists on its visionary nature; "for those painters only have right imaginative power who can set the supernatural form before us, fleshed and boned like ourselves."[63] He is clearly moving toward the mythopoeic imagination here, and this is evidenced by the fact that the immediately following chapter, "Of the Superhuman Ideal," concerns the problem of imaginative realization of supernatural beings. At this early stage of his thought on the subject he concludes that, by comparison with Christian divine images in such painters as Angelico, Giotto and Perugino, Greek mythic images have no "spirit-power" but merely "clay strength," for the Greek could not conceive a spiritual presence. This position he later repudiated as being a false Evangelical bias.

Put simply and in modern terms, Ruskin's central meaning is an outcry against the displacement of the awareness that Martin Buber has called "I-Thou" by that nonrelational, abstracting consciousness he calls "I-It." Myths and mythic symbols came to be important to Ruskin because they are, or were thought to be in his time, primordial expressions of the vital mystery, the relational bond between consciousness and being. For the vital mystery is the participatory urge that Ruskin detected beneath all tendency to "pathetic fallacy," whether in dead personifications at one extreme or living myths at the other. The plea for mystery is, it appears, ultimately a plea for "presences," for what Philip Wheelwright has called "presential reality." "A presence is a mystery— not an enigma that arouses our curiosity, but a mystery that claims our awe."[64] Much of the total meaning we are after here was conveyed by Wordsworth ("Little we see in Nature that is ours") in that famous heart-cry of Romantic paganism which Ruskin learned to quote in sympathy:

—Great God! I'd rather be
A Pagan suckled in a creed outworn;
So might I, standing on this pleasant lea,
Have glimpses that would make me less forlorn;
Have sight of Proteus rising from the sea;
Or hear old Triton blow his wreathéd horn.

Ruskin's famous autobiography, *Praeterita,* contains a number of such apocalyptic moments; generally they are remembered as points of transition in the growth of his mind. Many were selected and adapted from the less tendentious diary versions. Aesthetic objects and natural forms, especially sky effects, are the most common external correlatives of these experiences. However, the essential point about *Praeterita* is that Ruskin projects his identity, much as Wordsworth does his in *The Prelude*, as a pattern of critical moments of revelation, of authentic tidings of an invisible power. The moment of communion with the forming power in the aspen at Fontainebleau might be taken as typical of his epiphanies in the benign kind. Like his masters, Wordsworth and Carlyle, Ruskin views his life as an essentially religious but not always explicitly Christian progress. His awareness is more fundamentally Romantic than Protestant. Naturally he found his nursery Evangelicalism more and more constrictive. His religion spilled. There was a moment of renunciation in 1858, and he entered an important "pagan" or syncretic phase of spiritual growth. But the major components of the Romantic consciousness, nature as revelation, imagination as penetrative vision, translucence of symbols, the imperative to create a new mythos and a new order of life, come close to being the defining characteristics of Ruskin's awareness, if it is also understood that his was a Romanticism with a phenomenological bias. That is, while Ruskin was most often fascinated by intricately textured objects that had infinity, mystery, and organic unity in them, his concern was also to describe accurately their immediate appearances to the innocent eye. He constantly stressed the unified factual, poetical, and mystical power of pure seeing; however, his writing contains the further implication that such purity of sight is only attained at moments.

The question of Ruskin's Romanticism aside, I would simply reassert here that the stylistic strategy of *Praeterita* (and also of *Fors Clavigera*, in which the autobiography was begun) involves the speaker's seeing the determinants of his life as a sequence of apocalyptic moments, primary religious experiences or moments of "penetrative imagination." Further, and most important, these moments are generally confrontations with objective forms, especially skies, made translucent of a mythic presence. The translucence is developed stylistically by means of "pathetic fallacy" or by mythic allusion. Finally, this "presence," as we have seen, was by no means always benevolent. Gradually Ruskin came to see himself as the tragic interpreter of a cosmic crisis manifested in ordinary things. The "Night," implicit in his motto "Today" ("For the night cometh, when no man can work"), takes on a historical as well as a biographical significance. This sense he has of crisis in the god-stuff is the deeper meaning of the common identification of Ruskin as a Victorian "prophet." It appears, then, to judge from his own testimony in *Praeterita, Fors Clavigera*, the diaries, and other subjective writing, that

Ruskin was susceptible to religio-aesthetic moments of revelation, apocalyptic moments in which particular forms seemed to be manifestations of benevolent or malevolent "presences."

Of course it is neither possible nor necessary to prove here that Ruskin the historical person actually had such quasi-mystical experiences,[65] nor will it be necessary here to consider such experiences as possible results of filial bondage or thwarted love. (Of his parents he said, "Like visible powers of nature to me"; of love, with equal conclusiveness, "I was given nothing to love.") These matters concern the biographer. The interests of this study are primarily in parts played by myth, theory of myth, and mythical consciousness in his writings. When, for instance, he declares in *Deucalion: Collected Studies of the Lapse of Waves and the Life of Stones* (1875–83) that "Proserpine and Deucalion are at least as true as Eve or Noah; and all four together incomparably truer than the Darwinian theory" and further that "the reader may take it for a first principle, both in science and literature, that the feeblest myth is better than the strongest theory,"[66] he is appealing to a mode of awareness that has assumed increasing significance in his thought and style (since the early fifties) as the only restorative of the vital mystery of being, that "dearest freshness deep down things" as Hopkins called it, that was being neutralized by certain dangerous tendencies of the modern mind. What he is defending, of course, is mythical or presential consciousness. This consciousness, as Ernst Cassirer has observed, acts by animation, isolation, and interpenetration of its objects and so resolves the barrier that analytic consciousness erects between "inner" and "outer" aspects of experience. What interests us here is the way in which Ruskin, in the current of his thought and style, appears to have been driven to mythical consciousness (true "pathetic fallacy") as a last redoubt against what Whitehead called "the fallacy of misplaced concreteness," which must lead, Ruskin knew, to final disruption of the biosphere and all harmony of being.

This movement into myth appears to be conditioned in Ruskin's work by a confluence of factors: his interest in artistic myth-makers or other participants in the mythic consciousness, especially Homer, Dante, Turner, Wordsworth and Carlyle; the spiritual vacuum created by the failure of his early Evangelicalism; his special interest in the problem of form (as Coleridge had put it, "The idea which puts the form together cannot itself be the form.");[67] his friendship with the famous solar mythologist Max Müller; other possible encounters with the theory of myth; and last, most difficult to assess, the matter immediately before us, which is the actual representation in his writing of apparent moments of mythical consciousness when things seemed charged with presence. In such moments, Ernst Cassirer observes, "the I is oriented not immediately toward the outside world but rather toward a personal existence and life that are similar to it in kind. Subjectivity has as its correlate not some outward thing but rather a 'thou' or 'he,' from which on the one hand it distinguishes itself, but with which on the other hand it groups itself. This "thou" or "he" forms the true antithesis which the I requires in order to find and define itself."[68] In connection with this last point, self-definition in terms of mythic self-projection, it is important to reiterate, before taking up examples, something that was said in speaking of the "storm-cloud": increasingly as Ruskin aged the presence he encountered was hostile or diabolic, or expressed in terms of some archetypal antagonist; Python, frequently, or Ladon, or Medusa. That is, even the progress of anti-mythic neutralizing awareness was itself the manifestation of a presence. In Ruskin "the disappearance of God" was the appearance of the Fiend.

It is not, of course, possible to deal comprehensively with Ruskin's presential or apocalyptic moments here; but a few passages from *Praeterita* and the diaries will clarify my meaning and at the same time show first manifestations of that looming adversary which will ultimately manifest himself as the plague-cloud.

In the early chapters of *Praeterita* Ruskin, late in life, attempted to recreate the seed-time of his being. Images fastened themselves upon him in beauty and in fear; we observe the beginning of his "thirst for the visible fact."[69] His eye was seized as if in the "I-Thou" relation by the mystery of forms in carpet, counterpane, and wallpaper; he discovered a beatific calm in the outline of distant hills. Other images seemed to be recreated as if to give them nuances of the ominous for those who know the rest of his story. There is his fascination with water carts being filled "through beautiful little trap-doors, by pipes like boa constrictors; . . . [he] was never weary of contemplating that mystery, and the delicious dripping consequent."[70] There is a terrifying presence in the dark pools of the river Tay, in the "swirls of smooth blackness, broken by no fleck of foam, where the Tay gathered herself like Medusa."[71] Earlier in the same chapter the self-researcher introduced a long and strange quotation from his earliest literary production. It was, he says, "an extremely perfect type of the interwoven temper of my mind, at the beginning of days just as much as at their end."[72] The passage is apparently the climactic moment of his first "book," a little make-believe volume of forty hand-printed pages issued by the prophet at the age of seven. The tale is entitled "Harry and Lucy." The author explains that the work was composed under the joint influences of Jeremiah Joyce's *Scientific Dialogues* and Byron's *Manfred*, and that of four projected "volumes" only the first was completed. The excerpt is too long to reproduce here, but the shape of events is as follows: Harry is busy with a mountain drawing (Ruskin's first of the type) when Lucy calls his attention to "a great black cloud from the north which seemed rather electrical." Harry seizes an "electrical apparatus" given him by his father, and the great cloud charges his apparatus positively. Then a vast pillar of dust looms up from the ground and seems to follow the positive cloud and almost touch it. But meanwhile another great cloud trailed by cloudlets has approached and charged the apparatus negatively; when this cloud then approaches the positive cloud, lightning darts between them through the cloud of dust, whereupon the negative cloud dissolves in rain and clears the sky. This account of storm phenomena follows Jeremiah Joyce very closely, but the young Ruskin added something quite unscientific: after the rain Harry observes a rainbow and a presence, for the rainbow had "a rising mist under it which his fancy soon transformed into a female form." Finally, we are told that Harry knew the legend of the water-witch of the Alps, who could be raised by throwing a handful of water into the air and saying the mystic words. The point, we are told, is that the myth affected Harry now that he saw with his own eyes something like it in the clouds. Like *The Storm-Cloud of the Nineteenth Century*, "Harry and Lucy" shows the interweaving of empirical and mythopoeic, or at least relational, qualities of mind.

By his own testimony one of the most significant apocalyptic moments of Ruskin's youth occurred in the garden terrace of Schaffhausen one evening in the spring of 1833. Again he describes the event as a sky infused with mythic presence. The Ruskins had walked out that evening impatient for their first glimpse of the Alps, piously expecting to receive it, however, only after the "profane exertion" of a climb. But the vision surprised them. Suddenly, from an easy promenade west of town, the delectable horizon was there:

> There was no thought in any of us for a moment of their being clouds. They were clear as crystal, sharp on the pure horizon sky, and already tinged with rose by the sinking sun. Infinitely beyond all that we had ever thought or dreamed,—the seen walls of lost Eden could not have been more beautiful to us; not more awful, round heaven, the walls of sacred Death.[73]

Ruskin goes on to explain that this experience was a rite of passage in the growth of his mind, "his blessed entrance into life," but he adds also the mature reservation that the young initiate's temperament belonged to the age. And, of course, the experience—"A direct revelation of the benevolent will in creation," he called it—might be compared with other Romantic sacramental moments of communion with the supernal through the scenic. One thinks of Wordsworth's famous baptismal moment at Hawkshead, or of the sky-mountain visions of *The Prelude* or *The Excursion*. But Ruskin's account resembles more closely another such sacramental exposure, developed also in the age's temperament, but nearer in time and image. Here, published in the year of Ruskin's own Alpine vision, is Carlyle's Teufelsdröckh communing with the rose-lit peaks:

> He gazed over those stupendous masses with wonder, almost with longing desire; never till this hour had he known Nature, that she was One, that she was his Mother and divine. And as the ruddy glow was fading into clearness in the sky, and the Sun had now departed, a murmur of Eternity and Immensity, of Death and Life stole through his soul; and he felt as if Death and Life were one, as if the Earth were not dead, as if the Spirit of the Earth had its throne in that splendour, and his own spirit were therewith holding communion.[74]

As stylistic strategy, of course, these moments involve using the scene as the outward correlate of an inward renovation. The horizon becomes apocalyptic—in this case, of beatitude. Finally, it should be said that this particular image of the rose-lit peace of the high snows, the unction of mountain infinities, remains Ruskin's consoling image of possible sublimity, until it is gradually extinguished by the plague-cloud, the sign of possible malignity.

In *Praeterita*, writing from the perspective of half a century, Ruskin set 1837, his eighteenth year, as the year in which he "felt for the last time, the pure childish love of nature which Wordsworth so idly takes for an intimation of immortality."[75] A connected passage that Ruskin left in manuscript defines this feeling as "inexplicable, infinite, sacred: the sense of an awful life in things, an awful harmony; man made for Earth and Sky, and these for *him*."[76] The text continues: "It is a feeling only possible to youth, for all care, regret, or knowledge of evil destroys it. . . . The sense of the freedom, spontaneous, unpolluted power of nature was essential in it."[77] But also in the published passage there is a hint of retraction: "I am but the same youth, disappointed and rheumatic."[78] Now it should be apparent from the *Storm-Cloud* passages already quoted that Ruskin never ceases to commune with nature—But the pegs of that felt "harmony" are indeed gradually set down. The account in *Praeterita* and the diary entries show Ruskin of the forties and fifties becoming increasingly conscious of a malevolent as well as a benevolent will in things; the records—"moments"—show him entering the fallen world, becoming conscious of what Blake called the "contraries" of existence. The chiaroscuro of his imagery deepens correspondingly.

"The eye altering," Blake observed, "alters all." When we look into Ruskin's diaries of this period of initiation and at the uses of these memories in *Praeterita*, we confront such a projected alteration of the self in all its complexity of texture, fragmented into hundreds of separate impressions with daily interactions of mood and scene that it is impossible to paraphrase them. But within the rich fabric of this record woven of statement and intimation, immediacy and recollection—of facts, reflections, and scenes gathering into style—certain features make themselves felt. The dominant message is the intrusion of intimations of mortality, the humanizing of a soul by distress. In scenes described, there is progressive shadowing of what Wordsworth, in a similar mood, called "The light that never was, on sea or land." There are complaints of satiation with scenery, and there is some restless yearning for sublimity that is still occasionally gratified by the mountain glory or by clouds in solemn light. But if we supplement the deliberately therapeutic account in *Praeterita* with the more immediate records of *Fors Clavigera*, the diaries, and the later drawings, we see how his images of clarity and purity become, in the sixties and seventies, increasingly troubled by shadow and blight. Nature never becomes neutralized for him, never loses its symbolic power of reference to the ontological through the ontic; and his sense of "presence" in nature is more effectively articulated by means of myth. However, the face of existence becomes less benign and increasingly shadowed by that malignant antagonist whose ultimate manifestation is the plague-cloud. "I am always checked," he told himself in 1875, "in my natural history by the sense of failure or hostility. 'An enemy hath done this.' "[79]

In various places in the later writing he speaks of Python (in his view the Greek equivalent of Satan)[80] wreathing up against him. This is an allusion to the personal epiphany he had received from Turner's *"Apollo and Python"* while studying the painting for *Modern Painters*, volume 5. Here he is at fifty (1869), for instance, writing to his friend Mrs. Cowper, Lady Mount-Temple: "I am looking out as I write on a desolate little market-place—mere desolate chapel—desolatest hills above, sullen with rain, the Python gathering himself together, at me— Vain marketing—vainer prayer—Hills—to which no man lifts his eyes for—Help."[81] This Python-fighting appears to have two dimensions of meaning at once for Ruskin. At the subconscious level Python must be

connected with the serpent dreams he records in the diaries of the period
(for example, the entry for 1 November of the same year: "Had the most
horrible serpent dream I ever had yet in my life. The deadliest came out
into the room under a door. It rose up like a Cobra—with horrible round
eyes and had woman's, or at least Medusa's, breasts.")[82] And these
serpent dreams in turn are very likely connected with the fatal turn his
involvement with Rose was taking at the time, a crisis of the libido one
might suppose. At a more objective level participating in Apollo's
archetypal struggle with Python was simply another version of his
struggle with a great enemy in the skies. Hence to the same correspondent, Mrs. Cowper-Temple, he had written of the same enemy in a
different language two years earlier: "It is very frightful and wonderful.
The sense of demons in the dark air, and in the cold—joins strangely
with my own bitterness, as if all the black cold were sent for me only."[83]
Often in the works and diaries of the seventies and after Ruskin identifies
with mythic heroes of light (Apollo, Hercules, Perseus, Saint George,
and, on another plane, Turner) who engage in cosmic (and psychic)
struggles with the dark coils of fallen knowledge. Correlatively, his
criticism places greater emphasis upon visionary elements, "the visiting
and visible dream," in art; therefore he becomes increasingly anxious to
distinguish those "morbid states of intellect which are extremities of
noble passion, from those which are the punishments of ambition,
avarice, or lasciviousness."[84]

"Every day here," he told himself at Chamonix in 1854, "I seem to see
farther into nature, and into myself, and into futurity."[85] He was then at
work on the third and fourth volumes of *Modern Painters*. The progress
of insight that takes place in those and the later works defies accurate
expression in a few words. Broadly, he appears to have passed through
three primary but overlapping phases of concern: aesthetic,
socioeconomic, and prophetic or apocalyptic. His interests were chiefly
aesthetic in the forties and fifties, the period of *Modern Painters*, *The
Seven Lamps of Architecture*, and *The Stones of Venice*; primarily
economic and social analytical in the early and mid-sixties, the major
works being *Unto This Last*, *Munera Pulveris*, *The Crown of Wild
Olive*, and *Time and Tide*; and primarily prophetic of aesthetic, social,
and ecological doom from the late sixties to the end, especially in such
works as *The Queen of the Air*; *Fors Clavigera*; *The Art of England*; *The
Pleasures of England*; and *Fiction, Fair and Foul*. He evolved also three
relatively distinct styles as vehicles for each of these centers of concern.
The famous florid, sensuous word-paintings are the mark of the first
phase; it was a style he deliberately repudiated in favor of the com-

John Ruskin. *Greta*, 1876. Collection of the Art Institute of Chicago.

John Ruskin. *Ponte di Santa Trinità, Florence,* c. 1882. Courtesy of the Education Trust, Brantwood, Coniston

paratively spare expository and homiletic style of his socioeconomic period. This, in turn, gave way to a final style that tended to be cryptic, allusive, "tensive," and yet in its way more vehement. He called it his "riddling prose." Mainly he was attempting to escape the overblown descriptive prose for which he is still most generally known. This movement of style is coherent with the general drift of his interests from truths of sight to truths of vision, from things seen with, to things seen through, the eye.

He moves, in brief, from a conception of "Truth," basically mimetic and naturalistic, as an aesthetic norm in *Modern Painters*, volume 1, toward a more expressive theory of the same aesthetic value. A crucial development of his thought is reached in *Modern Painters*, volume 2, with his theory of the "penetrative or possession-taking" aspect of imagination, which "gets within all fence, cuts down to the root, and drinks the very vital sap of that it deals with,"[86] a theory which, as we have noted, appears to have affinities with the Coleridgean doctrine of coalescence of mind and nature in art. It is interesting that Ruskin repudiated most of the rest of this second volume, with its sacramental system of nature, as marred by "sectarian" narrowness. *Modern Painters*, volume 3, continues his interest in this matter of imaginative rapport or interpenetration of mind and nature in art, especially in the famous chapter entitled "Of the Pathetic Fallacy." Here and in the preceding chapter, called "Of Classical Landscape," myth becomes involved with his conception of nature. By the third volume he has taken up an inquiry into what I have been calling apocalyptic or mythopoeic awareness. By volume 5 of *Modern Painters* certain cloud forms are Gorgons or Graiae, and Turner has become a great myth-maker. It is especially significant to this study that the great moments of the last volume of *Modern Painters* should be given to mythic expositions: "The Lance of Pallas," "The Nereid's Guard," "The Hesperid Aeglé," even, in its way, "The Dark Mirror."

Already in *Modern Painters*, volume 5, some of the special qualities of his final style—indignant, cryptic, symbolic, apocalyptic features—were beginning to make themselves felt. The English were expected to understand that their condition was, for instance, this: "Thus in Athens, we have the triumph of Pallas; and in Venice the Assumption of the Virgin; here, in England, is our great spiritual fact for ever interpreted to us—the Assumption of the Dragon."[87] And the conditions of light and landscape under which, in Ruskin's view, Turner learned his art are clearly apocalyptic.

A goodly landscape this, for the lad to paint, and under a goodly light.

Wide enough the light was, and clear; no more Salvator's lurid chasm on jagged horizon, nor Dürer's spotted rest of sunny gleam on hedgerow and field; but light over all the world. Full shone now its awful globe, one pallid charnel-house,—a ball strewn bright with human ashes, glaring in poised sway beneath the sun, all blinding-white with death from pole to pole,—death, not of myriads of poor bodies only, but of will, and mercy, and conscience; death, not once inflicted on the flesh, but daily fastening on the spirit; death, not silent or patient, waiting his appointed hour, but voiceful, venomous; death with the taunting word, and burning grasp, and infixed sting.[88]

During his seventeen-year engagement with the five volumes of *Modern Painters* important objective changes had taken place. The diaries of the forties and fifties and the corresponding sections of *Praeterita* reveal the gradual erosion of his early Evangelicalism, a development that culminated in a revelational moment of 1858 that he identified as the moment of his "unconversion" and the beginning of a sixteen-year sojourn in what he came to call his "religion of Humanity." In the published works of the earlier period (to 1860) there is evident a gradual drift of his concern away from the problem of beauty toward the problem of its social matrix. Life, the vital mystery, was still the center of his quest, but he was now less concerned with the condition of life in the work than in the workman, and in the society from which he emerged. This shift of interest from the properties of vital art to those of a vital society that becomes apparent in *The Seven Lamps of Architecture, The Stones of Venice, Modern Painters,* volume 5, and especially *The Political Economy of Art,* culminated in 1860 with the appearance of *Unto This Last,* a work he considered pivotal in his career. The major works of the sixties, *Unto This Last, Munera Pulveris* (as *Essays on Political Economy,* [1862–63]), *Sesame and Lilies* (1865), *The Ethics of the Dust* (1866), *The Crown of Wild Olive* (1866), *Time and Tide* (1867), share a common difference from the works of his earlier and later periods: the banishment of nearly all consideration of specific works of art as such in favor of the more preliminary problems of social regeneration. Essentially they see life and landscape as locked in a struggle with dead wealth, much as in the earlier period he had seen life in art as threatened by formalism on the one hand and a Dutch sort of literalism on the other. In society and art his norm of perfection is the purposive coherence of infinitely varied parts, the mysterious unity of organic forms. Thus, for instance, in the social order as in the living thing the law of life is "help."

A pure or holy state of anything, therefore, is that in which all its parts are helpful or consistent. They may or may not be homogeneous. The highest or organic purities are composed of many elements in an entirely helpful state. The highest and first law of the universe—and the other nave of life is, therefore, "help." The other name of death is "separation." Government and co-operation are in all things and eternally the laws of life. Anarchy and competition, eternally, and in all things, the laws of death.[89]

But Ruskin's career had another major turn to take at the end of the sixties. It was a turn away from the primarily critical or analytic toward an increasingly prophetic or apocalyptic tone. Obviously there are external factors such as the indifference or hostility of readers to his socioeconomic theories, the duties of his first Oxford professorship in 1870, and the hostility of the La Touches that influenced the shift. This final style was announced by the publication in 1869 of *The Queen of the Air: Greek Myths of Cloud and Storm*, though it is clearly signaled by sibylline qualities in the fifth volume of *Modern Painters* and the difficult *Cestus of Aglaia* (1865–66). *The Queen of the Air* is ostensibly a trivial study of Greek myths undertaken in preparation for his professorship. But his remarks to Mrs. Cowper-Temple and others indicate that it had a special significance to him. ("I've done the best I could —The very best I could—with this book that chance set me upon," he wrote in 1869.[90] And four years later: "What a really grim book that *Queen of the Air* is! especially in its account of the life of Tantalus.")[91] Indeed, *The Queen* is an apocalyptic work, perhaps his deepest plea for the vital mystery, and as such it is connected not only with *The Storm-Cloud* but with all that is essential in his thought and style. I hope to make clear in a later chapter that Ruskin held this forgotten effort in such high regard because it was his myth of myths and that by this time the necessity of myth had become one of his central concerns. *Fors Clavigera*, perhaps the most tensive of all his longer works ("Ruskin's *Hamlet*, and also his *Apocalypse*," writes a contemporary)[92] fuses social and personal immediacy with mythic and apocalyptic sweep. The drifting, digressive style of this collection of homiletic letters to English labor defies brief description, but in general the letters are a melange of such materials as journal, autobiography, topical commentary, details of social and environmental distress, criticisms of art and interpretations of myths, principles and current business of St. George's Guild; these diverse materials are often linked thematically from letter to letter, and so gathered into signs and commands of destiny to the correspondent, who is the prophetic medium of the "Forses," feminine mythic powers modeled on the Greek Fates. The *Fors* letters are "radical" discourse in several senses: in their mythic roots, in their politics, and in their constant questioning of the signifying process through continuous subversion of their own discursive categories. Within the labyrinthine, constantly decentering text of *Fors*, Ruskin's prophetic effort, as the speaking center, is to create the apocalyptist's necessary intimation of an absolute center or system of transcendent signifieds (the worldly effects of the "Forses") so that his message will appear to be other than his own and his prophecy will be released from the limits of ordinary discourse; hence the Ariadne's thread of the work always leads back ultimately to the prophet's special relation to the quasi-mythic "Forses."

It is characteristic of Ruskin's writing in this final period that nearly all phenomena that came to his attention—art, nature, his own past—were drawn into some mythic field of force. (Even Rose, in his writing, seems more nearly a symbolic figure than a person.) It is as if he were echoing Blake's famous "I must create a system," for system is myth here, and myth mystery. This is why in *Proserpina: Studies in Wayside Flowers, While the Air Was Yet Pure among the Alps*, his *Systema Proserpinae* is both a detailed phenomenal description of these flowers as they relate to the human field of unaided vision and at the same time a renaming of them so as to evoke their individual mythic associations. These associations were important because they carried the primordial human or relational meaning of the plant seen by men as the expression of an informing spirit of life. Similarly, to him, the visible condition or form of life in the plant manifested the power of Proserpina "the Earth Mother, as Mother, and as *Judge*."[93] Therefore his mythic nomenclature would reconnect the visible form of the plant "with the loveliest fancies and most helpful faiths of the ancestral world—Proserpina be judge."[94] (But since Ruskin's flower names are feminine, and since Proserpina was linked in his later mind with Rose and Saint Ursula, the whole system is fraught with private significance.) *Love's Meinie* intended the same antiscientific, life-world oriented, descriptive system for English birds; and *Deucalion* was partly intended to carry the system into the common geological forms.

In these diffuse and fragmentary later works Ruskin appeared to be engaged in a vast and vaguely realized scheme to resystematize the forms of nature as they related to the unaided eye and the collective un-conscious: a kind of anti-Darwinian evolution of species that would free them from neutralizing theoretical classification and restore their vital, or lethal, mystery. The *Storm-Cloud* is perhaps only a special meteorological instance of this mythic systematizing in which all natural forms are seen as apocalyptic of a forming, or perhaps defor-ming, power. Here, as an example of this last, is an excerpt from the chapter of *Proserpina* devoted to "Brunella:"

If any of the petals lose their definite character as such, and become swollen, solidified, stiffened, or strained into any other form or function than that of petals, the flower is to be looked upon as affected by some kind of constant evil influence; and, so far as we conceive of any spiritual power being concerned in the protection or affliction of the inferior orders of creatures, it will be felt to bear the aspect of possession by, or pollution by, a more or less degraded Spirit.[95]

Possibly enough has been said about his career in this brief sketch to indicate that Ruskin gave himself more and more to mythic or apocalyptic expression after the sixties as he felt himself to be the bearer of authentic tidings of deterioration in the life of things. His voice, as I have already suggested, became mythic in several basic senses: first in Carlyle's sense of myth as an expression of "sincere communion of man with the mysterious invisible Powers visibly seen at work in the world around him";[96] next in the sense that it involved deliberate study of the myth-making impulse in man (possibly under the direct influence of his friend and Oxford colleague, Friedrich Max Müller) and hence the informed use of mythic symbols; and lastly in the sense that these symbols appear recurrently as conductors of his most significant experiences, becoming both personal and archetypal messages, as his Athena, his Saint George, or his plague-cloud.

When, in *Praeterita*, Ruskin speaks of Athena's admonition to him through the owls of Crossmount, he is using his mythic language of the 1880s to describe a moment of revelation that had occurred in 1847.

I must return for a moment to the clumps of pine at Crossmount, and their company of owls, because—whatever wise people may say of them—I at least myself have found the owl's cry always prophetic of mischief to me; and though I got wiser, as aforesaid, in my field of thistles, yet the Scottish Athena put on against me at that time her closed visor (not that Greek Helmets ever have a visor, but when Athena hides her face, she throws her casque forward and down and only looks through the oval apertures of it). Her adversity to me at this time was shown by my loss of Miss Lockhart.[97]

But though the language for the experience would acquire symbolic depth (Ruskin's studies in the meaning of Athena were a score of years away) the moment at Crossmount, like a Wordsworthian "spot of time," must have had at the time some revelational value: in owl's cry and the loss of Miss Lockhart must have lain a meaning, a message in nature that would not translate into Evangelical language. The process of his apostasy had begun.

I must introduce at this point an earlier and yet more significant apocalyptic moment that he recollects in *Praeterita* to dramatize the spiritual crisis ("modifying the untried faith of childhood") toward which he was moving in the forties and fifties, and that would determine the whole course of his work after the mid fifties. I have already indicated that this central experience was actually the waning and the transference of his inherited faith. The diaries of the period and *Praeterita* both record an increasing tension between his immediate emotional experiences and the Eden-world of Evangelical innocence in which he had been nurtured; but Ruskin never ceased to record religious experiences in the sense of encounters, or moments of reconciliation, of his own with a suprapersonal will. His conversion out of Evangelicalism was actually a conversion into a broader ground of faith where his concurrent discovery of the relevance of myth would play an important part. And this new syncretic religion in which, as he said, "the life of religion depended on the force of the faith, not the terms of it"[98] would determine new directions of his thought and style. It is, as I have said, his quest for and use of myth that is the subject of the following chapters. I must now place against these points the particular revelation alluded to at the beginning of this paragraph.

The chapter of *Praeterita* entitled "Cumae" is devoted to the effects upon Ruskin's spiritual development of a visit to Vesuvius and its environs in 1841. Although there is no similar record in his diary, he chose to recall having had, on that "spasmodic ground," several apocalyptic experiences that were in direct antagonism to the beatific vision of Mont Blanc and prophesied in their way the moment of his apostasy. It was, he wrote, "the first feeling of being in the presence of the power and mystery of the under earth," and, as such, "unspeakably solemn." The passages I wish to present here encapsulate those aspects of Ruskin's art and message that I pursue in the following chapters: physical existence seen in pathetic fallacy as a theater of conflict of vital and lethal forces communed with as mythic presences; finally, and most important, they show the sustaining infusion of mythic symbolism (here the voice of the birdless lake) as vehicles to be recharged with personal revelation. Briefly, then, these passages intimate the Ruskin as myth-maker and apocalyptist who is the subject of this study. First, of the global meaning to him of that volcanic experience, he has this to say:

> The first sight of the Alps had been to me as a direct revelation of the benevolent will in creation. Long since, in the volcanic powers of destruction, I had been taught by Homer, and further forced by my own reason to see, if not the personality of an Evil Spirit, at all events the permitted symbol of evil, unredeemed; wholly distinct from the conditions of storm, or heat, or frost, on which the healthy courses of organic life depended. In the same literal way in which the snows and Alpine roses of Lanterbrunnen were visible Paradise, here, in the valley of ashes and throat of

lava, were visible Hell. If thus in the natural, how else should it be in the spiritual world?[99]

There was also a visit to the Avernus Lake, which had, by way of Virgil, a double message for him concerning at once the reality of sibyls and of birdless places:

> But even now, what pieces I knew of Virgil . . . became all at once true, when I saw the birdless lake; for me also, the voice of it had teaching which was to be practically a warning Law of future life:

> > "Nec te
> > Nequidquam lucis Hecate praefecit Avernis"

> The legends became true,—*began* to come true, I should have said,—trains of thought now first rising which did not take clear current till forty years afterward; and in this first trickling, sorrowful in disappointment. "There *were* such places, then, and Sibyls *did* live in them!—but is this all?"[100]

Similarly, in the Dog's Grotto, "with its floor a foot deep in poisoned air that could be stirred with the hand," there was an augury of plague-wind and of earth ravaged by destroying laws. The common English traveler had seen, he concluded, only an earthly paradise at Naples, "But I knew from the first moment when my foot furrowed volcanic ashes, that no mountain form or colour could exist in perfection when everything was made of scoria, and that blue sea was little to be boasted if it broke on black sand."[101]

In the voice of the birdless lake, of the sibyl who rejected the embraces of Apollo, Ruskin heard a message that seemed to fix his own destiny as a teacher. The life-world must be saved, for if we lose it to poisoned air and ashes Paradise goes with it. It followed also that a religion that would cast away this world in hopes of another was merely a snare and a pious delusion. That his thoughts should turn toward "living myths" was inevitable. Of this search more must be said, because it is ours also.

THE STANDPOINT OF THIS STUDY

The text to be considered in this study is, within reasonable limits, the whole body of Ruskin's writing: aesthetic, economic, and prophetic; public and private; as represented primarily by the great Library Edition, the four published volumes of diaries, and several collections of letters. With the exception of the *Storm-Cloud* lectures, which were introduced first to indicate the direction of this study, I shall consider the major works in order of their composition to show the evolution of

Ruskin's interest in and use of myth and to place this subject in the broadening context of his thought. While I discuss all of the major works in some detail the treatment of them is not always proportionate to their general interest. Thus, for instance, the climax of this study is, appropriately, a reading of Ruskin's "myth-book" *The Queen of the Air* in the light of its probable sources in contemporary mythological theory and its antecedents in his own work. However, though his Athena has recently been called "one of the major myth-makings of the Victorian age,"[102] she has aroused only slight critical interest, and therefore the attention I have given to her here may at first seem disproportionate. On the other hand there is the more obviously significant *Fors Clavigera*, Ruskin's ninety-six letters to English labor, that is a labyrinthine tangle of policy, prophecy, allusion, and autobiography. While I discuss the mythic themes in it at some length in the final chapter, the work does not receive treatment appropriate to its literary value, nor could it, beside Ruskin's concurrent writing, unless a separate chapter were to be given to it.

Even within these limits this is necessarily a lengthy study. There are several reasons for this. One is the staggering diversity of Ruskin's interests; surely no other Victorian writer worked in such a range of topics. Aesthetics; painting, art history; techniques of drawing, of perspective, and of engraving; architecture; sculpture; etymology; mythology; literary criticism; education; the position of women; economics; museology; crystallography; geology; glaciology; meteorology; botany; and ornithology would be but a partial listing of his interests. And of course such a list cannot convey the depth to which a subject is pursued. Ruskin's study of modern painting led to the total study of Turner's art, and this necessitated a survey of the landscape tradition from which Turner emerged. His study of architecture led to the study of Gothic and the bases of its aesthetic, which led to Venetian history in which, for Ruskin, it culminated and fell; criticism of contemporary political economy led to the formulation of a countereconomics, the theory of an organic society, and eventually to his foundation and management of the Guild of Saint George to put the theory into practice.

Although it is inaccurate to say, as G. M. Young does, that Ruskin "is all dogma and no system,"[103] it is clear that this range of interests reflects a compulsion to gather up nearly every aspect of his experience in either dogma or system. These sometimes conflicting urges (broadly speaking, those of the prophet and the naturalist) drove him to a diffuse and voluminous output. In this respect he remained obedient to his rearing and to his "Master's," Carlyle's, injunction to "work" against the coming of the night.

There are, including one devoted to index, thirty-nine volumes in the Library Edition. These have been edited with filial loyalty and a meticulousness for which students of Ruskin will always be grateful. The quality of paper and print and the copious ancillary materials testify to the editors' devotion to Ruskin's teaching. Of these volumes, one is an index volume; two are given over to representative letters; another to materials relating to the Guild; and two more are taken up with exhibition catalogues, gallery notes, and materials edited by Ruskin. Still, when one adds to this bulk the four volumes of diaries now in print and an equal number of important collections of letters, it will be evident that the Ruskin corpus is of such length and scope that it does not invite brevity of treatment in any study that attempts to survey it.

It is also evident that Ruskin's uses of myth and apocalypse can be understood and are of interest only insofar as they are shown in their relation to the whole body of his work and are seen as vital to it. However, Ruskin is certainly the most neglected of the major Victorians; therefore it seems unreasonable to suppose that the reader has the kind of familiarity with his work that he might be expected to have with, say, Dickens, Arnold, or Browning. For this reason it seemed essential to represent much more of Ruskin's work by summary and quotation than would be necessary with the more familiar writers. This study is meant, therefore, to function secondarily as a general survey of Ruskin's writing given in his own words as often as possible.

Another contributory factor to the length of this study is a quality of Ruskin's mind and style that became increasingly evident after the mid sixties and continued to gain control of his work until his mind gave way in the late seventies. These are the qualities of digressiveness and allusiveness that gave to such works as *The Cestus of Aglaia* and *Fors Clavigera* their verbal density and labyrinthine complexity. This associative style, which Ruskin recognized as his "third way"[104] of writing, became characteristic of his work in the seventies and eighties, and with it there was a greater absorption of autobiographical matter into his public work, a tendency that culminated in *Praeterita*, where the style became more restrained and peaceful. In addition, after the mid sixties he relied mostly on short forms that were appropriate to the fragmentation of his efforts and mixed discursiveness and aphoristic urgency of his prose. Into such forms as the lecture, the letter, and the note he attempted to pack as much of his total message as possible, linking apocalyptic annunciation, social scheme, topical references, and personal revelation. The presence of so many fragmentary yet densely suggestive utterances makes his later work extremely difficult to represent with anything like completeness and brevity.

Yet within the whole of the diverse, diffuse, and unstable body of Ruskin's writing three interrelated mythic or archetypal themes are dominant and, in a sense, constitute his primary message. These are the Organic Model (Purity), the Fall, and the Hero-Serpent conflict. Ruskin's understanding of these themes altered with his religious development and with his sense of vocation. But a few words here will suggest the main meaning of this symbol-complex to him.

Ruskin employed the scheme of Judeo-Christian mythic history in a manner roughly analogous to that which M. H. Abrams has traced among other Romantics in his *Natural Supernaturalism* (1971). Nature, first in its sublime or high Alpine conditions and later in its formative laws (the organic model) represented, for Ruskin, a paradisaical condition of purity, unity, and harmony from which man had fallen into alienation, competition, and anomie. The historical moment of this fall was the Renaissance, when "science" replaced reverence and pure sight, with the consequence that art generated by pride of technique replaced that devoted to the truths of religion and of natural form. The sequelae of this original arrogance have appeared in such forms as Rembrandtean tenebrism, where purity of form is lost in shadow and glitter, and in the modern "science" of political economy, which opposes the supposed laws of the market mechanism to the natural affectional bonds that unify people. Quotation marks are used here to indicate that Ruskin finds certain kinds of science acceptable, particularly if they aim at the pure phenomenological description of the appearances of natural forms to the living eye. What he opposes is analytic, dissecting, or microscopic aspects of science that violate what he supposes to be a sacred bond between natural forms and the innocent eye.

For Ruskin, as for Coleridge, Carlyle, and other Romantics, the idea of organic form (inherently purposive and cohesive interaction of infinitely varied parts in a greater whole or composition) was of central importance, though he was more concerned to discern the presence of this model in nature and great art than to define it or theorize about it. However, it will be evident in the following chapters that organic form is the model of life for Ruskin, in nature, in art, and in society. Life is form, not force; and its essential law, help, is holy. By the operation of it the parts of an organic entity develop purity and consistency. Life, in this sense, is for him also the basis of value, the only true wealth. However, in human society the vital, forming power is opposed by important lethal adversaries such as codes of technique in art that deny the primacy of natural form directly observed, modes of knowing that interfere with the spiritual bond between the human mind and the visible thing, and ascetic religiosity that denies help in this life in the hope of another. But the most important of life's adversaries is selfishness or greed that creates, out of nature and the lives of others, pools of dead wealth—"illth," Ruskin calls it—that will not sustain life and are destructive of that which will. This human tendency (to selfish separation and therefore social death) taught by modern political economy and abetted by advances in mechanistic science (the "Plutocracy of Knowledge")[105] constituted, in Ruskin's view, the great crisis of his time: literally the struggle of life against lethal wealth. He saw its evidence literally and symbolically in the gradual advance of the chilling, hissing "hell sky."[106]

The Christian mythic scheme of Paradise, Fall, Redemption, and Last Judgment served more than any other as the ultimate horizon of meaning and dramatization of Ruskin's experience. It had been inculcated in his early religious teaching and remained, during much of his life, a matter of literal belief. Further, scripturalism is obviously an inseparable determinant of his verbal style and prophetic stance. Yet as his sectarian faith waned and became more syncretic, Greek mythology, as it was interpreted in his time, provided Ruskin with something the Christian scheme could not: personal symbolic figures expressive of his sense of conflict and crisis immanent in nature.

The Christian tradition of "physico-theology," exemplified by Thomas Burnet's *The Sacred Theory of the Earth* (1681–89), had infused the aesthetics of landscape with theological and moral concepts. The natural world had been looked upon as the wreckage of an original paradise and, as such, an apocalypse of God's judgment; aspects of landscape, beautiful or sublime, had been read as types of His infinity, power, and wrath. The diffused influence of this tradition was present in Ruskin's earliest efforts to interpret the landscape feeling. He set to work in this mode in the second volume of *Modern Painters*, confidently categorizing the phenomena of nature as types of divine attributes; but these allegorical types, though piously conceived, were bloodless abstractions, not presences or powers felt to be immanent in nature, so he later repudiated this portion of his work. This nature of theological types was essentially the "cold inanimate" nature of reason, not of intuition; it had no being in it, and said nothing of man's pretheological, preconceptual apprehension of nature. Ruskin's experience of nature, like Wordsworth's, demanded the sense of presences, needed angels, so to speak, not allegories. Men do not believe in allegories. But in the mythic symbol—at least in the Romantic idea of it as unmediated vision, revealing and concealing because never fully detached from its unconscious or preconceptual content—he found access to nature's primordial human meaning. This view is implicit in the warning he gave three times in his first series of Oxford lectures, that "the ruder the symbol, the deeper its intention."[107]

Yet, as George Landow has pointed out, Ruskin was an inveterate allegorist; that is, he frequently resorted to the hermeneutic of types. He did so, as we will see, in the repudiated sections of *Modern Painters*, volume 2, and on those occasions when he actually read or interpreted a painting for his reader; similarly, allegory enters his interpretations of particular myths. But his interest in the immediacy of sight, imagination, and vision drew him more fundamentally to the symbol, in the Romantic sense of it as the expression of preconceptual content, than to the type. Three observations may explain this apparent contradiction. First, the subjects of Ruskin's interpretations (of Dürer's *Melancholia* or his *Knight and Death*, for instance) were already allegorical, already conceptualized as types. On other occasions allegory served to lead him toward the depth and complexity of a controlling mythic symbol, that is, toward the revelation of what was not "mere allegory," as in his evocations of the Greek belief in Apollo and Athena. With myth, he could not *interpret* the preconceptual content of its symbols without conceptualizing them as allegory. Yet he realized that neither the actuality of belief in nor the deep truth of the mythic figure should be conveyed in this way but only conducted through the medium of his own myth-making.

From the beginning of his serious thought about myth, in the chapters on pathetic fallacy and classical landscape in *Modern Painters*, volume 3, Ruskin attempted to express the difference between actual Greek belief, the genuinely numinous landscape, and modern poetic allegories or sentimental pantheistic animations of nature. This perception, as Richard Jenkyns has recently observed, makes his discussion, at this point, of the nature of Greek belief "still illuminating after more than a hundred years."[108] Such illumination is a value that Jenkyns does not concede to many works in the vast tracts of Victorian Hellenism he so trenchantly assesses. But, while he praises Ruskin's efforts to convey the reality of the Greek religion and the "subtlety and lucidity" of his expositions of it, he judges that the prophet's attempts to reanimate his own landscapes with these mythic powers led him into bizarre and deranged pronouncements.[109]

For Ruskin, however, the right understanding of Greek belief led inevitably to the imitation of it. There were both religious and psychological reasons for this movement in his work. His first and intuitive comprehension of the Greek religion was rooted in his own early Wordsworthian experiences of numinous nature. This feeling that he actually shared in the Greek experience of nature led to his belief in his special capacities as interpreter of myths and, after 1858, to the sense in which he could speak of his own religion as being "old Greek." From this it followed that he must not only interpret myths but attempt to respeak them in such a way as to convey their continuous and inescapable truths. Psychoanalytically, it might be suggested that the projections of the anima in Ruskin led him inevitably through various representations of her in art, nature, and his private life, to the fullest symbolic expression of her in his mythic Athena, the queen of the air, breath, spirit, life—all the meanings of the anima, including her hostile Medusa's face of storm and chilling knowledge. It is this authenticity of his personal involvement with Greek belief, the religious and psychological plot of mythic symbols in his life and work, that is the special quality of Ruskin's Hellenism. But his uses of myth, though rooted in a complex of aesthetic, religious, and psychological needs, were nourished by his knowledge of current developments in mythology.

Contemporary mythological theory, which tended to assign natural meanings, often revealed by philological research, to mythic figures, provided him with certain advantages not available in Christian natural theology. For one thing, the "scientific" study of myth seemed to be disclosing a primordial basis for his organicism and his sense of the solidarity of all life. As a recent student of Victorian mythography has observed, "the dominant mid-Victorian conception of mythology was nothing if not organic."[110] Also the study of myth enabled him to detect deep and central truths in several important mythic subjects treated by Turner. The study of myth enabled him to transcend the narrowness of his sectarian piety without giving up religion in the larger sense at a time when he needed the sustaining power of a sacred tradition, allowing him a compromise in what he called his "religion of Humanity." Through his interest in myth he was in touch with an important intellectual movement of his age that was exploring the historical and linguistic origins of religion. While the mythic symbols retained personal implications for him, they had also the "scientific" authority of comparative philology behind them; they linked the facts of nature and of language. He could now see natural forms as "living myths" in terms of the ways they had entered the symbology of myth.

For Ruskin the most important of these "living myths" was the sky. Mythology enabled him to read the phenomena of his skies as apocalyptic symbols. In this he was aided by the prominent solar mythology of F. Max Müller. Such readings could suggest at once Biblical prophecy, the fate of the biosphere, and the struggle of organicity itself with an opponent power. In his mythic interests Ruskin was drawn primarily to the archetype in which the hero of purity and light opposes a dragon-serpent antagonist or antitype whose power is impurity, symbolized particularly by phenomena of storm or plague. There were private psychological implications in the importance of this symbolism to Ruskin, but objectively it meant that the organic model, the global unity of life was, in his view, threatened by the union of competitive greed with mechanistic knowledge: life against wealth. "To the romantic mind," as Albert S. Gérard has pointed out, "cognition was of two kinds: the dead and the vital."[111] Ruskin shared this sense of conflict between integrative and disintegrative knowledge; but his prophetic vision, unlike that of earlier Romantics, foresaw no joyous re-marriage of mind and nature. In the end, his was an apocalypse of disintegration signaled by a poison sky.

However, in the sphere of practical social action he fought the implications of his prophetic vision. He advocated a social order based on domestic and organic models and dedicated to the cultivation of vital wealth through minimal technology and maximum use of human resources, an economic system somewhat analogous to that proposed for emergent nations in our time by E. F. Schumacher.[112] In a recent study of Ruskin's socioeconomic thought James C. Sherburne[113] has pointed to the static quality of his organicism. This is so because his model is based upon the aesthetic ideal of fully integrated form and because it is ultimately a mythic model, locating man in a global whole that is the expression of a transcendent forming power.

Fifty years ago R. G. Collingwood[114] emphasized the historicism, holism, and dialectical contradictoriness of Ruskin's thought, comparing it with Hegel's. But Ruskin's organicism does not, like that of Hegel or Marx, see history as a self-infinitizing or self-integrating process in man. There is nothing like the materialist conception of history in his work. However, his comments on the modern dehumanization of labor do have something in common with Marx's idea that man is alienated from his own creative activity as laborer. He might even be said to have perceived something like Marx's view that man's self-realization in labor is opposed by his own tendency to self-aggrandizement through capital (Ruskin's "illth"). Like Marx's mythology[115] Ruskin's dramatizes the antagonism of vital and deadly forces which are global projections of man's self-conflict. Like Marx's, Ruskin's vision is organic, mythic, and moral; however, Ruskin's system is never truly atheistic. Though he prophesies revolution, Ruskin does not connect the return to the organic model ("the communism of God") with any inevitable historical process. Rather he looks to some moral change in individual men, or, failing that, to the infection and death of the whole system of the world and, presumably, its replacement by a new creation.

Three themes then, of which organicism is primary, enable us to see a unity in the diversity of Ruskin's work. Did he see so much system there? Although he said his only system was "the abhorrence of all that is doctrinal instead of demonstrable, and of all that is systematic instead of useful,"[116] he also declared that "neither Comte nor Mill nor Buckle have system so determined and arranged as mine; but mine is not easy for you to get at all the branches of, for the writing of it occupies now some twenty biggish volumes, and these written with the best care I could have never to throw a word away."[117] The arboreal metaphor implied in "branches" points to the sense in which he could think of his work as a system. It had the unity of organic form, every part of it implying connection with every other. Robert Hewison[118] has recently emphasized the unity and continuity of Ruskin's thought. He sees there the progressive and dialectical development of three modes of truth: truth of fact, of thought, and of symbol. The following chapters view these modes as being co-present in his earliest work, and they hold that the essential truth content of these modes is organicity, and that organicity determines the antithetical characteristic of his thought, the detection of disintegrative qualities or forces wherever they appear. To Ruskin, as Wendell Stacy Johnson has lately affirmed, "every part of nature is a symbolic expression—like a sacrament, not an icon—of the organic whole."[119]

There are several senses in which the principle of organicity may be taken as the controlling system of Ruskin's work. First, his "ocular and passionate" study of nature leads him to see not mere facts there, but facts of form; he sees the redundancy, mutual implication, and integration of forms. He sees these facts of form as fitted to human perception, particularly to sight, at the lived or preconceptual level. He sees these prehensive unities of form as expressions of the integrating intentions of a forming power with which he identifies. Consequently, as his work proceeds he attempts to integrate ever more expansive tracts of experience as he moves from aesthetics to global prophecy. In this effort of integration he is aided not only by organicism as root metaphor but by archetypal symbols, myths, and the poetics of apocalypse. There is also the pull of autobiographical integration; his works are, in a sense, branches of a great confession. His world, to echo Merleau-Ponty, is not what he thinks but what he lives through.[120] Finally, and related to this progress of the self, there is the antithetical element in his work. The integrating organic model, symbolized by vitality, purity, and light, has always its lethal opposite: darkness, disintegration, and death. As Ruskin's own psychic integration fails there is increasing outward vision of disintegration, a horror of great darkness, which culminates in his storm-plague symbolism. Of course, if we accept the position of Jacques Lacan, we must understand that such psychological contradictions arise necessarily as any subjectivity is constituted in the differentiation of the perceived from the perceiving *I*, and are the price of entry into language. The organic model, so viewed becomes, with all myths of universal structure, an effort to see in nature the reflected image of the lost wholeness of the imaginary or ideal ego which precedes all differentiation of self and other, symbol and referent.

CHAPTER 1

Apocalyptic Landscape

In a series of letters that W. B. Yeats and Sturge Moore exchanged in 1926 and 1927 they debated the mode of existence of a mystical something they called "Ruskin's cat."[1] The reference was to an incident described in Frank Harris's autobiography. Once, when Harris was visiting Ruskin, the latter suddenly dashed to the opposite side of the room, seized something not visible to Harris and hurled it out of the window. Ruskin explained that the invisible thing had been a demon in the form of a cat come to tempt him. Yeats related the story in support of one of his own in which he claimed to have watched a seer lift an imaginary stone from the ground and convey a totally convincing sense of its weight. Both stories were meant to attest the reality of visionary images.

The issue was a vital one. *A Vision* had just been published, and Yeats was understandably anxious to show that Ruskin's cat, like the seer's stone, could not be reasoned out of existence. Ruskin's spectral cat, he insisted, would have been as real to him as a house-cat. Yet the seer and his vision are one, and Yeats finally had to base his argument on what he called his own "special experience." This had shown him that there is no barrier between so-called objective forms and subjective images. He was convinced that, granted his "special experience," common sense did not justify the view that the one cat was any more external than the other.[2] And so throughout a year of epistolary debate with Moore, Ruskin's cat kept bristling in the way as the token of a special kind of "sense-datum" that must have had a "root" of some sort.

For one who is interested in Ruskin's work, however, this controversial cat may start up quite different, less metaphysical, trains of thought. The ontological status of this apocryphal demon-cat will interest him less than the implications of Yeats's Ruskin. Though he may be inclined to assign the strange encounter either to Harris's imagination or to Ruskin's latter-day derangement,[3] the visionary cat is likely to persist for him, if only because Yeats did not consider either of these obvious possibilities. Yeats, indeed, appears to have accepted Ruskin as a sharer of his own "special experience," as one of the literalists of the imagination: a judgment that casts an uncommon slant of light on Ruskin.

Ultimately Ruskin's cat invites us to think of Ruskin as one of those "who have given themselves up to images, and to the speech of images"[4] and entices us to reexamine this man's work not as a wreckage of doctrines but as a dynamic of styles, as an evolving complex of images and modes of giving himself up to them. Let Yeats's example of Ruskin ejecting the demon cat stand, then, for this neglected aspect of the most neglected of the great Victorians, *his imagination.*

By imagination I refer in particular to that essence of the poetic which the Romantics commonly understood to be, not merely a visualizing or synthetic capability, but a visionary or apocalyptic and, in its highest form, a mythopoeic power. Ruskin discussed this power as a theorist and obeyed it as a writer. It manifests itself early in his work as recreated moments of special religious or aesthetic experience. In the long view, however, to speak of Ruskin's use of—or use by—imagination is to speak of his giving himself up to images or symbols, especially mythic or archetypal, because they tended to bring into focus or to synthesize his experience, especially the miasmic experience of environmental degeneration.

The province of this study is the whole body of Ruskin's work, seen less as a development of ideas than as the incarnation of a mind being driven into myth and apocalypse to express its sense of a final struggle of life as organic purity with the lethal forms of "wealth." Aestheticism, radicalism, and apocalyptism were the basic movements of his mind, interwoven with such motifs as medievalism, Scripturism, scientific curiosity, and nature mysticism. But the core of his work is its involvement, in theory and style, with the special modes of awareness that the Romantics signified by imagination, revelation, and mythopoesis. This is the pulse and poetry of his writing, its controlling necessity and its ultimate relevance as a body of literature. His uses of imagination serve primarily to project, as symbolic action, the central discords of his being: his lust for form and life leading to a morbidly acute consciousness of the inroads of ugliness and blight.

The end of his work in incoherent apocalyptics and prophecy of ruin is prefigured in, even determined by, its beginnings in his discussion of Turner's "truth" of landscape in the first volume of *Modern Painters* and in the natural theology and the theory of imagination in the second. These two of Ruskin's books say little directly about myth or vision in art, but both themes gradually become inevitable in them. In fact the joint problems of imagination as inspired vision and of the representation of the "divine ideal" are introduced at the very end of this two-volume foray into the fundamentals of art as if they were the culmination of one stage of his thought and the threshold of another.

These two works, *Modern Painters*, volumes 1 and 2, therefore form a kind of unit within the first phase of Ruskin's work. They are separated from the later three volumes of *Modern Painters* by Ruskin's four-volume digression on Gothic architecture and its social bases, *The Seven Lamps of Architecture* and *The Stones of Venice*. They are also set off from the later volumes of *Modern Painters* by the confidently comprehensive and analytic way in which they chew into such basic aesthetic problems as the function of truth and beauty in art. (It was partly for this analytic arrogance that Ruskin later repudiated much of this earliest work.) Further, these two volumes were largely conceived before the important crisis of taste, connected with his discovery of Tintoretto, that Ruskin experienced during his Italian tour of 1845. Largely as the result of this experience, the progress of his aesthetics in these two volumes is climaxed by his first attempt to deal with the art of vision. Finally, though volumes 1 and 2 of *Modern Painters* are bound together in these respects they are separated by important differences in style and subject; these, however, can be presented more meaningfully as we move from the first work to the second.

But to begin this discussion with *Modern Painters*, volume 1 (1843), the first of his books to be published (he was twenty-four at the time), is to pass over, for the moment, a surprising amount of work that Ruskin had already completed before embarking on this undertaking. There are two substantial volumes of early short pieces in the Library Edition: a volume of negligible nature poetry, some of it composed as late as 1850; and another containing articles and essays. These include a series of papers written and published in 1837–38; *The Poetry of Architecture*, which partly anticipates the architectural sociology of *The Seven Lamps of Architecture* and *The Stones of Venice*; and "A Reply to *Blackwood's* Criticism of Turner" (written in 1836 but not published until 1903) in which the idea of *Modern Painters* is germinated. From the standpoint of this study, however, only one of these early works demands separate attention. This is *The King of the Golden River*, the pseudo-*Märchen* that Ruskin (then twenty-two) composed for Effie Gray in 1841 but did not publish until 1851. The tale belongs here because it foreshadows primary symbolic or imaginary aspects of his work while embodying clearly the vital-lethal antithesis (here, life against dead wealth) which is the dominant polarity of his thought. The closeness of the folktale to myth is another special anticipation, and in this connection it should be pointed out that the tale marks his first use of apocalyptic sky effects in prose and even his first, though unconscious, involvement with solar mythology.

1

Ruskin declared that the little tale was a compound of Dickens, Grimm, and a bit of "Alpine ecstasy" of his own. He might have added the parable of the Good Samaritan to his list. Of course it is the ecstatic element that most interests us here, and this appears in the tale in the form of animated sky-effects, which I call apocalyptic because they are the metaphoric vehicle by which a judging presence in nature is intimated. Further, *The King of the Golden River* conveys several other Ruskinian principles that appear later in discursive form during the radical phase of his work: the idea of the conflict of life with greed; the view that the first law of life (in organic as in social existence) is help, while the first law of death is alienation and competition; and, significantly, his view that the spiritual or moral landscape and the physical landscape are interdependent. But there is no conveying the fusion of ideas and imagery in the tale short of recounting it and quoting from it.

Gentle Gluck and his vicious older brothers, Hans and Schwartz, inhabit as their patrimony an Alpine Eden which because of its fruitfulness is known as the Treasure Valley. From a crag high above the valley a cataract plunges into the light in such a way that "when the sun had set to everything else, and all below was darkness, his beams still shone full upon this waterfall, so that it looked like a shower of gold. It was, therefore, called by the people of the neighborhood, the Golden River."[5] But the Golden River does not feed the valley, for it flows down to the plains on the other side of the mountains. Instead, the Treasure Valley is nourished by a benevolent blanket of clouds that clings to the snowy hills, protecting it from both drought and heat. But the economic system of the affluent Valley is thankless laissez faire. Hans and Schwartz relegate Gluck "to the honourable office of turnspit," rewarding him with the scraps of their plates for his fare, "and a wholesome quantity of blows, by way of education." They exploit their valley like rigorous utilitarians, killing everything that doesn't pay; they buy in the cheapest markets and sell in the dearest. Though they soon become immensely rich, they are without trace of charity toward their neighbors or gratitude to God; thus they earn their local nickname, the "Black Brothers."

The agricultural exploitations of the Black Brothers continue profitably for some time. Then, one soaking day they refuse hospitality to a little, rotund, ironic man dressed in a great conical cap and a superabundance of flyaway cape whose calling card identifies him as South Wind, Esquire. After this refusal the system of the brothers is reversed by an adversity of skies. Denied rain for an entire year, Treasure Valley is reduced to red desert, and the three brothers are driven to take what is left of their gold-hoards to seek their livelihood in the city. Because the remnant of their wealth is in the form of a few curious old pieces of plate, the brothers decide to become goldsmiths, "a good knave's trade." But their fortune continues to dwindle because their attempt to foist coppered gold on the public is a failure, and Hans and Schwartz take to drinking away their capital at the tavern next door, leaving young Gluck behind to melt what is left of their patrimony into bars.

On a certain day we find Gluck about to commit their last vessel into the melting pot. This is his own favorite mug (out of which, of course, he drinks nothing but milk and water). The mug is an odd piece of work, we are told, delicately wrought into a fierce little red gold face with searching eyes and wreaths of finely spun gold hair and whiskers. But the older brothers throw in the well-wrought mug without a qualm and set off for the tavern, leaving the boy to tend the pot. Sadly Gluck bids farewell to the familiar little face as it gazes up at him from the melting pot, and he turns disconsolately to gaze out of the shop window at the delectable vista of an Alpine sunset. As it happens the prospect includes the Golden River enveloped in Turnerian mysteries of light, and Gluck's gaze is drawn to "the rocks of the mountain tops, all crimson, and purple with the sunset; . . . bright tongues of fiery cloud burning and quivering about them; and the river, brighter than all . . . in a waving column of pure gold from precipice to precipice, with the double arch of a broad purple rainbow stretched across it, flushing and fading alternately in wreaths of spray."[6] But because Gluck's education in nature has been defective, the meaning of the sky vision is lost on him; his response to the "ecstasy" is innocent materialism: "Ah! If that river were really all gold, what a nice thing it would be." He is surprised to be corrected by a small metallic voice close behind him: "No it wouldn't, Gluck."

After some moments of confusion Gluck identifies the source of the corrective voice as the furnace and the very crucible into which, a few moments before, he had dropped his beloved mug. At the voice's insistence the lad tilts the crucible so as to pour forth to his surprise, not a stream of molten gold, but a tiny golden figure of regal bearing and the very features of the image into which the mug had been worked, particularly the same abundance of delicate curls in its hair and beard. This imperious dwarf announces himself as the king of the Golden River. Explaining that his previous mug-shape was the result of the enchantment of a stronger king from which the youth had freed him, he offers to serve Gluck for the goodness the boy has shown under the oppression of his wicked brothers. His immediate service is to propose the story's quest: " 'Whoever shall climb to the top of that mountain from which you see the Golden River issue, and shall cast into the stream at its source three drops of holy water, for him, and for him only, the river shall turn to gold. But no one failing in his first, can succeed in a second attempt; and if any one shall cast unholy water into the river, it will overwhelm him, and he will become a black stone.' "[7] Having thus defined the task, the king walks straight into the hottest part of the melting fire and disappears in a blaze of dazzling light.

As might be expected, the rest of the tale is built around the efforts of the three brothers to win the prize of the Golden River. Of course Gluck's innocent account of the disappearance of the mug at first procures cynical disbelief and a savage beating from his drunken brothers, but greed so spurs the growth of credence in them that swords are eventually drawn and a vicious fracas develops over which Black Brother is to have precedence in the attempt to gain the Golden River. The disturbance lands both brothers in jail, but Hans manages to escape, and, not without mocking Schwartz's confinement, takes up the quest.

The essence of the quest is, of course, trial of mercy, for the holy water which will have talismanic power over the Golden River cannot be sanctified by priests but only by acts of mercy. Each of the brothers starts his journey with what he assumes is holy water: Hans steals some; Schwartz buys it from a bad priest; Gluck obtains it for the asking, but the holiness of the water that is ultimately poured in the Golden River depends upon how it has been used along the way. Thus each traveler is tested by the deceptive surfaces of a glacier to be crossed, by the need to restrain his own thirst during the climb, and, most significantly, by the necessity of sharing the sacred, life-giving water with various beings who confront him with their anguished pleas for it. Though all three reach the river with the requisite drops of water, Hans and Schwartz both spurn the thirsting ones; hence they pour unholy water into the Golden River and are turned to black stones. However, the water Gluck brings is made holy by the quality of mercy which has triumphed over greed and personal thirst in him. But Gluck has a final lesson to learn: when the river receives the holy drops it does not turn to gold in the sense he had expected; instead it flows beneath the ground to refructify that wasteland which was once the Treasure Valley. Thus his patrimony is brought to abundance again.

Although this might be a good place to speak of *The King of the*

Golden River as a kind of Ruskinian "proto-myth"—or as an intimation of that myth-making which was to culminate in *The Queen of the
Air*—our interest at this point is not primarily in the tale's narrative or
thematic structure but in the most striking feature of its texture, in the
details of its style. We have already noticed Ruskin's observation that his
own contribution to the style of the tale is the quality of "Alpine
ecstasy." His allusion is, most probably, to the symbolic use of sky effects
in the tale; here, as throughout his work, Ruskin favors descriptions of
the active sky, particularly in its interplay with snowy peaks, as a way of
intimating the supernatural by the natural. And within sky-scapes and
other details of the story lies an emphasis upon contrasts between light
and darkness which is perhaps the story's fundamental mode of insistence.[8] Some of this verbal chiaroscuro should be apparent from the
foregoing summary. But this sketch is intended primarily to set the
context for some early excursions into sky contrasts in which Ruskin
approximates the stylistic device that I have called an apocalyptic sky.
He depicts the interaction of tones of solar light with cloudforms and
mountain masses so that they become vehicles of an ulterior prophetic
message, as was the tempest cloud that transformed the Schreckhorn at
the apocalyptic moment in *Sartor Resartus*.[9]

Consider how these ominous contrasts add a mythic dimension to the
quests of the two Black Brothers, "mythic" here because these sky
patterns, by altering in sympathy with narrative events, are obviously
meant to be authentic tidings of invisible powers. Thus as Hans sets out
for the Golden River he appears to be observed by a dimly animated
power figured in the interplay of lights and masses, a message from
nature that is without meaning for him at this point: "Far above, shot up
red splintered masses of castellated rock, jagged and shivered into
myriads of fantastic forms, with here and there a streak of sunlit snow,
traced down their chasms like a line of forked lightning; and, far beyond,
and far above all these, fainter than the morning cloud, but purer and
changeless, slept, in the blue sky, the utmost peaks of the eternal
snow."[10] But as he reaches the mysterious glacier, the presence is
awakened for Hans; there are intimations of presences, as lights play
among the spires of ice: "There seemed a curious *expression* about all
their outlines—a perpetual resemblance to living features, distorted and
scornful. Myriads of deceitful shadows, and lurid lights, played and
floated about and through the pale blue pinnacles, dazzling and con-
fusing the sight of the traveller."[11] For Hans the first of three mercy tests
is a dog near death from thirst. As Hans spurns the creature: "He did not
know how it was, but he thought that a strange shadow had suddenly

come across the blue sky."[12] Next he encounters a child languishing upon the rock; the sky message is ever more explicit: "And a dark grey cloud came over the sun, and long, snake-like shadows crept up along the mountain sides. . . . The leaden weight of the dead air pressed upon his brow and heart, but the goal was near." The final plea is from an old man who is prostrate in his path. As Hans steps over the body his un-heeded apocalypse is complete: "A flash of blue lightning rose out of the East, shaped like a sword; it shook thrice over the whole heaven, and left it dark with one heavy, impenetrable shade. The sun was setting; it plunged towards the horizon like a red-hot ball." Naturally, as he ap-proaches the Golden River to cast the unhallowed drops upon it, the waves are bloodied with the sunset light: "They shook their crests like tongues of fire, and flashes of bloody light gleamed along their foam."[13] Hans is about to become a black stone.

The skies attempt to communicate with Schwartz in the same way, though perhaps more emphatically. His quest commences under skies less eloquent and less propitious: "The day was cloudless, but not bright: there was a heavy purple haze hanging over the sky, and the hills looked lowering and gloomy." His first encounter is with the fair child, to whose agony of thirst he replies by raising his flask to his own lips. The skies promptly make a sign: "And as he went he thought the sunbeams grew more dim, and he saw a low bank of black cloud rising out of the West."[14] His next test is the old man lying in the path. When Schwartz flouts this plea the heavens threaten more distinctly: "Then again the light seemed to fade from before his eyes, and, he looked up, and, behold, a mist, of the colour of blood, had come over the sun; and the bank of black cloud had risen very high, and its edges were tossing and tumbling like the waves of the angry sea. And they cast long shadows, which flickered over Schwartz's path."[15] His final act of in-difference is to refuse water to the prostrate figure of his brother Hans, who stretches forth his arms in anguish from beside the path. Now the skies compose frightening but unheeded apocalypse above the impious Schwartz:

> And the bank of black cloud rose to the zenith, and out of it came bursts of spiry lightning, and waves of darkness seemed to heave and float between their flashes over the whole heavens. And the sky where the sun was setting was all level, and like a lake of blood; and a strong wind came out of that sky, tearing its crimson clouds into fragments, scattering them far into the darkness. And when Schwartz stood by the brink of The Golden River, its waves were black like thunder clouds, but their foam was like fire; and the roar of the waters below, and the thunder above, met, as he cast the flask into the stream.[16]

And then the river tumbled over "Two Black Stones."

2

Volume 1 of *Modern Painters*, which Ruskin probably began writing about the same time as *The King of the Golden River* (1841), has at least three qualities in common with his fairy tale. It too points to the disparity between two modes of awareness of nature, the materialistic and one-dimensional as opposed to the devout and relational. Here, also, discursive writing gives way to ecstatic moments of nature-painting where displays of clouds and light are prominent and are generally suggestive of an unseen power. But here, of course, the larger vehicle is not narration but criticism or aesthetics. And the nature-messages are verified by the genius of Turner. Yet the work will elude any attempt to paraphrase or summarize it, not merely because of its length and complexity, but because much of its meaning cannot be reduced to analytic language. It seems better to speak first of the volume's total effect and then to illustrate the kinds of materials that sustain it.

Primarily this first volume attempts to vindicate Turner from all charges of falseness to nature and to announce him as the greatest landscapist the world had yet known. More important, the volume's conclusions are such that he can be celebrated not simply as a copyist of nature but as her prophet, a reader, in Carlyle's phrase, of the "God-written Apocalypse."[17] He gives, one learns, something more than reality, and that is *truth*. With respect to the "material truth" of nature we are told that "J. M. W. Turner is the only man who has ever given an entire transcript of the whole system of nature, and is, in this point of view, the only perfect landscape painter whom the world has ever seen."[18] But in the painter's later and greater works there is a certain mystery that is a consequence of the fullness of his vision; "there was in them the obscurity, but the truth, of prophecy; the instinctive and burning language which would express less if it uttered more, which is indistinct only by its fullness, and dark with its abundant meaning."[19] And so, in the peroration of the volume, Ruskin directs a prayer, on England's behalf, to the living prophet-painter: "It is therefore that we pray him to utter nothing lightly; to do nothing regardlessly. He stands upon an eminence, from which he looks back over the universe of God and forward over the generations of men. Let every work of his hand be a history of the one, and a lesson to the other. Let each exertion of his mighty mind be both hymn and prophecy; adoration to the Deity, and revelation to mankind."[20]

Turner is defended as at once the great literalist and apocalyptist of nature. But the mind in the book is Ruskin's, not Turner's. The pseudonymous young "Oxford Graduate" was also using the painter's art as a vehicle for his own. There is demonstration of art as well as analysis of it in the book; Ruskin appears in his own right as literalist and revealer of nature—as well as of Turner—through the painterly nature of his prose. In the book's finest moments nature and Turner commune in Ruskin's style. But there is analytic as well as rhapsodic writing here. The ecstatic moments in which there is an attempt to fuse Turner and the *naturgeist* are prefaced by an elaborate aesthetic of landscape designed to oppose the practice of modern landscapists to the technique of the "ancients," chiefly Cuyp, Claude, and Poussin. The pervasive counterposing of methods was implicit in Ruskin's intended title for the volume, "Turner and the Ancients." The final title was suggested by his publisher.

Modern Painters, volume 1, is composed of four basic kinds of materials. First there is a general theory intended primarily to distinguish vital, or "truth"-oriented, from deadly, or imitative, tendencies in art. This sweeping aesthetic is developed in the first major division of the volume, headed "Part 1, Of General Principles." It is followed by more detailed theoretical materials that focus the aesthetic of truth toward more specific principles governing the practice of landscape painting. The central concern here is to accommodate Turner's luminism to the general theory developed earlier. The most important of these specific justifications are worked out in the first two sections of the second major division of the volume (part 2: "Of Truth," section 1: "General Principles Respecting Ideas of Truth" and section 2: "Of General Truths"). The third sort of material consists of Ruskin's rhapsodic or apocalyptic renderings of Turnerian effects described directly from nature or from particular paintings. Not confined to any particular section of the volume, these "purple patches" are most important because they show the primary bond of feeling between the two artists, especially in their handling of apocalyptic skies. Finally, there are materials in which Ruskin appears as a phenomenologist (as opposed to a priest) of nature. These sections, mainly chapters showing the landscapist how to see natural forms, make up the second half of the volume. A closer look at each of these aspects of the volume, and some of the relations among them, will help to clarify the early bearings of his work.

Ruskin grounds the volume's general aesthetic in the analogy between painting and language. Painting, he argues, is nothing more than a language, or *muta poesis*.[21] But the painter who is merely a master of technique has simply learned how to express himself in the medium; he is the competent versifier who is not yet a poet. For it is by the content, not the technique, that greatness in art is to be judged. Hence the Dutch realists, though they had perfected technique, are called mere "elocutionists" of painting. Ruskin's aesthetic appears to be essentially expressive at this point; art is a lamp not a mirror. But his definition of greatness blurs the distinction: "The art is greatest which conveys to the mind of the spectator, by any means whatsoever, the greatest number of the greatest ideas."[22] When the five possible "greatest ideas" are set forth they appear to fuse imitation and expression. They are ideas of power, of imitation, of truth, of beauty, and of relation.

For Ruskin the greatest of these is truth. It is the central aesthetic idea of the volume, and the last two-thirds of it are devoted to the elaboration of this concept through various aspects of the landscapist's medium and of the forms of life it hopes to represent. First, however, there must be preliminary chapters in which the five ideas are defined and distinguished from one another. Ideas of power are conveyed by art when the spectator is made aware of the mental or physical powers that produced it. This subject is important to Ruskin, he devotes four chapters to power in this volume and gives it, like truth, a place in his later work on architecture. Most important at this point is his observation that the direct sensation we have of power in a work and our intellectual estimate of that power, carefully weighing ends and means, are often contradictory. Because the feeling we have of power is proportionate to the evident inadequacy of means to ends in the work, we are most likely to be taken in by an imperfect work. Hence the intellectual assessment of a painter's power must be given priority over the direct sensation of it.

Though he assigns ideas of beauty a high rank among the others, Ruskin gives the subject short shrift in this volume. He will return to it at length in the two immediately following works, *Modern Painters*, volume 2 and *The Seven Lamps of Architecture*. At this point he merely asserts that ideas of beauty are instinctive, that no object of nature is incapable of conveying them to the receptive mind, and that they are the subjects of moral, though not of intellectual, awareness. Ideas of relation, on the other hand, are just those that must be received by the intellect. They refer apparently to the information related by art. But this subject too is merely acknowledged here, although with the greater justification that ideas of relation are of greater importance to historical than to landscape painting.

So much then for ideas of power, beauty, and relation in art. But the two remaining categories of aesthetic ideas, truth and imitation, are locked in an antithesis that is the key theory of the volume and is involved with that opposition of vital and lethal perception which I take to be Ruskin's central theme. When the volume appeared it challenged those readers who knew something of Turner and his critics with a paradox. This is the way Ruskin expressed it in his preface to the second edition: "For many a year we have heard nothing with respect to the works of Turner but accusations of their want of *truth*. To every observation of their power, sublimity, or beauty, there has been but one reply: they are not like nature. I therefore took my opponents on their own ground, and demonstrated, by thorough investigation of actual facts, that Turner *is* like nature, and paints more of nature than any man who ever lived."[23] He could resolve this apparent contradiction between Turner's art and nature by showing that there was a higher fidelity to nature than imitation as it was conventionally understood. This "faithful statement" of the facts of nature he calls truth. But to clarify the function of truth in art he had first to distinguish it from imitation and then to show that there was an order of priorities among the possible truths.

First let us look at his distinction between truth and imitation. Truth, in art, is "the faithful statement, either to the mind or senses, of any fact of nature."[24] Imitation he first identifies closely with deception. We receive an idea of imitation when a resemblance is perfect enough to approach deception, and yet at the same moment we are aware that it is a deception. Thus ideas of imitation are founded on contradictory impressions, deception and the penetration of it. With truth there is not even this momentary deception. But there are other differences. Ideas of imitation are limited to material things; truth can refer to ideas, emotions, moral values. Truth can be conveyed by symbolic forms that need not resemble something closely. Truth can be conveyed by only one attribute of an object, its outline, say, while imitation requires the presentation of most of the attributes by which the object is known when it is actually present. And in this respect imitation may be less accurate, for it requires only those aspects of resemblance usually perceived by the untrained senses. Thus the aims of imitation and of truth are incompatible. Pictures that attempt to deceive by imitation can never be true. "Hence, finally, ideas of truth are the foundation, and ideas of imitation, the destruction, of all art."[25]

But there was for Ruskin a deeper difference between ideas of truth and of imitation that none of these brisk distinctions quite comprehends. This finer distinction concerns the apocalyptic or revelational power of truth. The point is developed in a later chapter, one of seven in a section called "General Principles Respecting Ideas of Truth." Work-ing from the analogy between portraiture and landscape, Ruskin invites us to consider what would be the most truthful portrait of a particular man. Would it be the portrait that gives the physical features exactly, the accidents of flesh which the worm waits for? Would it be the one that, though blurring some features, gives the subject's particular flash of eye or radiance of lip "the stamp of the soul upon the flesh"?[26] Or would it be the portrait that caught the man's expression at the moment of his most intense experience "when the call and claim of some divine motive had brought into visible being those latent forces and feelings which the spirit's own volition could not summon, nor its consciousness com-prehend"?[27] It is much the same with nature: "She has a body and a soul like man; but her soul is the Deity." And there are three depths of likeness to her, dependent upon the acuteness of the painter and the judge.

> It is possible to represent the body without the spirit; and this shall be like, to those whose senses are only cognizant of body. It is possible to represent the spirit in its ordinary and inferior manifestations; and this shall be like, to those who have not watched for its moments of power. It is possible to represent the spirit in its secret and high operations; and this shall be like only to those to whose watching they have been revealed.[28]

This ultimate or apocalyptic truth of nature has been received only by spirits like Turner, Wordsworth, and, presumably, by the author himself.

Surprisingly, however, Ruskin is willing to call all three of these versions truth at this point. This is troublesome, because the first ver-sion, the body without the spirit, is difficult to distinguish from imita-tion. In fact Ruskin is not successful in keeping truth and imitation distinct throughout the volume. This difficulty is especially apparent in the latter half of the book where he undertakes to explain how the landscapist should give the truths of particular aspects of nature (for example, forms of clouds, mountains, water, and vegetation). Here, in order to mediate between truth and imitation, he frequently relies on a new term that plays little part in the theoretical groundwork of the volume. "Infinity"—the landscapist's ability to represent the hopeless intricacy of natural forms—tends to become his primary criterion for truth with respect to specific natural scenes: "If we wish, without reference to beauty of composition, or any other interfering cir-cumstances, to form a judgment, of the truth of painting, perhaps the very first thing we should look for, whether in one thing or another—

foliage, or clouds, or waves,—should be the expression of *infinity* always and everywhere, in all parts and divisions of parts."[29] But of course this reaching for infinity of finish carries the aims of truth perilously close to those of deadly imitation, "the destruction of all art."

Ruskin appears to have been aware of the inconclusiveness of his truth-imitation distinction, for he attempts to clarify it in the long preface to the second edition of the volume (1844). But the terms are shifted in such a way as to create, in effect, a new distinction. Here, in the second preface, he attempts to define the right way between methodized or generalized nature, the impious defect of early landscape, and mechanical literalism, a common defect of the moderns. It is truth or imitation refined now into the question of realism or idealism in art. Ruskin handles the problem by identifying the vital truth of natural forms with their "specific characters" or ideal forms. Thus landscape has its true ideal that is neither particular nature nor generalized or formalized nature. "The true ideal of landscape is precisely the same as that of the human form [among the Greeks]; it is the expression of the specific—not the individual, but the specific—characters of every object, in their perfection. There is an ideal form of every herb, flower, and tree, it is that form to which every individual of the species has a tendency to arrive, freed from the influence of accident or disease."[30]

This theory of specific form is a useful expedient given the terms of the idealist-realist problem as Ruskin states them here in the second preface. It suggests the compromise the landscapist is to make with living form; he is to give the details of the specific but not of the individual form. But the theory is of little use for those natural forms that have no species, for example, inanimate forms such as clouds, mountains and waves. Further, it says little about how forms are to be composed in a landscape, unless, of course, we are to conclude that true landscape consists of ideal forms in ideal relationships. But Ruskin is clearly opposed to this kind of deadly formalism. Quotations that follow will make it plain that he does not praise Turner for giving typical forms in typical compositions. On the other hand it is true that much of the latter half of volume 1 of *Modern Painters* is given over to the dreary business of attempting to classify the specific forms of things, not only of vegetation, but of clouds, water, and earth relieved here and there by ecstatic renderings of particular scenes or particular Turners. Hence in its content and style the book reveals the basic duality of Ruskin's work and an ambivalence of his aesthetic that continues throughout his later works. The prophet, poet, and phenomenologist remains one with the geologist, economist, and general systematizer. It is because of this tensive duality of his mind that his work gradually becomes fragmented into a multiplicity of projects reflecting both the intuitive and analytic aspects of his thought.

In the theory of art this ambivalence means that he is always clearer in his opposition to what he considers to be deadly extremes in realism or idealism than about the precise mean between them. The landscapist's true subject, clearly, is neither particular nor generalized nature but nature as the god-stuff, nature with the vital mystery in it. But what is this? Coleridge had argued that the artist must not try to convey "the mere nature, the *natura naturata*." This would be hopeless rivalry. Rather he should "master the essence," nature as creator, "the *natura naturans*, that presupposes a bond between nature in the higher sense and the soul of man."[31] Ruskin could have known of, may even have been influenced by, Coleridge's philosophic handling of this problem of the artist's reconciliation of the internal and external. But as a practical critic dealing with specific paintings he was forced to be particular, required to say just when truth has been given and when imitation. He was naturally driven into inconsistencies and ambiguities, for which his critics attacked him. However, he was convinced that he had pointed to a vital mean between deadly extremes, even though that mean could never be captured in theoretical language.

Among the manuscripts of *The Stones of Venice* Ruskin left a brief summary of his attempt to clear an aesthetic *via media* to truth between realist and idealist doctrines. Merging in later volumes with the problem of imagination, the issue he defines here became a theme that is central to the whole of *Modern Painters*. In vindicating the truth of Turner, he explains, he has had to meet

> two distinct classes of opponents, first and principally those who looked for nothing in art but a literal and painstaking imitation of the externals of Nature, as in the works of the Dutch school, against whom I had to prove that the truths thus sought were but a small part of the truth of Nature, and that there were higher and more occult kinds of truth which could not be rendered but by some sacrifice of imitative accuracy, and which Turner had by such sacrifice succeeded in rendering for the first time in the history of art. But in the second place and collaterally I had to meet those men who in their love of system or "composition" disregarded or denied the truth of Nature altogether, and supposed that Imagination was independent of truth. Against whom I had to assert the dignity and glory of Truth, and its necessity as the foundation of all art whatsoever.[32]

"The Truth of Greater Art" he defines as "that which the soul apprehended, not the sight merely." But how does the painter, particularly the landscapist, keep the truths of sight and soul together? What are those "higher and more occult kinds of truth" of nature for which imitation must be sacrificed? Truths of the *natura naturans*?

Because the issue here is not merely that of opposed techniques of painting but of two ultimately irreconcilable yet related modes of awareness—comparable, say, to Martin Buber's "I-It" and "I-Thou"— the answers of *Modern Painters*, volume 1, can be neither distinct nor final. This dialectic of sight and vision, of seeing with and through the eye, would dog Ruskin's work for the rest of his days. At that time, however, having defined truth and dissociated it from imitation, he moved confidently into the task of ranking possible truths in order of their importance.

His four chapters on the relative importance of truths (pt. 2, "Of Truth"; Sec. 1, "General Principles Respecting Ideas of Truth," chaps. 3 through 6) can be reduced to several propositions of priority among truths. The basic propositions are these: first, because of the infinity of nature total truth cannot be given; hence the need for priorities. Second, truths are valuable in proportion to their particularity, valueless in proportion to their generality. (Yet truths of specific form are prior to those which distinguish one individual of the species from another.) Third, nature's rare truths are more important than her common ones. "Her finest touches are things which must be watched for; her most perfect passages of beauty are the most evanescent."[33] Both the painter and the mystic are "commentators on infinity." Finally, truths of color are less important than truths of form; most important, however, looking toward Turner, is Ruskin's point that truths of chiaroscuro have priority over color because form is expressed by light and shade. "To make us understand the *space* of the sky, is an end worthy of the artist's highest powers; to hit its particular blue or gold is an end to be thought of when we have accomplished the first, and not till then."[34]

His next step is to measure, in a preliminary way, the whole development of landscape art against this scale of truths. His purpose is to provide his readers with a perspective on the eminence of Turner. Broadly speaking, he faults the earliest landscapists, particularly Claude, Salvator, and Poussin, for self-conscious and deceptive imitation instead of truth. He finds no evidence of their ever having gone to nature with any "thirst" or ever having surrendered themselves to her; consequently "there is no simple or honest record of any single truth."[35] There is some exceptional praise for the fragments of truth in Tintoretto; it is an appreciation that will deepen immensely in his later work. Here Tintoretto is seen as a precursor of Turner in rendering luminous and mysterious distances. The Dutch realists are scored for their "manual dexterities." Their influence is called "totally for evil"[36] and referred to later in the volume as "the Dutch infection."

In general he finds a far greater proportion of truths among the modern landscapists. Some of them have loved nature for herself. Fielding, Prout, and Stanfield are praised for their partial gifts of accuracy and feeling. Prout, for instance, is seen as the master of "that feeling which results from the influence, among the noble lines of architecture, of the rent and the rust, the fissure, the lichen and the weed . . . the confused hieroglyphyics of human history."[37] But none of these landscapists has the "intense all-observing penetration of a well-balanced mind," a quality which Ruskin illustrates by quoting Wordsworth.[38]

This survey chapter on evidences of love of nature in the progress of landscape painting culminates, of course, in an invocation of Turner. Ruskin is not yet ready for his technical defense of the painter; Turner is introduced simply in rhapsodic antithesis to the others. Yet there is a forecast of the later argument in the emphasis upon Turner as the painter who broke with the "gloomy principle" of the tradition, letting into his canvases the pure luminous infinity and the mystery of nature.

> The real colour of nature had never been attempted by any school; . . . of the actual, joyous, pure, roseate hues of the external world no record had ever been given. He saw also that the finish and specific grandeur of nature had been given, but her fullness, space and mystery never; and he saw that the great landscape painters had always sunk the lower middle tints of nature in extreme shade, bringing the entire melody of colour as many degrees down as their possible light was inferior to nature's; and that in so doing a gloomy principle had influenced them even in their choice of subject.[39]

As the first master of true aerial perspective and vital light, it followed that his special message would be the living sky. "Turner is the only painter, so far as I know, who has ever drawn the sky, not the clear sky, which we before saw belonged exclusively to the religious schools, but the various forms and phenomena of the cloudy heavens."[40] Further, he is the first painter who ever communed with the shapes of mountains and stones, the stems of trees, and the many moods of water. Finally, and most important, he is not the mere copyist but the apocalyptist of nature, standing, as Thoreau hoped to do, between eternities. He was sent, Ruskin declares in a passage which his *Blackwood's* reviewer thought blasphemous, "as a prophet of God to reveal to men the mysteries of His universe, standing, *like the great angel of the Apocalypse,* clothed with a cloud, and with a rainbow upon his head, and with the sun and stars given into his hand."[41]

3

Proving Turner true is the task of the rest of volume 1 of *Modern Painters* and the effort calls into play the three other categories of materials outlined earlier: discussions of landscape technique, prose renderings of Turnerian effects, and essays on the "specific forms" of primary natural phenomena. In terms of technique—truths of the medium in tone, color, chiaroscuro, and space—Ruskin finds Turner most true just where he had seemed most false with respect to the received style. He founds his defense on those innovations in light and space by which Turner had overcome the "gloomy principle" of the old masters. Further, if Turnerian light and aerial perspective could be defended as primary truths of technique they would point to a high position on the supreme scale of truths developed in the first half of the volume. Vital truths of specific form are dependent upon technical truths of chiaroscuro. Rare or evanescent truths, because usually given in sky effects, must depend upon true rendering of aerial perspective. But beneath the critical surface one senses that a thirst for light and spectacular skies was the primary empathic bond between Ruskin's work and Turner's.

It was essential and natural, then, in turning to practical truths, for Ruskin to take head-on the problem of Turner's rebellion against the tonal qualities of traditional landscape and build his defenses around Turner's most daring innovations. But the problem of tone (unity and veracity of light; "climate," or atmosphere, in a painting) is barely separable from problems of local color, chiaroscuro, and spatial perspective; thus they are grouped in a unit of chapters called "Of General Truths." Also implicit in this heading and in much of Ruskin's language is a broader message. The discussion of truths of landscape technique, which was Turner's victory over the gloomy tradition, is not simply about painting but about nature's teaching, as is *The King of the Golden River*. And here also the first lesson is in light.

To illustrate the kinds of implicit meanings Ruskin attaches to Turner's revelations in light I must shift for a moment to the third category of materials in this volume, namely, Ruskin's verbal paintings. Here, in one of the most impassioned passages of emotive prose, Ruskin tries to convey the dance of light-life in Turnerian chiaroscuro.

> Words are not accurate enough, nor delicate enough, to express or trace the constant, all-pervading influence of the finer and vaguer shadows

throughout his works, that thrilling influence which gives to the light they leave its passion and its power. There is not a stone, not a leaf, not a cloud, over which light is not felt to be actually passing and palpitating before our eyes. There is the motion, the actual wave and radiation of the darted beam: not the dull universal daylight, which falls on the landscape without life, or direction, or speculation, equal on all things and dead on all things; but the breathing, animated, exulting light, which feels, and receives, and rejoices, and acts,—which chooses one thing, and rejects another,—which seeks, and finds, and loses again,—leaping from rock to rock, from leaf to leaf, from wave to wave,—glowing, or flashing, or scin-tillating, according to what it strikes; or, in its holier moods, absorbing and enfolding all things in the deep fulness of its repose, and then again losing itself in bewilderment, and doubt, and dimness,—or perishing and passing away, entangled in drifting mist, or melted into melancholy air, but still,—kindling or declining, sparkling or serene,—it is the living light which breathes in its deepest, most entranced rest, which sleeps, but never dies.[42]

Notice the opposition of vital to dead light carried in part by projective, almost mythic, animation ("pathetic fallacy") by which the light takes on life of its own and becomes a "Thou."

In his more analytic prose Ruskin affirms the intensity and diffusion of daylight in living landscape and argues that "if a picture is to be truthful in effect of colour . . . it should tell as a broad space of graduated illumination,—not, as do those of the old masters, as a patchwork of black shades." Paint, of course, can never hope to reproduce the light of nature in the open air, but compared to nature and Turner the landscapes of the old masters are no more than "nature in mourning weeds."[43] Turner's canvasses are able to conduct more life through a higher and more perfect harmony of tone and aerial perspec-tive. This basic truth of technique is interfused with his veracities in local color, chiaroscuro, and the representation of distant forms. Ruskin defines and illustrates these limits of the medium, reached by Turner, in a difficult group of chapters, relying alternately on the analytic and the poetic dimensions of his prose. To follow him a way in this is to recover not only Ruskin's Turner, but the primary prehension of landscape upon which his critic's later work would be built.

First, there is the problem of tone. Aerial perspective, the right relation of tone to represented distance, requires that objects in a landscape be detached from each other by degrees of intensity propor-tionate to their distance. But nature infinitely surpasses paint in her gradational powers of light and shade. Art's highest light is white paper as opposed to sunlight; its deepest shades are black surfaces from which much light may be reflected, whereas nature's deepest shades are un-

J. M. W. Turner. *The Evening of the Deluge*. Courtesy of the National Gallery of Art, Washington, D.C. (Timken Collection)

reflective voids. "Here we are, then," Ruskin summarizes, "with white paper for our highest light, and visible, illumined surface for our deepest shadow, set to run the gauntlet against nature, with the sun for her light and vacuity for her gloom."[44]

With such a scale at her disposal nature can afford to throw dark material objects against the brilliance of her sky, and yet she can define their forms and distances with a thousand intermediate tones before losing them in gloom. But if the painter, with his dim skies and pale shadows, attempts to keep his material objects in the same relation of shade to distance as nature does, he quickly goes to the bottom of his scale of shadows with nothing left to represent nature's subtleties of perspective. The "gloomy principle" of the old masters, Ruskin insists, was to represent in true proportion of distance to shade only those steps that were most pronounced, such as from sky to foliage or from clouds to hills. But having exhausted their means in gross imitation they were forced to give up particular truths of space and form—leaving their trees, for instance, as "flat masses of mere filled-up outline"—in order to achieve general tonal coherence. They thus sacrificed vital truths of aerial perspective for gloomy harmonies of tone.

But Turner let new life and light into landscape by taking an expanded scale of illumination and strictly correlating intensities to degrees of distance.

> He boldly takes pure white (and justly, for it is the sign of the most intense sunbeams) for his highest light, and lamp black for his deepest shade; and between these he makes every degree of shade indicative of a separate degree of distance, giving each step of approach, not the exact difference in pitch which it would have in nature, but a difference bearing the same proportion to that which his sum of possible shade bears to the sum of nature's shade; so that an object halfway between his horizon and his foreground, will be exactly in half tint of force, and every minute division of intermediate space will have just its proportionate share of the lesser sum, and no more.[45]

Ruskin admits that by this innovation Turner sacrificed the harmony and richness of tone of the old masters but insists that he gained greater completeness, especially in rendering "aerial effects." That is, by giving up deceptive imitation he gained a thousand particular truths of form and distance.

There is also, in Ruskin's view, another fundamental way in which Turnerian tone improves on that of the old masters: his power of juxtaposing cold with warm light. However, in attempting to clarify the meaning of this association of light values he moves from the prose of statement to the prose of suggestion. He explains that the old masters "gave the warmth of the sinking sun, overwhelming all things in its gold, but they did not give those grey passages about the horizon where, seen through its dying light, the cool and gloom of night gather themselves for their victory."[46] But the cool purlieus of Turner's sunsets can carry a deeper, more ominous message than the mellow glows of Claude or Cuyp. Ruskin detects shadows of finality, apocalyptic voids, in the sky of the famous *Téméraire* (Plate I) that draw him into one of the volume's more ecstatic passages.

> That picture will not, at the first glance, deceive as a piece of actual sunlight; but this is because there is in it more than sunlight, because under the blazing veil of vaulted fire which lights the vessel on her last path, there is a blue, deep, desolate hollow of darkness, out of which you can hear the voice of the night wind, and the dull boom of the disturbed sea; because the cold deadly shadows of twilight are gathering through every sunbeam, and moment by moment as you look, you will fancy some new film and faintness of the night has risen over the vastness of the departing form.[47]

Having revealed the new truths of Turnerian light under the nebulous topic of tone, it is a simpler matter for Ruskin to trace his innovations in the related qualities of color, chiaroscuro, and spatial effect. The great dilemma of the colorist, we learn, is that the closer he approaches nature's color the farther he is from her light. Having to choose whether to be governed by color or by light, Turner chose the law of light. The result of this choice, Ruskin argues, is that no painter uses pure color more cautiously and sparingly, and yet he is distinguished by his ability to shed dazzling illumination through every hue. He has captured the palpitation and perpetual change of nature's color, but especially the luminous intensities of the sky. Compared with that of the common colorists of the Academy his system of color is "the chastity of fire to the foulness of earth."[48] However, this aerial glow is not the full message of his color. There is a kind of ironic countertruth, like the cold with the warm light. Ruskin detects "a general system or under-current of grey pervading the whole of his colour."[49]

Yet Turner's entire method of color is subordinated to an "inviolable law of chiaroscuro, from which there is no appeal. No richness nor depth of tint is considered of value enough to atone for the loss of one particle of arranged light."[50] In Ruskin's larger scheme of truths this means that Turner stands by definition of form, the highest truth, against force of color. The essential truth of chiaroscuro in landscape, he argues, is that distinctness of shadow is nature's primary means of expressing vividness of light. Nature is not indecisive about shadows; she marks the main transition from light to shade by "violent decision,"

not by subtle gradations, then varies the shade itself by complex gradation. Turner's chiaroscuro is an exquisite reading of nature's message:
"the sharpness, decision, conspicuousness, and excessively small quantity, both of extreme light and extreme shade, all the mass of the picture
being graduated and delicate middle tint."[51]

Taking up finally the general subject of spatial truth in landscape,
Ruskin holds that in his treatment of space Turner chooses truth over
imitation in two primary ways. First, he realizes that distinctness of
detail is dependent on the focus of the eye. If the foreground is distinct in
a landscape, truth requires that the background be vague, and vice versa,
because both cannot be distinct in the same focus. To strive for clarity in
both grounds at once is deceptive imitation. Turner takes the distance or
middle distance as his characteristic focus and innovates by honestly
subduing his foregrounds in favor of distance. Second, knowing that
nature is never either distinct or vacant, he uses his power, his "infinity"
of execution, to render both her mystery and her finish. He perceives that
the natural effect of distance is confusion, not annihilation of details. It
is not mist but mystery that is between us and the distant object. Thus
distant details in Turner appear to the untrained eye exactly as they
would in nature: "as an unintelligible mass." Near forms, especially of
vegetation, also dissolve in mystery and infinity. The painter cannot
hope to duplicate nature's infinity, but he can represent it by a lesser
order of infinity of his own. This is Turner's power with vegetation. It is
interesting that Ruskin uses the painter's late mythic subject *Mercury
and Argus* to illustrate not only his glowing aerial effects but his infinity
and obscurity in vegetation. In fact, in this volume he refers to it more
frequently than to any other particular work.

Such is the gist of Ruskin's defense of the modern master's rebellion
against the received limits of his medium in tone, color, chiaroscuro,
and distance. The basis of his impressionism in landscape is seen as a
new discipline in the uses of light. For Ruskin, the vital secret of
Turner's art is light, light defining form, allowing infinite mysteries of
gradation in aerial perspective, and infusing life into his color. But now
a concluding question wants to be answered. What message was the
painter's new medium bent on? Supposing Turnerian technique to be
capable of conveying the supreme moments of landscape (the rarest most
evanescent truths spoken of earlier in this volume) what expressions of
the god-stuff could best catalyze his powers into the highest art? Ruskin's
answer is that Turner is the great revealer of the moods of the upper
skies, especially of sunsets among the high clouds. He is the nearest to
mastery of those rose-lit moments that reveal, more than any other aspect

of nature, the "exhaustless operation of the Infinite Mind."[52] The living effect is inexpressible either in language or painting, but Ruskin must attempt to show, from his own impressions, what is painting's ultimate challenge.

> I speak especially of the moment before the sun sinks, when his light turns pure rose-colour, and when this light falls upon a zenith covered with countless cloud-forms of inconceivable delicacy, threads and flakes of vapour, which would in common daylight be pure snow-white, and which give therefore fair field to the tone of light. There is then no limit to the multitude, and no check to the intensity, of the hues assumed. The whole sky from the zenith to the horizon becomes one molten mantling sea of colour and fire; every black bar turns into massy gold, every ripple and wave into unsullied shadowless crimson, and purple, and scarlet, and colours for which there are no words in the language, and no ideas in the mind,—things which can only be conceived while they are visible; the intense hollow blue of the upper sky melting through it all, showing here deep, and pure, and lightless; there modulated by the filmy formless body of the transparent vapour, till it is lost imperceptibly in its crimson and gold. Now there is no connection, no one link of association or resemblance, between those skies and the work of any mortal hand but Turner's.[53]

4

The fourteen chapters—more than 250 pages—that comprise the latter half of the volume (sects. 3–6) consist almost entirely of materials of the fourth type, namely, instructions to the landscapist. Here Ruskin attempts to explain or describe, taking Turner as his standard, what the landscapist ought to see and paint: the "specific characters" of things in the four primary divisions of natural forms. He attempts, that is, to expound the "truths" of skies, earth, water, and vegetation. As might be expected, the section "Truth of Skies" is by far the longest. This subject is subdivided into truths of open sky and of clouds, cloud truths being further subdivided into those of the upper, middle, and lower regions of clouds.

In describing natural phenomena in *Modern Painters*, volume 1, Ruskin speaks first and most extensively of skies because he thinks of the sky as God's most articulate medium. "Sometimes gentle, sometimes capricious, sometimes awful, never the same for two moments together; almost human in its passions, almost spiritual in its tenderness, almost divine in its infinity, its appeal to what is immortal in us is as distinct, as its ministry of chastisement or of blessing to what is mortal is essential."[54]

This view was already implicit in the admonitory role assigned to the sky in the *King of the Golden River*. Most significant as a premonition of his later mythic interpretations of cloud forms is his observation that they "give to the scenery of the sky a force and variety no less delightful than that of the changes of mountain outline in a hill district of great elevation; and that there is added to this *a spirit-like feeling, a capricious mocking imagery of passion and life,* totally different from any effects of inanimate form that the earth can show."[55]

But if sky effects are the supreme fictions of the Deity, purple passages in "the God-written apocalypse," Turner is their prophet in painting. They are his primary way of calling in the Infinite. His new system of light led to his mastery of translucent effects of color and of the fullness and mystery of atmospheric space, making him, as Ruskin had shown earlier, the solitary master of the neglected upper skies. To find words for the message of the drifts of light in a high Turnerian sky Ruskin turns to one of the sky visions in Wordsworth's *The Excursion.* "But rays of light,/Now suddenly diverging from the orb/ . . . shot upwards to the crown."[56] The quotation is significant because, like Turner's and Ruskin's, Wordsworth's art leans heavily on the natural apocalypse, the technique by which some vast and evanescent effect of nature (as in the Simplon chasm or Snowdon passages of *The Prelude*) is described in such a way that it becomes the outward and visible metaphor for inward and spiritual revelation. The *Excursion* vision serves Ruskin twice in the volume as an image of Turner's "peculiar and favorite field," showing how "at all hours, in all seasons, he has followed its passions and its changes, and has brought down and laid open to the world another apocalypse of Heaven."[57] Later, in a characteristic passage of "Alpine ecstasy," Ruskin invokes the heavenly apocalypse and offers his vision in tribute to God, nature, and Turner.

> The rose-light of their silent domes flushing that heaven about them and above them, piercing with purer light through its purple lines of lifted cloud, casting a new glory on every wreath as it passes by, until the whole heaven, one scarlet canopy, is interwoven with a roof of waving flame, and tossing, vault beyond vault, as with the drifted wings of many companies of angels: and then, when you can look no more for gladness, when you are bowed down with fear and love of the Maker and Doer of this, tell me who has best delivered this His message into men![58]

But "His message" is not of Heaven only. It is necessary for the comprehension of Ruskin's later and more ominous skies to observe here what anyone familiar with Turner knows: his skies are often apocalyptic in a darker, more malevolent mode. Looking backward over his formative years in *Praeterita* Ruskin notices a significant irony in his having been given Turner's *Winchelsea,* with its fuliginous storm cloud, for his twenty-first birthday. Yet some of the most memorable rhetorical flights in this first volume are attempts to recreate the wrathful intimations of Turner's skies. The *Stonehenge*, for instance, he takes as a kind of paradigm of the painter's storm-work.

All its forms are marked with violent angles, as if the whole muscular energy, so to speak, of the cloud were writhing in every fold: and their fantastic and fiery volumes have a peculiar horror, an awful life, shadowed out in their strange, swift, fearful outlines which oppress the mind more than even the threatening of their gigantic gloom. The white lightning, not as it is drawn by less observant or less capable painters, in zigzag fortifications, but in its own dreadful irregularity of streaming fire, is brought down, not merely over the dark clouds, but through the full light of an illumined opening to the blue, which yet cannot abate the brilliancy of its white line; and the track of the last flash along the ground is fearfully marked by the dog howling over the fallen shepherd, and the ewe pressing her head upon the body of her dead lamb.[59]

And the magnificent *Slave Ship*, (Plate II) with its lurid sky and wild, corpse-encumbered sea, is invoked as a natural image of judgment over which the sun presides, as it had over the trials of help in *The King of the Golden River*.

The whole surface of sea included in the picture is divided into two ridges of enormous swell, not high, nor local, but a low broad heaving of the whole ocean, like the lifting of its bosom by deep-drawn breath after the torture of the storm. Between these two ridges the fire of the sunset falls along the trough of the sea, dyeing it with an awful but glorious light, the intense and lurid splendour which burns like gold, and bathes like blood. Along this fiery path and valley, the tossing waves by which the swell of the sea is restlessly divided, lift themselves in dark, indefinite, fantastic forms, each casting a faint and ghastly shadow behind it along the illumined foam. . . . Purple and blue, the lurid shadows of the hollow breakers are cast upon the mist of night, which gathers cold and low, advancing like the shadow of death upon the guilty ship as it labours amidst the lightning of the sea, its thin masts written upon the sky in lines of blood, girded with condemnation in that fearful hue which signs the sky with horror, and mixes its flaming flood with the sunlight, and, cast far along the desolate heave of the sepulchral waves, incarnadines the multitudinous sea.[60]

Ruskin will return to Turner's storm clouds in later volumes, in order to explore their mythic implications. In this connection, it should be observed that most of the major interrelated themes this study will trace in Ruskin's work: myth, imagination, natural theology, social and environmental protest, make little or no appearance in volume 1 of *Modern Painters*. Yet the taproot of his later thought is traceable here in the volume's constant opposition of truth to imitation. Within the general view of nature as an aesthetic norm Ruskin poses two modes of awareness of nature: the one is dynamic, unified, yet infinite, and mysteriously expressive of an immanent teleology with which the painter communes; the other is dead, mechanical, one dimensional, constituted in art by rules and deceptive techniques (in other words, nature as "Thou" and nature as "It").

"Atmosphere is my style," Turner told Ruskin in 1844.[61] He may simply have been pointing to his predilection for aerial effects. But in *Modern Painters* 1 his atmosphere means the mystery and infinity of landscape conceived organically and not mechanically, the feeling for nature as exhibiting, in Whitehead's phrase, "entwined prehensive unities, each suffused with the modal presence of others."[62] In Turner's foregrounds, no less than in his skies, the presence of the whole broods upon the infinity of parts. It is the master's skill, Ruskin explains,

> to trace among the grass and weeds those mysteries of invention and combination by which nature appeals to the intellect; to render the delicate fissure, and descending curve, and undulating shadow of the mouldering soil, with gentle and fine finger, like the touch of the rain itself; to find even in all that appears most trifling or contemptible, fresh evidence of the constant working of the Divine power . . . ; this, as it is the peculiar province and faculty of the master-mind, so it is the peculiar duty which is demanded of it by the Deity.[63]

5

Although *Modern Painters* 1 begins auspiciously enough with a bold catalogue of the qualities of great art, as a general aesthetic the volume suffers from serious defects even in the terms of its time. It gives short shrift to announced "Ideas of Beauty" in favor of those of "truth," merely acknowledging their importance and neglecting the traditionally important question of the relation between the two. It says little directly about the connection between art and morality, relying primarily on the moral implications of its idea of truth. The reader is left to assume that a faithful landscape is a moral assertion, which is a truth, perhaps, but hardly a sufficient one for those whose religion was more explicit than nature-worship. Imagination and symbolism, key topics of Romantic aesthetics, receive no explicit treatment. In brief, the whole expressive side of art is necessarily neglected in the volume in favor of the mimetic with mystical intimations. It was a satisfactory position, one might argue, as long as Ruskin restricted his interests to the Wordworthian-Turnerian landscape feeling, that is, to "modern" painters.

But before he could begin to appraise other, earlier, modes of "sacred" art than landscape—or even appreciate Turner's mythological subjects—he would have to reach more definite conclusions about the way art fuses internal with external vision, expressive with mimetic truths.

In writing volume 2 of *Modern Painters*, published in 1846, Ruskin attempted to remedy the general weakness in the subjective or "spiritual" aspect of his aesthetic that had limited the first volume. The second volume, as Cook observes, "sets forth the spiritual as opposed to the sensual theory of art."[64] The first volume had consisted of two major divisions: "Part 1, Of General Principles" and "Part 2, Of Truth." The second volume is appropriately subtitled "Part 3, Of Ideas of Beauty," but, superficially at least, it is less a continuation than a new beginning. Turner and the moderns virtually disappear and Tintoretto becomes the new protagonist, though the style and structure of the supporting context are quite different. The major topics are beauty, natural theology, and imagination, with a faint overture to the study of mythopoesis. If we are to recover the creative dynamic that drove Ruskin to explore these subjects, the course of his life during the period when he wrote the second volume must be retraced.

Despite the supplemental connections between the two volumes, to attempt to account for volume 2 merely in terms of the theoretical gaps in volume 1 would be to take a much too restricted view. To begin with, one cannot discount important biographical developments, some of which have already been touched upon in my introduction. Though it would be impossible to reconstruct precisely the state of Ruskin's mind at the time that he was writing the new volume, it is apparent from his own accounts that during the three years intervening the two volumes he had absorbed several new influences that he thought were apparent in the content and style of the new work. He described the period of its composition as the "moulting period" of his life, and it does indeed appear that the complex of influences to which he was exposed from 1842 to 1845 resulted in new dedication and direction, in an altered sense of the relationship between art and life and of his own calling as mediator between them.

It could be said, in the interest of brevity, that the shaping revelation of this period was the art of Tintoretto; he became, in a way, the Turner of volume 2. But this vastly oversimplifies the place of Tintoretto both in this phase of Ruskin's life and in the book. For his biographical accounts show that the effect of the encounter with Tintoretto and Venice can be seen as in some sense a secular reaction against his prior commitment to Florence and Florentine primitive painting. In the volume itself

Tintoretto's art is not as pervasive a norm as is Turner's art in volume 1 but is more a climactic illustration of human imaginative power. Ruskin's discussion of Tintoretto's art takes the form of an outburst of aesthetic empathy quite detached from the natural theology of the first half of the volume.

In the epilogue he wrote for volume 2 in 1883, Ruskin attempted to show how Tintoretto changed the course of his life and work. But this account should be supplemented by those in *Praeterita*, the *Fors* and personal letters, and the diaries, though no diary exists for the crucial tour-year 1845. For convenience of analysis the influences that shaped volume 2 might be sorted into three categories, though they are actually deeply interwoven and cumulative rather than separate. There are spiritual influences reflected in Ruskin's altering attitudes toward religion and nature; there are literary influences affecting his prose style; and there are aesthetic influences that were direct and theoretical influences upon his view of art.

Primary among the spiritual influences, of course, was his Evangelical faith, then essentially unshaken, founded on the habit of daily reading in, and learning by rote, the Bible and the "fine old Scottish paraphrases." This regimen, as Ruskin explains in the second chapter of *Praeterita*, had been taught him by his mother who required every sentence "to be said over and over again till she was satisfied with the accent of it."[65] The result of her teaching, he declares, was to establish his soul in life, and to bestow the gift of peace, obedience, faith and the habit of fixed attention. "My own faults or follies," he summarizes in the epilogue,

> only heightened my respect for the virtue and simplicity of the Scottish border race, as I then had known it; nor did either Byron or Shelley for an instant disturb my belief in John Bunyan, or my trust in the presence of an aiding God, in this world, and in the justice of His judgments in that to come. What formal obedience to my parents, and steady carrying out of my mother's way of reading, did for me, as farther safeguards I cannot estimate;—but the steady reading of a chapter of the Bible in the morning and evening, and at least the deliberate *utterance* of appointed prayer . . . gave me a continually increasing knowledge of the meaning both of Old and New Testaments, and of what prayer meant for Christians of old time: farther than this, all my love of the beauty, or sense of the majesty, of natural things was in direct ratio to conditions of devotional feeling.[66]

It was natural, then, that Ruskin should adduce this background to indicate that although he knew little of Christian art prior to the tour of 1845 he was solidly prepared in Christian faith. So firm, apparently, was

(Plate I) J. M. W. Turner. *The Fighting 'Téméraire' Tugged to her last Berth to be broken Up, 1838.* Reproduced by courtesy of the Trustees, The National Gallery, London.

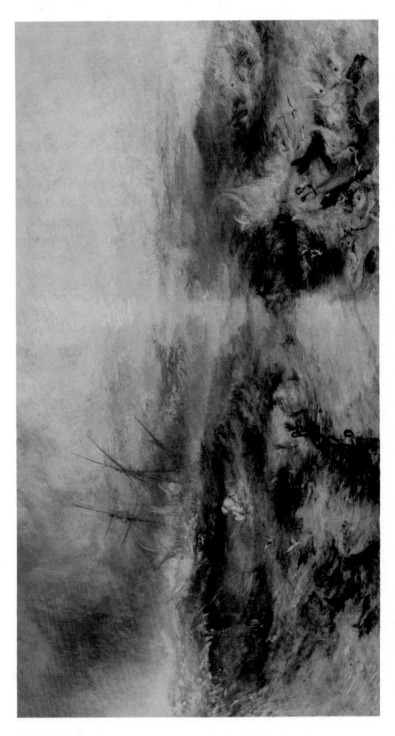

(Plate II) J. M. W. Turner. *Slavers Throwing Overboard the Dead and Dying—Typhon Coming on* [*The Slave Ship*]. Courtesy of the Museum of Fine Arts, Boston. (Henry L. Pierce Fund, 99.22)

his conviction at this time (or at least his urge to express conviction), and so strongly is this influence felt in the second volume, that as his faith waned after 1858 the volume became an embarrassment to him. He refused to include it in the revised works series he began in 1871.

In 1883, however, he reissued the volume in a special rearranged and annotated form. His comments at the time indicate that only the desperate need for a decisive countervoice to the amoral and autonomous aesthetics of the period, the "dissolytic,—dialytic—or even diarrhoeic—lies" to which the "general student" of art was then being exposed, persuaded him to republish the volume at all.[67] In a note to this edition, for instance, he points to his early rejection of the term *aesthetic* for the faculty, that perceives beauty because it signified a view that degraded this faculty, as he had said, "to a mere operation of sense, or perhaps worse, of custom." His note of 1883 goes on to explain that one of his main reasons for reprinting the work is "that it contains so early and so decisive warning against the then incipient folly, which in recent days has made art at once the corruption, and the jest, of the vulgar world."[68] However, the pervasive self-mockery of many of the notes to the rearranged edition also makes plain his intense dislike for the pietistic arrogance of the first two-thirds of the volume. It was written, he explained in *Love's Meinie*, "in affected imitation of Hooker, and not in my own proper style."[69]

But these remarks of Ruskin's on the Protestant bias of the second volume of *Modern Painters* do not account for the entire aesthetic of the volume nor do they fully express his spiritual condition in 1845. They might, for instance, explain the volume's natural theology and the interest in painters of what he would later call the "Purist Ideal," but they hardly account for the overwhelming influence of Tintoretto, a "worldly" painter, upon him. That fact is that Ruskin's spiritual growth was determined not only by his rearing and his reading but also by a certain number of apocalyptic encounters with his environment— by religious experience as well as religious thought. Since these experiences do not lend themselves to brief discursive analysis, I can only refer again to the "Cumae" chapter of *Praeterita* in which Ruskin recounts sibylline experiences of his own on volcanic ground near Naples in 1841, and to diary entries of the same time which occasionally show him receiving depressing intimations from scenery. It appears that by 1841 Ruskin was beginning to have revelations of the malefic as well as of the benevolent powers at work in existence, that he was becoming aware of the lethal as well as of the vital mystery, of the fallen world of "Experience," in Blake's sense, as well as that of "Innocence." This is how he phrased this awareness from the distant retrospect of *Praeterita*.

> The first sight of the Alps had been to me as a direct revelation of the benevolent will in creation. Long since, in the volcanic powers of destruction, I had been taught by Homer, and further forced by my own reason to see, if not the personality of an Evil Spirit, at all events the permitted symbol of evil, unredeemed; wholly distinct from the conditions of storm, or heat, or frost, on which the healthy courses of organic life depended. In the same literal way in which the snows and Alpine roses of Lauterbrunnen were visible Paradise, here, in the valley of ashes and throat of lava, were visible Hell.[70]

But if by the time of *Modern Painters*, volume 2 (1846), Ruskin was experiencing manifestations of a malevolent power in things, one does not receive these impressions from the natural theology of the volume; however, they may underlie the "Imaginative Verity" he felt in Tintoretto's *Last Judgment* and his invocation of that fearsome verity in the volume's most memorable passage. But more characteristic of the religious-aesthetic experience of nature upon which this and the immediately following volumes on the Gothic are built is the often-cited Fontainebleau revelation of 1842. In this "moment" of experience, related in *Praeterita*, Ruskin begins a dry and languid sketch of a small aspen outlined against the sky. But he finds, as we have noticed, that the lines of the tree insist on being traced; he is drawn into a kind of relation with the forming power in the tree, and sees "that they 'composed' themselves, by finer laws than any known of men." Not merely this, he sees in the beauty of these lines "the same laws which guided the clouds, divided the light, and balanced the wave." The whole experience is offered as testimony of "the bond between the human mind and all visible things."[71] The nature of this bond—the symbolic language of nature and the faculty which interprets it—is the major subject of the first part of volume 2 of *Modern Painters*.

Of course it is an illusory task to attempt to define precisely Ruskin's religious position in the 1840's. He was himself unable to do so at the time. In a letter of 1842, the twelfth of his *Letters to a College Friend*, he expressed his vacillation as the need to find a *via media* between the erroneous extremes of blind credence and private judgment instead of remaining "the *nothing* I am."[72] His religion at the time was compounded of two interacting aspects, scriptural and natural, both beginning to change. He had a church religion—Evangelicalism—that was still essentially unshaken but altering: "The flash of volcanic lightning at Naples, had brought me into a deeper and more rational state of religious temper," he wrote. But in the epilogue to *Modern Painters*, volume 2, he compares this temper with that of Bunyan; *Praeterita* and the letters to his mother speak of Herbert as his special teacher: "In the sincerity and brightness of his imagination, I saw that George Herbert represented the theology of the Protestant Church in a perfectly central and deeply spiritual manner."[73] His nature-religion, also altering, appears to be turning more toward nature as presenting symbolic forms conveying divine mystery which is sometimes ominous, away from what he considered to be the direct and sentimental Wordsworthian response to scenery. It was in 1837, he declares, that he felt "for the last time, the pure childish love of nature which Wordsworth so idly takes for an intimation of immortality." It was a feeling he could not help but lose, "for all care, regret, or knowledge of evil destroys it."[74] The same would also be true for the Evangelical faith of his childhood. Nature and religion would continue their joint influence but in deepening knowledge of the contraries, of the rose and the worm, in existence.

Literary influences on him during the period of *Modern Painters*, volume 2 cannot be effectively separated from the spiritual ones. His Bible reading, his Herbert, are both cases in point. Nor can the continuing primary literary influences of Homer, Aeschylus, Plato, Dante, Scott, Johnson, Wordsworth, Shelley, and Carlyle be entirely distinguished from the immediate impressions under which he wrote in the winter of 1845. Yet the special influence of Hooker's prose on the style of the volume, particularly of the first section, is pronounced and admitted by Ruskin.

> The style of the book was formed on a new model, given me by Osborne Gordon. I was old enough now to feel that neither Johnsonian balance nor Byronic alliteration were ultimate virtues in English prose; and I had been reading with care, on Gordon's counsel, both for its arguments and its English, Richard Hooker's *Ecclesiastical Polity*. I had always a trick of imitating, more or less, the last book I had read with admiration; and it farther seemed to me that for the purposes of argument, (and my own theme was, according to my notion, to be argued out invincibly,) Hooker's English was the perfectest existing model.[75]

So strong is this influence that much of the book seems unbearably sanctimonious and affected. His eventual repudiation of its theology and style is understandable in the light of his later work. In its theoretical content the book owes much to Plato, to the *Ethics* of Aristotle, and to Wordsworth's prefaces. But these theoretical debts, like the religious and stylistic influences, are really inseparable from those in our final and most important category, those moments of aesthetic illumination that, Ruskin says, shaped at this time the whole course of his study of art.

The aesthetic illuminations that Ruskin recalls as having been crucial to the period of composition of volume 2 of *Modern Painters*, during the fall and winter of 1845–46, belong to two opposed phases that might for convenience be called the Florentine experience and the Venetian experience. It is important to remember that these specific art influences, upon which Ruskin places the emphasis in his explanation of the temper of the second volume, are in reality closely interwoven with a whole complex of involvements with religion, nature, literature, and other art, as well as family and social life. But in his own account Ruskin is at pains to show how his critical impulses were polarized at this time by two revelational, life-altering encounters with specific works of art: first with Quercia's statue of Ilaria di Caretto at Lucca (the climactic Tuscan experience) and, later in the same summer, when he had gone to Venice, with the paintings of Tintoretto in the Scuola di San Rocco (the central Venetian experience and the climax of the tour of 1845). These points will need some explanation.

Ruskin had returned from his tour of 1844 with a nascent interest in early Christian art and a determination to study it further at first hand before proceeding with the second volume. Apparently he prepared himself in part by reading Rio's work on the poetry of Christian art.[76] But the essential point is that he returned to the Continent in April of 1845 with a whetted thirst for early religious art and a sense that his life had not yet been dedicated. In Italy, en route to Florence, a detour from the coast "to avoid the Pisan Maremma," led him to Lucca and to Quercia's sculpture of Lady Ilaria in peaceful repose upon her tomb. The work, for reasons that can hardly have been entirely aesthetic, came as a revelation to him and a new beginning in the study of art. This is how he remembered the experience in *Fors*, Letter 45 (1874): "Thirty years ago, I began my true study of Italian, and all other art,—here, beside the statue of Ilaria di Caretto, recumbent on her tomb. It turned me from the study of landscape to that of life, being then myself in the fullest strength of labour, and joy of hope."[77] He felt, and continued to feel, that it was in every respect a central example of medieval art, a perfect mean between formal rigidity and imitation. It "became at once," the epilogue affirms, "and has ever since remained, my ideal of Christian sculpture."[78]

The tour continued, yielding further revelations. Examples of Gothic architecture began to seize his sensibilities, first at Lucca and then at Pisa. "Absolutely for the first time I now saw what medieval builders were, and what they meant," he declared in *Praeterita*. "I took the simplest of all façades for analysis, that of Santa Maria Foris-Portam, and thereon literally *began* the study of architecture."[79]

Similarly, with an awe as much Christian as aesthetic he copied the legendary figures of the Campo Santo, to him a "veritable Palestine." Memmi, Giotto, Gozzoli, Orcagna their figures were, he said, "living presences" as well as beautiful forms. From Pisa he went to Florence where this phase of his religious-aesthetic pilgrimage culminated in devout copying of the Angelicos in the academy and his "discovery" of the Ghirlandajos in the apse of Santa Maria Novella. Lippi and Botticelli, he said, were still far beyond him, and yet it appears that the spell of Christian ideal art was as complete upon him as it would ever be. For the moment the art of Florence predominated over that of Venice in his mind. "At Venice," he says in *Praeterita*, "one only knows a fisherman by his net, and a saint by his nimbus. But at Florence, angel or prophet, knight or hermit, girl or goddess, prince or peasant, cannot but be what they are, masque them how you will."[80] And so, under the spell of the Florentines he turned northward again to meditate under Monte Rosa at Macugnaga. Here in his "cell" he spent a month in reading, mountain drawing, and literary "drudgery."

This meditative interlude was cut short by a letter from a friend, the painter J. D. Harding, proposing a joint sketching tour. Ruskin agreed and the two began an enchanted sweep of Italian towns that led from Baveno to Arona, to Bergamo, Brescia and Verona, and finally to Venice. The visit to Venice, he said, being "only for Harding's sake" that year. For a week they feasted in a rather aimless way on sights of the market and the harbor and on the play of light on the city and the sea, until "in the spare hour of one sunny but luckless day" fancy led them into the Scuola di San Rocco. Both were so stricken, at first, by the majesty of the Tintorettos before them that they had not strength to stand.[81]

Ruskin was swept away by the magnitude of what he saw into a new and deeper life, from the art-life of "Innocence" to that of "Experience." He must become an interpreter of the heights of human art in Venice, epitomized by Tintoretto, but also of its diseases and death. For he came to think of Tintoretto as closing the great arts of the world, the consummate talent of an epoch already tainted by death.[82] He sensed, as well, technical affinities between Tintoretto and Turner and, more deeply, found his prophetic imagination engaged by the special powers of the Venetian's *Last Judgment* much as it had been by Turner's *The Slave Ship*.

Bridging a gulf of almost forty years, Ruskin's account of that fateful encounter at San Rocco in *Praeterita* in tinged with regret as the actual encounter in 1845 could not have been.

But, very earnestly, I should have bid myself that day keep *out* of the

School of St. Roch, had I known what was to come of my knocking at its door. But for that porter's opening, I should (so far as one can ever know what they should) have written, *The Stones of Chamouni*, instead of *The Stones of Venice*; and the *Laws of Fésole*, in the full code of them, before beginning to teach in Oxford: and I should have brought out in full distinctness and the use what faculty I had of drawing the human face and form with true expression of their higher beauty.

But Tintoret swept me away at once into the "mare maggiore" of the schools of painting which crowned the power and perished in the fall of Venice; so forcing me into the study of the history of Venice herself; and through that into what else I have traced or told of the laws of national strength and virtue.[83]

6

In the late autumn of 1845 Ruskin returned to Denmark Hill and took up in earnest the writing of *Modern Painters* volume 2. His ends, he recalled, were twofold: "The first, to explain to myself, and then demonstrate to others, the nature of that quality of beauty which I now saw to exist through all the happy conditions of living organism; and down to the minutest detail and finished material structure naturally produced. The second, to explain and illustrate the power of two schools of art unknown to the British public, that of Angelico in Florence, and Tintoret in Venice."[84] He goes on to disclaim any knowledge of the extent to which the book accomplished these ends, but he complains that the book is generally read for its "pretty passages," its theory of beauty being generally ignored. This may be because no distinct theory of beauty is developed in it, for actually the work attempts much more, and Ruskin's account of it is more accurate when he speaks of it in *Deucalion* as setting forth "the first and foundational law respecting human contemplation of the natural phenomena under whose influence we exist."[85]

The book postulates and illustrates the operation of a contemplative faculty, called theoretic, that reads the primary aspects of nature as a system of symbols for the attributes of God, or a divine language. Depending on one's historical perspective this part of the work can be read as late natural theology or early environmental psychology. Theoria, the power that interprets the language of the God-stuff, is essentially an idealizing capacity of a Platonic cast. In art its operation is felt primarily in certain kinds of sacred, or purist, painting, especially in the work of Angelico. It appears that Ruskin may have been committed to this approach to "Ideas of Beauty" before his encounter with Tintoretto; for the latter part of the volume takes an unexpected turn (away from the contemplative, idealizing sense of beauty) and undertakes to examine the strange expressive and realizing capacity of the artist, namely, the imagination. At any rate, by this theory of imagination he was able to accommodate both Angelico and Tintoretto in the same volume and yet correct the naturalistic or "sensual" bias of his aesthetic of landscape in volume 1.

Structurally, as I have indicated, the second volume is presented as a third section of the whole of *Modern Painters*, continuing ostensibly the general subject of the ideas conveyable by art from ideas of truth to ideas of beauty. It is subdivided into two major topics, each devoted to one of the two "faculties" by which ideas of beauty are received, the "Theoretic faculty" and the "Imagination." In the first section, which is the longer and more blatantly tractarian of the two, Ruskin is concerned to define and illustrate the workings of "Theoria" in the perception of beauty. He begins by asserting that impressions of beauty are neither sensual nor intellectual but moral, and for the faculty that receives them no term can be more accurate than the Greek term "Theoretic." This "exulting, reverent, and grateful" perception of beauty is to be distinguished from "aesthesis," which is mere animal or sensual consciousness of pleasure in certain objects. These points lead him to the thesis of the first section: simply that the sense of beauty, being neither intellectual nor sensual, is dependent on a "pure, right, and open state of the heart."[86] Beauty can never be perceived by those who have become alienated from the life of God through any hardening of the heart, as, for instance, by materialism or "false taste" (taste built on mere fastidiousness and lust for novelty). Perception of beauty is devout awareness which participates in the life of God, transcending surfaces and self. But what are its objects?

The theoretic faculty, Ruskin argues, is able to receive impressions of beauty from two objective sources that he calls "typical beauty" and "vital beauty." Typical beauty refers to certain external qualities of natural forms by which they are read as "types" or symbols of divine attributes. Vital beauty derives from "the appearance of felicitous fulfillment of function in living things, more especially of the joyful and right exertion of perfect life in man."[87] These, he asserts, are the two modes of impression signified by the term *beauty*. Both are rooted in natural forms; all revelations of higher intentions are received through these. However, it should be noted in passing that Ruskin does take note of the elements of self-projection in our responses to external forms: "I believe that the eye cannot rest on a material form, in a moment of depression or exultation, without communicating to that form a spirit and a life,—a life which will make it afterwards in some degree loved or feared."[88] He has little else to say on the subject of projected being at this point, but the thought will develop later into concern with imagination, "pathetic fallacy," and myth.

He now proceeds to illustrate at length what is meant by typical and vital beauty as received by the theoretic faculty. The two chapters given to these illustrations are the primary content of the first two-thirds of the volume. Under typical beauty he explores six examples, devoting a chapter to each: nature's infinity seen as the "type" or symbol of divine incomprehensibility; organic unity as the "type" of divine comprehensiveness; repose the "type" of divine permanence; symmetry as the "type" of divine justice; purity the "type" of divine energy; and moderation the "type" of divine government by law. A few brief points will suggest how these illustrations of "typical beauty" serve to further the primary lines of Ruskin's thought.

Beneath its Christian reading of the *liber naturae*, the thrust of this section of volume 2 of *Modern Painters* is an attempt to systematize and also partly to Platonize and to mythologize the psychic effects of the natural environment. Ruskin is generally more concerned with the natural forms and those of our needs that they meet than in the deity they signify; he is more naturalist than theologian, even here. Further, he insists that although the metaphorical values of these organic forms are the result of meditation, the primary response to their beauty is instinctive: "Ideas of beauty are instinctive, and . . . it is only upon consideration, and even then in a doubtful and disputable way, that they appear in their typical character."[89] Finally, and most important, especially in relation to the attention given to them in volume 1 and in *The King of the Golden River*, it is interesting to note that space and light are the best defended of his examples of typical beauty.

Light as a source of typical beauty is discussed under two separate heads in the chapter "Of Infinity" as the type of divine incomprehensibility. The example of infinity is the calm, luminous distance of declining or breaking day over a comparatively dark horizon. In painting, this luminous distance ("heaven light") with its intimations of escape, hope, and infinity is to be distinguished from the claustrophobic glint and glitter of "object light." Ruskin conceives this bright distance of sky as absolutely necessary for life and art. Our delight in its beauty is instinctive; our souls feed upon bright space as the metaphor of some incomprehensible hope distinct from the imprisonments of life and the grave. But Ruskin is more concerned to capture the quality of sky itself than to define the heavenly rest he assumes it signifies.

Light appears again in the chapter on purity as the type of divine energy. Here the argument is that light signifies purity, which, in turn, signifies the energizing presence of the Deity, life. Our desire for light, he argues, is more instinctive than any other of our responses to beauty and quite distinct from our sense of its necessity for life. But, again, "it is not *all* light, but light possessing the universal qualities of beauty, diffused or infinite rather than in points; tranquil, not startling or variable; pure, not sullied or oppressed," that we desire.[90] Consequently, for Ruskin, "the utmost possible sense of beauty is conveyed by a feebly translucent, smooth, but not lustrous surface of white, and pale warm red, subdued by the most pure and delicate greys, as in the finer portions of the human frame."[91] This is beauty as purity in the perfect suffusion of light-life in matter. More generally, the sign of purity of life in matter is the "active condition" of it, the "vital and energetic connection among its particles" gathering into crystals or efflorescence. Death is separation, dissolution, dust. He observes also that there is a peculiar painfulness in all association of organic and inorganic matter.

Purity is a focal term for Ruskin. Like light, it is both a "type" and a state of reality; therefore it could point either to a spiritual or to a practical morality. As Henry Ladd observed, "it is the most pregnant seed of his whole moral and economic doctrine."[92] Suggesting to Ruskin at once life, light, and stainlessness, it links the organicist, luminist, and puritan tendencies of his thought. Here the concept of purity as "Divine Energy" relates directly to the other mode of beauty to which the theoretic faculty responds: "Vital Beauty."

Vital beauty is the empathic pleasure we feel in the apparent "happiness" of organic beings. This pleasure, of course, is conditioned by two factors: the purity of heart of the observer ("He who loves not God, nor his brother, cannot love the grass beneath his feet.")[93] and the appearance of pure and free vital energy in the organism. Our sense of happiness—of beauty—in the organism is destroyed, he argues, by all appearance of mechanism ("neatness of mechanical contrivance for the pleasure of the animal") or deformity in the creature. Vital beauty is less a coherent organic aesthetic than an account of Ruskin's own responses to living things expressed in analytic language, but his comment on the relationship between organic beauty and human intention is valuable for itself and consistent with the pervasive vitalism in his work. "The moment we begin," he insists, "to look upon any creature as subordinate to some purpose out of itself, some of the sense of organic beauty is lost. . . . It has become a machine; much of our sense of its happiness is gone; its emanation of inherent life is no longer pure."[94]

But, we ask, is the perception of vital beauty in organic forms

necessarily a moral perception? Does it not tend to make the perception
of beauty a functional or utilitarian rather than a moral impression? To
resolve this apparent dichotomy is his theory Ruskin must relate vital
beauty to the realm of ideal form, for it is evident that in its perception of
both typical and vital beauty his theoretic faculty is directed primarily
toward ideal or symbolic art. This was the kind of art that was engaging
his attention in 1844–45 just before his Tintoretto epiphany. He defines
ideal art as that which represents not the material object but the mental
conception of it. Un-ideal or realistic works represent existing things.
Ideal works are the result of an act of imagination and are good or bad
according to the health and power of the creating imagination. Here the
subject of imaginative capability is left vaguely connected with ideal art
because Ruskin is pursuing the theoretic faculty. It is the function of
theoria not only to perceive the happiness of living things but also to
compare and judge their fitness for the "duty" they have to perform.
Thus theoria arrives at the ideal of the species, the condition in which all
of its properties are fully developed. The task of the painter is to pursue
ideal form (specific form), especially, of course, that form in the highest
of the species. For *"there is a perfect ideal to be wrought out of every face
around us,"*[95] provided we can separate from it the signs of evil, of pride,
sensuality, fear, and cruelty. The intellect can never know the human
ideal, "only love can know and separate the signs of sin," and love is a
quality of the theoretic faculty, for its "perception is altogether moral
and instinctive, love clinging to the lines of light."[96]

So much, then, for the exposition of the theoretic faculty and its
receptivity to typical and vital beauty which occupied Ruskin for the
first two-thirds of volume 2 of *Modern Painters*. More than an aesthetic
in the usual sense (an attempt to define the common properties of works
of art), it was first an attempt to outline our relational involvement with
the life-world, and secondarily an attempt to accommodate this idea of
nature as a moral and aesthetic norm to those works of religious ideal art
that had seized his sensibilities in 1844–45 prior to his encounter with
Tintoretto. Although the tone of this portion of the work is confident, even arrogant, and its procedure systematic, the piety, the theory,
the derivative style all seem strained. Ruskin's judgment was sound
when, in a note of 1883 to this first section, he deplored its affectation and
its "morbid violence of passion and narrowness of thought."[97]

7

However, the second part of the book, titled "Of the Imaginative
Faculty," is quite different. The Hookerism, the sanctimonious confidence are both diminished. There is greater coherence of thought and

feeling. One senses that Ruskin had found his personal mode and vein of interest in this section and that it was specifically written to reflect the recent impact of Tintoretto upon him. Indeed, an evocation of this painter's power is the climax of the section. In a special introductory note to this part, written in 1883, Ruskin declared that in revising the book for republication he found less to be corrected and condemned in the second part than in the first, as well as more that he wished to add to it as the result of further thought. The little he did add in this note merely touches again upon a subproblem of imagination that became increasingly important to him as his own mind began to falter: the question of the vulnerability of imagination to disease, especially the distinction between morbid developments in strong imaginations as opposed to conditions resulting from mere weakness or deficiency. Though brief, the note at least suggests the continuing power of the subject over him. For us, Ruskin's imagination—his theory and practice of it—is a central topic, closely bound to his work in "pathetic" animation, myth, and vision.

Here, in *Modern Painters*, volume 2, the discussion of imagination brings the book back to the central nagging problem of the whole first phase of his works: the relation between realization and idealization in art. Just as *Modern Painters*, volume 1, never quite resolves its ambivalence over the relationship between mimetic precision of representation and truth (essentially expressive) as norms for art, so the second volume continues the dialectic under new heads by balancing the contemplative and idealizing theoretic faculty with another, imagination, conceived as active and "modifying." Ruskin does not appear to be entirely aware at this point that, by his own theory, the imagination is a realizing or particularizing function, really antithetical to his theoretic power. Therefore to describe their joint action he lapses into a vague metaphor: "The Theoretic faculty takes out of everything that which is beautiful, while the Imaginative faculty takes hold of the very imperfections which the Theoretic rejects; and, by means of these angles and roughnesses, it joins and bolts the separate stones into a mighty temple, wherein the Theoretic faculty, in its turn, does deepest homage."[98]

He divides the imagination into three primary functions: associative, penetrative, and contemplative. Each is given a chapter, but the first and third are rather feebly conceived, as if he were not entirely convinced that these belonged in the same dimension of perception with the central, penetrative, capacity of the imagination. Associative imagination is the unifying or combining power of artistic genius (comparable to Coleridge's "secondary Imagination")[99], it is the capacity to conceive perfectly coherent forms out of a multitude of separately defective parts. It is the power of simultaneous correlation of imperfect parts into organic wholes. Most important, Ruskin conceives of the associative imagination as a vital power by comparison with mere composition. The latter consists of fitting parts together according to external precepts, while associative imagination works by no law but its own internal purposiveness. It is, like organic growth, a vital mystery compared to the dead mechanism of formal composition. Among the possessors of this vital power Tintoretto stands supreme.

Contemplative imagination is the vaguest of the three concepts. It is not, Ruskin admits, part of the essence of imagination, "but only a habit of the faculty."[100] By it he appears to mean the abstracting, metaphor-making capacity. He speaks of the artist's ability to stamp one conception with the die of an image belonging to another, giving new value to both. This appears to be imagination's most idealizing tendency. Shelley, he notes, is most distinguished by it. Finally, for further insight into this aspect of imagination he refers us to Wordsworth, whose prefaces have obviously been among his sources.

But the core of Ruskin's theory is his view of the imagination as a penetrative or revelational power. In a note to the 1883 edition he impatiently cuts through the tangles of his early theory to get at the primary meaning of the term he had built upon in his later work, imagination as realizing vision: "I meant, and always do mean by it, primarily, the power of seeing anything we describe as if it were real."[101] And within the complexities of these early chapters is the central concept of imagination as a mysterious, prerational power, not consciously either associative or contemplative, but essentially intuitive, apocalyptic, and momentary. "The virtue of the Imagination is its reaching, by intuition and intensity of gaze (not by reasoning, but by its authoritative opening and revealing power), a more essential truth than is seen at the surface of things."[102] This "penetrating possession-taking faculty," he insists, "called by what name we will," is "the highest intellectual power of man." It is also closest to the Romantic, especially Coleridgean, doctrine of art as the reconciliation or coalescence of mind and nature; "there is no reasoning in it,"[103] though it seizes truth.

Penetrative imagination seizes the vital mystery of its materials: "It never stops at crusts or ashes, or outward images of any kind; it ploughs them all aside, and plunges into the very central fiery heart."[104] But having penetrated the vestures of things its messages are often obscure and enigmatic. "Hence there is in every word set down by the imaginative mind an awful undercurrent of meaning, and evidence and shadow upon it of the deep places out of which it has come."[105] That is, "the imagination sees the heart and inner nature, and makes them felt, but is often obscure, mysterious, and interrupted in its giving of outer detail."[106] And yet, for all its tendency to superficial incoherence, the imagination has no traffic in anything but truth. "Let it be understood once for all, that imagination never deigns to touch anything but truth; and though it does not follow that where there is the appearance of truth, there has been imaginative operation, of this we may be assured, that where there is appearance of falsehood, the imagination has had no hand."[107] From these remarks it should be plain that from the beginning Ruskin sees the central imagination as an apocalyptic power, but plain also that, like other Romantic theorists of imagination, he is left with very fundamental questions about the relation between imagination and reality, between the subjective and objective, and also active and passive aspects of imagination.

Is imagination, to bring the subject back to the central question in *Modern Painters*, primarily a realizing function, like Turnerian truth in the first volume, or is it primarily an idealizing capacity, like the "Theoretic faculty"? At this point Ruskin appears to conceive of it primarily as a kind of synthesizing insight that is under the discipline of the idealizing theoretic power. Vision, yes, but through doctrine; not vice versa.

Like Wordsworth and Coleridge before him, Ruskin considers also the problem of the relationship between imagination and fancy, but not with any deep interest. Essentially he concludes that fancy has the same three subfunctions as imagination but not its finer tone. For instance, fancy readily gives itself over to the trivial and the facetious, which the imagination by its very nature refuses: "She sees too far, too darkly, too solemnly, too earnestly ever to smile."[108]

A related question, but one much closer to Ruskin's interest, even in this early work, is the relationship between imagination (which always appeals to a "deep heart feeling" and is always "faithful and earnest" in contemplating its subject matter) and "that diseased action of the fancy which depends more on nervous temperament than intellectual power," which through "dreaming, fever, insanity, and other morbid conditions of mind" may give rise to daring and inventive conceptions. To the same category the youthful and pious Ruskin consigns "the visionary appearances resulting from disturbances of the frame by passion, and from the rapid tendency of the mind to invest with shape and intelligence the active influences about it, as in the various demons, spirits, and fairies of all imaginative nations."[109] This problem of the effects of pathos, piety, or insanity on imaginative vision becomes increasingly important to him; and it is in this connection that the nature of mythic awareness is first examined in volume 3 of *Modern Painters*. In the introductory note of 1883, written a year before the *Storm-Cloud* lectures, he takes this question of the distinction between healthy and morbid imagination to be more important than those hair-splitting distinctions among the various modes of fancy and imagination that had concerned him in his youth. Finally, it should be noted that at this point, in volume 2, the sectarian Ruskin is quite conservative about the matter of vision. All "involuntary" vision, he concludes, must be considered morbid "unless admitted to be supernatural," that is, having scriptural authority.[110]

On the subject of morbid vision, for the reader who has in mind Ruskin's own apocalyptic pronouncements, there is one point about the uses of imagination as they are discussed in volume 2 that seems singularly prophetic. The climax of practical criticism in the book is reached near its end when Ruskin uses his theory of penetrative imagination as the occasion to praise the paintings by Tintoretto that had seized his own penetrative imagination a few months before. (A corollary of his theory, incidentally, is that penetrative imagination in a work will speak to, coalesce with, the same quality in the mind of the viewer.) He describes several Tintorettos at length (the *Annunciation* of the Santa Maria Novella, the *Crucifixion* and *Massacre of Innocents* of the Scuola di San Rocco), emphasizing the painter's supremacy in actualizing imaginary events. But the painting, or the visionary event, which appears to have fastened upon his imagination in a special way so as to find its way eventually into his own skies, is the *Last Judgment* from the church of Santa Maria dell' Orto. His notes of the encounter indicate that it was this painting, with its air full of rising bodies, determined more than any other the new course of his studies. His description of the painting is probably the most spectacular passage in the second volume.

> The river of the wrath of God, roaring down into the gulf where the world has melted with its fervent heat, choked with the ruin of nations, and the limbs of its corpses tossed out of its whirling, like water-wheels. Bat-like, out of the holes and caverns and shadows of the earth, the bones gather and the clay heaps heave, rattling and adhering into half-kneaded anatomies, that crawl, and startle, and struggle up among the putrid weeds, with the clay clinging to their clotted hair, and their heavy eyes sealed by the earth darkness yet, like his of old who went his way unseeing into the Siloam Pool; shaking off one by one the dreams of the prison-house, hardly hearing the clangour of the trumpets of the armies of God, blinded yet more, as

Tintoretto. *The Last Judgment*. Madonna dell' Orto, Venice. (Alinari Editorial Photocolor Archives)

they awake, by the white light of the new Heaven, until the great vortex of
the four winds bears up their bodies to the judgment-seat: the Firmament
is all full of them, a very dust of human souls, that drifts, and floats and
falls in the interminable, inevitable light; the bright clouds are darkened
with them as with thick snow, currents of atom life in the arteries of
heaven, now soaring up slowly, and higher and higher still, till the eye and
the thought can follow no farther, borne up, wingless, by their inward
faith and by the angel powers invisible, now hurled in countless drifts of
horror before the breath of their condemnation.[111]

In a sense this is the Turnerian apocalyptic sky again, put to the uses of
religious vision by imagination. Like Ilaria di Caretto in sculpture it is a
consummate fusion of naturalistic truth and symbolizing theoria
through penetrative imagination.

By the end of volume 2 of *Modern Painters* Ruskin has invoked three
primary standards of excellence in art: naturalistic truth in volume 1;
theoria in the first part of volume 2, by which nature is seen as beautiful
in its mediation of divine attributes; and finally imagination, especially
penetrative imagination, which sees clearly things that never were.
These criteria, as contemporary critics noted, were to some extent contradictory and seemed more meant to justify Ruskin's meandering
enthusiasms than to be an internally consistent aesthetic. Truth for
Turner; theoria for Giotto and Angelico; imagination for Tintoretto.
But could he accommodate Turner and Angelico or Giotto under any
single standard? Imagination, of course, had theoretical possibilities as a
mediating standard between Turnerian naturalism and Angelican
idealism, for imagination could be thought of as the power either to
idealize the real or to realize the ideal. But this kind of equivocating
could not produce any solid measure for weighing individual greatness.
In which of these two painters, given the differences of their subjects, do
the real and the ideal achieve the finer harmony? (Which, that is, shows
the more perfect power of imagination?) To resolve such questions
Ruskin must come to some conclusion about imagination's involvement with the real and the ideal. Is imagination, once again, primarily a
realizing or an idealizing capacity? Is it essentially mimetic or expressive? What, particularly, is its relation to external nature? At the end
of volume 2 of *Modern Painters*, he is much less clear about the imagination's ability to see, ultimately, for itself than about its ability to
serve the idealizing theoretic faculty. In speaking of the penetrative
imagination he does conclude that it must be "fed constantly by external
nature." There must be something in nature worth penetrating, but
then "Imagination is a pilgrim on earth—and her home is in heaven."[112]

Not only is imagination in the service of heaven—as opposed to the human present—but her heaven is exclusively the Christian abode. Pagan imagination, for Ruskin at this point, is a contradiction in terms. In the last chapter of the volume, entitled "Of the Superhuman Ideal," he takes up in a preliminary way the crucial question of the interaction of imagination and theoria in representing "Divine ideality," that is, in limning divine figures. Thus he is brought, for the first time, directly to the problem of myth. He is aware that the subject involves, as he says, "questions of great intricacy respecting the development of mind among those Pagan nations who are supposed to have produced high examples of spiritual ideality."[113] But he pushes the matter off with the promise of future treatment and turns to the less fundamental but more immediate question of the representation of supernatural figures in painting and sculpture. He will inquire "by what modifications those creature forms to us known . . . may be explained as signs or habitations of Divinity."[114] How, for instance, will idealizing theoria and realizing imagination be balanced in their creation?

His interest is not in those symbolic indications of deity that might surround the figure, but in the superhuman form itself and in the means by which it is possible "to raise that form by mere inherent dignity to such a pitch of power and impressiveness as cannot but assert and stamp it for superhuman."[115] One would expect him to be forced to allow the superiority of Greek god-figures as supreme works of visualizing imagination in his own terms, but his sectarian piety will not permit such an admission at this time. The limitations of his view, the heavy constraints of theoria upon imagination, are indicated by the fact that he finds the angels of Benozzo Gozzoli in the Pisan Campo Santo to be exemplary work in the superhuman ideal, by comparison with which all forms of the pagan divine ideal are dangerously defective because dangerously real.

The Greek mythic ideal in art, he believes at this point, is too materialized, too human, indicating some defect in imaginative vision. In the Apollo Belvidere, for instance, "the sandals destroy the divinity of the foot, and the lip is curled with mortal passion."[116] He does not conceive yet that this humanizing of the deific ideal (form) could actually be a testimony to the veracity of the Greek faith or vision. "The Greek," he argues, "could not conceive a spirit; he could do nothing without limbs; his God is a finite God, talking, pursuing, and going on journeys. . . . No spirit power was in the vision; it was a being of clay strength, and human passion, foul, fierce, and changeful; of penetrable arms, and vulnerable flesh."[117]

At this point the sectarian Ruskin is involved in an inconsistency that betrays a bias against Greek art, for he has stated definitively in the preceding chapter that "those painters only have the right imaginative power who can set the supernatural form before us, fleshed and boned like ourselves."[118] A note to the 1883 edition explains that the "false bias" of this view was sufficiently corrected in *The Queen of the Air*.[119] Actually it will be plain that his understanding of the Greek mythic ideal and of the imagination are deepened together in the third volume of *Modern Painters*. But between volumes 2 and 3 of *Modern Painters* came the Venetian or Gothic digression in which Ruskin moves away down the bole of art to its social roots. There is a general deepening of his view of the world to encompass social problems from apocalyptic landscape to apocalyptic history.

CHAPTER 2

Life and Death in Architecture

The second volume of *Modern Painters* appeared in 1846; the third not until 1856. During the intervening decade Ruskin was drawn into an urgent digression on architecture and its social determinants that generated four major volumes: *The Seven Lamps of Architecture* (1849) and the three volumes of *The Stones of Venice* (1851–53), with ancillary materials. Moreover, the magnum opus was none the worse for this decade of delay in which it was never entirely absent from his plans.

Among the controlling themes and images of his work some were explicitly deepened or developed during these years; others were in abeyance, present only in the sense that they determined the limits of the phase. Myth, for instance, although introduced briefly at the end of *Modern Painters*, volume 2, was seldom treated directly in these architectural works; nevertheless the subject is indirectly present here for the modern reader in at least two important senses. First, architecture was, for Ruskin, an index of the vitality of a people's belief, of their mythology, especially insofar as it revealed a holy bond between that mythology and nature. Secondly, Ruskin's whole theology of the Gothic, including his use of it for the interpretation of the spiritual history of Venice, must be regarded as a personal "myth." However, the further development of mythology as an explicit topic in his work was awaiting changes in Ruskin's religious outlook; and further work with Turner, imagination, and landscape was waiting on his interest in myth.

In referring to Ruskin's major architectural work as being inherently "mythic" we are obviously using the word in a more diffuse and dangerous sense than that which will apply to his interpretations, in volume 5 of *Modern Painters*, of Turner's symbolism in his *Apollo and Python* or *The Garden of the Hesperides*. Ruskin was not at this point deliberately reanimating symbols drawn from Greek mythology, yet we do need the term *mythic* to express his way of seeing all architectural choices, even minor decorative details, as symbolic of a conclusive moral drama at work in human history. We are therefore using the term in much the same sense that Robert Tucker, for instance, does in referring to the mythic vision of the world in Karl Marx and placing him among those "obsessed with a moral vision of reality, a vision of the world as an arena of conflict between good and evil forces."[1] Similarly, Ruskin's architectural work is mythic in the sense that his subjective experiences of quality in real architectural forms (which were for him generally details of ornamentation, architectural sculpture) were ultimately referred to a decisive moral conflict in history and to such primal concepts (reducible to mythic terms) as these: (1) the idea that the "laws" of organization in natural forms manifest divine intention when the forms are wedded to the human spirit; (2) that the moral condition of a society—the victory in it of vitality, purity, and beauty over their opposites—depends upon the society's intuitive obedience to these organic laws; (3) that this condition may be read out of a society's artifacts, particularly its architecture, by a mind that is properly attuned to the forming laws; (4) that there has been some earlier, comparatively paradisal state of purity and unity, revealed in architecture, from which art and society have fallen and to which they can return only through the reintuition and restoration, in practice, of the bond to natural form.

Apocalypse, the rhetoric of revelation in which real objects are so described that they seem to bear authentic tidings of spiritual processes or of the accomplishment of sacred history, continued to be the essential prophetic device of Ruskin's style. But now the natural or landscape apocalypse was replaced by an architectural version as Ruskin read the fate of nations in the carving of a capital and focused these adumbrations into moments of prophetic utterance. Because his vision was fundamentally mythic or prophetic rather than technical and structural it tended to focus attention only on small portions of the buildings he studied.[2] The wholes with which he was concerned were organic and mysterious, not mechanical and logical. From his organicist's standpoint the past participates in and can therefore reveal by a kind of critical biopsy the state of health of a moral organization of which the building itself is but a symbol. His most important theme during this phase was that of the antagonism between vital and lethal awareness (often supported by light-darkness imagery) which I take to be the core of Ruskin's thought on art. Essentially he set out to show us how to read the signs of life and death in architecture and, through architecture, in the society that produced it. The vital-lethal antithesis became more critical as Ruskin's interests were drawn from painting and abstract aesthetics to matters of greater social urgency.

Tracing the intricacies of the development of Ruskin's personal interests is the task of the biographer; yet there is no need to separate the life and the work simply because the life can never be as fully known. Therefore we begin by tracing the lines of avowed interest that led Ruskin to the first work of this series, *The Seven Lamps of Architecture*.

1

Ruskin's first study of architecture had appeared a decade earlier, when he was eighteen. *The Poetry of Architecture; or the Architecture of the Nations of Europe Considered in its Association with Natural Scenery and National Character* appeared serially in J. C. Loudon's *Architectural Magazine* in 1837–38. It was signed "Kata Phusin," a phrase (from Heraclitus, fragment 1) meaning "according to nature." This first nom de plume, Ruskin explained in *Praeterita*, was "equally expressive of the temper in which I was to discourse alike on that and every other subject"[3] and was meant to refer to instinctive rightness of judgment. The essay appeared in two parts: the first, consisting of six chapters, was devoted to the poetics of the cottage; and the second, in seven chapters, dealt with the villa. He intended to extend his analysis to nobler forms of architecture but the *Architectural Magazine* ceased publication after the second installment.

Commenting on these youthful essays from the prospective of 1886, Ruskin praised their essential rightness—as far as they went—and the "Johnsonian symmetry and balance" of their style.[4] More important, they show his early commitment to certain views of architecture that not only forecast the bias of *The Seven Lamps* and *Stones* but suggest what compulsion drew him into the subject. First, there is his distinction between architecture and mere building: architecture should be thought of as "a science of feeling more than of rule"; its ministry is to the mind more than to the eye; "no man can be an architect, who is not a metaphysician."[5] "Poetry" in architecture is, primarily, "unity of feeling."[6]

This unity is both internal and external; it means organic coherence and harmony of the parts of the building and also its "unison" with its setting. The young Ruskin deplored the use of cheap, inorganic, and false materials in construction; the application of superfluous decoration incongruous with the spirit of the whole building; and, most important, the frequent incompatibility of buildings with the repose of the landscapes in which they were set and with the regional character of their builders. He perceived the contrast between the natural, organic building growing out of character and scenery (the living building) and the building that is a mere statement of the wealth, pride, imitative skill, and technology of its builders (the dead building). He valued complexity of texture derived from imitation of natural forms as well as from ruggedness and delapidation; and he perceived the impossibility of imitating or restoring any work generated by imaginations of the past.

There can be no true Greek architecture without Greek belief; so far is a building like a visible myth. "It is utter absurdity to talk of building Greek edifices now; no man ever will, or ever can, who does not believe in Greek mythology; and, precisely by so much as he diverges from the technicality of strict copyism, he will err."[7]

There is at least one very important aspect of Ruskin's later thought about architecture that does *not* make itself felt in these youthful essays, and this is his insistence on the dependence of all great architecture on the condition of life of the laborer. To pick up this important thread of concern we must go to a later period of his life, 1845–48.

In the preceding chapter I noted that Ruskin remembered the tour of 1845 as the beginning of a new direction in his life. He spoke of this rededication as stemming from two supreme moments of aesthetic revelation experienced that year: the one inspired by a sculpture by Quercia and the other by a painting by Tintoretto. Although these experiences influenced primarily his views on painting, other remarks indicate that they also prompted a new beginning in his study of architecture. The statue of "sleeping" Ilaria di Caretto at Lucca, "the most beautiful extant marblework of the middle ages," turned him, he said, from the study of landscape to the study of life.[8] What is at first curious is that he began this study of life with medieval architecture.

From the Ilaria he turned to the close study of the facade of Santa Maria Foris-Portam at Lucca "and thereon literally *began* the study of architecture."[9] That is, he opened a new direction in the interpretation of architecture. He had made in medieval marble a connection he had not seen in his architectural studies of 1837–38: that the life of the builders could be read in the texture of the building.

The other major aesthetic revelation of the tour also drew him from art to architecture and through architecture to "the study of life." In a passage of *Praeterita* quoted earlier Ruskin explains that the fateful turn into the Scuola di San Rocco led not only to the revelation of Tintoretto to him but also to *The Stones of Venice*.[10] That is, his admiration for the painting led him to inquire into the moral history of the society whose artistic development culminated and terminated in such works as the *Paradise* and *Last Judgment* of Tintoretto. And, of course, since his earliest writing on the subject, architecture had been for Ruskin a general reflection of national character, so he understood how it could be used to document the spiritual progress of a society.

His new researches into the life forms of medieval architecture were presumably left in an incipient state when he turned homeward in the fall of 1845, and they had to be set aside during the winter in favor of the more pressing task of writing *Modern Painters*, volume 2. Yet there were features of that work itself, which, though not architectural, must have played their part in directing his attention toward architecture. The essential work of that volume had been to set forth a general, "spiritual," theory of beauty as the "instinctive" perception of the God-stuff in things, that is, perception of the divine "types" and vital qualities such as health, energy, and free growth in natural phenomena or in art. Beauty became the instinctive experience of purity and vitality in nature and of the natural in art. But the internal dynamic of Ruskin's aesthetic was bound to lead in a certain direction when coupled with a developing interest in architecture. First, having a general aesthetic, he would be understandably anxious to extend it to an art not covered in the second volume. And the general theory of *Modern Painters*, volume 2, does in fact make its appearance in *The Seven Lamps*. Second, and more important, his aesthetic formula carried excellent possibilities for being read in reverse: the comparative quantity of vital or typical beauty in a work could be read as an index of the spiritual condition of its creators. And if the creator were not an individual but a society, as in the case of medieval architecture, the study of beauty could be used as a measure of the vital energy of the building society. The transition from the study of landscape to the study of life would have been effected. But why Ruskin actually chose during the period from 1846 to 1856 to begin to explore the architectural and social implications of his aesthetic (instead of further developing his theory of Imagination, for instance, or writing about Tintoretto) cannot be understood in terms of internal continuities in his work alone. We must also glance at the relation of this new socioarchitectural focus of his work to certain aspects of his being-in-the-world: to his ways with objective evidence, to the social movements of the period, and to his personal spiritual development.

The *Seven Lamps of Architecture* was written during the winter of 1848–49. The diaries and notebooks for 1845–48 indicate an increased attention to architectural detail, both in the number of verbal accounts and in the number of drawings and graphic notes of architectural features: moldings, traceries, crockets, capitals, cusps, et cetera. The more finished drawings of architecture, like the studies from nature, manifest his desire to represent the intricacy and unity of organic texture. In his diary for 1843 he had entered this observation by his friend, the painter Thomas Richmond: "He says my chief aim in art is infinity, which I think a clever guess, if it be a guess."[11] In the diary for 1846, the comments most preoccupied with architecture show that he was also comparing his own observations with those of Robert Willis's *The Architecture of the Middle Ages* (1835) and Joseph Woods's *Letters of an Architect* (1828). Joan Evans has noted that he was particularly taken with the style of Lord Lindsay's *Sketches of the History of Christian Art* (1846–47), which he reviewed for the *Quarterly* in 1847.[12]

There were two tours abroad between volume 2 of *Modern Painters* and *The Seven Lamps*. The aesthetic and social experiences they provided must have informed the new book in ways which can only be suggested here. From April to November 1846 he traveled abroad with his parents, reworking much of the same ground he had covered the previous year. Between August and October 1848, accompanied by his bride, Euphemia Gray, he carried on his architectural studies and noted the signs of social malaise in Normandy. Earlier that summer the two, accompanied by the senior Ruskins, had begun what was apparently to have been a tour of English cathedrals, but the expedition ended abruptly and abortively at Salisbury with Ruskin working himself into a fever and the party being ordered back to Denmark Hill by mother Ruskin. Hence, for reasons not entirely aesthetic, the idea of examining English Gothic was given up.

Yet these tours were crucial despite their not being governed by exhaustive or systematic research, because they enabled him to draw; touch; trace; measure; and, more important, commune with the buildings about which he would write; and Ruskin's writing was largely determined by direct experience. Characteristically, whether in works or diaries, he did not write of a neutral object but of his experience of the object, though this experience was sometimes treated as a quality of the object. Experiences, in turn, were always being gathered in his work into larger wholes or systems of belief, personal myths; in this loose sense Ruskin was nearly always myth-making, even in the diaries. Although he frequently recorded dates, measurements, proportions, quantities, styles, and other abstractions about a building, his characteristic mode as a writer was not to deal with the great building as a structural abstraction but as a vital or emergent presence; or, in the case of defective architecture, as a vital form oppressed by morbid encrustations. Here, for instance, is a diary fragment from the abortive Salisbury visit, a passage that would reappear in *The Seven Lamps*. Essentially it contrasts his experiences of the cathedrals of Salisbury and Florence, mainly in terms of a difference of textures.

> On the whole, the carving of this cathedral, more especially of the west front, is, as compared with a piece of that of Florence, perfectly savage, and reminds one of the carvings of an Indian's paddle. What a contrast between the swarded space, all sounding over with nibbling of sheep, and the rising out of it of the grey walls like old steep rocks out of a green lake, and the weedy and shadowy recesses between the transepts, and the rude, mouldering, massy, roughgrained, shafts, and triple lights without tracery or other ornament than the martins' nests in the height of them—and that populous, trodden, history haunted square, that worn, bright, smooth marble seat against the wall, that jaspery variegated surface, those spiral shafts of glittering mosaic and leafy mouldings, rich with birds and fruit, those fairy traceries of white, faint, crystalline lines of alabaster, that companile, coloured like a morning cloud and chased like a sea shell.[13]

However, although it could be argued that the tours were a determinant, actually making his architectural work possible, as the recorded experiences and observations of buildings show, the diaries do not suggest that they were undertaken for the sake of studying architecture. We do not have the sense that Ruskin was dashing about seeing buildings to test hypotheses or to compile a definitive catalogue of Gothic buildings. Indeed architectural features are so immersed in the larger fund of impressions of people, paintings, sunsets, and spiritual states that one has the impression that the architecture is only a part of some larger study of life. It will be necessary to return to some of these wider impressions, but first let us see what Ruskin's way of observing architecture, as revealed in his diaries, can show us about the causes and the urgency of his digression into architecture.

The most obvious things that the diaries, especially that of 1846, indicate about Ruskin's way of working with architectural evidence have already been suggested: the dependence of his generalizations upon immediate personal experience; his primary interest in the textural detail—the sculpture—of a building as opposed to its total structure; his tendency to invoke a building as a presence, a moment of revelation. Other aspects of his point of view as revealed by the diary entries show why his involvement with architecture, once begun, had to run its course before *Modern Painters* could be resumed.

One of the most revealing of these journal entries is not explicitly about architecture at all but is a record of his reaction to a display of shells seen at the British Museum on 20 December 1848. (The passage just quoted indicates that sea shells had been on his mind in comparing the texture of Giotto's tower with that of Salisbury.) Here the remembrance of the shells is converted into a working hypothesis on the relationship between structure and texture in organic form. Ruskin concludes:

> Now I think that Form, properly so called, may be considered as a function or exponent either of Growth or of Force, inherent or impressed; and that one of the steps to admiring it or understanding it must be a comprehension of the laws of formation and of the forces to be resisted; that all forms are thus either indicative of lines of energy, or pressure, or motion, variously impressed or resisted, and are therefore exquisitely abstract and precise.[14]

So much for form "properly so called," form as overall shape or structure of the object; however, variegation of texture such as Hopkins's "pied beauty" is a special problem for the student of form: "Variegation, on the contrary, is the arbitrary presence or absence of colouring matter and the beauty is more in the colour than the outline. Hence stains, blotchings, cloudings, etc. in marble, on skins and so on, and their beauty of irregularity." Of these dappled forms in particular the important point is their "impossibility of imitation . . . except by great freedom of hand and then imperfectly."[15]

Having distinguished between these two modes of form, structure and textural variegation, Ruskin moves forward in the same diary entry to consider their interrelation in the total or final form. In so doing he introduces another sort of form; so we have now three kinds: "that of mere stains on a surface, shells and skins; that of organic structure on a surface, serpent scales up to the most beautiful plummage; and real form, the most precise of all in muscular or other separate developments." Coming finally to the central question of how these modes of organic form are combined, he suggests this general principle: "Each form is imperfect in proportion to its subjection" to a higher category. He seems to mean that a form of the less inclusive class will be less perfect in proportion as it must be subordinated to the perfection of a form of the more inclusive class. Thus, in his example, the scales (second-class form) of a snake's head will be less perfect, less symmetrically arranged, than those of the body (a "ruder organism") in order not to detract from the perfection of the "nobler" inclusive form, the head. The same principle, he notes, applies to a shell: its essential form is drawn twice; once in the final outline of the shell and again, rudely, in the pattern on its surface. Between outline and pattern there is, it would appear, a kind of tension as between statement and implication in a poem. "This . . . very imperfection, as I thought, becomes as it were a piece of higher design, an example of restrained power to a given purpose."[16]

Of course Ruskin was not trying to work out a definitive aesthetic of forms in this diary entry. He must have been deeply engrossed at the moment with the *Seven Lamps of Architecture.* But he was obviously struck, in examining shells that day, by the idea of a vital law of gradation of imperfections that governs the internal relation of organic subforms, a law of coherence by subjection in which lesser forms support higher by relative imperfection, with the result that "all *final* forms, as of animal bodies, or of shells, are absolutely perfect." He was not concerned in the diary to trace the implication of this law of subjection beyond skins and shells to architecture; this was for his books to detail. He simply concluded with this expansive hint: "The same principles apply to the patterns and forms of G[ree]k vases and to mosaics and frescoes, etc."[17]

What is important about this entry is that it contains the germ of Ruskin's theory of the Gothic, and, as such, contains the essential point of many specifically architectural entries too numerous and fragmentary to be meaningfully cited here. But from what follows it will become apparent that Ruskin regarded the pure Gothic building as a "final form," and "absolutely perfect" in the sense that a shell is: a perfect, internal coherence of imperfect subforms. Perfect Gothic is formed in obedience to the principles of organic form, its beauty governed by the principles of "vital beauty" as set forth in the second part of *Modern Painters,* volume 2, where we are told that "the pleasure afforded by every organic form is in proportion to its appearance of healthy vital energy"[18] or that "the moment we begin to look upon any creature as subordinate to some purpose out of itself, some of the sense of organic beauty is lost. . . . It has become a machine; some of our sense of its happiness is gone; its emanation of inherent life is no longer pure."[19]

Because he regards Gothic architecture as an organic form, his main interest when he analyzes a piece of Gothic architecture in his notebooks and diaries is in the degree of purity, the health, of its subforms. Is this, he seems always to be asking, a pure and unpolluted form, a coherent and internally purposive whole built of natural and freely varied subordinate forms? Or is the shell somehow diseased, contaminated by a superimposed style, by excrescences or accretions, or by the restorations of later dwellers? He is able to test for signs of disease by close examination of a few architectural details such as a section of molding, a few capitals, or a tracery, and their interrelationship; he is seldom interested in a building as a total structure or as an engineering problem, especially if the building is impure in ornamentation. In the diaries of 1846, for instance, "vicious" is an important negative term, occurring in about half the architectural notes for that year and generally applied to some feature of style or workmanship which Ruskin regards as noxious to the Gothic spirit. "The Chapel of Colleone," he noted, "is one of the most vicious specimens of 15th century work. The windows are filled up with columns of which . . . the effect is as if they had been brought together by accident, while each is individually of vulgar proportion and more like a candlestick than a column."[20] Similarly, in a long note entered as "Chatillon-sur-Seine" he attempted to trace the geographical spread of a Swiss-French regional style that seemed a particularly vicious corruption of the Gothic, because in it the vital lines of moldings were lopped into sections for specious structural reasons.

> I should call this architecture generally, sectional or inter-sectional, its distinguishing character being . . . that the moldings, instead of uniting with or arising out of each other, cut each other and form inelegant interstices, or are themselves violently truncated, as in my examples at Lucerne and Sursee. . . . At Besançon the style appears in great perfection, more elegant than in Switzerland, but quite as vicious.[21]

In similar contexts Ruskin was likely to use such equivalents as "morbid" or "corrupt" generally in opposition to such positive terms as "vigorous," "pure," "rich," or "varied." The prevalent implicit metaphor of these notes is an organic one, the struggle of a vital forming principle, the Gothic spirit, with the lethal influences of mechanical efficiency, pride of technique, mere functionality, careless workmanship, or deceitful restoration.

This, then, is the message of the journals concerning the urgency of Ruskin's Gothic digression: he was not merely tracing the evolution of a style or enunciating certain architectural shibboleths; he was tracing from symptom to symptom the life-death struggle in art, a struggle epitomized for him in the architecture of Venice during the thirteenth and fourteenth centuries. Since he regarded Venetian architecture of this period as the greatest material efflorescence of the human spirit, he had to trace the whole cycle of its life: root, flower, and fall. To the extent that the conflict he perceived had much in common with the opposition of the visible to the conventional in the landscape aesthetic of volume 1 of *Modern Painters*, it was not a digression at all but a development and reapplication of a basic organic aesthetic. The important difference lay in the fact that he was now reading the signs of life and death in a social art; by the measure of Gothic art he could begin to read symptoms of disease in any society, medival or modern, whose architecture lacked the perfect imperfection, the organic vitality, of pure Gothic work.

This might suggest that Ruskin's interest in society was indirect, developed and manifested only by his study of its artifacts rather than of its people. In fact he would assume, by 1865, that the primary index of a society's spiritual condition was its taste, the language of things it liked. "Taste," he would declare, "is the ONLY morality." And his "tell me what you like, and I'll tell you what you are"[22] would be meant for nations as well as individuals. Obviously in things as objectified spirit he had something with a wholeness and an inherent intentionality that his own mind could penetrate and compare with those qualities of organic forms. However, it is also clear from his letters and journals that in 1848, in Normandy, Ruskin observed the symptoms of spiritual malaise not merely as imprinted in Gothic forms of medieval and Renaissance times but as revealed directly in the lives of a people in the midst of social upheaval. The preface to *The Seven Lamps* speaks of his haste to study churches threatened by both revolution and restoration. More important, the historical moment of social crisis, convulsion, and reconception in which *The Seven Lamps of Architecture* was conceived and written appears to have determined the content of the book. Its subject is social as much as physical architecture; it prescribes the moral structure that must precede the one of stone.

It would be difficult and probably unnecessary to set a precise date for the awakening of Ruskin's social conscience. In a chapter of *Praeterita* called "The Feasts of Vandals," Ruskin reveals that he first became aware of the exploitation of labor around 1845 and attributes the origin of this awareness to his encounters with the Domecque family, producers of "double-cross sherry," who had taken on Ruskin's father as their English partner. Peter Domecque, whose lifestyle Ruskin described as luxurious but not extravagant, maintained a house in Paris primarily for the education and establishment of his five daughters, for whom (including Adele, who became the object of Ruskin's first disappointed infatuation when the girls came to stay at Herne Hill in 1836) he arranged marriages with the French elite. Some years later (in 1845 or 1846) when two of the daughters, now well married, visited his father at Denmark Hill, Ruskin remembered being struck by the way these gentle ladies spoke of their French tenants and Spanish laborers, "with no idea whatever respecting them but that, except as producers by their labour of money to be spent at Paris, they were cucumbers of the ground." Their attitudes, he recalls, "gave me the first clue to the real sources of wrong in the social laws of modern Europe; and led me necessarily into the political work which has been the most earnest of my life." With this revelation came the darker intimation of something rotten in the state kept at Denmark Hill itself: that the life and labor of Andalusia was being drained to create wealth at London and Paris: "That its precious wine was not for them, still less the money it was sold for; but the one came to crown our Vandalic feasts, the other furnished our Danish walls with pictures, our Danish gardens with milk and honey, and five noble houses in Paris with the means of beautiful dominance in its Elysian fields."[23]

Of course Ruskin was not an entirely reliable narrator of his own experience in *Praeterita*; the shadows of recollection, mental disturbance, repressed bitterness over the unattainable Adele, and other factors may account for his linking of awakening social concern with the visit of the Domecque daughters sometime in the mid forties. Nothing of this appears in the diaries. We do know that on tour in France with Effie in the year of the Revolution he felt the imminence of social crisis, the life-wealth conflict about to become overt. From Calais in August he wrote an often-cited letter to W. H. Harrison, his editor, that showed clearly the social tension he perceived there.

> At Rouen, where we stayed about three weeks, the distress though nearly as great, is not so ghastly, and seems to be confined in its severity to the class of workmen. There seems, however, everything to be dreaded both there and at Paris—and the only door of escape seems to be the darkest— that which grapeshot opens. I do not see how another struggle for pillage is avoidable—a simple fight of the poor against the rich—desperate certainly—and likely to be renewed again and again. . . . Vagabonds and ruffians—undisguised—fill the streets, only waiting—not for *an* opportunity, but for the *best* opportunity of attack. And yet even from the faces of these I have seen the malice and brutality vanish if a few words of ordinary humanity were spoken to them. And if there were enough merciful people in France to soothe without encouraging them, and to give them some— even the slightest—sympathy and help in such honest efforts as they make—few though they be—without telling them of their Rights or their injuries—the country might still be saved.[24]

When news of the proclamation of the Second Republic in Paris reached England in late February 1848 it completely altered the English view of the virulence of the European social upheaval. Until then it had seemed that the revolutionary threat was essentially a German and Italian problem, that unrest in Paris would be more easily repressed than in 1830, and indeed that Paris might even assist Vienna, Berlin, and Rome in silencing their rebels. But the news of February repealed all this. Paris now appeared to be the heart of a vast social convulsion spreading throughout central Europe; first to the southern states of Germany; then, by mid-March, to Hungary and Austria; to Prussia a few days later; and finally to Italy and Sicily. Economic paralysis followed in its wake, reviving labor agitation in England. Chartism, which had embodied the English revolutionary impulse for a decade, took new encouragement not only from the victories of revolution abroad but from the revival of economic troubles at home. There was, of course, genuine anxiety, especially in the minds of those who could remember the disturbances following the French upheaval of 1830, that the revolution would reach England. And in effect, as Elie Halévy points out, it did, but in the gradual forms of suffrage reform and social legislation.

In April of 1848, the forces of protest in England organized for action. The Chartists moved on London where they planned to march 500,000 strong accompanying their National Petition (a huge scroll supposedly containing almost six million signatures) from Kensington Common to Westminster, where it was to be presented to Parliament. The date set for this confrontation was 10 April, Ruskin's wedding day, as it happened. Fear of revolution was naturally greater by now than it had been over presentation of the petitions of 1839 and 1842. The royal family and many middle-class families fled the city, the streets were deserted and the shops shuttered. In a letter to his wife, Carlyle described London on the day of expected "Revolution."

> Piccadilly itself, however, told us how frightened the people were. Directly at Hyde Park Corner one could see that there was something in the wind. Wellington had his iron blinds all accurately down; the Green Park was altogether shut, even the footpaths of it, the big gates of Constitution Hill; and in the inside there stood a score of mounted Guardsmen privately drawn up under the arch—dreadfully cold, I dare say. For the rest, not a single fashionable carriage was on the street . . . omnibuses running, a few cabs, and even a mud cart or two; nothing else; the flag pavements also nearly vacant, not a fifth of their usual population there, and those also of the strictly business kind; not a gentleman to be seen, hardly one or two of the sort called *gents*.[25]

On this ominous day Ruskin and Effie were married at Perth in the room in which Ruskin's grandfather had committed suicide. But the "Revolution" (like the marriage) was not consummated. Of a half-million demonstrators expected, only twenty-five or thirty thousand appeared, and these were met by 170,000 special constables and general public hostility. The police forbade the crowd to march on Westminster; it dispersed without incident, and the petition was sent on to Westminster in a cab. "The same evening," Halévy writes, "a jubilant middle class walked the streets of London singing *God Save the Queen*. 'God save the shops is what they ought to be singing,' the Chartists muttered as, swamped in the crowd, they witnessed the collapse of their hopes."[26]

The picture of capitalist exploitation of labor projected by Friedrich Engels's *Condition of the Working-Class in England in 1844* was itself based upon the famous "Blue Books" of the various Parliamentary Committees and Royal Commissions of inquiry which succeeded the Poor Law Commission of 1832. Particularly appalling is the Blue Book of the Royal Commission on the Employment and Conditions of Children in Mines and Manufactories that appeared in 1842 and depicted naked children of both sexes harnessed to trucks in the mine tunnels or at work among the unguarded belts and flywheels of the factories for fifteen-hour days. In that year the second Chartist petition containing more than three million signatures demanding "six points," including universal suffrage (one man, one vote, one value) and legislation restricting hours of work in factories, was rejected amidst widespread agitation. Revolution, even "anarchy" had seemed imminent. It was at the close of this year of protest and revolt, capped by the Manchester Insurrection, that Carlyle addressed *Past and Present*, his "tract for the times," to an England that seemed "dying of inanation" and "asphixied soul." He scored the alienating "Gospel of Mammonism" and the social incoherence it bred in terms that Ruskin would echo in the sixties.

> True, it must be owned, we for the present, with our Mammon Gospel, have come to strange conclusions. We call it a Society; and go about professing openly the totalest separation, isolation. Our life is not a mutual helpfulness; but rather, cloaked under due laws-of-war, named "fair competition" and so forth, it is a mutual hostility. We have profoundly forgotten everywhere that *Cash-payment* is not the sole relation of human beings; we think, nothing doubting, that *it* absolves and liquidates all engagements of man.[27]

And yet, he exhorted, if sick England could but swallow the "Morrison's Pill" of corrective legislation, ending the empire of Mammon, there might follow after the passing of these convulsions a new industrial order led by enlightened, working "Captains of Industry." "One sees Organisms enough in the dim huge Future," he wrote, "and 'United Services' other than the redcoat one; and much, even in these years, struggling to be born!"[28]

Less oracularly, but in a vein that resembles Ruskin's doctrine of the sixties, Charlotte Tonna's *Perils of the Nation* (1842) called attention to four primary defects of English society. These, were, in G. M. Young's summary, "(a) defective conceptions of national wealth; (b) exorbitant power of the employing class; (c) unwillingness to legislate between employer and workman; (d) competition, which had (i) destroyed the notion of fair wage, fair price, and fair profit, (ii) lowered the quality of goods."[29] Carlyle's intuition of the imminence of change was not entirely incorrect. Out of the life-wealth catharsis of the forties there began to emerge a new conception of the responsibility of the state in socioeconomic relations. "By 1845," Young observes, "it was becoming evident that the line between what the State may do and what it must leave alone had been drawn in the wrong place, and that there was a whole world of things where the individual simply could not help himself at all."[30] The real turning point of social reconstruction in the century, Young observes, was not the repeal of the Corn Laws in 1846 but the passage of the Factory Act of 1847. In the debates over the act, he continues, "we can see the waning of the economics of pure calculation" in favor of "that preoccupation with the quality of life which is dominant in the next decade."[31] D. C. Somervell reads this same development of a countereconomics in the growing list of "exceptions" to laissez-faire that were gradually added to John Stuart Mill's *Principles of Political Economy* in successive editions after 1847.[32] These emendations to his chapter "The Grounds and Limits of The *Laissez-faire* or Noninterference Principle" are significant because the work remained the standard treatise for the rest of the century.

In France, one movement toward social reconstruction combined a relatively coherent program with a kind of religious rededication, the Comtist "Religion of Humanity." I mention this in passing, not because there is any resemblance between Comte's program and the social architecture of *The Seven Lamps*, but because the idea of a religion of humanity did, as I shall show later, have a certain oblique influence on Ruskin's own spiritual development. The Positivist Society was not founded in France until 1848, but during the thirties and forties Comte had been attempting to develop a philosophy for the reorganization of society based on the uses of scientific knowledge.

Comte's positivism was a system of social doctrine derived from the "positive" sciences. Although based on empirical knowledge, its ultimate aim was the spiritual regeneration of humanity through knowledge of humanity gained by a course of positive science leading to a "subjective synthesis" in which the needs of man appear self-evident. A religious reorientation would then take place based on the urge to serve humanity and cure its manifest ills. Systemization and spiritualization of social life was the hope, giving it coherence instead of competition and bending social activity to the services of a spiritual end as had been

true in medieval times. In this respect, desiring the spiritual regeneration and reorganization of society through cooperation instead of
through economic liberalism and individualism, Ruskin and Comte
would be working in the same direction as were the Saint Simonians, the
English Tory and Christian Socialists, and the various "communist" or
utopian socialist movements that were springing up at this time.

But in the final analysis no one can define the precise temper of social
anxiety that, among other elements, had its effect upon the writing of
The Seven Lamps and *Stones of Venice*; all we can assert is that the
analogy between architectural and social organization was important
and that the mood of *The Seven Lamps* is less pessimistic, or more naive,
about the possibility of achieving the moral regeneration necessary for
"architecture" on the Gothic model than the mood of the third volume
of *Stones* and later works. It appears that Ruskin had first systematized
the moral imperatives of architecture while aware of the prevalence of
social unrest but as yet relatively blind to the roots of its causes. Publicly
at least, he was still committed to Evangelical piety and consequently
committed to the view that great architecture could be founded on the
Protestant ethic. As with *Modern Painters*, volume 2, Ruskin later
condemned the book (he did not republish it with his collected works of
1871) for its sectarian bias and enthusiasm, referring to it in one of his
notes to the 1880 edition as "this wretched rant of a book,"[33] and
elsewhere as "the most useless I ever wrote."[34] Naturally Ruskin's later
abuse of his early work need not be taken at face value. His editor notes
that he was fond of running down those of his books which the public
liked best. My own view is that he found it hopelessly naive, though it
became the "germ," as he admitted, of much later work.

E. T. Cook suggests that the sectarian bitterness of *The Seven Lamps*
(the defect Ruskin himself refers to as its passages of "rabid and utterly
false Protestantism" and "pious insolence")[35] are in part due to his
desire to dissociate Gothicism from "Romanism" and from the "High
Ritualism" with which the Gothic revival, underway in England since
the late thirties, had become associated. Augustus Pugin, for instance,
whose *True Principles of Gothic Architecture* (1841) and *Apology for
the Revival of Christian Architecture in England* (1843) as well as his
practical work as an architect had made him the dominant figure in the
architectural revival before Ruskin, confessed that he had actually been
converted to Catholicism by Gothic architecture. Examination of the
particularly "rabid" passages does reveal that in these Ruskin was in fact
anxious to show that Catholicism was not a concomitant of the Gothic
spirit. There is also appendix 12 to the first edition of *The Stones of*

Venice in which he attacks Pugin's churches as theatrical Romanist lures.

Of course, when Ruskin excised certain specifically anti-Romanist passages in 1880 he was himself, as will be seen, passing through something like a Catholic phase in his spiritual development. By then, indeed, he had also condemned the pietism of volume 2 of *Modern Painters*. The pious confidence that he condemned in the book goes deeper than anti-Romanism. It is clear on internal grounds that he regarded the pure Gothic spirit as a vital efflorescence, a physical myth, with a life of its own and powers of social regeneration quite apart from its connection with the church as an historic institution. He had intuited that the Gothic spirit was itself a faith, an expression of organic awareness (like Turnerian "truth") not limited to any sect. Therefore, the Protestant rhetoric of the book shortly appeared to be a subversion of his own larger purposes in advocating Gothic.

I say *shortly appeared* because, as I have mentioned in the previous chapter, Ruskin was passing through a personal religious crisis whose exact stages are difficult to determine, but it was one that within a decade would make all of his earlier expressions of Evangelical certitude seem innocent. It would be convenient to know just how far this erosion of faith had progressed by 1848. Some remarks about his spiritual anxiety in the forties recorded in *Praeterita* and the diaries suggest that the pietism of the works he published during this period was actually an objective reaction against private doubt (another possible explanation of his strong condemnation of their religious tone). In closing a chapter of *Praeterita* dealing with events of 1845, he describes having and losing the "happy sense of direct relation with Heaven": "Whether I was capable of holding it or not, I cannot tell; but little by little, and for little, yet it seemed invincible, causes, it passed away from me. I had scarcely reached home [Denmark Hill] in safety before I had sunk back into the faintness and darkness of the Under-World."[36] Most commonly, of course, Ruskin's moments of spiritual exaltation and depression were so closely tied to conditions of scenery that it is difficult to isolate the true subjective basis for these moods. Harking back to a stay at Ambleside in 1847, he remembered a depression that seemed especially premonitory and protective: "But there, whether it was the grilled salmon for breakfast, or too prolonged reflections on the Celestial Hierarchies, I fell into a state of despondency till then unknown to me, and of which I knew not the like again till fourteen years afterwards. The whole morning was painfully spent in balancing phrases; and from my boat, in the afternoons on Windermere, it appeared to me that the water was leaden, and the hills were low."[37] It should be noted that Ruskin was at this time vaguely considering marriage with Charlotte Lockhart ("become a Scottish fairy, White Lady, and witch of the fatallest sort")[38] whom he did not love. In the diary for the same year we have another striking record of a moment of spiritual dread, again connected with thoughts of a woman and vaguely projected upon scenery. At Dunkeld in August he recorded "the saddest walk this afternoon I ever had in my life." Partly, he attributed this depression to his not having seen Effie Gray, and "in far greater degree, as I found by examining it thoroughly, from thinking that my own pain was perhaps much less than hers, not knowing what I know." Outwardly the feeling became "strange deadly shadow over everything, such as I hardly could comprehend; I expected to be touched by it, which I was not, but then came a horror of great darkness—not distress, but cold, fear and gloom."[39] So behind the confident piety, the "pious insolence" that he came to deplore in *The Seven Lamps*, lay private intimations of doubt and dread; and these suggest, in part, why, despite its popularity, he did not revise this work until 1880.

In this section I have attempted to recover part of that complex of experiences that influenced the writing of *The Seven Lamps* and *The Stones of Venice*. Obviously such an endeavor can never fully account for a work; its function is mainly to dispel the discomfort we feel when attempting to study the work in a social or psychological vacuum. Before turning to an internal analysis of the work itself, however, I must touch on two matters that are strictly biographical. A good deal of critical effort has been spent on the sensational question of why Ruskin did not consummate his marriage. While this is a question of great interest in the reconstruction of the historical Ruskin, its relevance to the substance of his work is not so easy to show unless one were to argue that Effie was somehow too earthy for Ruskin and so was inversely responsible for the mythical girl-queen who makes many appearances in his work and was most nearly realized for him in the person of Rose La Touche. Joan Evans concludes that "it was still a child rather than a woman whom Ruskin desired as his wife."[40] His frustrated youthful passion, especially for Adele Domecque, "made him admire girls hardly yet nubile, a fixation that was to become a dominant factor in his life." I have proposed in my introduction that the Jungian concept of the anima, the feminine archetype of soul-projection, best links this "dominant factor," the personal and mythological aspects of Ruskin's idealization of the feminine, to his other efforts to find privileged symbols, residences of the soul, in his world. But these are subjects to which we must return, though briefly, in considering Effie's suit for nullity, Ruskin's unused statement in defense of his behavior toward her, and his relationship with Rose. For the moment, as the other biographical matter just mentioned, we may wish to have in mind the description of Ruskin's appearance written about this time by F. J. Furnivall.

> After a short chat with the wife, I saw the door open, and John Ruskin walkt softly in. I sprang up at once to take the outstretcht hand, and then and there began a friendship which was for many years the chief joy of my life. Ruskin was a tall, slight fellow, whose piercing frank blue eye lookt through you and drew you to him. A fair man, with rough light hair and reddish whiskers, in a dark blue frock coat with velvet collar, bright Oxford blue stock, black trousers and patent slippers—how vivid he is to me still! The only blemish in his face was the lower lip, which protruded somewhat: he had been bitten there by a dog in his early youth. But you ceast to notice this as soon as he began to talk. I never met any man whose charm of manner at all approach Ruskin's. Partly feminine it was, no doubt; but the delicacy, the sympathy, the gentleness and affectionateness of his way, the fresh and penetrating things he said, the boyish fun, the earnestness, the interest he showd in all deep matters, combined to make a whole which I have never seen equalld.[41]

2

The Seven Lamps of Architecture has as much to do with social as with physical architecture. A society that could build by Ruskin's seven primary commandments would itself be a utopian order. His architectural dicta are generally, though not exclusively, concerned with prescribing the social and environmental matrix of a living architecture, not with detailing techniques of construction or even with laying down aesthetic criteria for good design. His essential effort, though he was not entirely conscious of it, was to project a moral order through the medium of an ideal building largely informed by his conception of the Gothic cathedral and the mode of life its stones implied. In this sense Ruskin's ideal building was a quasi-mythical entity for him, because he had read its Gothic models as myths in stone and because the architecture prescribed was really a metaphor for a coherent body of ultimate social values. Each of the seven lamps, not merely the fifth, is a law of life; and the creation they generate is not so much a "building" as an organic community in which art, nature, and social ends come together.

Ruskin suggested the analogy between the social and the physical building in his introduction to the volume (the same analogy would be used in his *Notes on the Construction of Sheepfolds*).[42] Both modes of building, he remarked, were being threatened by materialistic habits of thought that were increasing as the age advanced. The most urgent need was "to determine some constant, general, and irrefragable laws of right"—laws based upon man's nature, not his knowledge—that would not be peculiar to any art but will apply to the "entire horizon of man's action." His title, therefore, refers to "lamps" of architecture because, as in Scripture, "The Law is light." Further, he insisted that, properly understood, the relationship between architectural and social laws is closer even than analogy. There is "no branch of human work whose constant laws have not close analogy with those which govern every other mode of man's exertion." However, the more we simplify those laws the more they transcend mere analogy and become "the actual expression of some ultimate nerve or fibre of the mighty laws which govern the moral world."[43] In their ultimate simplicity the laws of life and art are one.

Despite his emphasis in his introduction on the universality of the laws governing all human work, Ruskin opened the discussion of the first of his lamp laws ("The Lamp of Sacrifice") by distinguishing architecture from building, a distinction he had made earlier in "The Poetry of Architecture" and would reaffirm in later books. Architecture addresses the mind of man; building is for his physical being only. Ruskin's note to the edition of 1880 points to "the mental ἀρχή . . . which separates architecture from a wasp's nest, a rat hole or a railway station."[44] Architecture and building have a relationship analogous to that between a poem and its paraphrase, or between a painting and its subject. Works of architecture are not merely machines for living (What is living?) but symbolic forms or expressions of human feeling with the kind of life of their own that myths have. They are expressions of life, not merely vehicles for it. This conception of architecture is more supportive to the particular concurrence of vital laws Ruskin wished to illustrate. He was not interested in possible analogies between the laws of engineering and those of society, his earlier emphasis on the oneness of *all* laws notwithstanding. He appears to have meant that the laws of all "organic" works are one.

Having distinguished between architecture and building, Ruskin moves forward to his first topic: architecture as expression of the social life-principle of sacrifice. Of the five types of architecture, devotional, memorial, civil, military, and domestic, it is to the first two, he claims, that the concept of sacrifice is most relevant. But it is the problem of devotional architecture as expression of sacrifice that interests him most; this is because devotional architecture best makes his point about the kind of social expression architecture should be. The gift here is in the act of giving: God has no need of a rich church. "It is not the church we want; but the sacrifice . . . Not the gift, but the giving."[45] The sacrifice should be in loving labor, then. This, of course, is of no use to God either, but it *is* of use to the society: the society needs the sacrifice though God does not. Building thus is both an expression and an instrument of social harmony through sacrifice. If architectural sacrifice were taken to mean rich adornment of building, one might expect it to be discussed last; but of social architecture it is the first law (appearing later as his law of help): that primary rebellion against self-interest and the profit-motive which is the beginning of social cohesion.

On the building itself the sign manual of sacrifice should be the expenditure of labor in the expression of nature's unity, variety, and mystery in stone. Such ornamentation, Ruskin argues, is never overcharged when good, and always overcharged when carelessly or mechanically executed. As for classical understatement and simplicity in ornament, these are but "the rests and monotones" in the solid music of architecture;

> it is to its far happier, far higher, exaltation that we owe those fair fronts of variegated mosaic, charged with wild fancies and dark hosts of imagery, thicker and quainter than ever filled the depth of midsummer dream; those vaulted gates, trellised with close leaves; those window-labyrinths of twisted tracery and starry light; those misty masses of multitudinous pinnacle and diademed tower; the only witnesses, perhaps, that remain to us of the faith and fear of nations.[46]

The discussion of "The Lamp of Truth" begins rather obliquely with a reference to the analogical relationship between the shadow zones of moral and solar light. Though the passage bears only indirectly on the rest of the chapter, it explores a motif, the light-darkness archetype, that permeates Ruskin's work. The following evocation of the shadow-line metaphor should be connected with the emphasis on the distinctness of Turner's shadows in volume 1 of *Modern Painters* and the discussion of light as a "sacred symbol" of purity and energy in volume 2, as well as the light-law metaphor implicit in the title of *The Seven Lamps*: "There is a marked likeness," he observes,

> between the virtue of man and the enlightenment of the globe he inhabits—the same diminishing gradation in vigour up to the limits of their domains, the same essential separation from their contraries—the same twilight at the meeting of the two: a something wider belt than the line where the world rolls into night, that strange twilight of the virtues; that dusky debatable land, wherein zeal becomes impatience, and temperance becomes severity, and justice becomes cruelty, and faith superstition, and each and all vanish into gloom.[47]

Similarly, a few pages farther on, Ruskin propounds a distinction between imagination and deception that belongs more to the theme of imagination as a mode of truth that he was and would be developing in *Modern Painters* than to the immediate subject of truth in architecture. There is no deception in imagination, he argues, for its power depends on our recognition of the things it conceives as absent or impossible. When imagination deceives it becomes madness, he declares in 1849, but a note of 1880 adds that diseased imaginations may be as true as the healthiest provided we *know* that they are diseased; "a dream is as real a fact, as a vision of reality: deceptive only if we do not recognize it as a dream."[48] Imagination is no deception, then, but is a painting? Only when it strives to realize its subject completely, he asserts, reemphasizing a distinction that had troubled him in volume 1 of *Modern Painters*. But in the social art of architecture more contemptible violations of truth are possible than in painting.

These subjects, the light metaphor and imagination as truth, though important to the totality of his work, are tangential to the central concerns of the chapter: the possibilities of deceit in architecture. By architectural deceits Ruskin means "a direct falsity of assertion respecting the nature of material, or the quantity of labour."[49] In other words, they are palpable lies about the amount of social sacrifice embodied in the building and can be read as signs of "moral delinquency" in the builders. Ruskin identifies three categories of such architectural deceits: structural, surface, and operative. Structural deceits occur whenever a building manifests some false mode of structure or support. The building need not exhibit its actual structure but must not suggest a false one. The danger inherent in the use of metals for construction lies in their potential in aiding structural deceits. For Ruskin, "true architecture does not admit iron as a construction material";[50] that is, "metals may be used as a *cement*, but not as a *support*."[51] In insisting that the builder use wood and stone, which are materials of the visible landscape, for construction and that the building possess no superfluous structure, Ruskin is insisting that the building be organic in two senses. This implicit organicism is supported in the chapter itself by analogies with animal structures. Another mode of deceit occurs when architectural surfaces are painted to represent some material or ornament that has not actually been supplied. The law of life here is that "no form nor material is to be *deceptively* represented."[52] Paintings are permissible so long as the painting is confessed and not used to represent materials or forms supposed to be real.

The final and most significant are the "operative deceits." These occur when cast or machine work is substituted for that of the hand. Such work, Ruskin teaches, is both aesthetically and socially bad. However, it is the social evil only that concerns him at this point, and his remarks on it are the core of this chapter. We receive the pleasure we take in ornament (and architecture for Ruskin *is* ornament) from two separate sources: its abstract beauty as form (presumably the same whether made by hand or machine) and our sense of the amount of human labor expended upon it. Thus labor is part of a building's intrinsic value.

The idea that part of the value of an ornament or building rests in the imprint it bears of living labor, of human struggle, is crucial to Ruskin's architectural theory. This view has several important implications. It points to a mode of sacrifice that cannot really be falsified and one that tends to ensure maximum social involvement in architecture, namely, maximum distribution of creative labor in making it and maximum recreative value in observing it, because the forms produced most nearly approach the psychological satisfaction offered by nature itself. He sees the gradual loss, through mechanical deceits, of the labor-value of art as a threat to both society and art. Buildings ornamented by free handwork have in them a kind of life that derives from the process of becoming and that shares the quality of perfect imperfection of organic forms. Once any ornamental technique has been mechanically perfected to the point of self-consciousness, so that the architecture becomes a vehicle for the display of technical facility, the architecture is dying of inanition. These are implications that Ruskin explores elsewhere in this volume and in *The Stones of Venice*. For the moment he is content to end his chapter on architectural truth with one illustration of architectural death through deceit: the decline of Gothic through over refinement of technique leading to the final deceptive flexibility of Gothic tracery.

The decline of Gothic architecture may be read, he proposes, in the evolution of window traceries and their gradual infection by deceit. It is "inexcusably absurd" he argues, following Willis's *Architecture of the Middle Ages*, to regard Gothic tracery as having been derived from "vegetable form." Indeed, the older and purer the Gothic the *less* it imitates organic forms.[53] (It is, of course, another thing to say that the Gothic building *is* an organic form, obeying organic principles of coherence and assymetry, or that it may symbolize nature in its ornamental carving.) Looking through its "lights" (windows) we may see that the Gothic style reached its acme at the instant "when the light had expanded to its fullest, and yet lost none of its radiant unity, principality, and visible first causing of the whole."[54] Up to this point the architect's eye is on the apertures themselves. The moment he turns his attention from mass to line, from the lights to the technique of tracery, the system is doomed. The plain truth of the window form, characterized

by rigidity, falls into the "deliberate treachery" of attempting to represent silken tendrils of tracery in stone. Thus the Gothic died of enervation. The relations of these deadly operative deceits to social decline are
clarified in *The Stones of Venice,* and the "feverish" enervation of
flamboyant Gothic is diagnosed in a lecture he delivered in 1869.[55].

Having declared that the older and purer the Gothic, the less it imitates organic form, Ruskin moves to rest his third lamp, "The Lamp of
Power," on the apparently contradictory assertion that "whatever is in
architecture fair or beautiful is imitated from natural forms."[56] As in
volume 1 of *Modern Painters* and elsewhere in his work, the difficulty
turns on the meaning of *imitation*. At this point he chooses to give
imitation the very open meaning of "sympathy"; his concern is with
architectural power generated by the sympathy of human intervention
"with the vast controlling powers of Nature . . . [now] little felt or
regarded by architects."[57] This tapping by sympathetic invention of
nature's power of the sublime is yet another sense of life in Ruskin's
archetypal building. It has its implications for the social building as
well. Ruskin would have his architect study among the mountains; thus,
his designs would be mass media conducting messages of nature's
awesome power to citizens of the plains.

Among the various architectural messages of power considered
(magnitude, sheer verticality, use of square form, et cetera), the emphasis
placed upon power in the play of light and shade is most characteristic of
Ruskin. The impression of "abstract power and awfulness" depends
primarily upon bold expanses of unbroken surface. So long as they are
natural, the materials of construction are to a large extent irrelevant.
Here the architect builds with weight and light ("the light of heaven
upon it, and the weight of earth in it are all we need") and leaves a cliff
for us "to mark the play of passing light on its broad surface, and to see
by how many artifices and gradations of tinting and shadow, time and
storm will set their wild signatures upon it."[58] Similarly, a few pages
farther on, Ruskin attempts to formulate both the aesthetic and social
value of chiaroscuro in architecture. Directly after sheer magnitude, size
and weight, "the Power of architecture may be said to depend on the
quantity (whether measured in space or intentness) of its shadow"; and
its social influence lies in its expression of sympathy with the human
condition "by a measure of darkness as great as there is in human life."[59]
In sum, the young architect must learn to flesh his structures in living
light and shade "not looking at a design in its miserable tiny skeleton;
but conceiving it as it will be when the dawn lights it and the dusk leaves
it."[60]

Of special interest in the light of Ruskin's later opinions is the attack on Greek architecture and society to which this discussion of architectural chiaroscuro leads him. Although the patterns of line on Greek capitals are much more artful, Byzantine handling of chiaroscuro is "incontestably more grand and masculine" because it is based on pure gradations of solar light on massive natural forms, such as thunderheads and mountain forms. Study of their lighting will reveal the same "great and honoured law" of diffusion of light for which Byzantine ornamentation was designed; furthermore, it will "show us that those builders had truer sympathy with what God made majestic, than the self-contemplating and self-contented Greeks."[61] How much Ruskin had yet to learn about Greek belief (and his own) is suggested by his correction in 1880 of this early impression of "self-contented" Greeks. "A noble Greek," he then writes, "was as little content without God, as George Herbert, or St. Francis; and a Byzantine *was* nothing else than a Greek,—recognizing Christ for Zeus."[62]

At the outset of "The Lamp of Power" Ruskin had indicated two natural sources of architectural life: *power* derived from the expression of "sympathy" of human capability with the gloom and mystery of nature's more awesome forms, and *beauty* of line directly adapted from organic forms. Although this sweeping division of the subject may seem to imply as much, these are by no means the only modes of harmony between architecture and nature to which Ruskin appeals. However, the development of his subject requires him to show why and how architecture must derive its beauty of line from nature. This is the light of the fourth lamp, "The Lamp of Beauty." His main postulates are these: that man cannot advance the invention of beauty without direct imitation of natural forms (this does not mean that forms copied from nature are automatically beautiful, but that man cannot conceive beautiful forms unaided by nature); forms *not* derived from natural objects are necessarily ugly; and, finally, there is a relationship between the visible frequency of a form and its beauty: the more frequent, the more natural, and thus the more beautiful. By *"visibly* frequent" forms Ruskin wishes to exclude those forms normally hidden from the unaided human eye. Obviously, the value of these pronouncements turns on the meaning assigned to the word *beauty.* But Ruskin has no time in *The Seven Lamps* for the whole aesthetic that would have to be written around that word. He is anxious to move on to other dicta concerning the practical application of these laws in architectural ornament and to the social implications of faulty ornament.

First he proceeds to cite several classical forms of architectural ornament that violate his law of frequency. The Greek fret, for instance, is attacked as representing a form infrequent in nature; hence it is lifeless and ugly. (However, a note of 1880 explains that this fret, representing the labyrinth, possesses "a deep meaning which I did not then know."[63]) The Greek egg-and-dart molding, because it was derived from common forms, he finds as beautiful as the other is painful. He objects to ornamental ribands and scrolls, particularly ribands, on the same grounds, as being unnatural and affected. With garlands and festoons the problem is more complicated, for these are unnatural arrangements of natural forms. Here Ruskin must appeal to another essentially unexamined concept, that of organic coherence, often implicit in the book. In imitating natural objects the architect is bound to place them where nature herself would have done so. Yet he must not imitate complete natural arrangements to justify the positions of objects. There is no need, that is, to run stems up a column to account for the placement of exuberant vegetation on the capital. This discussion of the natural placement of natural objects leads to a brief attack on social affectation in the use of ornament. It is absurd to decorate (as architecture) buildings that are utterly defined by function, such as shops and railway stations: let these confess their functions, miserable as these may be, and not pretend to spiritual appeal where none exists.

Having dealt with the considerations on which the placement of ornament should depend, Ruskin's next concern is with the principles by which the objects themselves are made compatible with architecture. These are considered under two heads: proportion and abstraction. On proportion his essential point is that one member of any composition must be dominant. There can be no principle of proportion among equals. In physical as in social architecture, he notes, the laws of reason and nature are against equality; the law in both is proportion and submission. In abstraction of imitated natural forms, the law is that while increasing completion marks the progress of art, absolute completion is the sign of its decline. Perfect execution of ornament, though not always wrong, is always dangerous.

Ruskin's final topic in "The Lamp of Beauty" concerns the uses of color in architectural ornament. The subject is treated under two heads: polychromatic effects and monochromatic carved design. His remarks on the former are significant in revealing, more than elsewhere, his overall organic conception of the building. Just as the architect must look to nature for instruction in form, so must he also with color. No architecture, Ruskin considers, can be perfect without color. Thus, color should be where possible the color of natural stones, even at the sacrifice of intricacy of design. But there is a more important reason for giving up intricacy of form for unity of color. Since the building is to be thought of as "a kind of organized creature," it should be "coloured as Nature would colour one thing." However, organic color has a life of its own; it "never follows the form, but is arranged on an entirely separate system."[64] That is, though the boundaries of organic forms are always delicately and precisely drawn, their patterns of color, while roughly symmetrical, are generally blurred in outline, imperfect, irregular, or blotched. Turning to the architectural uses of monochromatic design, Ruskin attempts to outline the law of relationship between color and carving in the entire range of architectural ornamentation. The general principle is that the more fully carved the natural form the less concurrent should its color be with form: organic form requires organic color. Thus at one end of his scale we have "organic form dominant" (as in independent sculpture or high relief), with color "in a system not concurrent with the form"; then, as we pass down through "organic form sub-dominant" (low relief) and "organic form abstracted to outline" (monochromatic design), color becomes increasingly congruent with form, until organic forms give way to geometrical patterns and color and form are united.[65]

The building invoked in these two chapters, the "organized creature" of power and beauty, is more nearly a mythic projection of a socioaesthetic ideal expressed in architectural language than a complex of practical design criteria. In fact, Ruskin concludes his chapter by pointing out that only one building in the world comes near to fully expressing the essential characteristics of power and beauty: Giotto's campanile at Florence. He invokes it in a passage that parallels the apocalyptic comment entered into his diary at Salisbury. Once again the tower by contrast with the gray starkness of Northern Gothic, appears like a vision in light

> that bright, smooth, sunny surface of glowing jasper, those spiral shafts and fairy traceries, so white, so faint, so crystalline, that their slight shapes are hardly traced in darkness on the pallor of the Eastern sky, that serene height of mountain alabaster, coloured like a morning cloud, and chased like a sea shell. And if this be, as I believe it, the model and mirror of perfect architecture, is there not something to be learned by looking back to the early life of him who raised it?[66]

But his primary purpose in introducing Giotto's campanile in the concluding paragraphs of "The Lamp of Beauty" is to offer this work as proof of a doctrine that underlies all the others, namely, his view that architectural ideas of power and beauty must be nurtured in the wilderness. So it was, he insists, with Giotto. "Not within the walls of Florence, but among the far away fields of her lilies, was the child trained who was to raise that headstone of Beauty above her towers of watch and war."[67] So with the introduction of the idea of the supreme architect schooled among the fields, Ruskin prepares us for his next chapter, "The Lamp of Life."

Each of the "lamps" discussed so far is, in effect, a lamp of life: "Sacrifice" of life in labor; "Truth" forbidding deception as to the amount of labor and natural material in the building; "Power" derived from adaptation of organic form. Because "The Lamp of Life" restates and deepens concepts of life already expressed by Ruskin's utopian building, it is the most significant in the volume. It is part of the thematic core of his work, presenting the vital-lethal antagonism.

Ruskin anchors his argument to the concept of "vital beauty" he had developed in volume 2 of *Modern Painters*. The principle, he reminds us, is that the sense of beauty is involved with the sense of life in or expended on things. That is, the impression of beauty depends largely "on the expression of vital energy in organic things, or on the subjection to such energy, of things naturally passive and powerless."[68] It is the second phrase that has particular relevance to architecture, and Ruskin proceeds to develop it. Objects that bear the impress of human creative life take their nobility (Ruskin's word) from the amount of creative energy that they visibly reveal. The inert materials of architecture, he reiterates, "depend for their dignity and pleasurableness in the utmost degree, upon the vivid expression of intellectual life which has been concerned in their production."[69] This emphasis on the visual impression of creative life left on the stone is the central principle of *The Seven Lamps* and of all Ruskin's theory of architecture; it is also, of course, the most vital nexus between architecture and society. But what, to continue, is this "life"?

With all other forms of vitality save that of the human mind, Ruskin explains, there is no doubt about when there is life and when not. There is "no mechanism or galvanism" by which the lower organisms can counterfeit their own lives, but human imagination, "rejoicing in its own excessive life," may project vital sensibility into forms that do not have it, an activity which Ruskin would later call "pathetic fallacy." Man's being alone seems to have a "fictitious counterpart," a kind of antilife, "which it is at his peril if he do not cast off and deny."[70] So now, in a very important section, Ruskin sets out to distinguish the true from the false life of the mind. The "true life," like that of lower forms of being, is an independent assimilative force, which, while it lives, never surrenders its own integrity as a shaping principle; never forfeits its power to judge and assimilate what it must to fulfil its existence. (Unless, as we now know, its whole environment has been altered.) "False life" is life determined by custom or accident, by assent without comprehension or conviction, "life which is overlaid by the weight of things external to it,"[71] life shaped by what it cannot assimilate—uncomprehended existence, we might say. Continuing his organic metaphor, Ruskin sees this inauthentic state of being represented in the effect of hoar frost crystalized upon vegetation; a metaphor that recurs at significant points in his later writing. "Brittle, obstinate, and icy," unable either to bend or to grow, this frostbitten life must be rebelled against, "must be crushed and broken to bits, if it stand in our way." False being is "but one of the conditions of death or stupor," he observes, a comment the Ruskin of 1880 singles out for reappraisal and reformulation in more urgent language: "The real question is only—are we dead or alive?—for, if dead at heart and having only a name to live in all our actions, we are sowing the seeds of death."[72]

Moving from the signs of individual life toward his proper subject, societal and architectural life, Ruskin compares the flow of national vitality to the flow of lava, "first bright and fierce, then languid and covered, at last advancing only by the tumbling over and over of its frozen blocks."[73] This terminal condition of national torpor is saddening to look upon, and it is more strikingly apparent in the arts and architecture than in any other aspect of national growth. Evidently referring in part to the Gothic revival, he notes that there has been some faint stirrings of architectural life in England of late, thought by many to mark the beginning of a new era, but to him this new efflorescence has a "sickly look," a view that his note of 1880 heartily reaffirms with a twinge of remorse for the effort he himself had expended on its behalf. But he thinks it a mistake to assume that the chief sign of death in present architecture is its derivativeness; art is dying only when it borrows without paying interest, adapts without assimilating. Thus in Lombard architecture imitated Byzantine elements were at first incoherent and inorganic with its own innate life; gradually, however, these adopted forms were assimilated and fused into a perfect final organization, "all the borrowed elements being subordinated to its own primal, unchanged life."[74]

What, then, are the signs of healthy, as opposed to deadly, imitation in architecture? Ruskin reminds us first that while it may be comparatively easy to list its signs, life cannot be defined or communicated. Two primary signs of vitality in imitation are frankness and audacity. But frankness itself does not excuse indolent imitation any more than audacity excuses unwise adaptation. No, it is necessary to seek more positive signs of vitality in architecture, signs that will be independent of originality or adaptation, signs that will mark every "determinedly progressive" style, whether original or derivative. Perhaps the most important of these, he continues, is a certain involuntary or intentional contempt for finish, "visible subordination of execution to conception."[75] A perfect finish belongs only to perfected art; "a progressive finish belongs to progressive art; and I do not think that any more fatal sign of a stupor or numbness settling upon that undeveloped art could possibly be detected, than that it had been taken aback by its own execution, and that workmanship had gone ahead of the design."[76]

Here is the heart of Ruskin's theory of architectural vitality; living architecture will be marked by visible signs of struggle, of becoming or emergence, in the work (a distinction parallel to that between the *natura naturans*, which Coleridge said was the proper subject of art, and the *natura naturata*, the nature of soulless imitation). Except for rare moments of perfection, there will be an evident separation between the sculptor's, or builder's, conceptions and his capacity to execute them. Live work will be marked by rebelliousness, by constant impatience with the old clothes (as Carlyle might have put it) of technique, and by "a restless disdain for all qualities which appear either to confess contentment, or to require a time and care which might be better spent."[77]

Living architecture, like nature, will generally not show perfect symmetry or exact reduplication of forms; a higher perfection proceeds from the sum of imperfect parts. As an illustration of this organic contempt for symmetry and uniformity, Ruskin introduces measurements showing the asymmetry and irregularity, the higher subtlety of proportioning, in the front facade of the Duomo of Pisa. It is the only piece of architectural evidence examined with any care in *The Seven Lamps*, and it is the book's principal illustration of living architecture. "There is," Ruskin concludes, "sensation in every inch of it, and an accommodation to every architectural necessity, with a determined variation in arrangement, which is exactly like the related proportions and provisions in the structure of organic form."[78] In the same terms of organic subtlety in variation and imperfection, in a brief foretaste of *The Stones of Venice*, he cites the letters of Joseph Woods as an example of a professional architect's failure to appreciate the perfect imperfection of Saint Mark's and the Ducal Palace in that city. The builders of these worked with feeling, not simply with wealth and technique, and consequently "there is this marvelous life, changefulness, and subtlety running through their every arrangement"[79] as there is in the incomprehensible loveliness of trees.

But the great building for Ruskin is a social growth, not merely in the general sense of being a material expression and repository of social values such as truth, beauty, and sacrifice, but in the more explicit sense that it must be built by hand; it cannot be built by men who have become the tools of their tools. No great building can be built by machines or by men who work as machines. On the other hand, as long as free men work as men, he argues, no matter how unskilled they may be, "there will be that in the handling which is above price." It is not coarse or blunt cutting of ornament that is death to architecture, "it is *cold* cutting . . . the smooth, diffused tranquility of heartless pains."[80] *"High finish"* in ornament "is the rendering of a well intended and vivid impression; and it is oftener got by rough than fine handling."[81] The feeling is primary, yet "you cannot get the feeling by paying for it—money will not buy life."[82]

In sum, Ruskin's mythical building is alive in *two* senses: in organic subtlety of variation, and with the intricacies of texture growing out of the free creative efforts of ordinary men; it is a kind of existential building. The bond between such a building and its social matrix would be extremely deep both economically and spiritually. "The Lamp of Life" concludes with a metaphor that must be noticed here for the apocalyptic power it acquires in his later writing. Life is imaged in a glowing, precious cloud or vapor (James 4: 14) liable to pollution: "There is dreaming enough, and earthiness enough, and sensuality enough in human existence, without our turning the few glowing moments of it into mechanism; and since our life must at the best be but a vapour that appears for a little time and then vanishes away, let it at least appear as a cloud in the height of Heaven, not as the thick darkness that broods over the blast of the Furnace, and the rolling of the Wheel."[83]

Ruskin's last two lamps, those of memory and obedience, are more distinctly social in reference than the lamp of life. In "The Lamp of Memory" he ties society's need for architecture to its need for history. Architecture, as distinct from building, is visible history. A society can live without architecture, he insists, but it cannot remember without it. Thus architecture is the great time-binding art of the people, preserving a society's sense of continuity and being rooted in cultural duration. Gothic architecture, of course, he finds uniquely suited to function as social memory, for its intricacy of structure can admit unlimited richness of record.

It follows that for Ruskin the true perfection of both civil and domestic architecture can be reached only when buildings become both memorial and monumental. Even the ordinary family dwelling, built with feeling, might become a kind of temple sanctifying and sanctified by the life in them through time and memory. These considerations lead Ruskin to a vehement attack upon the shoddy, ephemeral, and hence alienated, dwellings which then seemed to be choking London and desecrating the landscape. This suburban sprawl seemed to him an ominous symptom of social degeneration. I quote at length, for its own value, what may be the finest stretch of indignant rhetoric in *The Seven Lamps of Architecture*.

> And I look upon those pitiful concretions of lime and clay which spring up, in mildewed forwardness, out of the kneaded fields about our capital—upon those thin, tottering, foundationless shells of splintered wood and imitated stone—upon those gloomy rows of formalised minuteness, alike without difference and without fellowship, as solitary as similar—not merely with the careless disgust of an offended eye, not merely with sorrow for a desecrated landscape, but with a painful foreboding that the roots of our national greatness must be deeply cankered when they are thus loosely struck in their native ground; that those comfortless and unhonoured dwellings are the signs of a great and spreading spirit of popular discontent; and they mark the time when every man's aim is to be in some more elevated sphere than his natural one, and every man's past life is his habitual scorn; when men build in the hope of leaving the places they have built, and live in the hope of forgetting the years that they have lived; when the comfort, the peace, the religion of home have ceased to be felt; and the crowded tenements of a struggling and restless population differ only from the tents of the Arab or the Gipsy by their less healthy openness to the air of heaven, and less happy choice of their spot of earth; by their sacrifice of liberty without the gain of rest, and of stability without the luxury of change.[84]

The earth is not ours to plunder or to encumber with wasted work: "God has lent us the earth for our life; it is a great entail. It belongs as much to those who are to come after us, and whose names are already written in the book of creation, as to us; and we have no right, by anything that we do or neglect, to involve them in unnecessary penalties, or deprive them of benefits which it was in our power to bequeath."[85]

The chapter concludes with some famous strictures against restoration of ancient buildings. "It is *impossible*, as impossible as to raise the dead, to restore anything that has ever been great or beautiful in architecture."[86] This doctrine may seem unduly severe and even inconsistent with Ruskin's love of pure medieval Gothic, unless one remembers that he regards these buildings as organically coherent living entities that received their life directly from the hand of the ancient workman, and "that spirit which is given only by the hand and eye of the workman, can never be recalled."[87] Ruskin would, of course, wish the society to invest its creative energies in new great architecture rather than in attempts to embalm what must ultimately be lost. However, to what extent he would have distinguished mere repair from restoration is unclear.

With the seventh lamp, "The Lamp of Obedience," Ruskin is perhaps at his farthest remove from physical architecture and closest to the social structure from which it is, in his view, derived. And, as before, he again attempts to set forth a joint social and architectural law of life. In all nature, he argues, the obvious principle of creation is law not liberty; so also it must be with society and architecture. Liberty is a treacherous illusion, a death principle, not a life principle.

But obedience procured by enslavement or subjugation he sees as also a fatal alternative: society, like architecture, must incorporate sufficient freedom to release individual creative energies; yet, in both, creativity can be perfected only by restraint. The highest art is never to be found through the pursuit of originality for its own sake; the greatest work is always the fusion of individual energy and the restraint of law, much as the grammar of a language both permits and restrains the creativity of individual speakers. Practically, this means that the architecture of a nation can achieve greatness only when the efforts of individual architects are restrained by the principles of a national style that are as universal and established as those of its language. At this point in the manuscript Ruskin wrote a very interesting passage linking Blake and Turner as examples of "magnificent and mighty innovators" whose art "would have been greater if they had appeared in a time of law."[88] As the mythic, prophetic, and apocalyptic elements in his own work begin to emerge it may be well to bear in mind this evidence of Ruskin's early awareness and approbation of Blake.

Characteristically, the chapter (and the volume) end in a kind of apocalyptic peroration fusing solar imagery with mythic, in this case biblical, resonance. Ruskin has been decrying the modern practice of expending the social energy of labor in the building of tunnels and trestles or in the manufacture of artless luxuries that return neither satisfaction to the laborer nor dwellings for his spirit. The whole alienating tendency is seen as darkly connected with the advance of knowledge and technology, and so he concludes:

> There is something ominous in the light which has enabled us to look back with disdain upon the ages among whose lovely vestiges we have been wandering. I could smile when I hear the hopeful exultation of many, at the new reach of worldly science, and vigour of worldly effort; as

if we were again at the beginning of days. There is thunder on the horizon
as well as dawn. The sun was risen upon the earth when Lot entered into
Zoar.[89]

In reviewing the essential argument and imagery of *The Seven Lamps
of Architecture* I have tried to emphasize the features that mark the basic
thrust of Ruskin's work, the central coherence from which will spring
apparently opposed branches. In its fusion of social and aesthetic interests, the book clearly indicates his deepening social concern, for it is
not so much an attempt to set forth the laws of great architecture as to
define the relationships that must exist between architecture and society
if either is to be great. Strains and tones that were to be more fully
developed in his later work make their appearance here. The admission
of imagination as a mode of truth is important to "The Lamp of Truth"
and underlies the emphasis on the free creative energy of the workman in
"The Lamp of Life." Myth, of course, is not discussed objectively in the
book but is implicit in the scriptural and prophetic resonance of
Ruskin's style and, more significantly, in the fact that the socioarchitectural building defined by Ruskin's seven lamps is an impossible entity
belonging to the realm of vision or prophecy. The life-death struggle,
the core of Ruskin's awareness of things, pervades the work in that each
of the lamps sets forth one or more senses of life in the interaction of
society and architecture and defines by implication the contrary mode of
death: life as sacrifice of precious labor in the building; life as design
with, not servile imitation of, organic form; life as uses of organic
materials; life as power derived from continued sympathy with
manifestations of power in nature; life as beauty through rejection of
meretricious forms not derived from nature's "vital beauty"; life in the
multitudinous expressions upon the stone of the free creative energy of
the workman; life in the building as expression of social continuity,
memory, and as embodiment of the creative restraint of a national style
to be understood by analogy with its language.

Obviously no postindustrial, fragmented, and mechanistic people
could build Ruskin's radically organic architecture until they had first
built his radically organic society. Even if something like the
socioaesthetic integration he desired had been realized in the climatic
moment of medieval Gothic, as the perfect churches seemed to testify, it
should have been clear to him from the first, as it partly was, that such
architecture could no more be revived than restored. It is obvious to any
reader of *The Seven Lamps* that the pure, sculptured organic architecture it describes could never be built by an urban industrial society.
Given this truth it is hard to understand how Ruskin could have been

even momentarily deluded by the Gothic revival, but it is entirely easy to see why he was so bitterly disillusioned by it.[90] There could be no Gothic architecture without a revival of a Gothic society. To impose Gothic artifices upon modern building techniques and modern towns would be to produce stillborn monstrosities and not the vital architecture Ruskin envisioned.

Of course, he would have to think more deeply about the death of the Gothic, as he was to do in *The Stones of Venice,* and to see with his own eyes the buildings that the perversion of his principles helped to create, in order to arrive at the state of embittered comprehension that caused him to see *The Seven Lamps,* one of his most popular works, as a useless and even harmful book. Actually the "organic" architectural mission of Frank Lloyd Wright seems nearer to Ruskin's deeper principles than were the largely decorative efforts of the Gothic revival. Wright shared Ruskin's hostility to the Renaissance and to the "pseudo-classic mask," the grand opera posturings it imposed on the development of architecture. Like Ruskin he contrasted the organic character of the Gothic architecture with that of the Greeks, which he believed had no organic feeling whatever. Unlike Ruskin, however, Wright sought to free architecture from all derivative styles; he did not contemplate any return to the Gothic. Yet, for Wright as for Ruskin, architecture was a mode of poetry, and they share an acute sense of the distinction between mere building and truly creative architecture. They had in common a deep and ultimately indefinable conception that a building should be involved with nature. For Wright this meant that a building should grow out of its situation, its function, the native materials, and something else—its own internal and unique coherence. A building is "something out of the ground . . . conditioned by the nature of the materials and the purpose of the thing done, as something having a fresh integrity."[91]

Because he was a practicing architect, Wright was concerned with a building's overall structure while Ruskin conceived his organic architecture largely in terms of details of ornament or texture, as if these determined structure. Therefore, Wright was not led, as Ruskin tended to be, into the fallacy that an architecture becomes organic by the use of ornamentation based on natural forms. And yet he seems to have shared Ruskin's delight in the infinite complexity of natural textures. A more fundamental agreement is their radical and prophetic comprehension of the close relationship between architectural and social forms; both see their architectural conceptions as instruments of profound social change: reintegration with nature, decentralization of cities, and redefinition of wealth. "What we call organic architecture," Wright declared, "is no mere aesthetic nor cult nor fashion but an actual movement based upon a profound idea of a new integrity of human life wherein art, religion, and science are one: Form and Function seen as One, of such is Democracy."[92] Ruskin's architecture is, in a sense, the more radical, because it is concerned with the development of free, creative labor. Yet Wright perceived that there could be no organic architecture without an organic society. This is a truth that Ruskin intuited in *The Seven Lamps of Architecture*, but its implications would be tested and clarified in *The Stones of Venice*.

CHAPTER 3

Venetian Approaches

Viewed as a literary design, *The Stones of Venice* appears primarily as an effort in the prophetic or apocalyptic uses of art history. Within the profusion of architectural detail, Ruskin discloses the development of the Venetian spirit in art in such language that the historical process becomes a vehicle for the revelation of divine judgment upon a society; a Gothic paradise blooms and is lost. Furthermore, the Venetian "Fall" serves ultimately as a mirror in which Victorian society might perceive darkly certain grim lineaments of its own destiny. In the immediate context of Ruskin's thought, *Stones* is a case study in the operation of those principles of relationship between architecture and society which had been set forth in *The Seven Lamps of Architecture*. By correlating sculpture and ethical history he attempts to trace the life cycle of a vital architecture and its social matrix. Accordingly, the work perceives its subject in terms of three organic phases: the Byzantine roots, the Gothic infusion and efflorescence, and the Renaissance frost and fall.

There are other important aspects of the book, of course. In its concentration on the particulars of workmanship, especially in the details of Gothic decoration, *Stones* presents touchstones of quality in any architecture. In order to show what the Renaissance destroyed, Ruskin had to refine his general conception of the Gothic into distinct qualities of mind and style; this is the substance of the most familiar chapter in the three volumes, "The Nature of Gothic." Further, in its close readings of the sculpture of certain buildings, notably Saint Mark's and the Ducal Palace, the work could function simply as a guide to the appreciation of these structures as the culmination of a tradition opposed to the classical spirit in design. At the same time Ruskin shows his readers how to feel about this architecture, not simply what to know about it. Although the style of *Stones* is generally more restrained than that of *The Seven Lamps*, there are moments of epiphany in which Ruskin's direct encounter with the living building in its setting takes precedence over more objective analysis, and there are passages in which the feeling of a natural scene is invoked and charged with historical or

religious associations. Finally, because changes in architectural form
are, for Ruskin, ultimately rooted in belief, he is drawn closer to the
problem of myth here than in any of his earlier books.

1

Although *Stones* is in some respects a sequel to *The Seven Lamps*, a
natural outgrowth of his desire to redefine and document certain dicta
set forth there, especially Ruskin's generalizations in "The Lamp of
Life" about the uniquely vital power of Saint Mark's and the Ducal
Palace, the work was not the product of theories elaborated in an
experiential vacuum. Impressions derived from his personal experience,
particularly those of contemporary Venice received while he was gathering and arranging the materials of his book, obviously affected its course
and conclusions. I say obviously, first, because Ruskin made a point of
working from the stones as they stood, decaying and abused in the flood
of modern life, by sketching, measuring, and touching; secondly,
because the work itself compounds the prose of value with that of fact.
However, to correlate all we know of Ruskin's subjective experience
during the years from 1849 to 1852 with the theories and tones in the
book he was writing would be a task beyond the scope of this study. It is
possible here merely to set down a few representative impressions drawn
from those he recorded in his diaries, letters, and, much later, in
Praeterita, in the hope at least of keeping this analysis of his work in
touch with the Ruskin of flesh, spirit, and situations. To give these
impressions a semblance of order it seems wise to group them into two
broad but related categories: impressions of nature and of Venice and
impressions of his own spiritual development.

In the summer of 1849 Ruskin traveled to Switzerland with his
parents. Effie, his bride of a year, remained behind in Perth with her
mother to recover from the death of her young brother and other shocks
of loss that had apparently weakened her health. Ruskin felt optimistic
but responsible: "I trust that she is now gaining strength" he wrote,
"and that when she is restored to me, or as I feel almost inclined to say,
when we are married next time, I hope to take better care of her."[1] On the
Continent that summer he kept a copious journal of impressions of
skies, notably, and of geological formations—the beautiful and fearful
in nature, images of mountain glory and gloom that would find their
way into the later volumes of *Modern Painters*. It was a meticulous
record of scenery and sensation to work from, but there is nothing, of
course, of marital strain or the duress of separation. "I wonder at the
lightness of these entries, now;" he wrote as he quoted from them in

Praeterita, "but I was too actively, happily, and selfishly busy, to be thoughtful, except only in a scholarly way."[2]

But though Ruskin's feelings may have been comparatively disengaged, or were remembered as having been so, not all the entries were marked by lightness. Some, like the Naples impression of 1842, bear witness to a malevolent power at work in nature.[3] One entry, for instance, written at Saint Martin in July 1849, noted a "strange contrast" between the stricken valleys thereabouts, "with their overwrought richness mixed with signs of waste and disease, and their wild noon-winds shaking their leaves into palsy and their black clouds and dark storms folding themselves about their steep mural precipices" compared with the "pastoral green and ice, and pure arguilles and white fleecy rainclouds of Chamouni."[4] Years later Ruskin selected this passage for quotation and analysis in *Praeterita*, adding then that the action of this "malignant" noon wind caused not only distortion in vegetation but "abortion of human form and mind" in the region.[5] This sense of nature, not as perfection of organic form but as ominous, destructive, perhaps apocalyptic manifestations, figures in a number of other entries from the Swiss tour of 1849. From among these I wish to cite one other that Ruskin also drew upon for this portion of his autobiography. Here is his impression of the fall of the Arveron against a Turnerian background of "grisly clouds."

I got out, however, before dinner to-day, during a fair blink which lasted just long enough to let me, by almost running and leaping all the streams, reach the end of the pinewood next the source of the Arveron. In order to see the waterfall, I had then to turn to the left to the wooden bridge over the Arveron; when behold a sight new to me. An avalanche had evidently taken place from the glacier into the very bed of the great cataract and the consequence was that the stream was as nearly choked as could be with *balls and ellipsoids* of ice, from the size of its common stones to that of a portmanteau, which were rolling down with it wildly, generally swinging out and in of the water as it waved; but when they came to the shallow parts, tumbled and tossed over one another and then plunging back into the deep water like so many stranded porpoises, spinning as they went down and showing their dark backs with wilder swings after their plunge—white, as they emerged—black, owing to their clearness, as seen in the water; the stream itself of a pale clay colour, opaque, larger by one half than ever I saw it and running, as I suppose, not less than ten miles an hour; the whole mass, water and ice, looking like some thick paste full of plums, or ill-made pineapple ice with quantities of fruit in it; and the whole, looking like a solid body (for the nodules of ice hardly changed their relative position during the quarter of a minute they were severally in sight) going down in a mass, thundering and rumbling against the bottom and the shore, and the piles of the bridge. It made one giddy to look at it;

and this the more, because on raising the eye, there was the great cataract itself, every time it was seen, startling one as if it had just begun, or were increasing every instant, like a large avalanche; bounding and hurling itself hither and thither, as if it was striving to dash itself to pieces, not falling because it could not help it—and behind, there was a fearful storm coming up by the Breven, its grisly clouds warping up, as it seemed, against the river and cataract, and pillars of hail behind. I staid till it began, and then crept back in the pinewood, running from one tree to another. With a few pauses I got through it, thanks to the small leaves of the pines, and there is really, now, a bit of blue sky over the Pavillon, and a general lightness in the clouds, which look more hopeful than anything these five days.[6]

An earlier passage in the same diary entry casts considerable light on the source of the apocalyptic tone in Ruskin's description of the cascade. Commenting on his activities of the preceding day, Ruskin wrote, "I have been abstracting the book of Revelations." This remark is followed immediately by a parenthetical comment on the progress of the revolution and outbreaks on the continent: "They say the French are beaten again at Rome, and another revolution in Paris; many signs seem to multiply around us, and yet, my unbelief no more yields than when all the horizon was clear." And then back to Revelations: "I was especially struck with the general appelation of the System of the world as the Mystery of God, in Chap. X.7, compared with Hebrews XI.6, which chapter I read this morning in our usual course. Theme enough for the day's thought."[7] Ruskin's note to this same passage as it is used in *Praeterita* makes clear what larger theme he had in mind as he went out to the cascade. It invites us to read in succession Revelations 10:5, 6, and 7, the conclusion of which is that when the trumpet of the seventh angel begins to sound, "the mystery of God should be finished."[8]

Mystery, in the sense of an infinite complexity and subtlety of textures in an obscure design, an awful process of disintegration, was, like that of the cataract, Venice's hold upon Ruskin, mystery rather than mere beauty, sentiment, or romance. "You know I promised them no Romance, I promised them stones," he told his father, justifying the rarity of "fine writing" in *Stones*. "Not even bread. I do not *feel* any Romance in Venice. It is simply a heap of ruins, trodden under foot by such men as Ezekiel describes, XXI. 31; and *this* is the great fact which I want to teach,—to give Turneresque descriptions of the thing would not have needed ten days' study or residence. I believe that what I have done will be found useful at last."[9] Of course this condescending allusion to Turner would not have been possible after the understanding he would reach in the later volumes of *Modern Painters*; however, the reference to

Venice as a decaying city delivered to the wrath of God suggests that the city he had in mind to reveal in *Stones*, is an apocalyptic city, a city of the last days, its mystery nearly finished. Similarly in a letter written to Norton seven years later in 1859 he recalled that by the time his analysis of the city was completed he had lost nearly all joy of the place, that it had presented itself "merely as so many 'mouldings' " with "provocation from every sort of soul or thing in Venice at once."[10] What Ruskin actually did come to feel about Venice by 1852, as distinct from what he actually set down in *Stones*, cannot be reconstructed here, so great is the quantity of material he has left us in his diaries, letters, and ancillary matter to *Stones*.[11] Yet it is vital to give the reader some sense of the raw impressions he recorded for possible use. These too are part of his writing.

Although Ruskin declared that the materials for *Stones* had been gathered during six visits to Venice between 1835 and 1852, the main research for the book was carried out on the scene during the winters of 1849–50 and 1851–52. They were seasons of intense, unremitting, and sometimes agonizing work. He remembered, much later, the "pain of frost-bitten finger and chilled throat as [he] examined or drew the window-sills in the wintry air; puzzlement from said window sills which didn't agree with the doorsteps, or back of house which didn't agree with front."[12]

Effie accompanied him both seasons, and during the second winter the couple even set up house in a furnished apartment on the Grand Canal. The intervening season in London (1850–51) had seen the Ruskins involved in a social life of increasing complexity and elevation, the most relevant feature of which was their relationships with Carlyle and Millais. Similarly, in Venice, now Austrianized, there were evenings of elegance and glitter that saw Effie reigning and John retiring at half past ten. But this is a story that has been told elsewhere. We need merely observe here that so much gaiety must have been a strain, part of the "provocation," to the writer feverishly attempting to systematize an infinity of "mouldings" searching for the signs in stone of the cohesion and dilapidation of a once vital society.

The record of the diaries has little or nothing of this evening levity but is heavy with the weight of eroding textures closely read. There is copious evidence of his intense and intimate examination of his objects; of his sketching, measuring, and touching. And more, the diaries show that Ruskin and the objects of his study were both caught, like Thomas Mann's Aschenbach and Tadzio, in a larger situation brimming with ominous implications. For the diaries record not only the physical decline of nineteenth-century Venice evidenced by the inundation of its stones but also its moral decay, and the inevitable consequence of this combination casts its shadow over the aesthetic evolution Ruskin wishes to trace. Cook rightly discerns several implications in the title of *Stones*: touchstones of architecture, beautiful and vicious; dilapidation; the hardness of the subject. Of the many notes suggesting the dimensions of his subjective awareness of Venice (Ruskin himself declared that some six hundred quarto pages of notes remained unused when the book was finished), I must limit myself to a mere handful set down with minimal commentary so as to indicate the problem of coherence he faced.

An entry for late November 1849, describing the ruins of a Venetian house, shows two qualities of his Venetian notes, tragic yet picturesque dilapidation of the fallen city coupled with close observation of sculptured detail especially in terms of its naturalism.

> This house—one of the most neglected—is also one of the loveliest in Venice. The sun, in winter, touches only the angle of the court into the depth of which it is withdrawn; and when the light is warm on the fondaco de'Tedeschi, the dews of the night still hang upon the eagle wings of its capitals, and the heavy moisture makes its broken stair slippery and cold, and brings out into continual green the wild herbage of its crannies. There is deeper green than theirs in the Verd antique, precious, and veined with pure white, which surrounds its peaked windows as if with a moat of the Venetian sea; the golden brown of their dentils, and the rich dark ornament of the arch beside them are set with a Titian-like warmth and mystery beside those bands of green. One prism of pure white only shines in the point of one of these arches; but all in the last stage of habitable ruin. The wind whistles through the rotten door which protects the access to the staircase, withered flowers and broken flowerpots lie in heaps about the landing, and the rain from the granite dripstone soaks into the mud and sand which has choked its pavement.[13]

The entry for 30 December 1849 attempts a verbal Turner in its imagery of environmental decay under solemn red light, serene sky, and Alpine horizon far above.

> I was to-day rambling—or rather running—among the quiet and melancholy canals which extend between the Madonna dell' Orto and Sta. Fosca: the winter sun glowing on the deep red brick, and the canal beneath turned into a chasm of light, divided into sharp squares of blue and vermillon, as if the houses were standing on a scarlet carpet. They are lonely and stagnant canals, bordered for the most part by the dead walls of gardens—now waste ground—or by patches of dark mud, with decayed black gondolas lying keel upmost, sinking into the putrid and black ground gradually; or by remnants of palace wall, never finished, of which the doors and the angle shafts alone remain. Farther on one comes to detached groups of low and filthy houses, with mud paths trodden hard

between them; but through their dark alleys I saw the horizontal brightness of the lagoon sunshine and over the hard frozen snow made my way down to the shore. The sky was all serene white blue; the lagoon, as calm as a mirror, reflected it in a metallic aqua marine; only its strong tide was seen gliding and curdling in one flat mass of shallow water that seemed to move altogether, without break or wave, and the far away islands seemed gliding the opposite way. The water was not bright, only lustrous and of delicate metallic colour, for the sun was too low to make it luminous, and the lower sky was hazy, and all of deep tone—so deep that Murano and St. Cristoforo, which caught the sunset light full, seemed coming out of the dark haze in one long bar of crimson light, which the eye felt—even when it was directed elsewhere—in its constant and intense presence. Far away out of the mist, the endless range of the Alps lifted their jagged ridge of silver: melting into orange light towards the west, where the flat mainland showed its dark line across their ghostly distance, the single square mass of the Church of Mestre being the only object that broke its monotony. Close beside me, the green clear sea water lay quietly among the muddy shingles of the level shore, so calm that it made a little islet at the edge of it, of every stone: as clear as a mountain stream, and with here and there a large block of marble marking the outmost foundations of Venice.[14]

The entry for 10 January 1850 presents the kind of architectural revelation that was central to the thematic development of *Stones*.

> CAPITALS—FRIEZES. I saw in St. Mark's to-day the entire derivation of the Byzantine from the Corinthian capital. From the Byzantine comes the leaf frieze, directly; the cornices of Murano, St. Mark's and Dandolo's house are *nothing* but the leaves of a Byzantine imitation Corinthian, unrolled and laid along. Now to show this properly I must draw one of the St. Mark's capitals in its foliage part, thoroughly, (with the steps). Then, the capitals gradually become Lombardic, and the plinths take the *rose*, and become luxuriant; and when they have become rich, they are again twined round the capital and form the luxuriant Venetian as the other formed the Corinthian. Thus in Venice nothing can be more simple than the derivation of their Gothic—whatever it may be in the north.[15]

Another part of the same entry records another architectural revelation; in this case Renaissance moral decline is being read out of the characterization of children on two sequences of capitals (Gothic against Renaissance, presumably) of the Ducal Palace.

> The Doge's Palace: Series of Capitals. . . . It is highly interesting to compare the children on this fourth [capital] with those on the Piazzetta side. Those on the fourth are full of childish life, playful, human, affectionate, full of *sensation* and vivacity, with much manliness and firmness, and not a little treachery, and perhaps some hardness and cruelty lurking under all; but they will be thorough men when they grow up; they will do great things and fierce ones—and perhaps some vile ones. But those on the

other side are dull, curly haired, barbered dunces, without a spark in their dim eyes or a meaning line in their fat stolid cheeks. They will grow up into perfumed coxcombs and will spend their lives in thoughts of snuff and brocade, or in gambling and fiddling.[16]

Further on in the same entry the character of contemporary Venice is disclosed in a description of the wares being sold at the portals of Saint Mark's. A vendor of toys and a bookseller block Ruskin's work at the church door, and his reaction is to note the ironic contradiction of values represented by the titles of the books displayed against the church.

As I was measuring the northern or atrium door [of St. Mark's] I was grievously impeded on one side by a seller of children's playthings—baby services of pewter spoons and wooden dishes being mixed with dolls in black masks (about 6 inches high, for the carnival) and on the other side by a bookseller, whose store of literature was laid out in goodly show between the square bases of the shafts. I noted down the titles of the first row, or group, as they lay, thus:
Storia del Testamento vecchio
Brevissima parafrasi de' Salmi di David
Commedie Buffe in Prosa del Sig. Carlo Goldoni . . . .[17]

The entry for 13 October 1851 offers a strange vignette describing a Venetian seaman, a kind of primitive, glad and big, in a street encounter with three cadaverous degenerates of the day.

Yesterday I was walking from the Rialto to the Apostoli, and a man came after me—the noblest fellow I have yet seen in Venice. His face, in expression something like Brockedon's, but one fourth as large again; the eyes large and black, the hair of negro blackness, like charcoal; the complexion like a hazel nut, or darker—between toast and chocolate; a grey round cap of rough cloth on the head, a rich brown rough thick jacket—the ordinary fisherman's—thrown over his shoulders, his arms not in it, but in the sleeves of a pink thinly striped shirt, quite clean, down even to the wrists, and full over his breast; his trousers of coarse blue cloth, quite clean, and strong, though like some good sails, not without mending, a huge patch, especially behind.
He was rolling along the street with a sailor gait, throwing a word of jest right and left to every one as he passed. At last he broke heavily into a group of three thin, dirty, ragged men, in the sort of dress that would be worn by gentlemen—coats and hats, &c.—but all ragged, greasy, worn, filthy and foul, and ill put on—unbuttoned; not from poverty, but the look that the dress of a man gets who is always in the lowest dissipation. They were smoking and spitting, the animals, sallow faced and small, and I suppose within a few years of their graves at five-and-thirty or thereabouts. My brown friend rolled in among them, and they tried to banter him, and pulled open a paper parcel he had in his hand, containing a goodly steak just bought at the Beccaria. He took hold of one of them by the long beard, gathered up the dirty piece of tow in his brawny fist till he had screwed the

man's jaws into a regular lock, and shook him—though good humouredly always—till I thought the cadaverous wretch would have gone into powder like a Prince Rupert's drop. But the giant quitted his hold of him just in time, and rolled away down the narrow street, jesting as before. The sufferer relaxed his features into a laugh and made the best of it.[18]

On 19 November of the same year Ruskin catches the effect of a Turnerian sunset on Venice and the viewer.

> There was a lovely scene this evening out by San Giorgio in Aliga. It had been raining nearly all night, and was very foul weather to-day and wretchedly cold, and the snow was down on the hills, nearly to the plains; and there was the strange snow mist upon them, not cloud, but a kind of dense light breaking into flakes and wreaths; and the upper precipices came gleaming out here and there fitfully in the haze, their jagged edges burning like lightning, then losing themselves again in blue bars of cloud; to the north disappearing altogether in one mass of leaden grey, against which the whole line of Venice came out in broad red light. As the sun set, there were fiery flakes and streams of long cloud brought out from this grey veil, and the lagoon flowed and rippled under them in great sheets of rose colour, with ripples of green. The seagulls were sailing and flitting by towards the south; not the common shrieking gull, but one that gives a low, clear, plaintive whistle of two short notes, dying upon the salt wind like a far away human voice. And at last, as the sun went down, he sank behind a bank of broken clouds which threw up their shadows as on the opp[osite] page [sketch], on dark grey, horizontal, soft bands of vapour, the clear sky seen through—shadowless. When the sun had sunk, the shadows disappeared, but the grey bands became blood colour, and so remained, glowing behind the towers of St. Eufemia, as I rowed back up the Giudecca, grown purpler and darker gradually, till their deep crimson became a dark colour on the clear sky behind. Note that at this time of evening, one may have down on the horizon grey cold clouds, and across them bars of dead crimson of a depth which is *light* upon the grey cloud, but dark against the soft amber of the sky.[19]

The last entry for the year is, simply, "Turner buried."[20]

2

The painter had died on 19 December with, Ruskin heard, the last rays of the setting sun on his face; his murmured final words were "The sun is God." Ruskin would comment later on the significance of these words as a testament of Turner's solar faith, but at this point he was himself still such a Sabbatarian that he had yet to draw his first sketch on "The Day of the Sun." Despite the aggressive sectarianism of his *Notes on the Construction of Sheepfolds*, published that year, his letters and diaries of this period (1849–1853) show that his fervid Protestantism had begun to erode. On the other hand his private religious studies deepened as he became discontented with public observances. At Venice, for instance, while at work on *Stones,* he also wrote for his own uses a ninety-page commentary on Job.

In "The Grande Chartreuse" chapter of *Praeterita* Ruskin dismisses, with retrospective exaggeration, the whole decade of the fifties as "for the most part wasted in useless work" but chronicles with some care the gradual breakdown of his faith as being of greatest interest to his readers.[21] And so it is, for the vacuum left by the disappearance of his Protestant fervor was to be filled by a growing interest in myth and a deepening social awareness. We will trace this changing commitment in greater detail as we proceed; for the present some quotations from his diaries will serve to suggest some of the nuances of Ruskin's religious position during the writing of *The Stones of Venice.*

Among the diary entries of this period a number deal explicitly with impressions of religious observance (as distinct from comments on scripture or nature). These include several memoranda of sermons heard while he was at home during the spring and summer of 1850. In April he accompanied his mother to hear Henry Melvill preach on the text "Behold I have given him for a Witness." (Isaiah 55:4) "Quoting the prophecy that the word should be preached for a witness among all nations and then shall the end come, he showed that the word was a Witness wherever it was preached, asserting, in a most awakening and glorious way, the manner in which both the pastor and the Bible shall judge at the last day, those who have not received the word. I was myself deeply struck by his assertion that the Spirit was always present to guide the Word, if we would not Grieve it. . . ." Ruskin went on to say that he felt this sermon laid to his heart and promised himself either to get a copy of it or to write it out more fully, closing the entry with "Turner. Errors in. See if he draws sunlight diverging to horizon." The next entry (he had not written another until July 1850) speaks of a sermon on the text "My people shall never be ashamed" and of his own determination to "live so as to be able to preach unblushingly," but then tells of the transience of these impressions: "I have forgotten the *above* sermon."[22]

If these two entries record comparatively soothing, even uplifting, experiences with sermons, the next on this subject (not made until late August) expresses his disgust with bad preaching. At Edinburgh he heard two grating sermons: "one from pure Scotch, the other high Puseyite—the former the most offensive, the latter the least useful." While the Scotsman mispronounced his words and padded his time with specious divisions and pious excelsior, the Episcopalian "in a quieter and more decorous, but still more trashy and drivelling, fashion spoiled Deuteronomy." The experience launched Ruskin, still in the same entry, into a brief sermon to himself on the endurance of "dead Talk" from the pulpit.

> Really I believe the only good of such sermons is the self-denial exercised in hearing them. How wrong our whole system is—when people come together at ringing of a bell, to hear a man talk for an hour in set phrases about something on which he has nothing to say. That something being, however the most important of all somethings; and sitting patiently under a piece of dead Talk which would not be endured for one instant if it regarded any real business of life and is only endured because Christianity is not considered business at all. I wonder how St. Paul would have liked being shown up into a box and told that he might talk about Christ till lunchtime—if he would do it decorously. I wish we had the old synagogue habit again—men and brethren—'If you have any word of exhortation for the people, say on—on until midnight if you will—but if you have not—(in the name of Time and Eternity both) go about your business where you have it if such creatures as you have business anywhere.'[23]

Among the letters of this period, one written to his father from Venice in January 1852 is particularly interesting for the position Ruskin took on the relation between the form and content of revelation. Replying to some religious doubts intimated by his father, Ruskin endeavored to set forth the state of his own mind with regard to religion. He said he did not, as John James did, find such mysteries as the Trinity or Redemption at all threatened by "abstract reasonings." He could accept these *as* mysteries. "But on the other hand," he continued,

> while I am ready to receive any amount of mystery in *What* is revealed, I don't at all like mystery in the *manner* of revealing it. The *doctrine* is *God's* affair. But the revelation is *mine,* and it seems to me that from a God of Light and Truth, His creatures have a right to expect plain and clear revelation touching all that concerns their immortal interests. And this is the great question with me—whether indeed the Revelation *be* clear, and Men are blind, according to that "He hath blinded their eyes and hardened their hearts"; or whether there be not also some strange darkness in the manner of Revelation itself.[24]

His circular conclusion is that this shadowing of the mystery is by design. That revelation is dependent upon conduct. The more man strays from God's ways, the more revelation is obscured and vice versa. The darker the revelation, the greater has been our deviation.

Another letter, also to his father, written on Good Friday of that year, described Ruskin's state of spiritual depression and anxiety about his own health. Examining his past work he finds it selfish: it was undertaken for ambition, "or to gratify my affections in pleasing you and my mother," nothing really done "for God's service." Thoughts of his scriptural investigations give him no comfort either ("For there seemed to me nothing but darkness and doubt in it"), and the more he dwells on these matters the more his health seems to sink. Sleepless and queasy at two o'clock in the morning, deeply anxious lest another respiratory attack should cut short his research in Venice, he yields up religious questions in despair: "So I considered that I had now neither pleasure in looking to my past life, nor any hope, such as would be any comfort to me on a sick-bed, of a future one. And I made up my mind that this would never do."

But the letter goes on to explain how further meditation induced a mildly regenerative experience. It could hardly be called a leap of faith. Considering, he writes, that "to disbelieve the Bible was quite as difficult as to believe it," and that there were mysteries either way, he determined at least to gamble on the Bible's truth. "I resolved that at any rate I would act as if the Bible *were* true." He would take "Christ for a Master" in life and let that gift be a sufficient comfort. This conclusion reached, he fell into peaceful sleep and awoke the next morning in good health. Since this experience, he assures his father that everything had seemed to go well with him, "all discouragement and difficulties vanishing even in the smallest things."[25]

Continuing with the same subject two days later, on Easter Day, Ruskin appears secure enough in the spiritual shelter he has just erected to attempt a kind of antiscientific postscript. Had it not been for the experience just related, he declared, he might have taken the position of the modern scientific men, who, while they may accept the necessity of believing in "a God," give up the Bible as unscientific (not "arranged in a scientific manner, or capable of being tried by scientific tests") "and are fortified in their infidelity by the weaknesses and hypocrisies of so-called religious men." Such men give up nearly all hope of futurity and set themselves to improve this world as best they can. But Ruskin, his letter seems to be saying, finds nothingness harder to accept than the Bible: "I cannot understand the make of minds that can do without a hope of the future." So despite immense difficulties of belief felt at the moment ("No scientific difficulty will ever be cast in my teeth greater than at this moment I feel the geological difficulty: no moral difficulty greater than that which I now feel in the case of prophecies so obscure that they may mean *anything*, like the oracles of old."), he has chosen, after deep meditation on death, the road of belief as the least difficult for him. The regenerative experience described in the previous letter has convinced him that this is his God-appointed road: "Which having taken, I do not intend, with His help, ever to look back."[26]

Despite his protestation of spiritual comfort, these letters do not suggest a secure spiritual position but rather a man adrift on pieces of religious wreckage. He is confessing, here in 1852, to a faith by inversion rather than affirmation: he must believe in an afterlife because he cannot do without it; he will behave as if the Bible were true because he finds it more difficult to behave as if it were not. His belief, he appears to be saying, derives from dependence on certain mental comforts. He has moved to the position of a man with certain vestiges of religion but without positive foundations of church and creed. Thrown back upon personal religious experience, he is desperate for some kind of revelation; this is why he clutches rather pathetically at the overnight recovery from the apparent onset of a cold (on Good Friday) as a manifestation of God's will for him. On the other hand, he seems to have acknowledged the discontinuity between reasoned faith and lived faith; his religion was becoming more existential, following that process of development toward a religion of the lived-world he described much later in *Praeterita*: "I grew also daily more sure that the peace of God rested on all the dutiful and kindly hearts of the laborious poor; and that the only constant form of pure religion was in useful work, faithful love, and stintless charity."[27] Finally, this urge to integrate, somehow, belief and being would lead Ruskin not only to such attempts to set forth the principles of a belief in life (as opposed to a belief in death and beyond) but further, sustained by his continuing interest in the iconology of art, to a far more liberal sympathy with the universal and archetypal manifestations of man's religious experience. He would develop a tolerant curiosity about the expressions of any system of belief, whether Catholic, Greek, or Islamic, by which men have lived.

The fact that Ruskin's religious thought was moving toward this kind of pan-mythic liberalism by 1852 is shown by an astonishing passage in the chapter he devoted to the church of Murano in the second volume of *Stones*. The whole building, he concludes after a long appraisal, is "simply a temple to the Virgin: to her is ascribed the fact of Redemption, and to her its praise."[28] But are we, he asks himself, to look back upon this time of fervid Mariolatry with reverence and regret for its loss? Insofar as the Virgin was worshipped instead of God, by no means; but insofar as this building signifies worship and the sense of numinous presence, yes.

> For there is a wider division of men than that into Christian and Pagan: before we ask what a man worships, we have to ask whether he worships at all. . . . Therefore, there is first the broad division of men into Spirit

worshippers and Flesh worshippers; and then, of the Spirit worshippers, the farther division into Christian and Pagan,—worshippers in Falsehood or in Truth. I therefore, for the moment, omit all inquiry how far the Mariolatry of the early Church did indeed eclipse Christ. . . . Let that worship be taken at its worst; let the goddess of this dome of Murano be looked up as just in the same sense an idol as the Athene of the Acropolis, or the Syrian Queen of Heaven; and then, on this darkest assumption, balance well the difference between those who worship and those who worship not.[29]

Not perhaps, to us, a remarkably liberal perspective, but a surprising departure from the Protestant narrowness that marred *The Seven Lamps of Architecture*. Only one worship is allowed to be true, but any worship is nearer to truth than no worship. This awakening pan-mythic interest opened the way to more profound questions about belief and art than the strict sectarian could admit.

3

The primary importance of Ruskin's religious perspective to *Stones* is revealed by his own explanations of the work's purview. From these it appears that he saw art through religion, and social history through art; that is, in its large outline *Stones* is apocalyptic social history, a vast metaphor in which the vehicle is Venetian art and the tenor is Ruskin's religion. Looked at more closely the book is much more, for its focus is on particulars and on the poetics and techniques of organic architecture. But his résumés of the book's structure, though misleading as to its texture, will provide a good point of entry into our discussion of it.

The preface that Ruskin wrote for the first edition (1851) does not contain a structural analysis of the work. Instead it calls attention to two of its important textual features: its authority, deriving from first-hand observation, and its simplicity of style. The reader, he supposes, may notice certain discrepancies between his observations and those of predecessors: "for which discrepancies I may be permitted to give this single and sufficient reason, that my account of every building is based on personal examinations and measurement of it."[30] (Of course he does not consider that what truly mattered in his account were those correlating impressions that could not be measured, or, strictly speaking, observed.) His defense of the work's comparative plainness of style is that he is more anxious to be understood than enjoyed: "Though I may often be found trite or tedious, I trust I shall not be obscure. I am especially anxious to rid this essay of ambiguity, because I want to gain the ear of all kinds of persons."[31]

The second preface, that to the third edition (1874), was written in the bitter knowledge that the work had in fact gained many ears but had been misheard by most of them. While Ruskin admits that no book of his has had so much influence on contemporary art as *Stones* has had, he deplores the fact that this influence derives entirely from the third part of the book and is therefore perverse, the main part of the book's message having been largely ignored. In order to explain this he gives a brief summary of the work, showing how it was meant to be read.

By way of introduction to this analysis, and, as it were, explaining the need for it, he gives two brief illustrations of his own encounters with the book's abortive influence; both are interesting as ironic symbols. In the first instance, while traveling through Ealing and watching the ominous "red light fade through gaps left between the rows of new houses which spring up everywhere," he is startled by what appears to be a piece of fine Italian Gothic looming up between himself and the fading radiance. Aha! This architect has read his *Stones of Venice*, thinks Ruskin. "But this good and true piece of brickwork was the porch of a public house, and its total motive was the provocation of thirst, and the encouragement of idleness."[32]

In the second instance, walking over the Kew Bridge at twilight and having in mind the speech of the Thames river god in Pope's *Windsor Forest*, he is surprised to see what appears to be a circular temple, lately built, thirty or forty times the size of the temple of Vesta (so called) at Rome or that of the sibyl at Tivoli and resembling both in a general way. "Its dark walls and singularly tall and narrow columns rose sublimely against the twilight at the extremity of the longer reach of the stream, and presented at once a monument to the art and religion of the children of the Thames." This "temple" on closer inspection turned out to be "no less beauteous a work of peace than the new gasometer of (I presume) the Bentford Gas Company, Limited." Finally, the two instances are drawn together in a bitter assault on the very possibility of art in a nation that so desecrates the gifts of its God; "which mimics the architecture of Christians to promote the trade of poisoners; and imagines itself philosophical in substituting the worship of coal gas for that of Vesta."[33]

It must be remembered that the prophetic irony, the opposition of ancient and modern modes of "worship," and the solar images are those of a later Ruskin whose religion and hopes have altered and who has lived to be derided by his own influence. This experience is evident in the brief analysis of *Stones* that follows in this preface, where emphasis shifts away from the Gothic style and Christian faith as particular models to the more general terms of the relation of the workman to his work and the morality of a state to the quality of its architecture. The first volume is described as being simply "an analysis of the best structure of stone and brick building, on a simple and natural scale."[34] It is recommended to any youth who wishes to understand the basic principles of noble building but is dismissed as being "of no use to any modern builder" because it ignores all uses of iron except as a means of bonding stone to stone. The other two volumes, he explains, "show how the rise and fall of the Venetian builder's art depended upon the moral or immoral temper of the State."[35] This he observes, but without reference to Christianity here, was the main work of the book. However, it accomplished along the way two subsidiary purposes: on the basis of medieval practice it explained the necessary relation of any worker to his work, and it traced the evolution of Venetian Gothic from earliest Romanesque forms to its decline in the classical revival of the sixteenth century. But modern readers have ignored the first two themes, the "chief subject" and "most important practical principle" respectively, in favor of the third and *least* significant message of the book, "its exhibition of the transitional forms of Arabian and Byzantine architecture adopted by the Christian faith and Gothic mind."[36] They have simply used the book as a resource piece for style, ignoring the deeper message of the style with such pernicious results as the Gothic pub and temple of gas mentioned earlier.

If this thematic analysis of *Stones*, which is the main point of the preface to the third edition, may be said to de-emphasize the religious in favor of the moral and social implications of the work, quite the opposite is true of the two résumés that Ruskin incorporated into the work itself at the time of its original publication. In these summaries Ruskin appears to see the progress of Gothic architecture in medieval Europe almost entirely in terms of a conflict of religious (or mythic) forces.

Along with the third volume of *Stones* Ruskin published a "Venetian Index" in which he attempted to list all buildings of any significance in or near Venice and to provide brief critical notices of all those which he had not dealt with in the text itself. As part of the "Explanatory Note" prefixed to the Index he attempted a formal résumé of the whole of *Stones* partly, as he said, to spare the reader the trouble of interpretation and partly to forestall such efforts by his reviewers. A reviewer for *The Builder*, for instance, had announced with an air of "discovery" that "if Mr. Ruskin be right, all the architects, and all the architectural teaching of the last three hundred years, must have been wrong."[37] But this is precisely the case, and further, Ruskin insists, it is a point he had made over and over again in the book: "I believe the architects of the last three centuries to have been wrong; wrong without exception; wrong totally, and from the foundation."[38] It is to prevent such conclusions from being either overlooked by readers or co-opted by critics that he attempts in this résumé to put his entire thesis into "unmistakable form." A glance at it would serve the dual function of showing what Ruskin hoped he had proved at the time and the extent to which his thesis was determined by his religious perspective.

He begins this summary of *Stones* by confidently setting aside all architecture down to the time of Christ. Although many of these pre-Christian styles were good considering the times and races from which they derived, none was so near to perfection as to be worthy to become the one style for all time. However, "the advent of Christianity for the first time rendered possible the full development of the soul of man, and therefore the full development of the arts of man." Not only did Christianity give birth to a new and superior architecture, Ruskin proposes, it also conceived the first perfect and permanent architecture, "demonstrably the best architecture that *can* exist; perfect in construction and decoration, and fit for the practice of all time."[39] Now this Christian architecture, he continues, generally called "Gothic," although perfect in ideal conception, never actualized its full perfection because of various extraneous corrupting influences; however, about the close of the thirteenth century it came nearest to perfection, and by this, Ruskin believed, it indicated the peculiar vitality of the European Christian mind at the time. During the course of the fifteenth century, however, through causes that are traced in *Stones*, "The Christianity of Europe was undermined; and a Pagan architecture was introduced, in imitation of that of the Greeks and Romans." This "Pagan" architecture had once been natural and coherent with the uses of its time and place, but the derivative classical architecture, first introduced in the fifteenth century and practiced since, could never be good or natural. "It was good in no respect, and for no time. All the architects who have built in that style have built what was worthless; and therefore the greater part of the architecture which has been built for the last three hundred years, and which we are now building, is worthless." In this Ruskin sounds like Frank Lloyd Wright, but not in his conclusion: we must give up this pseudoclassical style utterly "and build henceforward only in that perfect and Christian style hitherto called Gothic, which is everlastingly the best." This, he concludes, "is the theorem of these volumes."[40]

There is no need to enlarge here on the point that when Ruskin gets down to particulars on the Gothic he plainly derives his theory of its permanence (the only style that *can* be) from its organic integrity and purity rather than from its Christian associations. Yet to judge from this résumé alone one would think he really saw architecture only as a manifestation of the struggle for supremacy among mythologies. One gets a similar impression from the survey of his subject included in the first chapter of *Stones* itself. He opens his chapter, entitled "The Quarry," with a general historical sketch of Venice from 421 to 1508, drawing the primary conclusion that the failure of Venetian political ascendency was precisely coincident with the loss of private religion. The cause of this joint decline was the stopping short of personal faith when it appeared likely to influence national policy, a condition, he suggests, that is strikingly correspondent "with several characteristics of the temper of our present English legislature."[41] Turning from political to aesthetic history, he finds that between the birth dates of Bellini and Titian the "vital," though not the formal, religion of Venice expired. This change is manifested in Venetian painting by the gradual subordination of religious subjects to the temporal purposes of decoration and portraiture for the world's sake. It is a principle of treatment that governs even the work of Tintoretto, though his mind, Ruskin allows, "casts the solemnity of its own tone over the sacred subjects it approaches, and sometimes forgets itself into devotion."[42] With architecture the conditions of decline are more complex yet equally determined by the currents of national faith.

The Greek Doric and Corinthian orders were the roots of all European architecture, he explains. These two orders, which were clumsily imitated and varied by the pagan Romans, solidly improved upon in the West by Roman Christians, and illuminated by the idolatrous "corpse-light" of the Byzantine Christian imagination in the East, finally settled into an embalmed repose. Thus, as the empire declined, two great branches of Christian architecture developed: Romanesque and Byzantine. Both, Ruskin argues, as true continuations of the Roman tradition, might be called Christian Romanesque, "an architecture which had lost the refinement of Pagan art in the degradation of the Empire, but which was elevated by Christianity to higher aims, and by the fancy of the Greek workmen endowed with brighter forms."[43] A note to this section in the edition of 1879 corrects the "great error" of grouping the Byzantine and Romanesque together "for simplicity." The Byzantine, he had by then realized, was "pure Greek in decline" and the Roman "was sensualized and brutalized into forms which developed the Northern fleshly or naturalist instincts."[44] While the pure Romanesque was being practiced in languid refinement at Rome and Constantinople, he continues, "patois" forms of it were being carried by inferior workmen to the barbarous outskirts of the empire; so, even as the refined forms were becoming enervated by sensuality and idolatry, "the living light rose upon both horizons, and the fierce swords of the Lombard and Arab were shaken over its golden paralysis."[45] It was the business of the Lombard architects, Ruskin argues, to give vitality and system to the enfeebled architecture of Christendom, and of the Arab architects to purge it of all traces of idolatry: the former by adding lavish use of life imagery; the latter by banishing the same. Hence two powerful stylistic streams, alike in energy but opposed in purpose, converged upon Italy from the North and South and collided at Venice (at different periods): "The very centre of the struggle, the point of pause of both, the dead water of the opposite eddies, charged with embayed fragments of the Roman wreck, is VENICE." The Ducal Palace represents the Roman, Lombard, and Arab styles in equal proportions and is "the central building of the world."[46]

This convergence of styles did not take place at once, of course, but during successive historical periods. The succession of Venetian styles began with a primitive phase of pure Romano-Christian architecture of which few if any traces remain. This was followed by a Byzantine-Arabic period that was the *first* true Venetian style and is the subject of the first division of Ruskin's book. This style, he believed, was succeeded by a "transitional" style, still more distinctly Arabian, but limited to secular architecture and centered on the year 1180. Underlying both Eastern styles, however, was a strange and primitive (Southern) system of Gothic that made its way into ecclesiastical architecture. Gradually, under Northern or Lombard influence, the transitional style of civil and domestic architecture was transformed into Gothic, and a *second* or Gothic style, consisting of two separate systems, flourished in high purity between the thirteenth and fifteenth centuries. Then, suddenly, this Gothic efflorescence became diseased: "All Gothics in existence, southern or northern, were corrupted at once,"[47] the chief symptoms of this infection being extravagant and meaningless ornamentation. This *third* phase was the plague of Renaissance rationalism which kept the arts but cast out their religious content. "Instant degradation followed in every direction,—a flood of folly and hypocrisy. Mythologies ill understood at first, then perverted into feeble sensualities, take the place of the representations of Christian subjects. . . . Gods without power, satyrs without rusticity, nymphs without innocence, men without humanity, gather into idiot groups upon the polluted canvas, and scenic affectations encumber the streets with preposterous marble."[48]

The myths themselves do not corrupt; the Renaissance mind corrupts the myths, for it does not believe in any power but its own. This is a condition, as the other résumé makes clear, that Ruskin believed had continued to his own day, but whose whole development was epitomized at Venice. "Now Venice, as she was once the most religious, was in her fall the most corrupt, of European states; and as she was in her strength the centre of the pure currents of Christian architecture, so she is in her decline the source of the Renaissance." And so the prophetic task before him is clear: "It is in Venice, therefore, and in Venice only that effectual blows can be struck at this pestilent art of the Renaissance. Destroy its claims for admiration there, and it can assert them nowhere else. This, therefore, will be the final purpose of the following essay."[49]

It should be apparent that each of Ruskin's own analyses of *Stones* differs from the others in important respects, though together they serve us well as an introduction to the subject. All stress the importance of architecture as an index of moral and mythological crisis. The résumé of the "Venetian Index" is most dogmatic in identifying the purity of architecture with Christianity; the résumé of "The Quarry" is less Christian in its emphasis and focuses attention on the perverse effects of rationalism; while the preface of 1879 points more liberally to the moral temper of the state and the involvement of the laborer. But where, among these, is the real meaning of *Stones*? One point is clear: Ruskin cannot convey the full meaning of the work in his summaries alone, because this meaning derives from implication as well as statement. Like any work of literature it comprises an interaction of structural and textural effects. The larger meaning of the work is not in its argument but in the way its truths are made to glimmer in epiphany through closely observed architectural details.

Ruskin himself gives an example, later on in his first chapter, of the way this kind of meaning works in the book. He is comparing the workmanship in two pillar capitals of the Ducal Palace, the ninth and twenty-ninth in his system of numbering. The ninth is a respectable piece of fourteenth-century work, the twenty-ninth an inferior fifteenth-century imitation. They are decorated with figures representing the eight Virtues. In the earlier capital the Virtues are characterized as "hard featured" yet "vivid and living" in expression, but in the Renaissance copy the virtues have lost their hard features and vital expression; they have gained instead Roman noses and curled hair. More particularly, he comes to focus on the representation of Hope. In the fourteenth-century capital "Hope is praying, while above her hand is seen emerging from sun-beams—the hand of God (according to that of Revelations, 'The

Lord God giveth them light')." In the fifteenth-century version all the actions and symbols are preserved, Ruskin notices, "until we come to Hope; she is still praying, but she is praying to the sun only; *The hand of God is gone.*" This, he continues, may be taken as a sign of the spirit that was then dominant in the world, that had forgotten to see God's hand in the light. "Such," he concludes, "is the nature of the accidental evidence on which I shall depend for the proof of the inferiority of character in the Renaissance workmen."[50] Taken together from the perspective of the present, Ruskin's own various assessments and advertisements of *The Stones of Venice* appear to challenge us, in rereading his long argument, to hear him out on two primary matters: first, to note carefully what he takes to be the distinguishing features of vitality in architecture, especially of that one eternal style; second, to weigh as we go that "accidental evidence" of symbolic detail that he wishes us to receive as a revelation of decline. Stated more objectively, the central critical question about *Stones* is how does Ruskin's art make architecture seem apocalyptic of moral life and death?

4

The first volume of *Stones*, however, is of slight interest as literature or social thought. Ruskin seems to have felt compelled, perhaps over-compelled, to lay an absolute (objective) ground for further discussion by making his first volume a crystalline exposition of inevitable principles of organic construction in natural materials. It is only in the volume's final chapter, "The Vestibule," where he leaves off technical abstractions and, after declaiming prophetically the right relationship between mind and nature, proceeds to take his reader by gondola into the actual looming presence of the Venice he knew, that his writing takes on color and becomes rich in overtones. Yet there are a few details in the stonier chapters that require notice because they are not simply descriptive of building technique but shaped by Ruskin's special bias.

The volume's first chapter, built around the historical survey already discussed, is followed by another introductory chapter, "The Virtues of Architecture." After censuring modern architecture for its hypocrisy (our builders do not build what they like but what they think they ought to like), he proceeds to lay down the two primary virtues of architectural decoration: "first, the signs of man's own good work," his honest taste; "secondly, the expression of man's delight in better work than his own."[51] Decoration—and decoration, as we have noted, *is* architecture for Ruskin,—should thus be "natural" in two basic senses. From this point the volume divides into two broad categories of discussion, principles of construction and of decoration.

Construction as a general subject leads Ruskin successively into six major "Divisions of Architecture": walls, piers, arches or lintels, roofs, buttresses, and apertures. These, in turn, are generally broken into subtopics according to the constructional features of the architectural element, that is, "The Pier Base," "The Shaft," "The Capital." In all, seventeen chapters are devoted to the logic of wood and stone construction. Although there is little stylistic color in this section and next to nothing about the actual practice of medieval builders, the chapters are redeemed from utter dreariness by Ruskin's determined simplicity and prescriptive arrogance. A few points from these chapters require emphasis here because they have a bearing on our understanding of his peculiar consciousness. One minor but characteristic point is the language he uses to describe the necessary vitality of walls. "A wall," he insists, "has no business to be dead. It ought to have members in its make, and purposes in its existence, like an organized creature, and to answer its ends in a living and energetic way; and it is only when we do not choose to put any strength or organization into it, that it offends us by its deadness."[52] Further on he intuits an important distinction between the Greek and Gothic spirit from their handling of square elements in building. The Greek, it seems, prefers to set a square evenly, the Gothic, if he can, will set it obliquely. On the subject of capitals Ruskin becomes especially dogmatic: "As far as structure is concerned, the moment the capital vanishes from the shaft, that moment we are in error: all good Gothic has true capitals to the shafts of its jambs and traceries, and all Gothic is debased the instant the shaft vanishes. It matters not how slender, or how small, or how low, the shaft may be: wherever there is indication of concentrated vertical support, then the capital is a necessary termination."[53] Among the forms of cathedral windows he finds the rose window to be most beautiful, not only for its ability to pattern and diffuse the admitted light, but also for its symbolic sympathy with the source of light itself. Finally, it is notable that he considers the purest forms of Gothic traceries, the early pierced forms, to be completely independent of any authority of tradition; they are simply "eternal forms, based on laws of gravity and cohesion" until they disintegrate in self-conscious luxuriance and flamboyance.[54] With these subjects, however, Ruskin has reached the other major division of his book, "Of Decoration."

Ornamentation is taken up under three primary heads, the material of ornament, its treatment, and its placement. The materials of ornament, its sources and design, are in all God-created forms; Ruskin will not permit images of man-made things as ornamental forms unless they are subordinated to the human figure as subject. He provides a catalogue of twelve systems of inorganic and organic forms, in descending order of frequency of occurrence, from "abstract lines" to "mamalian animals and man." Abstract lines, the most common contours abstracted from natural objects when the object itself is not imitated, are most beautiful because, as he had argued in volume 2 of *Modern Painters*, they are, like natural gradation, types of divine infinity. His discussion extends to the ornamental suitability of the generic forms of earth, water, fire, clouds, shells, and fish, et cetera. The Greek dolphin motif, for instance, is praised as one of the most beautiful uses of animal form; and, although he credits Christian architecture with the discovery of the full implications of leaf form in decoration, he allows that the "roots" of leaf ornamentation are in the Greek acanthus and Egyptian Lotus. In the treatment of ornamentation, "subordination" is, for Ruskin, the central criterion. It is essentially another idea of organic coherence; a thing is beautiful in its place and nowhere else; the beauty of the part is interdependent with that of the whole. He does not object to Greek ornamentation per se at this point so much as to the deadly imitation of it by modern architects or the attempt to engraft its forms upon the alien tissue of contemporary structures. "Find your Phidias first," he demands, if you want a true Greek architecture.[55] But the questions of coherence or subordination of ornament he admits to be among the most difficult he has yet tried to work out for any branch of art. The great decorative abstractions of architecture "are the deep and laborious thoughts of the greatest men, put into such easy letters that they can be written by the simplest."[56]

One problem touched on at considerable length is that of "aesthetic distance" in nature and ornamentation, a question of the conciliation of object intention and observer intention in design. "Are not all natural things as lovely near as far away?" His answer is one of the few passages of Ruskinian purple rhetoric in the volume.

> Nay, not so. Look at the clouds, and watch the delicate sculpture of their alabaster sides, and the rounded lustre of their magnificent rolling. They were meant to be beheld far away; they were shaped for their place, high above your head; approach them, and they fuse into vague mists, or whirl away in fierce fragments of thunderous vapour. Look at the crest of the Alp, from the far-away plains over which its light is cast, whence human souls have communion with it by their myriads. The child looks up to it in the dawn, and the husbandmen in the burden and heat of the day, and the old man in the going down of the sun, and it is to them all as the celestial city on the world's horizon; dyed with the depth of heaven, and clothed with the calm of eternity.[57]

Every form in nature appears to have its fitting distance for aesthetic observation. So also in architecture the perfection of ornamentation depends upon its being suited to its distance from the eye. In landscape there is a different system of forms for every distance from eye, subtly entwined and graduated into a whole of infinite complexity. In architecture "all good ornamentation is . . . *arborescent,* as it were, one class of it branching out of another and sustained by it . . . every order subordinated to a greater, simpler, and more powerful."[58] If this subordination is not complete the ornament is bad. Among the various comments on the decorative uses of natural symbols that conclude this section, one must be singled out for its bearing on the general cast of his thought. Characteristic of his continual involvement with light-darkness archetypal symbolism is this passage, based on Lord Lindsay, on the decorative uses of light in dentils, frets, and billet mouldings. "The opposition of good and evil, the antagonism of the entire human system . . . the alternation of labour with rest, the mingling of life with death, or the actual physical fact of the division of light from darkness, and of the falling and rising of night and day, are all typified or represented by these chains of light and shade, of which the eye never wearies, though their true meaning may never occur to the thoughts."[59]

Having disposed of the sources and treatment of ornament in two longish chapters, Ruskin now takes up the structural placement of it in eight brief but comparatively arid chapters devoted to such topics as the proper decoration of angles, edges, fillets, rolls, recesses, bases, shafts, cornices, capitals, and so on. A great deal of technical detail is assembled in these chapters, most of it of interest here only insofar as it reveals that same strong empirical bent that is apparent in his studies in geology and botany. There is much collection and correlation of data on decorative forms, giving these technical chapters an aura of objectivity in keeping with their restrained style.

In his chapter "The Base," for instance, he assembles profile drawings of twenty-eight varieties of Gothic base moldings, eighteen of them from Venice, arranged in sequence to show the individuation and evolution of their curvatures. But data, dogma, and symbolism are intermixed here; Ruskin believes that the later moldings of the sequence clearly show the decadence of flamboyant Gothic as their rolls become more lavishly rotund. He even sees a sign of this in the resemblance of these later curves to the profile of a breaking wave. Despite this degeneration, he is convinced of "the ineffable superiority of these Gothic bases, in grace of profile, to any ever invented by the ancients."[60]

His early bias against classical architecture appears in certain elements of inconsistency in the chapter, as above, where classical base moldings are condemned for imaginative restraint, while later Gothic bases are repudiated for their lack of it. Similarly, under "Shafts," Greek caryatid columns are rejected, along with all Gothic and Renaissance efforts in elaborate sculpturing of shafts, as being "fantastic" and as compromising the strength of the shafts. On the other hand, he finds the disciplined severity of classical capitals to be repressive of imagination with a tendency to degenerate in the hands of indolent workmen into dead formalism. In the same mood (and apparently forgetful of what he had said earlier about the Greek architectural abstraction as deepest thoughts put in signs the feeblest hands could execute) he dismisses the Greek egg-and-dart cornice as "conventionalized into a monotonous successiveness of nothing."[61] Similarly, in the volume's last chapter, he reproduces a bit of Greek spiral design in order to mock the Greeks for reducing the infinite irregularity of the sea to a sterile scrollwork.

Clearly he was still insensitive to the "reserved variation" and symbolic depth of Greek ornament, a defect of taste he acknowledged and repaired in later work. Yet when, at this point, he examines some Venetian cornices decorated with realistically carved leafage he immediately feels vital subtleties of expression there and can easily read in them signs of religious struggle. "Here are two great new elements visible; energy and naturalism:—Life, with submission to the laws of God, and love of His works; this is Christianity, dealing with her classical models."[62] But he must be quoted at somewhat greater length to show how the precise degree of purity of Christianity in the carver is revealed to him in the curve of a sculptured head.

> Now look to the last cornice (g). That is Protestantism,—a slight touch of Dissent, hardly amounting to schism, in those falling leaves, but true life in the whole of it. The forms all broken through, and sent heaven knows where, but the root held fast; and the strong sap in the branches; and, best of all, good fruit ripening and opening straight towards heaven, and in the face of it, even though some of the leaves lie in the dust.
>
> Now, observe, the cornice (f) represents Heathenism and Papistry, animated by the mingling of Christianity and nature. The good in it, the life of it, the veracity and liberty of it, such as it has, are Protestantism in its heart; the rigidity and saplessness are the Romanism of it.[63]

Here, in effect, is the Evangelical aspect of the message of *Stones* in a couple of cornices.

In this comparatively subdued foundational volume Ruskin strives hard to attain "objectivity" through restrained, imageless style and adherence to the logic of Gothic construction. In dealing with the aesthetics of ornamentation he tries to elucidate his precepts of naturalism, variation, organic coherence, and submissiveness in ornamentation by merely pointing to contrasting forms and leaving the reader, he supposes, free to choose. "The reader has decorated but little for himself as yet"; he concludes, "but I have not, at least, attempted to bias his judgment. Of the simple forms of decoration which have been set before him, he has been always left free to choose; and the stated restrictions in the methods of applying them have been only those which followed on the necessities of construction previously determined. These having been now defined, I do indeed leave my reader free to build; and with what a freedom! All the lovely forms of the universe set before him, whence to choose."[64] But when, as in the cornice passages quoted above, he comes to the ultimate problem of the mythic submissiveness of art "to God's laws" it is clear, even in this relatively cool volume, that Ruskin is not primarily either an architect or an aesthetician, but a prophet and an apocalyptist. He is a revealer, not an analyst.

It is to this mode that he returns in the brief concluding chapter of the volume, "The Vestibule" (meaning the approach), in several senses, to Venice. Here he shifts from the prose of knowledge to that of power, in De Quincey's usage. Summing up the subject of decoration, he hymns the infinity and perfection of nature as a source of ornament. There is material enough in a single flower to decorate a score of cathedrals, but we should rather build ten cathedrals to illustrate a single flower than waste our efforts in attempting to design new forms. The designs of nature, he warns, may be illustrated but not improved, except in the sense that a preacher may be said to "improve" upon his text: "Just such difference as there is between the sense in which a minister may be said to improve a text, to the people's comfort, and the sense in which an atheist might declare that he could improve the Book, which, if any man shall add unto, there shall be added unto him the plagues that are written therein; just such difference is there between that which, with respect to Nature, man is, in his humbleness, called upon to do, and that which, in his insolence, he imagines himself capable of doing."[65]

Since art cannot improve nature, Ruskin continues, he who cannot love both must choose nature. Modern men, penned in cities, have not this choice to make; yet men need nature, he knows, for psychological survival. They need the space, the peace, the subtleties of texture, and the immanence of purpose, in short, the environment of "typical" and "vital" beauty he had described in volume 2 of *Modern Painters*. Hence it becomes the function of architecture to bring, as far as possible, the beauty of nature to urban man: "to tell us about Nature; to possess us with memories of her quietness; to be solemn and full of tenderness, like her, and rich in portraitures of her; full of delicate imagery of flowers we can no more gather, and of the living creatures now far away from us in their own solitude."[66] Knowing that architecture must have the peace and mystery of nature in it, we can now easily tell the living from the dead in it; "for, as surely as you know that meadow grass, meshed with fairy rings, is better than the wood pavement, cut into hexagons; and as surely as you know the fresh winds and sunshine of the upland are better than the choke-damp of the vault, or the gaslight of the ball-room, you may know . . . that the good architecture, which has life, and truth, and joy in it, is better than the bad architecture, which has death, dishonesty, and vexations of heart in it, from the beginning to the end of time."[67] So ends the peroration of volume 1, with Ruskin driving home in prophetic puritan tones his sense of the fatefulness of taste.

Ruskin has laid his foundations in areas of construction and ornament and paid obeisance to technical objectivity here, yet he comes to focus attention in the end on a deep crisis in architectural choice: it must revere nature or die. However, the work of the volume is not yet finished. He must bring his long-patient reader into "The Vestibule," the lagoon of Venice, with the city lying low and obscure on the horizon, as his accompanying drawing shows. Therefore, in a brief epilogue, he lapses into the idiom of the travelogue, soothing but with ominous undertones, as he takes us first along the low banks of the Brenta: "A muddy volume of yellowish-grey water, that neither hastens nor slackens, but glides heavily between its monotonous banks, with here and there a short, babbling eddy twisted for an instant into its opaque surface, and vanishing, as if something had been dragged into it and gone down. Dusty and shadeless, the road fares along the dyke on its northern side."[68] We reach Mestre, where Ruskin dwells for a moment on the bleak environs of its little inn: "The view from its balcony is not cheerful: a narrow street, with a solitary brick church and barren companile on the other side of it: and some conventional buildings, with a few crimson remnants of fresco about their windows: and, between them and the street, a ditch with some slow current in it." Then to the lagoon where we are to embark for Venice: "We have but walked some two hundred yards when we come to a low wharf or quay at the extremity of a canal, with long steps on each side down to the water, which latter we fancy for an instant has become black with stagnation; another glance undeceives us,—it is covered with the black boats of Venice."[69] Once we are in our gondola, Ruskin unwinds the volume's final and most moving paragraph. The distant Venice he unveils is no romantic anticipation but a threatened scene caught between rail causeway and brooding smoke:

> Another turn, and another perspective of canal; but not interminable. The silver beak cleaves it fast,—it widens: the rank grass of the banks sinks lower, and lower, and at last dies in tawny knots along an expanse of weedy shore. Over it, on the right, but a few years back, we might have seen the lagoon stretching to the horizon, and the warm southern sky bending over Malamocco to the sea. Now we can see nothing but what seems a low and monotonous dockyard wall, with flat arches to let the tide through it;—this is the railroad bridge, conspicuous above all things. But at the end of those dismal arches there rises, out of the wide water, a straggling line of low and confused brick buildings, which, but for the many towers which are mingled among them, might be the suburbs of an English manufacturing town. Four or five domes, pale, and apparently at a greater distance, rise over the centre of the line; but the object which first catches the eye is a sullen cloud of black smoke brooding over the northern half of it, and which issues from the belfry of a church.
>
> It is Venice.[70]

CHAPTER 4

The Judgment of Venice

The lagoon journey that concludes volume 1, giving a promise of Venice already diminished by ominous disharmonies, continues in the first chapter of volume 2 of *The Stones of Venice*. But now the life-death antithesis is emphasized and becomes the subject of direct comment. His city, Ruskin reminds us, is not to be the Venice of Romantic fiction and drama, the Venice of Byron, but the discordant city that the modern visitor sees. For the Venice of the Doges now lies "hidden behind the cumbrous masses which were the delight of the nation in its dotage; hidden in many a grass-grown court, and silent pathway, and lightless canal, where the slow waves have sapped their foundations for five hundred years, and must soon prevail over them forever." His task will be to gather out of this wreckage a faint image of this lost city, "more gorgeous a thousandfold than that which now exists."[1]

However, Ruskin's immediate subject in this chapter is not the city proper but "The Throne," the favored yet precarious geographical site of Venice that has dictated the labor and character of its inhabitants for twenty centuries. In a typically apocalyptic passage he envisions its creation, imagining the providential action of geological forces in weaving its unique web of channels and islands on which a people might settle and begin a culture shaped by its peculiar intimacy with the sea.

> If, two thousand years ago, we had been permitted to watch the slow settling of the slime of those turbid rivers into the polluted sea, and the gaining upon its deep and fresh waters of the lifeless, impassable, unvoyageable plain, how little could we have understood the purpose with which those islands were shaped out of the void, and the torpid waters enclosed with their desolate walls of sand! . . . How little imagined that in the laws which were stretching forth the gloomy margins of those fruitless banks, and feeding the bitter grass among their shallows, there was indeed a preparation, and *the only preparation possible*, for the founding of a city which was to be set like a golden clasp on the girdle of the earth.[2]

He suggests that the base of Venetian creative power was a geological miracle; precise margins of tidal variation defined the unique estuarine environment which was the real foundation of Venetian greatness.

> Had there been no tide, as in other parts of the Mediterranean, the narrow canals of the city would have become noisome, and the marsh in which it was built pestiferous. Had the tide been only a foot or eighteen inches higher in its rise, the water-access to the doors of the palaces would have been impossible; even as it is, there is sometimes a little difficulty, at ebb, in landing without setting foot upon the lower and slippery steps; and the highest tides sometimes enter the courtyards, and overflow the entrance halls.[3]

But there is, finally, another, less objective, natural determinant of Venetian life that Ruskin wishes to describe. Still approaching by gondola, he tries to recapture the psychological effect on the ancient settlers of these labyrinthine waterways as seen at dusk.

> The scene is often profoundly oppressive, even at this day, when every plot of higher ground bears some fragment of fair building: but, in order to know what it was once, let the traveller follow in his boat at evening the windings of some unfrequented channel far into the midst of the melancholy plain; let him remove, in his imagination, the brightness of the great city that still extends itself in the distance, and the walls and towers from the islands that are near; and so wait, until the bright investiture and sweet warmth of the sunset are withdrawn from the waters, and the black desert of their shore lies in its nakedness beneath the night, pathless, comfortless, infirm, lost in dark langour and fearful silence, except where the salt runlets plash into the tideless pools, or the sea-birds flit from their margins with a questioning cry; and he will be enabled to enter in some sort into the horror of heart with which this solitude was anciently chosen by man for his habitation.[4]

So be it, but one may also recognize this as yet another Ruskinian poetic excursion into archetypal light-darkness contrasts.

1

The second volume of *Stones*, like the first, is divided into two major topics, the Byzantine and Gothic periods of Venetian architecture. Byzantine remains are the essential subject of four successive chapters devoted to Torcello, Murano, Saint Mark's, and the Byzantine palaces. The chapters on the cathedrals of Torcello and Murano contain little of interest to this study that has not already been considered. Perhaps their chief relevance is the light they throw on the extent to which Ruskin was able, at this time, to acknowledge Greek (that is, pagan mythic) roots for the Byzantine art he admired so much in Venice.

In a note to the 1880 edition of *The Seven Lamps* (cited above in chapter 2)[5] Ruskin claims that he and Lord Lindsay were the first English critics to appreciate the beauty of Byzantine architecture. This note, as we have seen, makes it clear that by 1880 Ruskin was more than willing to identify the Greek with the Byzantine spirit. ("A Byzantine *was* nothing else than a Greek,—recognizing Christ for Zeus.")[6] But in *The Seven Lamps* and *Stones* he makes a crucial distinction between the Greek and the Byzantine-Christian spirits in architecture. In "The Lamp of Power" he had judged that the Byzantine felt a greater sympathy with nature's power than the "self-contemplating and self-contented Greek." Now, among the Greek-Byzantine remains at Torcello, he is convinced that the Christian carvings exhibit a greater vitality than their classical models. The sculptor of the acanthus capitals at Torcello has captured, he believes, the "elasticity and growth" of the natural foliage. These are "not very like the acanthus," of course, "but much liker than any Greek work."[7] In this same cathedral he feels a special sympathy with the builders' liberal admission of sunshine; the result is another characteristic light-darkness piece:

> They did not need the darkness; they could not perhaps bear it. There was fear and depression upon them enough, without a material gloom. They sought for comfort in their religion, for tangible hopes and promises, not for threatenings or mysteries; and though the subjects chosen for the mosaics on the walls are of the most solemn character, there are no artificial shadows cast upon them, nor dark colours used in them: all is fair and bright, and intended evidently to be regarded in hopefulness, and not with terror.[8]

In the light of this passage, it is interesting to consider that as *Stones* progresses Ruskin moves further and further from the arid analytic prose in which he founds the first volume and becomes increasingly committed to making the external internal and more deeply involved in the revelation of objects in terms of the builders' presumed state of mind or of his own. Prose of statement, that is, gives way increasingly to prose of impression. This development is evident in several places in the chapter on Murano and its church. Ruskin begins it with an organic metaphor of decay setting in at the extremities of dying Venice.

> The decay of the city of Venice is, in many respects, like that of an outwearied and aged human frame; the cause of its decrepitude is indeed at the heart, but the outward appearances of it are first at the extremities. In the centre of the city there are still places where some evidence of vitality remains, and where, with kind closing of the eyes to signs, too manifest even there, of distress and declining fortune, the stranger may succeed in imagining, for a little while, what must have been the aspect of Venice in her prime. But this lingering pulsation has not force enough anymore to penetrate into the suburbs and outskirts of the city; the frost of death there

has seized upon it irrevocably, and the grasp of mortal disease is marked daily by the increasing breadth of its belt of ruin.[9]

Such a diseased extremity is Murano. Approaching it from Venice, Ruskin paints a panorama of sky effects and their reflection, in the midst of which the ruin seems suspended; a smoke cloud hovers over its glass furnaces. There are other images of the town's fallen state, followed by examined details of the remains of Byzantine ornamentation in the cathedral. The study culminates in the curious passages, noticed earlier, on its Greek Madonna and on the function of the building as a "Temple" where the Virgin is worshipped instead of God. Most interesting is Ruskin's impression, which is quite irrelevant to his subject, of the abjectness of her modern suppliants.

> If we return to-morrow we shall find it filled with woeful groups of aged men and women, wasted and fever-struck, fixed in paralytic supplication, half-kneeling, half-crouched upon the pavement; bowed down, partly in feebleness, partly in fearful devotion, with their grey clothes cast far over their faces, ghastly and settled into a gloomy animal misery, all but the glittering eyes and muttering lips.[10]

By such means the argument of *Stones* becomes a spiritual quest for the lost vitality of Venetian architecture. The early chapters on the principles of Gothic construction are barren of poetic effects. As Ruskin moves into the theory of decoration the impressionistic factor in the style increases slightly, but still the emphasis is on object analysis and the formulation of aesthetic law. Content here is, of course, heavily subjective, but the style is restrained. Things are seldom dealt with, in those early chapters, as felt presences (I-Thou) but as objects of abstract aesthetic value. Then in the last chapter of volume 1, "The Vestibule," Ruskin begins to carry his readers, by imagination, into the actual presence of Venice, and beyond this by "penetrative" imagination into the city's still-vital cores, as the revelational or apocalyptic note in his prose takes hold. Through construction, decoration, lagoon passage with ominous causeway, formless and gloomy prehistoric site, decayed Torcello and Murano; from technical abstractions and discordant landscapes, relieved here and there by touches of living beauty glimmering through dead forms, Ruskin carries his reader inward toward the vital centers of his Venice. The movement is carried by increasing impressionism in the prose, by developing emphasis on presential moments in which the object is not analyzed but revealed. In such moments we are drawn into sudden penetration of disorder, decay, or abstraction into the complex living presence of the beautiful thing. This impressionistic undercurrent in the book culminates in the famous chapter on Saint Mark's in volume 2.

Before bringing his reader into the actual presence of Saint Mark's Ruskin conducts him, for purposes of contrast and as a kind of prelude to the vision, into the precincts of an imaginary English cathedral compounded of details from Canterbury and Salisbury. His emphasis in describing the English scene is on the coherence of the cloistered setting with the mood of the cathedral itself. There is "the inner private-looking road or close, where nothing goes in but the carts of the tradesmen who supply the bishop and the chapter, and where there are little shaven grass-plots, fenced in by neat rails, before old-fashioned groups of somewhat diminutive and excessively trim houses, with little oriel and bay windows jutting out here and there."[11] Approaching the imaginary cathedral itself, he pictures the gray grotesques of its sculpture and the general somberness of its aspect, both to be contrasted with Saint Mark's; yet it has in common that "infinity" of texture that is Ruskin's prime criterion of vitality in architecture:

> . . . the great mouldering wall of rugged sculpture and confused arcades, shuttered, and grey, and grisly with heads of dragons and mocking fiends, worn by the rain and swirling winds into yet unseemlier shape, and coloured on their stony scales by deep russet-orange lichen, melancholy gold; . . . the bleak towers, so far above that the eye loses itself among the bosses of their traceries, though they are rude and strong.[12]

But Saint Mark's is not cloistered in "small formalisms" or "secluded, continuous, drowsy felicities." The approaches are pulsating with secular urban life, oblivious to its mysterious presence. In the first phase of his vision, Ruskin brings us toward the cathedral by way of a narrow, teeming alley lined with close-set shops. The eye is met by a riot of textures: goods, shop fronts, green leaves gleaming here and there; the ear is assailed by the shrieks of vendors. Yet as he conducts us past the various doors, Ruskin has us survey, with Protestant condescension, the ways the Madonna is remembered in a sampling of shops:

> . . . the light in all cases entering at the front only, and fading away in a few feet from the threshold into a gloom which the eye from without cannot penetrate, but which is generally broken by a ray or two from a feeble lamp at the back of the shop, suspended before a print of the Virgin. The less pious shopkeeper sometimes leaves his lamp unlighted, and is contented with a penny print; the more religious one has his print coloured and set in a little shrine with a gilded or figured fringe, with perhaps a faded flower or two on each side, and his lamp burning brilliantly. Here, at the fruiterer's, where the dark-green water-mellons are heaped upon the counter like cannonballs, the Madonna has a tabernacle of fresh

laurel leaves; but the pewterer next door has let his lamp out, and there is nothing to be seen in his shop but the dull gleam of the studded patterns on the copper pans, hanging from his roof in the darkness.[13]

And so he continues, suggesting in these images the contemporary state of Venetian religious observance. As one might expect, the fruiterer's piety is greater than the pewterer's.

We move on out of the alley toward the piazza through other harmonies and disorder of nineteenth-century Venice. Passing what was then the Black Eagle Inn we glance "through the square door of marble, deeply moulded, . . . we see the shadows of its pergola of vines resting on an ancient well, with a pointed shield carved on its side."[14] But at the entrance to Saint Mark's Place, the Bocca di Piazza, we note that "the Venetian character is nearly destroyed, first by the frightful façade of San Moisè . . . and then by the modernizing of the shops as they near the piazza, and the mingling with the lower Venetian populace of lounging groups of English and Austrians." But we push fast through these contaminations and soon "forget them all" in an architectural epiphany. For suddenly, between the pillars at the end of the way "there opens a great light, and, in the midst of it, as we advance slowly, the vast tower of St. Mark seems to lift itself visibly forth from the level field of chequered stones; and, on each side, the countless arches prolong themselves into ranged symmetry, as if the rugged and irregular houses that pressed together above us in the dark alley had been struck back into sudden obedience and lovely order."[15] Thus the second stage of the vision is begun.

Revelation intensifies as we move forward now, and at first no discord enters. Well may those straggling buildings appear to fall back into obedient ranks, he continues, "for beyond those troops of ordered arches there rises a vision out of the earth, and all the great square seems to have opened from it in a kind of awe, that we may see it far away."[16] In this central phase of the vision, Ruskin moves us gradually closer so that we become aware of the pulsating infinity of the building's texture, far removed from that of the grim English Gothic by its richness of color and the scope of its symbolism. In these famous descriptive passages Ruskin seems to be trying to show all the lamps of architecture burning at once, but the essence of his vision is the interaction of mythic symbolism, color, variegation, and entwined organic forms in living architecture. The vision is apocalyptic in that, insofar as he can make it so, Ruskin's Saint Mark's is a vision of paradise in terms of architecture.

A multitude of pillars and white domes, clustered into a long low pyramid of coloured light; a treasure-heap, it seems, partly of gold, and partly of opal and mother-of-pearl, hollowed beneath into five great vaulted porches, ceiled with fair mosaic, and beset with sculpture of alabaster, clear as amber and delicate as ivory,—sculpture fantastic and involved, of palm leaves and lilies, and grapes and pomegranates, and birds clinging and fluttering among the branches, all twined together into an endless network of buds and plumes; and in the midst of it, the solemn forms of angels, sceptred, and robed to the feet, and leaning to each other across the gates, their figures indistinct among the gleaming of the golden ground through the leaves beside them, interrupted and dim, like the morning light as it faded back among the branches of Eden, when first its gates were angel-guarded long ago. And round the walls of the porches there are set pillars of variegated stones, jasper and porphyry, and deep-green serpentine spotted with flakes of snow, and marbles, that half refuse and half yield to the sunshine, Cleopatra-like, "their bluest veins to kiss"—the shadow, as it steals back from them, revealing line after line of azure undulation, as a receding tide leaves the waved sand; their capitals rich with interwoven tracery, rooted knots of herbage, and drifting leaves of acanthus and vine, and mystical signs, all beginning and ending in the Cross; and above them, in the broad archivolts, a continuous chain of language and of life—angels, and the signs of heaven, and the labours of men, each in its appointed season upon the earth.[17]

In the third phase of the vision, ominous discords of the fallen world reappear as we approach still nearer and are taken inside the building itself. The apocalypse of life gives way to that of death. What, Ruskin now asks, is the effect of this vision in stone on the people whose lives go on around it? "You may walk from sunrise to sunset, to and fro, before the gateway of St. Mark's, and you will not see an eye lifted to it, nor a countenance brightened by it."[18] There is not merely indifference to its beauty, but, ironically, the church seems to act as a magnet attracting idleness and degradation. Ruskin sees a square lined with cafes where idle Venetians peruse empty journals and the martial music of Austrian bands jams the organ sounds from the church, "the march drowning the miserere." Against the building itself drifts the flotsam and jetsam of the social wreck:

And in the recesses of the porches, all day long, knots of men of the lowest classes, unemployed and listless, lie basking in the sun like lizards; and unregarded children,—every heavy glance of their young eyes full of desperation and stony depravity, and their throats hoarse with cursing,—gamble, and fight, and snarl, and sleep, hour after hour, clashing their bruised centesimi upon the marble ledges of the church porch. And the images of Christ and His angels look down upon it continually.[19]

Regarding the building not only as a vestige of another time but also of another order of social life, Ruskin assumes that we will share his impulse to speculate about the manner of men who built it; and so he conducts us still inward away from the disorder and degradation of the square into the peace and harmony of the ornate, vaulted tomb where the image of the Doge Andrea Dandolo reclines on its canopied sepulchre.

> Let us look also, and thank that gentle light that rests upon his forehead for ever, and dies away upon his breast.
> The face is of a man in middle life, but there are two deep furrows right across the forehead dividing it like the foundations of a tower: the height of it above is bound by the fillet of the ducal cap. The rest of the features are singularly small and delicate, the lips sharp, perhaps the sharpness of death being added to that of the natural lines; but there is a sweet smile upon them, and a deep serenity upon the whole countenance.[20]

We note the decoration of the room in which he lies, it is an architectural paradise ravaged by time.

> The floor of it is of rich mosaic, encompassed by a low seat of red marble, and its walls are of alabaster, but worn and shattered, and darkly stained with age, almost a ruin, . . . the ravaging fissures fretting their way among the islands and channelled zones of the alabaster, and the time-stains on its translucent masses darkened into fields of rich golden brown, like the colour of seaweed when the sun strikes on it through deep sea.[21]

Finally, to conclude the vision, Ruskin's eye falls upon an image with a special apocalyptic message: "Upon the walls, again and again repeated, the gaunt figure of the Baptist, in every circumstance of his life and death." But the essential meaning of the message which the "old Greek" has formed on the wall of this "Baptistry" is simply that "to be baptized with fire, or to be cast therein . . . is the choice set before all men," Ruskin concludes. "Venice has made her choice."[22]

Everything else in the chapter and perhaps in the entire volume is subsidiary to this revelation of the former power and present punishment of Venice. There is a kind of epilogue to the vision; in this we leave the tomb and enter the church itself. Ruskin gives a brief account of the forest of imagery that surrounds the observer, entwined branches of symbols leading the eye upward toward the central mystery of the cross. But his main concern is to show, with good Protestant indignation, how this vital structure has become the setting for the tawdry theatrics of a decadent Christianity.

> Darkness and mystery; confused recesses of building; . . . artificial light employed in small quantity, but maintained with a constancy which seems to give it a kind of sacredness; preciousness of material easily comprehended by the vulgar eye; close air loaded with a sweet and peculiar odour associated only with religious services, solemn music, and tangible idols or images having popular legends attached to them,—these, the stage properties of superstition, which have been from the beginning of the world, and must be to the end of it, employed by all nations, whether

openly savage or nominally civilized, to produce a false awe in minds incapable of apprehending the true nature of the Deity, are assembled in St. Mark's to a degree, as far as I know, unexampled in any other European church.[23]

All this proceeds in indifference to the living testament which is written in the building itself.

Having carried us by a tour de force in the prose of invocation and revelation to a pure but beleaguered source of vital architecture in Venice, Ruskin devotes the remaining two thirds of the chapter to an analysis of the structure and purpose of Saint Mark's. Predictably, the rich impressionistic style of the opening of the chapter becomes more subdued and matter-of-fact. Surprisingly, however, he does not carry over the construction-decoration pattern of analysis developed in the first volume. Instead he proposes to deal with the structure in two categories: Saint Mark's as architecture, treating its constructional and decorative merits as a work of art; and the fitness of Saint Mark's for its function as a place of worship. Clearly the pursuit of this second topic would carry Ruskin beyond the aesthetics of architecture into the nature of worship, of the religious experience itself, a subject implicit in the passage just quoted on the uses of the interior of the cathedral.

It is neither possible nor relevant here to examine the whole of this long two-part discussion of Saint Mark's; however, a few points must be mentioned because they are among his basic precepts. For instance, in his treatment of Saint Mark's as architecture, his chief emphasis is on the vitality of its color. The Venetians, he explains, were the first Europeans to sympathize fully with the Eastern instinct for color. At first, of course, they had to import Byzantine craftsmen to design their mosaics, "but they rapidly took up and developed, under more masculine conditions, the system of which the Greeks had shown them the example."[24] This Venetian aptitude with color Ruskin takes as proof that their early architecture was alive; for love of color, he insists, is "one of the essential signs of life in any school of art," and the loss of color sense presages a dying art: "I know it to be one of the first signs of death in the Renaissance schools, that they despised colour."[25] In sum, it is not merely because of the abundance and delicacy of its sculpture but also because of the vitality of its encrusted color, "the most subtle, variable, inexpressible colour in the world," that Saint Mark's has a density of texture rivaling nature herself. "It would be easier to illustrate a crest of Scottish mountain, with its purple heather and pale harebells at their fullest and fairest, or a glade of Jura forest, with its floor of anemone and moss, than a single portico of St. Mark's."[26]

But is such splendor of ornament proper for a place of worship? Can Saint Mark's be considered an ecclesiastical and Christian building? These are the questions raised during the second phase of Ruskin's critical discussion of the church. He does not so much answer them as use them as the occasion for laying down dogma on the relationship between religion and architecture. A style "must be practised in the dwelling before it can be perfected in the church, and it is the test of a noble style that it shall be applicable to both."[27] Indeed it is doubtful whether aesthetic sensibilities that have been starved all week should suddenly be feasted at church. As for Saint Mark's, we must remember that when it was built its general style was ubiquitous. The style of a church, then, ought not to be segregated from that of its community, and in its time Saint Mark's was not. But what of its brilliant pictorial mosaics? What is the effect of these upon Christian piety? Ruskin opens this issue by noting that the structural character of Byzantine architecture, as opposed to Gothic, requires the decoration of large plain surfaces, and this decoration only reaches its highest potential when it becomes pictorial. Hence the question broadens to "What effect upon religion has been or may yet be produced by pictorial art, and especially by the art of the mosaicist?"[28]

Taking up this larger question, he allows at the outset that men whose faith is entirely secure seem to have no particular need or care for art. Surprisingly, however, he observes that English Protestants, being unwilling to accept from Catholic painters any of the little artistic aid they do allow, have been reduced to aesthetic beggary, that is, to accepting the art of those who do not believe at all, "but who read the Bible in search of the picturesque." But what is the sign of faith in art? Rude intensity, it appears. Whenever the human mind is in the right state of belief, he continues, it has the "childish power" (childish because most common in youth) "of raising into sublimity and reality the rudest symbol which is given to it of accredited truth."[29] But the Renaissance put an end to accredited religious truth; hence the painter is no longer regarded as the narrator of mythic truths but as the inventor of artistic ideas. Since the Renaissance, he argues, art has lost the symbolic intensity by which powerful truths could be conducted through rude forms and has given itself over to the interests of perfection and polish, dead ends for art. Further, it follows that if the technique-oriented standards of art derived from Renaissance science were to be abandoned, great reservoirs of creative power would be released from the common people; for "there are many peasants on every estate, and labourers in every town, of Europe, who have imaginative powers of a high order, which nevertheless cannot be used for our good, because we do not choose to look at anything but what is expressed in a legal and scientific way."[30] Ruskin returns from this digression to point out that the mosaics of Saint Mark's are thus not decorations in our sense at all, but "the actual Table of the Law and the Testimony, written within and without." The church as a whole was "at once a type of the Redeemed Church of God, and a scroll for the written word of God."[31]

Having dealt with the Byzantine churches, Torcello, Murano, and Saint Mark's, Ruskin concludes the Byzantine first half of volume 2 by taking up "Byzantine Palaces," only six of which he considered to be in assessable condition. In studying these he not only rounds out his subject but documents his earlier assertion about the continuity of style between ecclesiastical and secular structures. The major points of his discussion here had been made in earlier chapters: the eye is influenced, perhaps *most* influenced, by subtleties of texture of which it is not conscious; such is vital art, and its only sufficient model is living nature, not traditional forms. Byzantine capitals have more "Life" and "Breath" than Greek capitals. Though rudely worked, these carvings show "the mind of the workman to have been among the living herbage, not among Greek precedents."[32] Some of these designs may lack the grace of the Greek prototypes, he admits, "but they are indisputably more *natural*, than any Greek ones, and therefore healthier, and tending to greatness."[33] This emphasis on imitative naturalism implies a contradiction with what he had said in the previous chapter about the power of rude symbols to convey accredited truth to faithful minds; the old issue of the mimetic or expressive function of art is still unresolved. Similarly, in taking up the reasons for our delight in Arabian woven or perforated designs, he speaks not only of our absorption in its mazy texture but maintains further that our direct visual pleasure in it is "increased and solemnized by some dim feeling of the setting forth, by such symbols, of the intricacy, and alternate rise and fall, subjection and supremacy, of human fortune."[34] Again, this counter interest in the symbolic as opposed to the mimetic aspect of art emerges in Ruskin's affirmations as to the sacredness of color. There is, he is convinced, a direct relation between the faith of a painter and the purity of his expression in color. "So surely as a painter is irreligious, thoughtless, or obscene in disposition, so surely is his colouring cold, gloomy, and valueless."[35] Again, "I know of no law more severely without exception than this of the connexion of pure colour with profound and noble thought."[36] Most interesting, in terms of the later development of Ruskin's mythic interests is the reason he gives for the certainty of this

law: the "statutes of colour" (to be connected with Greek myth in
Modern Painters, volume 5) are directly sanctified by solar light. Hence
he suggests that the seriousness of the love of color in the Byzantine mind
stems from the solar origins of Oriental religion, from "taking the stars
from the rulers of its fortune, and the sun for the God of its life."[37] And
so, lapsing finally into prophetic prose, Ruskin invokes the evidence of
direct mythic involvement with nature, long since perverted by
knowledge, of which the intense symbology of Venice's Byzantine remnants are a testament.

> That mighty Landscape, of dark mountains that guard the horizon with
> their purple towers, and solemn forests that gather their weight of leaves,
> bronzed with sunshine, not with age, into those gloomy masses fixed in
> heaven, which storm and frost have power no more to shake or shed;—that
> mighty Humanity, so perfect and so proud, that hides no weakness
> beneath the mantle, and gains no greatness from the diadem; the majesty
> of thoughtful form, on which the dust of gold and flame of jewels are
> dashed as the sea-spray upon the rock, and still the great Manhood seems
> to stand bare against the blue sky;—*that mighty Mythology*, which fills the
> daily walks of men with spiritual companionship, and beholds the protec-
> ting angels break with their burning presence through the arrow-flights of
> battle;—measure the compass of that field of creation, weigh the value of
> the inheritance that Venice thus left to the nations of Europe, and then
> judge if so vast, so beneficent a power could indeed have been rooted in
> dissipation or decay.[38]

Having described and assessed the remains of Byzantine architecture
at Venice, Ruskin is now ready, midway in the second volume, to take up
the Venetian Gothic. But at this point a new foundational chapter is
needed because the principles of construction and decoration set forth in
volume 1 are too diffuse, abstract, and restrained in presentation either
to convey the Gothic feeling or to define its vulnerability to the
Renaissance. The dialectic of *Stones* requires that the Gothic be set
before the reader now in its form and spirit, like a living thing that the
Renaissance will infect and destroy. Answering this need is the famous
chapter carefully entitled "The Nature of Gothic" and divided, as if to
preserve the life metaphor, into Gothic spirit and Gothic form.

In the preface he wrote for it in 1892 William Morris assessed this
chapter as one of the most important of Ruskin's works and one that "in
future days will be considered as one of the very few necessary and
inevitable utterances of the century."[39] Taken at full value, the essay is
much more than an attempt to set forth the principles of the Gothic
aesthetic. It is also Ruskin's most systematic effort to define the conditions under which vital art can be created and to describe the features

by which it may be recognized. As such it is an extension of the distinction between truth and imitation developed in volume 1 of *Modern Painters*, the chapters on "Vital Beauty" in volume 2 of *Modern Painters*, and the "Lamp of Life" in *The Seven Lamps of Architecture*. Of course the roots of vital art are, for Ruskin, not simply technical but social and spiritual. Because the essay also expounds the conditions of creative labor it becomes his first substantial effort at direct social criticism. More important here, the essay explores (or creates) what might with some justice be called the Gothic myth, in that it looks within Gothic work to recover its organic world-view, a primordial harmony with nature that the architecture appears to embody. In this sense the chapter anticipates Ruskin's later studies in Greek mythopoesis, though at this point he conceives the Gothic mind as totally antithetical to the Greek. In support and illustration of these points it will be necessary to review Ruskin's argument briefly. This is no easy task because the chapter is long and sometimes works in three dimensions at once: aesthetic, social, and religious.

Ruskin begins by making it clear that the Gothic he is attempting to define here is not merely that of Venice but "universal Gothic"; indeed, one of the tasks of *Stones* will be to discern later how near Venetian Gothic approaches to the universal or ideal Gothic. More important, Gothic cannot be defined in terms of the presence or absence of such structural elements as pointed arches, vaulted roofs, flying buttresses, grotesque sculpture, and so forth; Gothic occurs only when some or all of these elements, and many others, "come together so as to have life."[40] As with any living thing, the Gothic creation has its "Form" but also its "Power and Life," and it is this "Mental Power" or "Expression" of the Gothic builders that Ruskin tries to define and to which he devotes the major part of his attention in this chapter. Here, as in *The Seven Lamps of Architecture*, he shifts freely among various senses of Gothic: Gothic as aesthetic object with certain formal characteristics; Gothic as social order in which such objects could be made; Gothic as a mythic state of mind underlying both the social order and the objects.

For "Savageness" or "Rudeness," the first of these "mental" characteristics of Gothic, he finds two sources. It expresses sympathy and struggle with the terrain and climate of northern Europe; hence there is "this look of mountain brotherhood between the cathedral and the Alp; this magnificence of sturdy power, put forth only the more energetically because the fine finger-touch was chilled away by the frosty wind, and the eye dimmed by the moor mist, or blinded by the hail."[41] More important, however, the Gothic expresses the medieval Christian mind's refusal of all "Servile ornament," characteristic of Greek, Ninevite, Egyptian, and much modern work. In consequence of its high tolerance for imperfection, Gothic work can be a vehicle for free individual creativity and an instrument of social cohesion; it is a tribute to the Gothic schools "that they thus receive the results of the labour of inferior minds; and out of fragments full of imperfection, and betraying that imperfection in every touch, indulgently raise up a stately and unaccusable whole."[42]

This line of thought about the social involvement of Gothic architecture launches Ruskin into his famous diatribe on the spiritual condition of the modern English laborer vis-a-vis that of the Gothic laborer. The English mind, he argues, shares with the Greek a desire for perfection in all things and is forgetful of the truth that "the finer the nature, the more flaws it will show through the clearness of it."[43] While the drive to perfection *is* imperative, this does not mean that we are to settle for the lesser thing perfected in place of the nobler imperfect thing. The greatest danger is that in dealing with men we will neglect the finest work they can do, the soul work, because it is necessarily flawed and will reduce them to the lowest mechanical work in the interest of perfection. Hence, in a fine stretch of rhetoric, he brings into focus a life-death choice for modern society, embellishing his prophecy, as he frequently does, with a cloud-light metaphor.

> You must either make a tool of the creature, or a man of him. You cannot make both. . . . All the energy of their spirits must be given to make cogs and compasses of themselves. All their attention and strength must go to the accomplishment of the mean act. . . . On the other hand, if you will make a man of the working creature, you cannot make a tool. Let him but begin to imagine, to think, to try to do anything worth doing; and the engine-turned precision is lost at once. Out come all his roughness, all his dullness, all his incapability; shame upon shame, failure upon failure, pause after pause: but out comes the whole majesty of him also; and we know the height of it only when we see the clouds settling upon him. And, whether the clouds be bright or dark, there will be transfiguration behind and within them.[44]

But the modern English have chosen to make men tools and the tools of tools; this enslavement of souls to trivial perfection is the ultimate slavery, "a thousand times more bitter and more degrading than that of the scourged African, or Helot Greek. Men may be beaten, chained, tormented, yoked like cattle, slaughtered like summer flies, and yet remain in one sense, and the best sense, free. But to smother their souls within them, to blight and hew into rotting pollards the suckling branches of their human intelligence . . . This is to be slave-masters indeed." It is important to note here that Ruskin speaks of the "animation" of England's multitudes being "sent like fuel to feed the factory smoke";[45] thus, early in his work industrial smoke becomes an emblem of the consumption of life in the interests of wealth. Moreover, this industrial slavery has bred not only wealth, idleness, and junk, but concommitantly with these a social malaise, an ungratifiable desire for freedom and satisfaction that turns in frustration into the further pursuit of wealth.

> It is verily this degradation of the operative into a machine, which, more than any other evil of the times, is leading the mass of the nations everywhere into vain, incoherent, destructive struggling for a freedom of which they cannot explain the nature to themselves. . . . It is not that men are ill fed, but that they have no pleasure in the work by which they make their bread, and therefore look to wealth as the only means of pleasure.[46]

By the so-called division of labor, then, it is not the labor that is divided, but men, ground into mere fragments and crumbs of their full selves. It is a condition, he prophesies, that humanity will not long endure.

But what can be done to ease this vicious cycle of mindless manufacture that is eating up the souls and resources of the earth? Ruskin proposes a simple program of consumer resistance against all servile production; the essence of it is that we should prefer invention to finish. We must not buy or encourage the manufacture of any item that is not absolutely necessary unless the "Invention" of the laborer has been engaged in its production. "Above all, demand no refinement of execution where there is no thought, for that is slave's work, unredeemed."[47] This precept, of course leads back to architecture and the Gothic, for the architect has the same choice as the manufacturer; he must either make slaves of his workmen and degrade his work to slaves' capacities or free their minds and "let them show their weaknesses together with their strength, which will involve the Gothic imperfection, but render the whole work as noble as the intellect of the age can make it."[48]

Having given these essentially social arguments for the necessity of imperfect work, Ruskin concludes his explanation and defense of Gothic "Savageness" by placing it under a general aesthetic axiom: *"the demand for perfection is always a sign of a misunderstanding of the ends of the art."*[49] This is for two reasons. The great artist's conception is always ahead of his powers of execution, and he never stops working until these powers have failed him; more important, however, is the point that "imperfection is in some sort essential to all that we know of life."[50] Flaws of becoming are the sign of life in all organic forms.

Imperfection, which to Ruskin is the outward sign of free creative growth, becomes in this section the universal law of life in society, art, and nature. And Gothic becomes at once a demonstration of this general law and the one human enterprise that successfully unifies these three forms of life. His last point, imperfection as the sign of the *natura naturans*, leads Ruskin directly to another facet of Gothic work: "Changefulness." Again this is seen as a linking law for nature, art, and society, a law of which the Gothic is an application and an emblem. The merest glance at a piece of architecture, he argues, will reveal the amount of degradation the laborers suffered in building it.[51] If it is characterized by uniformity of parts (capitals all alike and moldings unvaried, as in a Greek building) we may know that the degradation of the workman was complete; but "if, as in Gothic work, there is perpetual change, both in design and execution, the workman must have been altogether set free."[52] But this is not simply a social ideal, this notion that the freedom of the workman is tied to the aesthetic imperative of variation, for the aesthetic law is, in turn, sanctified by nature. We derive no more pleasure from a monotonously regular building than we would from a universe in which the clouds and trees were all perfectly uniform sizes and shapes. In fact, says Ruskin, introducing a point to be developed in volume 3 of *Modern Painters*, the monotony of cities has fostered the "peculiar" modern love of landscape. Increased knowledge and perfected technique tend to produce spiritual complacency and artistic uniformity, but the law of life in architecture, felt exquisitely by the Gothic builders, is love of change.

> The vital principle is not the love of *Knowledge*, but the love of *Change*. It is that strange *disquietude* of the Gothic spirit that is its greatness; that restlessness of the dreaming mind, that wanders hither and thither among the niches, and flickers feverishly around the pinnacles, and frets and fades in labyrinthine knots and shadows along wall and roof, and yet is not satisfied, nor shall be satisfied. The Greek could stay in his triglyph furrow, and be at peace; but the work of the Gothic heart is fretwork still, and it can neither rest in, nor from, its labour, but must pass on, sleeplessly, until its love of change shall be pacified for ever in the change that must come alike on them that wake and them that sleep.[53]

The third primary aspect of the Gothic mind, naturalism, is implicit in the first two. But here Ruskin turns to more exclusively aesthetic issues, though larger moral implications are present as usual. Explicitly he moves toward a resolution of the mimetic-expressive dichotomy left open in the first two volumes of *Modern Painters*. Here, as if to clear up the issue, he explains that the noblest art is a perfect union of the abstract value and imitative power of forms and colours. But this precise union of imitation and expression, "fact" and "design," is seldom achieved in actuality. To show this Ruskin proposes two spectra of artistic power. The first represents technical capabilities only. "On the right side, are the men of facts, on the left the men of design, in the centre the men of both," these types passing into each other by subtle gradations.[54] Apparently each of these capabilities is liable to disease, but the danger is greater as we approach the extremities of talent: the men of facts despising design and vice versa. But these disorders of capacity are not of equal danger to society: "The morbid state of the men of design injures themselves only; that of the men of facts injures the whole world."[55] But this division of artists is in terms of technique only; there is an analogous division to be made in terms of the moral (or perhaps mythic) awareness expressed in their works. Here we have first the purists, who picture the good and leave the evil. "Out of whatever is presented to them, they gather what it has of grace, and life, and light, and holiness, and leave all, or at least as much as possible, of the rest undrawn." Angelico, Perugino, and Giovanni Bellini are painters of this group. In the center are the naturalists, the greatest men, who "render all that they see in nature unhesitatingly," whether good or evil. Giotto, Tintoretto, Turner, and (at this time) Michelangelo are placed in this group. "Their subject is as infinite as nature."[56] On the left are the sensualists, men like Salvator Rosa, Zurbaran, Teniers, and especially Rembrandt, who "perceive and imitate evil only."[57] We note especially Ruskin's point that "the greatest spaces of their canvasses are occupied by *darkness*."[58]

This grouping of artists, implying a particular mythic world-view dependent on archetypal light-values, is especially important in the development of Ruskin's thought and will be taken up later. Here Ruskin refers to them merely to show that the men at the extremities of the scale are all false, though at this stage he believes that "the Purists, in their sanctity, are less separated from these natural painters than the sensualists in their foulness."[59] The problem of clarifying the effects of sensualism on landscape painting is, he admits, a difficult one, but he promises to work the subject out fully in the continuation of *Modern Painters*. For the present, however, his case is simply that between the two extremes of purism and sensuality there is a vital center, true to nature, where the Gothic builders belong; that is, they "belong to the central or greatest rank in *both* the classifications of artists which we have just made; that considering all artists as either men of design, men of facts, or men of both, the Gothic builders were men of both; and that again, considering all artists as either Purists, Naturalists, or Sensualists, the Gothic builders were Naturalists."[60] As a final and curious point he observes that this naturalism of the Gothic workmen is so "peculiarly manifested" in the fondness for vegetation forms as to be an even more distinctive characteristic than the naturalism itself.

Savageness, changefulness, naturalism are for Ruskin the primary coordinates of the Gothic mentality, and he devotes by far the greatest amount of space to them. All three are regarded as expressions of life and indicative of the close bond between the Gothic mind and nature. Insofar as Ruskin here attempts to penetrate Gothic architecture so as to understand how the Gothic builders perceived their work, "The Nature of Gothic" looks forward to his analysis of the mythopoeic landscape in volume 3 of *Modern Painters*. There are, of course, three other characteristics of the Gothic spirit: grotesqueness ("Disturbed Imagination"), rigidity, and redundance. Of these three, rigidity and redundance are both treated briefly, but both are also thought of as life expressions. Gothic rigidity means "not merely stable, but *active* rigidity; the peculiar energy which gives tension to movement, and stiffness to resistance . . . as much seen in the quivering of the lance as in the glittering of the icicle."[61] It is vital rigidity, "a stiffness analogous to that of the bones of a limb, or fibres of a tree; an elastic tension and communication of force from part to part."[62] Even redundance is thought of as an expression of life; it means "the uncalculating bestowal of its labor," indicating "that humility, which is the very life of the Gothic school."[63] But the remaining characteristic, grotesqueness or disturbed imagination, Ruskin must not have thought of as compatible with the vitality of the others, for he deferred his discussion of it until volume 3, remarking simply that one of the Renaissance schools was "morbidly" influenced by it.

In this first and much the longest part of "The Nature of Gothic" Ruskin concerns himself essentially with what he considers to be its "Inner Spirit." But in the last fourth of this chapter of nearly ninety pages he turns to the "Outward Form" or structural definition of this architecture, a matter of secondary concern to us as it was to him. There are, he declares, only three possible good architectures: architecture of the lintel, the Greek; architecture of the round arch, the Romanesque; and architecture of the gable, the Gothic. Structurally, then, Gothic is distinguished as that construction " 'which uses the pointed arch for the roof proper, and the gable for the roof-mask.' "[64] Its ornamental system derives primarily from the principle of foliation copied from the leaf; hence Ruskin's full final definition of Gothic becomes " '*foliated* architecture, which uses the pointed arch for the roof proper, and the gable for the roof-mask.' "[65] He concludes the chapter with two four-point structural and qualitative tests for true Gothic. It need only be noted here that the qualitative tests are based on the "absolute" aesthetic law of organic coherence, which is "that a composition from which anything can be removed without doing mischief, is always so far forth inferior."[66]

This introductory chapter, "The Nature of Gothic," is followed by two chapters on secular Gothic buildings at Venice, "Gothic Palaces" and "The Ducal Palace." These long and detailed chapters bring the second volume to a close. Although there is a wealth of explicit structural description here of interest to the student of both architecture and Venice, these chapters, except for one point to be considered below, contribute relatively little to the development of Ruskin's thought and style. Most of the major critical points have already been anticipated in the preceding chapter and elsewhere. One expects, for instance, his view that the Renaissance palaces are sterile, deriving their picturesqueness from the sea life around them and from the proximity of Gothic palaces; similarly predictable, is his assertion that the latter actually "exhaust their own life by breathing it into the Renaissance coldness,"[67] as is his pronouncement that the Gothic temper of the thirteenth century "is the life-blood of all manly work thenceforward in Europe."[68]

From allusions he has already made to it one expects that the Ducal Palace will be pivotal to Ruskin's discussion of Venetian Gothic, much as Saint Mark's is to his analysis of Venetian Byzantine. In point of fact, he divides the stylistic development he is to survey into two periods: the first, a so-called transitional period in which various Gothic tendencies are evident but do not cohere into any satisfactory domestic architecture; the second, a phase in which consistent domestic Gothic suddenly springs into bloom under the direct influence of the Ducal Palace. Hence the palace is seen as the chef d'oeuvre of the Gothic imagination at Venice and in fact the focusing agent of her entire architectural imagination, since it was built in three successive styles, Byzantine, Gothic, and Renaissance. "Considered as the principal representation of the Venetian school of architecture," he declares, "the Ducal Palace is the Parthenon of Venice, and Gradenigo its Pericles."[69] But Ruskin's thesis requires him to show not simply that the Ducal Palace epitomizes the architecture of Venice, but that the lethal chill of the Renaissance mind, the fall of art, is actually visible in the sculptured texture of the building. This, of course, can be accomplished only by the projection of values through style; and his major effort of this kind in these two chapters is a quasi-apocalyptic presentation of a portion of the palace's decoration to which he gives the appropriate name the "Judgment Angle." By apocalyptic presentation here I mean that he comes to focus on a piece of sculpture in such a way as to make its ordinary defects seem to reveal some extraordinary disaster for mankind, a "national lesson" written in stone.

Ruskin first establishes the general significance of the sculptured angles of the Ducal Palace by explaining that at the time of their construction they represented "a more definite concession to the Gothic spirit than any of the previous architecture of Venice."[70] Thus the sculptured angles epitomize the condition of the Gothic spirit at Venice as the palace itself embodies the whole Venetian achievement. Since one of the four angles is concealed, only three are decorated. Ruskin designates these as the "Fig-tree Angle" (depicting the Fall of Man), the "Vine Angle" (The Drunkenness of Noah), and the "Judgment Angle" (The Judgment of Solomon). The fig-tree and vine angles belong to the old or true Gothic palace, which built between 1301 and 1340 but partially demolished for new construction beginning in 1424, a fateful act of demolition, in Ruskin's view, "the first act of the period properly called 'Renaissance.' "[71] It was the death sentence of the architecture of Venice, and of Venice herself. The third or judgment angle belongs, ironically enough, not to the Gothic palace but to the Renaissance restoration of it. Hence its symbolic significance: "At the first two angles, it is the Gothic spirit which is going to speak to us; and, at the third, the Renaissance spirit."[72]

Ruskin now proceeds to remind us that the chief characteristic of the Gothic spirit is its open admission of weaknesses in its tolerance of rudeness and imperfection of work, whereas the Renaissance spirit is characterized by complete confidence in its own wisdom. So perfectly, he proposes, is this distinction in feeling portrayed in the two Gothic angles as opposed to the Renaissance fabrication, that it appears as if the whole Ducal Palace had been built in various periods and preserved to his time merely to teach us the fateful difference between these two modes of work (Ruskin had noted earlier the coincidental resemblance between his own name and that of the first architect to oppose the complete demolition of the palace after it was gutted by fire in 1574, Giovanni Rusconi).

Thus, by statement and suggestion Ruskin makes it appear that the whole destiny of European art, of the Western mind in fact, is inscribed upon these three angles and that he is their elected prophet or interpreter. What he reads in these stones is, as we might expect, that in the vine and fig-tree angles the sculptor has rendered his foliage truthfully and with exquisite care. "Nothing can be more masterly or superb than the sweep of this foilage on the Fig-tree angle; the broad leaves lapping round the budding fruit, and sheltering from sight, beneath their shadows, birds of the most graceful form and delicate plumage."[73] But in the judgment angle, the Renaissance sculptor partly copied his fig-tree from that of the fig-tree angle, and even so "it is of immeasurably inferior spirit in the workmanship; the leaves of the tree, though far more studiously varied in flow than those of the fig-tree from which they are partially copied, have none of its truth to nature: they are ill set on the stems, bluntly defined on the edges, and their curves are not those of growing leaves, but of wrinkled drapery."[74]

Having set forth the prophecy of the primary angles of the palace, Ruskin turns to the thirty-six capitals of its lower arcade. Here the focus of revelation is not on the workmanship but on the fact that the vices and virtues are personified on these capitals. The motif of the fig tree, with its borrowed branches, is interwoven, giving further resonance to the sculptured prophecy of the angles. To begin with, the mere fact that the subjects of the capitals are vices and virtues reveals to Ruskin a dangerous difference in the tone of the Renaissance mind. They indicate the self-interested and analytic tendency of Renaissance belief. Instead of contemplating the Redeemer and his works, he argues, the Renaissance mind shifts to self-analysis and the counting of virtues like money. This introversion of belief, he believes, has its roots in the profound interest of the best scholars of the period in heathen literature and philosophy. This long-developing interest is "that root of the Renaissance poison-tree, which, of all others, is deepest struck."[75]

An important stem of this poison tree grew from the misguided attempt to graft the Christian system of ethics onto the pagan one, but like the fig tree of the judgment angle, the tree was a lifeless mutation. The "cardinal" virtues of Prudence, Justice, Courage, and Temperance, derived from Plato by way of Cicero, Ruskin supposes, were given a restraining or guiding function in Christian thought. "But in Pagan ethics, they were not only guiding, but comprehensive. They meant a great deal more on the lips of the ancients than they now express to the Christian mind."[76] One notes that here Ruskin not only assumes that his own comprehension of the classical sources is deeper than that of the Renaissance scholars but finds no ultimate evil in the pagan ethical system at its source ("Plato, indeed, studied alone would have done no one any harm").[77] What is assaulted here is not the Greek root but the Renaissance attempt to graft a product of the pagan mind onto the living stem of Christian belief: "At first . . . they tried to graft a Christian system on the four branches of the Pagan one; but finding that the tree would not grow, they planted the Pagan and Christian branches side by side; adding to the four cardinal virtues the three called by the schoolmen theological, namely, Faith, Hope and Charity; the one series considered as attainable by the Heathen, but the other by the Christian only."[78] In this manner the study of classical literature led the Christian writers to "the unfortunate love of systematizing, which gradually degenerated into every species of contemptible formulism, but it accustomed them to work out their systems by the help of any logical quibble, or verbal subtlety, which could be made available for their purpose."[79]

In their matter, then, namely, the system of vices and virtues, the capitals of the Ducal Palace are to Ruskin a sign of the dangerous analytic tendency of the Renaissance mind. But another equally morbid tendency is signaled by their manner: personification. "This general tendency to a morbid accuracy of classification was associated, in later times, with another very important element of the Renaissance mind, the love of personification; which appears to have reached its greatest vigour in the course of the sixteenth century, and is expressed to all future ages, in a consummate manner, in the poem of Spenser." He makes an immediate and important distinction between personification and the more intense and primordial communication, symbolism. "Symbolism is the setting forth of a great truth by an imperfect and inferior sign; . . . and it is almost always employed by men in their most serious moods of faith, rarely in recreation. Men who use symbolism forcibly are almost always true believers in what they symbolize." Personification is the deadly reverse, however; it is the "bestowing of a human or living form upon an abstract idea: it is, in most cases, a mere reaction of the fancy, and is apt to disturb the belief in the reality of the thing personified."[80]

Having settled these important matters for the moment, Ruskin moves on to a brief description of most of the thirty-six personifying capitals of the lower arcade of the Ducal Palace. His main purpose is to distinguish, as he proceeds, between Gothic and Renaissance workmanship, but the process gives him an opportunity for incidental commentary on the meaning of the ethical factor personified. Avarice, for instance, depicted on the fifth side of the tenth capital, draws forth the comment that covetousness, "the sin of Ahab, that is, the inordinate desire of some seen or recognized good,—thus destroying peace of mind,"[81] is very likely productive of much more misery than avarice itself, "but covetousness is not so inconsistent with Christianity."[82] He continues his account of capitals on through the eighteenth, at the fig-tree angle, ending appropriately at the thirty-sixth, in his numbering, which is under the judgment angle and devoted to Justice. Here the incidental comment is on the possibly hypocritical relation between the subject of this capital and the secret trials that characterized later Venetian justice, signifying the attempt, he suggests, to administer justice in an age of violence. From the capitals of the lower arcade he proceeds to those of the upper, but here he has to admit that although their designs are varied and curious, an inadequate knowledge of ancient symbolism prevents him from describing their subjects.

Ruskin's comments on the lower capitals, which are in some ways revealing of his ethical and iconographic interests, cannot be examined here. But the essential point about their design has already been made: in their subjects (vices and virtues) and in their approach (personification) they reveal the chilling, analytic, and abstracting tendencies of the Renaissance. However, he concludes that some of the earlier sculptures of the palace (distinguished by "freshness, elasticity, and softness of their leafage, united with the most noble symmetry and severe reserve,—no running to waste, no loose or experimental lines, no extravagance, and no weakness")[83] reveal the state of Gothic work in Venice at the acme of its period, about 1350. "After this time, all is decline,—of what nature and by what steps, we shall inquire in the ensuing chapter; for as this investigation, though still referring to Gothic architecture, introduces us to the first symptoms of the Renaissance influence, I have considered it as properly belonging to the third division of our subject."[84]

2

The "ensuing chapter" on the etiology of the Renaissance decline turned out to be a volume of some two hundred pages. Although the main lines of argument in this third volume are implicit in the second, Ruskin attempts here to place them in the context of historical process and to give them something like definitive statement. Accordingly the book is subtitled "The Fall" and divided into four stages or chapters: "Early Renaissance," "Roman Renaissance," "Grotesque Renaissance," and a "Conclusion" in which the implications of this "Fall" for modern society are developed. The work wants some detailed consideration here for several reasons. In his analysis of the effects of Renaissance "science," Ruskin is really defending the Gothic again, but this time he does so in terms of the developments that the Gothic mentality opposed: development of the megamachine of integrated knowledge and technique; subjection of and alienation from nature; servile specialization of labor; centralization of skills around wealth and power with consequent dissociation of art from the common people;

despiritualization of art, and so forth. Further, in his exposition of the nature of true or "terror grotesque" Ruskin ties his work on the Gothic to his earlier theory of imagination, and a shift in his interest away from the mimetic toward the symbolic and apocalyptic functions of art becomes apparent. Finally, the relevance of Gothic to the needs of modern life is restated, now from the standpoint of the beholder as well as of the laborer.

The first important point that Ruskin has to make in his "Early Renaissance" concerns the continuity of Renaissance architecture with that of the nineteenth century. From the Grand Canal to Gower Street stretches one unbroken tradition such that, for Ruskin, the Renaissance means the modern tradition in architecture as well; hence the importance of examining the stages by which this style emerged. However, the first of these stages is, contradictorily, marked by enervation of the Gothic style itself, "extravagances and corruptions" of its forms for which "the plague" was in no wise responsible. Venetian Gothic, he argues, declined of itself in two distinct modes: it "fell back first upon Byzantine types, and through them passed to the first Roman,"[85] and it drifted into overluxuriant, languid, and flamboyant forms of ornament. There are two causes of natural decline in any school, Ruskin suggests, overrefinement and overluxuriance. Byzantine infusions into Gothic illustrate the former; flamboyant corruptions of it illustrate the latter. The chapter contains some important illustrations of this overluxuriant and sensuous Gothic in which "excitement and interest are sought for by means of violent and continual curvatures wholly unrestrained, and rolling hither and thither in confused wantoness."[86] To Ruskin they obviously suggest an effete or jaded response to nature.

> It is as if the soul of man, itself severed from the root of its health, and about to fall into corruption, lost the perception of life in all things around it; and could no more distinguish the wave of the strong branches, full of muscular strength and sanguine circulation, from the lax bending of a broken cord, nor the sinuousness of the edge of the leaf, crushed into deep folds by the expansion of its living growth, from the wrinkled contraction of its decay. Thus, in morals, there is a care for trifles which proceeds from love and conscience, and is most holy; and a care for trifles which comes of idleness and frivolity, and is most base.[87]

On top of these internal diseases of Gothic came the Renaissance desire for "universal perfection" at the expense of free creativity and tenderness. This perfective chill is to be distinguished, Ruskin insists, from the social demand for classical *forms* of perfection that grew out of the burgeoning interest in classical literature. Nonetheless the ultimate effect of this new enthusiasm was to destroy the entire system of Gothic craft and knowledge. *"The Renaissance frosts came, and all perished!"*[88] (The frost metaphor—along with clouds, light-darkness, plague, serpents, and roses—reappears continually and with increasing significance as Ruskin's work progresses.) What the frost killed was not merely a style but an entire world of awareness founded on a spiritual bond to nature, the continual perception of typical and vital beauty in things outlined in volume 2 of *Modern Painters*. To underline this fact, Ruskin reintroduces the major thesis of that volume, that all beautiful forms are also types or symbols of God's laws. One example of this is the law that the most perfect unity is to be obtained by the integration of one nature into another, a law which is written for us everywhere by nature's subtle gradations of light and shade:

> It is perfectly inconceivable, until it has been made a subject of special inquiry, how perpetually Nature employs this principle in the distribution of her light and shade; how by the most extraordinary adaptations, apparently accidental, but always in exactly the right place, she contrives to bring darkness into light, and light into darkness; and that so sharply and decisively, that at the very instant when one object changes from light to dark, the thing relieved upon it will change from dark to light, and yet so subtly that the eye will not detect the transition till it looks for it.[89]

Ruskin gives other moral readings of the coloring and dappling of things in nature, but the essential point is that lost with the Gothic mind was its perception of nature's moral code and the social coherence founded upon it. The subjection of nature, as opposed to the devout reading of it, had begun.

In his second chapter, "Roman Renaissance," Ruskin attempts to classify the main destructive forces which unite to create the socioarchitectural system of the central Renaissance. These are four: pride of science, pride of state, pride of system, and infidelity. They are dealt with successively in this order with the greatest attention being given to the first two.

Pride of science, of knowledge, closely bound to the drive for perfection, is "the first notable characteristic of the Renaissance central school."[90] Forms introduced into ornament show evidence of careful study, especially study of anatomy and perspective. This is based on the assumption that to advance knowledge is to advance art, whereas in fact they are "so opposed that to advance the one is . . . to retrograde the other."[91] Much like a modern phenomenologist, Ruskin insists that nothing must come between the artist and the direct apprehension of his object: "Nothing must come between Nature and the artist's sight; nothing between God and the artist's soul."[92]

He must now attempt to formulate the distinction between science and art. Essentially, science presents objective or neutral facts, art human or relational facts. "Science deals exclusively with things as they are in themselves; and art exclusively with things as they affect the human sense and human soul."[93] Art is concerned with the relations and appearances of things to man, with "eye-witness"; that is, "science has to do with facts, art with phenomena."[94] Further, it is by no means true that the more a man knows the more he sees. Knowledge structures perception and blocks immediate experience. "The mind retires inward, fixes itself on the known fact, and forgets the passing visible ones"; so that, "for one visible truth to which knowledge thus opens the eyes, it seals them to a thousand."[95] Not only does knowledge narrow immediate perception, it limits experience in another sense because time spent learning is not spent perceiving things; consider, he suggests, in a passing jab at contemporary education, the life-cost of knowledge.

> Let each man answer for himself how far his knowledge has made him this, or how far it is loaded upon him as the pyramid is upon the tomb. Let him consider, also, how much of it has cost him labour and time that might have been spent in healthy, happy action, beneficial to all mankind; how many living souls may have been left uncomforted and unhelped by him, while his own eyes were failing by the midnight lamp; how many warm sympathies have died within him as he measured lines or counted letters; how many draughts of ocean air, and steps on mountain turf, and openings of the highest heaven he has lost for his knowledge; how much of that knowledge, so dearly bought, is now forgotten or despised, leaving only the capacity of wonder less within him, and, as it happens in a thousand instances, perhaps even also the capacity of devotion. And let him,—if, after thus dealing with his own heart, he can say that his knowledge has indeed been fruitful to him,—yet consider how many there are who have been forced by the inevitable laws of modern education into toil utterly repugnant to their natures, and that in the extreme, until the whole strength of the young soul was sapped away; and then pronounce with fearfulness how far, and in how many senses, it may indeed be true that the wisdom of this world is foolishness with God.[96]

Is it any wonder, he concludes, that even Bacon recognized a certain "venomousness" in the nature of knowledge. In the Renaissance this venom was spread primarily by grammar as a conceptual model; so all branches of knowing were reduced to grammars; this led to pride of system. However, Ruskin would allow at this time that early in the period, before science and system developed their full effects and faith was still possible, science, especially anatomical study, had actually assisted the artistic perceptions of men like Leonardo and Michelangelo (though not Raphael). But

> the dull wondering world believed that their greatness rose out of their new knowledge, instead of out of that ancient religious root, in which to abide was life, from which to be severed was annihilation. And from that day to this, they have tried to produce Michael Angelos and Leonardos by teaching the barren sciences, and still have mourned and marvelled that no more Michael Angelos came; not perceiving that those great Fathers were only able to receive such nourishment because they were rooted on the rock of all ages, and that our scientific teaching, nowadays, is nothing more nor less than the assiduous watering of trees whose stems are cut through.[97]

Gothic art had been good for the worship of God, but Renaissance art promoted the worship of man, aided the cultivation of what Ruskin calls pride of state. Gothic art, he argues, was natural, imperfect, and universal. It was as suited in style and workmanship to the cottage as to the cathedral. It was a folk art bound to God and nature by humble craft. But classic art was by its nature cold, rigid, erudite, perfect, and thus suited to and only possible to the places of power and wealth. It was thus an enslaving art, ironically reaching its highest perfection in the decoration of tombs.

> But of all the evidence bearing upon this subject presented by the various art of the fifteenth century, none is so interesting or so conclusive as that deduced from its tombs. For, exactly in proportion as the pride of life became more insolent, the fear of death became more servile; . . . we find the early tombs at once simple and lovely in adornment, severe and solemn in their expression. . . . But the tombs of the later ages are a ghastly struggle of mean pride and miserable terror.[98]

For Ruskin, the three Renaissance prides, science, state, and system, had in common the limitation of social and artistic freedom. Knowledge, fusing with Gothic excesses, begot perfectionism, specialization of labor, and the consequent limitation of personal expression and creativity. The formalized and erudite art that was produced, gravitated to the centers of wealth and power; so there was no longer any free and universal style, no power for the people in art. The lamp of life in it dimmed. Mental manacles were being forged everywhere, led by grammar, which became first among the sciences. Learned men were busy codifying everything; "so that the whole mind of the world was occupied by the exclusive study of Restraints."[99] And all the creative efforts of mankind were being reduced to "so many different forms of fetter-dance" because men had forgotten that inspiration, not method, is the life of art; that "the letter killeth, but the Spirit giveth life."[100]

With reference to his later work, it should be emphasized that Ruskin's characteristic metaphors for these degenerative Renaissance inputs are poison, venom, or plague. Also, what Ruskin says here about the art of this period must be qualified by bearing in mind that there were, in his view, certain artists of the time, most notably Giotto, who remained essentially uncorrupted by the Renaissance spirit. Further, the persistence of Renaissance values into modern times seemed to be confirmed by the hostility of contemporary criticism to the Pre-Raphaelites, whom Ruskin saw as the inheritors and sole practitioners of the untainted style. "Giotto was, perhaps, of all painters, the most free from the infection of the poison, always conceiving an incident naturally, and drawing it unaffectedly; the absence of posture-making in the works of the Pre-Raphaelites, as opposed to the Attitudinarianism of the modern school, has been both one of their principal virtues, and of the principal causes of the outcry against them."[101]

These infections could not, presumably, have taken such hold on the mind and art of the Renaissance period had religion not become debilitated. Renaissance "Infidelity," Ruskin holds, took two distinct forms: "corruption" of Catholicism and "respect" for Paganism. On the one hand, "the Church had become so mingled with the world that its witness could no longer be received"; thus, when the Protestant movement came it was "in reality, not re-*formation* but re-*animation*."[102] In the meantime, classical myths were beginning to absorb some of the displaced religious energy; "the systems of Pagan mythology began gradually to assume the places in the human mind from which the unwatched Christianity was wasting . . . and it did not matter in the least, as far as respected the power of true religion, whether the Pagan image was believed in or not, so long as it entirely occupied the thoughts." This contradictory creed of "Christianity confessed and Paganism beloved"[103] effectively eliminated all true belief. Better, Ruskin concedes, with Wordsworth, "to have been 'a Pagan suckled in some creed outworn,' than to have stood by the great sea of Eternity, and seen no God walking on its waves, no heavenly world on its horizon."[104] The effect of this spiritual dryness on art was disastrous; all the energies that had once been put to the uses of faith were now expended on fiction. "In old times, men used their powers of painting to show the objects of faith; in later times, they used the objects of faith that they might show their powers of painting."[105] Christianity, then, was undermined on the one hand by its own worldly corruption and on the other by the allure of classical literature. The religious ruin, which had begun at a scholarly level, was abetted by Renaissance sensuality; the characters of the classical deities so suited the manners of the time that "Paganism again became, in effect, the religion of Europe."[106] Such, in Ruskin's view, were the determinants of the central phase of Renaissance decline: "From pride to infidelity, from infidelity to the unscrupulous and insatiable pursuit of pleasure, and from this to irremediable degradation, the transitions were swift, like the falling of a star."[107]

The last act of Ruskin's Renaissance tragedy is appropriately called "Grotesque Renaissance." In discussing the six aspects of the Gothic mind he had left one, Gothic grotesque or disturbed imagination, unelaborated because he planned to show how the Renaissance mind battened morbidly upon the sole Gothic feature that it did develop. Of course, whatever the actual case, this aspect of architecture serves the structure of *Stones* nicely as the ugly denouement and final revelation of the Renaissance decline. What appears on the surface as a comparatively objective choice of topic, governed by the interests of architectural and historical completeness, is in fact a stylistic choice dictated by the work's larger strategy of revelation. Ruskin's style rises frequently to the rhetoric of prophetic indignation and apocalyptic symbolism appropriate to the cultural disaster he envisions.

The long chapter opens with a sweeping condemnation of late Renaissance architecture and an attempt to define the essential feature of its grotesques. "The architecture raised at Venice during this period is among the worst and basest ever built by the hands of men, being especially distinguished by a spirit of brutal mockery and insolent jest, which, exhausting itself in deformed and monstrous sculpture, can sometimes be hardly otherwise defined than as the perpetuation in stone of the ribaldries of drunkenness."[108] A few pages further on Ruskin focuses his attention on one particular carved head, ironically situated on a keystone at the base of the tower of the church of Saint Mary the Beautiful, that epitomizes the final Renaissance degradation. We are forced to take his word for it, since he considers the image literally too dangerous to dwell upon: "A head—huge, inhuman, monstrous,—leering in bestial degradation, too foul to be either pictured or described, or to be beheld for more than an instant: yet let it be endured for that instant; for in that head is embodied the type of the evil spirit to which Venice was abandoned in the fourth period of her decline."[109]

Thus defined, this final Renaissance quality of "idiotic mockery," so horrible that he "cannot pollute this volume by any illustration of its worst forms,"[110] must now be distinguished from the noble Gothic grotesque. In general, Ruskin continues, grotesques are composed of two primary elements, the ludicrous and the fearful; therefore, grotesque forms tend to polarize into either, "sportive grotesque" or "terrible grotesque," depending upon which element is emphasized. To understand the former type and its degeneracy we must know that men fall into three degrees of play: wise, necessary, and inordinate. Inordinate play is the play of those who make amusement the sole object of their existence. Sportive grotesque, then, is the art form of inordinate play. "Incapable of true imagination," this degenerate art, "will seek to supply its place by exaggerations, incoherences, and monstrosities; and the form of the grotesque to which it gives rise will be an incongruous chain of hackneyed graces, idly thrown together,—prettinesses or subtleties, not of its own invention, associated in forms which will be absurd without being fantastic, and monstrous without being terrible."[111] Ruskin apparently had no taste for sculpture that stuck out its tongue at existence.

The source of the true or "terrible grotesque," he continues, is fear; and to understand its function in art one must first consider God's apparent messages of terror. It seems evident from nature that it is the Divine intention to make us often feel profound fear, "not the sudden, selfish, and contemptible fear of immediate danger, but the fear which arises out of the contemplation of great powers in destructive operation, and generally, from the perception of the presence of death."[112] Then, in an enlightening instance, he urges us to consider the moral power of a thunderstorm. First, he explicitly distinguishes the larger judgmental or apocalyptic effect of the storm on us from the more immediate effect produced by our knowledge that several persons may be struck dead by it. This local confrontation with death would produce no more than "momentary sadness" in our busy minds.

> But the preparation for judgment, by all that mighty gathering of the clouds; by the questioning of the forest leaves, in their terrified stillness, which way the winds shall go forth; by the murmuring to each other, deep in the distance, of the destroying angels before they draw forth their swords of fire; by the march of the funeral darkness in the midst of the noon-day, and the rattling of the dome of heaven beneath the chariot wheels of death; . . . . The lurid colour, the long, irregular, convulsive sound, the ghastly shapes of flaming and heaving cloud, are all as true and faithful in their appeal to our instinct of danger, as the moaning or wailing of the human voice itself is to our instinct of pity. It is not a reasonable calculating terror which they awake in us; it is no matter that we count distance by seconds, and measure probability by averages. That shadow of the thunder-cloud will still do its work upon our hearts, and we shall

watch it passing away as if we stood upon the threshing-floor of Araunah.[113]

Here and in several accompanying passages of apocalyptic prose Ruskin strives to invoke the "Holy Fear" produced in us by the destructive powers of nature and to distinguish this emotion from the more limited dread we feel at the sight of those who have suffered from these "ministries of judgment." Natural apocalypses of hell (characterized by dark imagery) appear to be answered in nature by those of heaven (light imagery). "Wrath and threatening are invariably mingled with love; and in the utmost solitudes of nature, the existence of Hell seems to me as legibly declared by a thousand spiritual utterances, as that of Heaven. . . . Gerizim and Ebal, birth and death, light and darkness, heaven and hell, divide the existence of man, and his Futurity."[114]

But, returning to the psychology of the grotesque, the mind in which the "terrible grotesque" appears is one that develops a strange fixation "upon certain conditions of terribleness, into the complete depth of which it does not enter for the time." As for these "conditions of terribleness," Ruskin merely notes that the proper subjects of our fear are forms which suggest the power of death or the nature of sin, and he offers as an example the archetypal significance of the serpent, an important symbol in his own later work. When he turns to the psychic state that foists up the "terrible grotesque," he argues that it always contemplates "some expression of vice or danger" but does so in a "peculiar temper." These strange moods generally belong to one of three types: "predetermined or involuntary apathy," "mockery," or "diseased and ungoverned imaginativeness." That is, as he had noted at the outset, the grotesque always appears to incorporate some degree of playfulness, but the "terrible grotesque," unlike its opposite, involves playing with terror, the mind summoning images "of which, either in weariness or in irony, it refrains for the time to acknowledge the true terribleness."[115]

Ruskin now passes to a separate discussion of each of the three moods in which masters of the terrible grotesque appear to contemplate objects of terror: apathy, mockery, and disturbed imagination. Only the last of these conditions is of particular importance here, but two brief points about the others should be made in passing. First, true grotesque can emerge, in his view, from the languid play of a solemn mind but never from even the full exertion of a frivolous mind, yet there is a kind of grotesque which can emerge from the apathetic toying with terror in a deep mind. Second, among examples of terror grotesque rooted in mockery or satire, Ruskin pays tribute to those of Dante, Spenser, and Dürer. He seems to have been particularly impressed by the dragons of Dürer's Apocalypse illustrations and by his *Knight and Death*; in these, he notes, "there is neither play nor apathy; but their grotesque is of the ghastly kind which best illustrates the nature of death and sin."[116]

The third source of terrible grotesque, "disturbed imagination," is particularly important, because it connects the true grotesque with his earlier general theory of imagination and raises again the special problem of visionary or disturbed imagination that had worried him in volume 2 of *Modern Painters* and would continue to do so. He approaches the subject by pointing out that the most intelligible yet most ignoble instances of this kind of grotesque are those which appear to all men in their troubled dreams. The imagination, he insists, is not the same as the dream; yet imagination at its highest shares with the dream an involuntary or unrefusable quality, and this is the source of its prophetic authority.

> The imagination is never governed; it is always the ruling and Divine power: and the rest of the man is to it only as an instrument which it sounds, or a tablet on which it writes; clearly and sublimely if the wax be smooth and the strings true, grotesquely and wildly if they are strained and broken. And thus the *Iliad*, the *Inferno*, the *Pilgrim's Progress*, the *Faerie Queen*, are all of them true dreams; only the sleep of the men to whom they came was the deep, living sleep which God sends, with a sacredness in it as of death, the revealer of secrets.[117]

In a sense, then, the greatest art is, as he would put it later in volume 4 of *Modern Painters*, the "Art of *Dreaming*."[118]

Ruskin's recurrent image for the inevitable dimness and distortion of such truths as men are able to perceive is Saint Paul's metaphor "through a glass darkly." But here, the subject being grotesques, he uses the metaphor to point to the difference between dimness and distortion in the glass. "Most men's minds are dim mirrors, in which all truth is seen, as St. Paul tells us, darkly; this is the fault most common and most fatal; dullness of heart and mistiness of sight, increasing to utter hardness and blindness; Satan breathing upon the glass, so that if we do not sweep the mist laboriously away, it will take no image."[119] But even when the glass will take an image there is still the danger of distortion, for "the fallen human soul, at its best, must be as a diminishing glass, and that a broken one, to the mighty truths of the universe round it; and the wider the scope of its glance, and the vaster the truths into which it obtains an insight, the more fantastic their distortion is likely to be." The vaster the scope of imaginative vision, then, the greater the danger of distortion, of the disturbed grotesque. "It would seem to be rare that any very exalted truth should be impressed on the imagination without some grotesqueness. . . . Nearly all the dreams recorded in the Bible,— Jacob's, Joseph's, Pharoah's, Nebuchadnezzar's—are grotesques; and nearly the whole of the accessory scenery in the books of Ezekiel and the Apocalypse."[120]

At this point he is thinking particularly of symbolic grotesques in biblical deep-dream visions: "the kine of Pharoah eating each other, the gold and clay of Nebuchadnezzar's image, the four beasts full of eyes, and other imagery of Ezekiel and the Apocalypse";[121] but he must bring his theory of distortion in deep imagination back toward ordinary experience. First, he qualifies his judgment of the examples just given by suggesting that these might be placed in a special category of "Symbolical Grotesque." Yet the element of awe so strongly enters the symbol, or into its deep meaning when the vision itself is not terrible, that their classification with the terrible grotesques is justified. Further, "this mingled doubt, fear, and curiosity" enters into all our responses to symbols; however, the "Divine fear" that accompanies the perception of deep meanings is true not merely of invented symbols but of all the forms of nature, for they are types of eternal truths. Thus terrible or apocalyptic grotesques can be read in ordinary nature through the necessary distortions of deep imaginations. The distortion is induced, not by the superficial subject itself, but by the depth of imaginative penetration; yet "it is the trembling of the human soul in the presence of death which most of all disturbs the images on the intellectural mirror, and invests them with the fitfulness and ghastliness of dreams."[122]

This tangled line of reasoning leads to Ruskin's final formula for the terrible grotesque. It appears when, in contemplation of death, the imagination ("fancy") "is brought into morbid action by terror, accompanied by the belief in spiritual presence, and in the possibility of spiritual apparition. Hence are developed its most sublime, because its least voluntary, creations, aided by fearfulness of the phenomena of nature which are in any wise the ministers of death, and primarily directed by the peculiar ghastliness of expression in the skeleton."[123] Note that along with imagination and symbol, especially a death symbol, a new element has crept into Ruskin's definition: "spiritual presence." But why, in the end, has such an extended analysis of the grotesque been necessary at this point in *The Stones of Venice*? Because Ruskin wishes to show that there is no more certain test of a period's greatness or moral vision than the quality of its grotesques. In this respect Dante is, and remains, the absolute standard of the moral imag-

ination for Ruskin; he is "the central man of all the world, as representing in perfect balance the imaginative, moral, and intellectual faculties,
all at their highest"[124]; and in him the grotesque reaches its supreme
perfection. He is not only, of course, the central man of the central time
of European art, but also the master of mythic and apocalyptic symbolism, for whom allegorical abstractions become embodied presences.

Ruskin's chapter entitled "Grotesque Renaissance" is complex and
confused, but what it appears to assert is that all true grotesque is
apocalyptic, the unrefusable vision of a great imagination induced by
holy dread in the contemplation of sin, death, and the lethal powers of
nature. The medieval and early Renaissance minds possessed the moral
capacity for true terrible grotesques, but the late Renaissance lacked this
vision and its grotesques became merely ludicrous or obscene. This
failure of the true grotesque at Venice is, for Ruskin, a visible and ironic
index of her moral decrepitude. Of course it might be said that he
supplies the moral awareness so that Venice's false grotesques, centered
on the head with which the chapter opens, become true terrible grotesques for him personally. Finally, because Renaissance Venice could
envision no true grotesques, she was deprived of their prophetic warning of the fearful affinity of sin and death, and thus her fate was sealed.

> Thenceforward, year after year, the nation drank with deeper thirst from
> the fountains of forbidden pleasure, and dug for springs, hitherto un-
> known, in the dark places of the earth. . . . That ancient curse was upon
> her, the curse of the Cities of the Plain, "Pride, fulness of bread, and
> abundance of idleness." By the inner burning of her own passions, as fatal
> as the fiery rain of Gomorrah, she was consumed from her place among the
> nations; and her ashes are choking the channels of the dead, salt sea.[125]

The "Conclusion" to *The Stones of Venice* does not so much look
backward over the book as forward through analogies toward the present. Its subject is the special and continuing dangers of vanity of
knowledge. Particularly notable is the chapter's emphasis upon the way
art's participation in the ancient language of symbols is opposed by the
aesthetic of naturalism. The scientist, Ruskin begins, teaches us to look
forward to the imminent "manhood of mankind" after six thousand
years of infancy; but little real progress has been made, and this not
without much risk. In "social science," for instance, the basic principles
are so little understood "that doctrines of liberty and equality can be
openly preached, and so successfully as to infect the whole body of the
civilized world with apparently incurable disease."[126]

There are two primary and presumably related dangers inherent in
any period of change such as the nineteenth century: "pride of vain

knowledge" and "pursuit of vain pleasure." These are the divisions of
the book's final chapter. In earlier chapters Ruskin had shown how the
Renaissance vanity of science had led to a thirst for perfection and, in so
doing, had invalidated that rude energy of the workman which was the
life of Gothic art; for the Renaissance mind "preferred science to emotion, and experience to perception."[127] Turning to his own time, Ruskin
concedes that the modern mind possesses more extensive and substantial
knowledge and is therefore less vain, but in the cultivation and creation
of art he finds its errors as great or even greater than those of the
Renaissance. It shows no sign of comprehending "the great principle to
which all that has hitherto been stated is subservient,"[128] namely, that
great art is the expression of a great soul, and the soul cannot be enlarged
by knowledge. Its natural language is "that great symbolic language of
past ages, which has now so long been *unspoken*."[129] Though he
complains that the modern spirit of formalism, descended from the
Renaissance, is unable to appreciate either the faithful naturalism of the
Pre-Raphaelites or the penetrative symbolism of the medieval painters,
his particular interest here is in the way the symbolic functions in
aesthetic preception. When he says that the modern artist wants emotion
and perception, not experience and science, he appears to be making a
distinction between conceptual and relational awareness, between
representation and expression. The artist's fundamental concern is not
with direct copying of the object but with enabling the object to say what
it must say; yet to supply the object with its necessary language the artist
must be aware of what it has said to others, be a speaker of the symbolic
language of past ages. This competence can not be given by analytic
knowledge of the object or by techniques of representation. What can
science tell the artist about the ways in which a natural object, say an
olive tree, has traditionally been perceived or "intended" by observing
consciousnesses? To the artist, the olive tree is not merely a living thing
perceived in a neutral way but a living symbol, an object-for-
consciousness that includes not only his immediate perception of the
real object but also any awareness of its mythic or symbolic significance
he may possess. This is why "no art is noble which in any wise depends
upon direct imitation for its effect upon the mind." A point, Ruskin
notes, that he had made in volume 1 of *Modern Painters*, but not upon
the highest grounds."[130] Great art, then, never falls into the error of
realizing its subject so completely that it fails to converse with the
beholder's imagination.

   This larger section of the chapter, his analysis of the dangerous
confusion of knowledge with art and a plea for a return to symbols as the

language of the soul in art, ends with an apocalyptic peroration in which, under the right comprehension of "the holier nature of the art of man," the erstwhile "dead" symbols of the world give up their souls to our awakened eyes

> as the world opens to our sight, lo! far back into all the depths of time, and forth from all the fields that have been sown with human life, how the harvest of the dragon's teeth is springing! how the companies of the gods are ascending out of the earth! The dark stones that have so long been the sepulchres of the thoughts of nations, and the forgotten ruins wherein their faith lay charnelled, give up the dead that were in them; and beneath the Egyptian ranks of sultry and silent rock, and amidst the dim golden lights of the Byzantine dome, and out of the confused and cold shadows of the Northern cloister, behold, the multitudinous souls come forth with singing, gazing on us with the soft eyes of newly comprehended sympathy, and stretching their white arms to us across the grave, in the solemn gladness of everlasting brotherhood.[131]

The second phase of his final argument in *Stones* deals with the dangers of illusory pleasure to which the modern mind, like that of the Renaissance, is exposed because in our knowledge we have lost the childlike freshness of vision. The contemporary fondness for medieval settings in romantic novels and for landscape painting suggested to Ruskin a continuing human hunger for the simple pleasures of organic color and form that goes mostly unfed in denatured modern life. This need had partly been filled in simpler times by Gothic architecture. In fact "the English school of landscape, culminating in Turner, is in reality nothing else than a healthy effort to fill the void which the destruction of Gothic architecture has left."[132]

Most ordinary practical men are unable to fill this lack in life with impressions drawn from romances and landscapes, and the capacity for romantic imagination, if one possess it at all, is a quality of youth. Therefore, in the light of common day no art form answers the romantic thirst so well as Gothic architecture, which, just as it can absorb the creative energies of every degree of workman, can also address every mood and character in its spectators. And so Ruskin concludes his long defense of the Gothic with a plea for a return to it as a focusing agent for labor and delight in modern life, an architecture rich in natural imagery that will please like delectable landscapes worked in stone.

> It is hardly possible at present to imagine what may be the splendour of buildings designed in the forms of English and French thirteenth century *surface* Gothic, and wrought out with the refinement of Italian art in the details, and with a deliberate resolution, since we cannot have figure-sculpture, to display in them the beauty of every flower and herb of the English fields, each by each; doing as much for every tree that roots itself in

our rocks, and every blossom that drinks our summer rains, as our ancestors did for the oak, the ivy, and the rose. Let this be the object of our ambition, and let us begin to approach it, not ambitiously, but in all humility, accepting help from the feeblest hands; and the London of the nineteenth century may yet become as Venice without her despotism, and as Florence without her dispeace.[133]

3

Concurrently with the researching and writing of *The Seven Lamps of Architecture* and the three volumes of *The Stones of Venice*, Ruskin was engaged in dismaying amount of peripheral work. By this I do not refer merely to his daily routine of drawing, letter writing, and diary keeping; nor to the preparation of those ancillary materials to *Stones*, the appendixes, "Venetian Index," and *The Examples of the Architecture of Venice* already mentioned in passing, but to a considerable range of other writing not yet touched on here. During this period of major architectural work, Ruskin produced, among other lesser things, two long reviews for the *Quarterly*, a hefty theological tract, a course of four comprehensive lectures on his work, and, most important, a barrage of material in defense of the Pre-Raphaelites that may have prevented the movement from being extinguished by hostile criticism. The editors of the Library Edition have collected these incidental writings of 1844–54 (thirteen in all) into a volume of more than six hundred pages.

Because there are so many primary works to be examined it is impracticable to attempt to recreate the explicit biographical contexts of these minor works. Moreover, this has been adequately accomplished by others. What must be done is to relate the more important of these writings to the developing central awareness and expressive drive we have been tracing. This incorporation is necessary because some of these works can be called "minor" only from a restricted point of view. They are minor, that is, in the sense of being shorter, largely occasional, and built of more subdued, less fully orchestrated prose, but not minor in the sense of scope or breadth of synthesis undertaken. Even these by-works show Ruskin's urge to create comprehensive, even quasi-mythic systems or to survey massive tracts of human values.

Consider, for instance, *Notes on The Construction of Sheepfolds*, the only published work of this group not at all concerned with art. The title sounded sufficiently mundane that some readers apparently purchased it under the misapprehension that the author of *The Seven Lamps of Architecture* would now prescribe the ideal enclosures for sheep. But the architecture intended by *Sheepfolds* is even more removed from physical structures than that of *The Seven Lamps. Sheepfolds*, of course, means "churches," not church buildings but mystical and political enclosures of flocks signified by such expressions as High Church or Low Church, Catholic Church or Christian church.

Ruskin explains that the tract was begun as part of an appendix to *Stones* in order to clarify his assertion that the Venetian attempt to separate church and state was vain and impious, but the inquiry deepened to matters of interest to a more general readership. In fact, the essay undertakes to deal with three profound questions: What is the church, in the spiritual and hierarchical senses, considered in terms of the doctrinal or disciplinary authority it expresses? What is the necessary relation between church and state? Considering the meaning of the church, how can the Protestant schism in England be healed? Ruskin proposes to answer these questions directly from scriptural authority, but the bias of his tract is clearly anti-Anglican and, of course, anti-Catholic. It is a narrowness he remarks in his brief preface to the work's third edition (1875): "I had only got the length of perceiving the schism between sects of Protestants to be criminal, and ridiculous, while I still supposed the schism between Protestants and Catholics to be virtuous and sublime."[134]

To enlarge his readers' conception of *church*, Ruskin begins by marking the distinction between the church invisible and the church visible. The invisible church is the indiscernible body of true believers in the myth itself, signified by such expressions as the *communion of saints* or the *mystical body of Christ*. The absolute number of this flock is known only to God, yet its members can occasionally be discerned by their consistently Christian or "sheeplike" behavior. But questions of membership in the visible church are no less difficult, since its members spend so much time haggling over details of baptism, sacraments, and other mysteries of membership in the visible church that they fail to act upon the clear and palpable signs of belonging or nonbelonging. That is, Christians should be prepared to excommunicate any man convicted of and unrepentant of any un-Christian act, "of any dishonourable conduct or wilful crime, of any fraud, falsehood, cruelty, or violence."[135] This concept of ejection from the fold leads directly to large questions of church authority. What authority, Ruskin asks, do the churches, invisible or visible, have in the declaration of doctrine or the enforcement of discipline?

In declaration of doctrine the invisible church is infallible by definition. A mythic system never fails its believers. Similarly, it is absolute but invisible in its enforcement of discipline. But the visible church, because it is an alloy of "the small wisdom and light weight of Invisible Christians with the false wisdom and contrary weight of Undetected Anti-Christians"[136] (meaning Puseyites) has no authority whatever in doctrine. "We might as well talk of the authority of the morning cloud."[137] But through the action of "common consent" of the flock the visible church has immense authority in discipline, if it would exercise it and purify the fold through excommunication. The visible church, then, has disciplinary but no doctrinal authority. But in what officers should the essentially disciplinary power of the visible church be vested?

This leads Ruskin to the two final practical questions that evoke the main points of his essay: Who are the clergy? and What is their authority over the church? His main point here (again anti-Anglican) is that the clergy may be called deacons, bishops, elders, evangelists but never *priests*, for "all members of the Invisible Church become, at the instant of their conversion, Priests."[138] The functions of the clergy are to be twofold: "Teaching; including doctrine, warning, and comfort: Discipline, including reproof and direct administration of punishment."[139] But "their authority never supersedes that of either the intellect or the conscience of its simplest lay members. . . . Truth is to be discovered, and Pardon to be won, for every man by himself."[140] These, he argues, are the central principles of religion: that truths can be discerned only by action (seeking) and they can be revealed individually to the simplest man. Again, ultimate authority goes back to the invisible church, the mythic unity rooted in personal religious experience. But in matters essentially of social discipline Ruskin would give the visible church and its officers frightening power. Again he emphasizes the uses of excommunication as the main feature of the structure of sheepfolds.

> There ought, I think, to be an ecclesiastical code of laws; and a man ought to have jury trial, according to this code, before an ecclesiastical judge; in which, if he were found guilty, as of lying, or dishonesty, or cruelty, much more of any actually committed violent crime, he should be pronounced Excommunicate; refused the Sacrament; and have his name written in some public place as an excommunicate person, until he had publicly confessed his sin and besought pardon of God for it. The jury should always be of the laity, and no penalty should be enforced in an ecclesiastical court except this of excommunication.[141]

Within all, Ruskin appears to be arguing that the visible church cannot tell a man what to believe; this is between man and myth. The church must not come between the individual conscience and God, but it can tell him how to behave if he is to belong to the visible church. But since he has claimed that doubts can be resolved only by action, his argument circles; and we see that the visible church, by controlling behavior, would intrude between the individual conscience and the invisible church. This contradiction becomes more severe in the last phase of his argument where it appears that Ruskin will permit no separation of church and state. "Throughout the whole of Christendom, the Church (or society of professing Christians) *is* the State."[142] (But which church is meant, the visible or invisible?) The best form of government will be monarchical and paternal, acting *for* the people not as an expression of their opinions. And while this governmental father will have no absolute authority to compel visible religious performance from his children, he will have

> indisputable authority to procure for them such religious instruction as he deems fittest, and to recommend it to them by every means in his power; he not only has authority, but is under obligation to do this, as well as to establish such disciplines and forms of worship in his house as he deems most convenient for his family: with which they are indeed at liberty to refuse compliance, if such disciplines appear to them clearly opposed to the law of God; but not without most solemn conviction of their being so, nor without deep sorrow to be compelled to such a course.[143]

It appears that, although the visible church has no absolute doctrinal authority (over conscience), its business is to make itself as visible as possible through excommunication, teaching, and self-propagation with state assistance. Thus, while Ruskin admits the existence of a mystical as well as a political church, he allows the former little practical influence upon fold-building; in fact his visible fold would half create his invisible fold.

This is why, although his tract concluded with strong words about the Protestant schism in England, he did not, as he thought, know how to heal it. He wanted, rightly, to bring the visible and invisible churches together through appeal to scripture or, at the least, to achieve a unified Protestantism, which was the same thing for him at this point. But the very sectarian bias of his language shows how far he was from seeing that no attempt to define the visible church would bring it closer to the vital but invisible church. "The real difficulty, nowadays," he argues, "lies in the sin and folly of both parties; in the superciliousness of the one, and the rudeness of the other. Evidently, however, the sin lies most at the High Church door, for the Evangelicals are much more ready to act with Churchmen than they with Evangelicals."[144] His formula for unity is explicit, the Anglican church, for instance, "*must* cut the term Priest entirely out of her Prayer-book, and substitute for it that of Minister or Elder; the passages respecting Absolution must be thrown out also, except the doubtful one in the Morning Service, in which there is no harm; and then there would be only the Baptismal question left, which is one of words rather than of things, and might easily be settled in Synod, turning the refractory Clergy out of their offices, to go to Rome if they chose."[145] But, though his intentions were noble, Ruskin did not see that if his scheme were carried through, instead of the "two great sects of paralyzed Protestants" of which he complained there would simply be three great sects of paralyzed Protestants. The best that can be said is that Ruskin's desire for social order and decency was such that he would evict religion to tighten the fold.

The same effort to systematize large subjects is evident also in most of Ruskin's incidental writings on art during this period. But in the first of these, his view (1847) of Lord Lindsay's *Sketches of the History of Christian Art* (1847), Ruskin had to demolish a system much like one of his own and at the same time propose another. Lindsay, whom Ruskin acknowledged as his own "first master in Italian art,"[146] had built his art history around an analysis of human faculties into three primary racial qualities: sense, intellect (subdivided into imagination and reason), and spirit. In an earlier work, *Progression by Antagonism* (1846), Lindsay had attempted to show that human progress is the result of dialectical antagonisms among these ethnic aspects of the mind. It is his attempt to use art history as a demonstration of this theory which Ruskin finds most objectionable in Lindsay's *History*. The historian had assumed that phases of sense, intellect, and spirit in art were in exact correspondence with the same phases in the historical development of man. Thus, in Lindsay's system, the massive architecture of Egypt expresses the "ideal of Sense or Matter" characteristic of all descendants of the race of Ham; the sculpture of Greece is the "very voice of Intellect and Thought" characteristic of the line of Japhet; while the great Christian painting is the language of the immortal spirit in conversation with its God in the manner of the Jews, the race of Shem. Finally, and most important, for Lindsay the proof of continuous progress in the arts is in the fact that, out of earlier antagonism of sense and intellect resulting in phases of progress and decline among the sister arts, all three arts finally emerge in perfect synthesis in Christian Europe.[147]

Although Lindsay's scheme, a mixture of mythology and criticism, sounds like one of his own, Ruskin had to attack it because at bottom it was deeply antagonistic to his conception of the development of art. Superficially, yet sensibly, he first objected to Lindsay's system for its intellectual fuzziness and incoherence: "The writer's evil genius pursues him; the demand for exertion of thought is remorseless, and continuous throughout, and the statements of theoretical principle as short, scattered, and obscure, as they are bold.''[148] Later, however, Ruskin rounds upon the system itself, inviting his reader to perceive

> the bold fallacy of this forced analogy—the comparison of the architecture of one nation with the sculpture of another and the painting of a third, and the assumption as a proof of difference in moral character, of changes necessarily wrought . . . by the advance of mere mechanical experience. Architecture must precede sculpture, not because sense precedes intellect, but because men must build houses before they adorn chambers, and raise shrines before they inaugurate idols; and sculpture must precede painting, because men must learn forms in the solid before they can project them on a flat surface.[149]

Briefly, to the abstract intellectual system that relates the development of art to the internal spiritual development of man, Ruskin gradually opposes his own more existential system in which the progress is related to material or environmental conditions from which various nations had to form their art. Egyptian art differs from Greek, not because the one was a nation of Sense and the other a nation of Intellect, but because

> no singing winds nor shaking leaves or gliding shadows gave life to the line of their barren mountains—no Goddess of Beauty rose from the pacing of their silent and foamless Nile. One continual perception of stability, or changeless revolution, weighed upon their hearts—their life depended on no casual alternation of cold and heat—of drought and shower; their gift-Gods were the risen River and the eternal Sun, and the types of these were forever consecrated in the lotus decoration of the temple and the wedge of the enduring Pyramid.[150]

At root, the difference between Lindsay's myth of the development of art and Ruskin's version is, as we might expect, that while Lindsay's was mentalist, Ruskin's depended upon the interrelationships of the human spirit and nature, considered as climate, scenery, or materials of art. Finally, and most important, Lindsay's scheme implied that continuous perfection of art would follow upon the spiritual and intellectual refinement of man, but for Ruskin this was a conclusion vigorously denied by the condition of modern art. If the advance of art were tied to the awakening of consciousness, as Lindsay thought, we could never have too much knowledge for the good of art. To Ruskin, however, the contemporary synthesis of refined theology and advanced technology looked more like the dead end of art than the high vitality that one might extrapolate from Lindsay's history. Hence the importance of an apparently irrelevant early passage defining the plight of modern art:

> In proportion to the increasing spirituality of religion, the conception of worthiness in material offering ceases, and with it the sense of beauty in

the evidence of votive labour; machine-work is substituted for hand-work, as if the value of ornament consisted in the mere multiplication of agreeable forms, instead of in the evidence of human care and thought and love about the separate stones; and—machine-work once tolerated—the eye itself soon loses its sense of this very evidence, and no more perceives the difference between the blind accuracy of the engine, and the bright, strange play of the living stroke—a difference as great as between the form of a stone pillar and a springing fountain. And on this blindness follow all errors and abuses—hollowness and slightness of frame-work, speciousness of surface ornament, concealed structure, imitated materials, and types of form borrowed from things noble for things base; and all these abuses must be resisted with the more caution, and less success, because in many ways they are signs or consequences of improvement, and are associated both with purer forms of religious feeling and with more general diffusion of refinements and comforts.[151]

My comments here can hardly do interpretive justice to Ruskin's long and complex review; I merely want to show that the work, though incidental, is not trivial and that it opposes a meliorist concept of art history with another that might be called phenomenological in that art-consciousness is not seen through some other mode. Although Ruskin is kinder to Charles Eastlake's *Materials for a History of Oil Painting* (1847), his review (1848) employs much the same strategy of replacing the author's system with his own more phenomenological approach.

At the opposite extreme from Lindsay's spiritual history, Eastlake's work is not a history of the art but of its materials and their direct influence upon technique. It is really a history of invention centered upon Van Eyck's discovery of the process of mixing solid color with varnish and the effect this had upon the practice of laying on color, chiefly among the Northern painters. Ruskin praises the book's generally meticulous scholarship and its value in placing the techniques of the ancients before contemporary painters. But, though he allows its value as a contribution to the technology of painting, he concludes that such a study, "grounded merely on the invention or amelioration of processes and pigments," is really of limited interest to the student of art.[152]

For Ruskin, what is essential to art is not in the course of "mechanical" improvements traced by Eastlake (and reexamined by himself with surprising scholarship) any more than in the scheme of human development imposed by Lindsay; what matter are the recurrent verities of greatness that can only be deduced from the practice of the masters themselves through comparison of their work with nature. In examining the "transparent" technique of the early Flemish masters in which the color had to be built up by successive steps from a design laid on pure white ground, Ruskin finds that the enduring quality was not in the chemistry but in the *discipline* the system demanded, especially careful drawing and absolute decisiveness in the chiaroscuro.

> The reader cannot but see that the *eminent* character of the whole system is its predeterminateness. From first to last its success depended on the decision and clearness of each successive step. The drawing and light and shade were secured without any interference of colour; but when over these the oil-priming was once laid, the design could neither be altered nor, if lost, recovered; a colour laid too opaquely in the shadow destroyed the inner organization of the picture, and remained an irremediable blemish; and it was necessary, in laying colour even on the lights, to follow the guidance of the drawing beneath with a caution and precision which rendered anything like freedom of handling, in the modern sense, totally impossible. Every quality which depends on rapidity, accident, or audacity was interdicted; no affectation of ease was suffered to disturb the humility of patient exertion.[153]

Most important, however, is the point that licenses in shadow were impossible: "Shade was not to be had at small cost; its masses could not be dashed on in impetuous generalization, fields for the future recovery of light. They were measured out and wrought to their depths only by expenditure of toil and time; and, as future grounds for colour, they were necessarily restricted to the *natural* shadow of every object, white being left for high lights of whatever hue."[154]

But even in early practice, after the white ground had been prepared and the design traced, it was customary to lay in the shadows with a transparent brown pigment in an asphaltum base. In Ruskin's system, based on the archetypal significance of light-values, this brown shadow ground, was the crux of painting technique. "As the art advanced, the lights were more and more loaded, and afterwards glazed, the shadows still being left in untouched transparency. This is the method of Rubens."[155] "The great advantage of this primary laying in of the darks in brown was the obtaining of an unity of shadow, throughout the picture, which rendered variety of hue, where it occurred, an instantly accepted evidence of light."[156] But the infusion of brown was also a deadly practice, especially as underdrawing ceased to be defined with the pen.

> When, by later and more impetious hands, the point tracing was dispensed with, and the picture boldly thrown in with the brown pigment, it became matter of great improbability that the force of such a prevalent tint could afterwards be softened or melted into a pure harmony; the painter's feeling for truth was blunted; brilliancy and richness became his object rather than sincerity or solemnity; with the palled sense of colour departed the love of light, and the diffused sunshine of the early schools died away in the narrowed rays of Rembrandt.[157]

Finally, having elaborated Eastlake on the Flemish practice and added some commentary on its relation to Italian color technique, Ruskin deduces only one absolute of practice common to all great colorists:

> It appears from the evidence now produced that there are at least three distinct systems traceable in the works of good colourists, each having its own merit and its peculiar application. First, the white ground, with careful chiaroscuro preparation, transparent colour in the middle tints, and opaque high lights only (Van Eyck). Secondly, white ground, transparent brown preparation, and solid painting of lights above (Rubens). Thirdly, white ground, brown preparation, and solid painting both of lights and shadows above (Titian); on which last method, indisputably the noblest, we have not insisted, as it has not yet been examined by Mr. Eastlake. But in all these methods the white ground was indispensable.[158]

This scheme was presented as an objective interpretation of the history of painting based upon careful examination of the paintings themselves, but of course one may read in it that emphasis on purity of light which is characteristic of Ruskin's thought.

Ruskin's critical support of the Pre-Raphaelites between 1851 and 1854 took the form of four letters to the *Times*; a pamphlet entitled *Pre-Raphaelitism* (1851); and a lecture delivered at Edinburgh in 1853, the fourth of a series. He was also, of course, personally involved with members of the movement at this time, but it is what he wrote that concerns us here. At first it would appear that this group of miscellaneous pronouncements could hardly display the systemizing urge, closely related to mythologizing, which I take to be the most interesting feature of these incidental writings. Yet when one studies these Pre-Raphaelite commentaries in the order of their appearance it is plain that their total effect is an attempt to incorporate the Pre-Raphaelites into the system of *Modern Painters*, as far as it had gone. Ruskin attempts to show that they are Turnerian naturalists, in the sense of *Modern Painters*, volume 1, and at the same time believing medievalists in the manner of *Modern Painters*, volume 2. His defense of the Pre-Raphaelites allowed him to clarify and reiterate certain points of his aesthetic, especially his concept of truth, and make their work appear to be a living vindication of it. At the same time, however, the whole engagement, and the palpable limitations of Pre-Raphaelite art itself, pointed to difficulties still unresolved in the developing argument of *Modern Painters*. That is, the Pre-Raphaelite controversy of 1851 to 1854 made apparent to him what the next volume of *Modern Painters* would have to do. Mainly it would have to clarify the relation between imitation and "invention" in painting.

On 7 May 1851 the *Times* had printed a review of paintings by Millais and Hunt exhibited at the Royal Academy. The reviewer assaulted the painters for, among other things, their "antiquated style and affected simplicity," their "servile imitation of the cramped style, false perspective, and crude colour of remote antiquity," and, in general, a "morbid infatuation" which caused them to sacrifice "truth, beauty, and genuine feeling to mere eccentricity."[159] Ruskin's first defense, a letter printed in the *Times* six days later, is very restrained. He has no wish "in any way to dispute or invalidate the general truth"[160] of the review. He will, however, remonstrate with the reviewer over his assertion that these painters sacrifice *truth* for eccentricity. He does happen to know that the water plant, *Alisma plantago*, appearing in one of the paintings (Charles Collins's *Convent Thoughts*) had been painted with absolute botanical accuracy despite the painting's other failings. Further, he finds "not one single error in perspective in four out of the five pictures in question." Finally, anyone who knew much about the early art these painters are said to imitate would see that it is not ancient art to which they return but ancient honesty. "They intend to return to early days in this one point only—that . . . they will draw either what they see, or what they suppose might have been the actual facts of the scene they desire to represent, irrespective of any conventional rules of picture-making."[161] They will not sacrifice "stern facts" to make fair pictures. But Ruskin's next letter to the *Times*, printed on 30 May of the same year, involves him in a partial contradiction. Here he objects to the "commonness of feature in many of the principal figures."[162] He hopes they will remedy this "false choice of feature" by choosing nobler models. They are to paint real images of ideal human forms and yet give the truth.

Ruskin did not write to the *Times* again about the Pre-Raphaelites for three years. Then, on 5 May 1854, that paper published a letter from him offering a close interpretation of Hunt's *The Light of the World*. At the time he pronounced it "one of the very noblest works of sacred art ever produced in this or any other age,"[163] and he continued to refer to it as a major religious vision in his later works. His emphasis on interpretive rather than technical analysis implies what anyone who has followed this discussion thus far would suspect: that Ruskin valued the painting not for its technical excellence so much as for its visual exploration of light as a Christian symbol. Technically he emphasizes Hunt's meticulousness in representing the precise fusion of clarity and mystery which would be in the cone of vision of a person actually observing the scene from the given point of view—each object becoming realized at the proper distance. That is, true Pre-Raphaelite work "represents all objects exactly as they would appear in nature in the position and at the distances which the arrangement of the picture supposes. The false work represents them with all their details, as if seen through a microscope."[164]

Later in the same month Ruskin sent to the *Times* an interpretation of Hunt's *The Awakened Conscience*. Here Ruskin is so touched by the image of the girl portrayed ("the countenance of the lost girl, rent from its beauty into sudden horror; the lips half open, indistinct in their purple quivering; the teeth set hard; the eyes filled with the fearful light of futurity, and with tears of ancient days") that he is willing to allow that all the intricacies of detail contribute to, instead of detract from, its total pathos. He insists that in this instance the overfinished treatment is based on a "truer principle of the pathetic than any of the common artistical expedients of the schools."[165] This principle of pathos is that even trivial details tend to force themselves with almost unendurable vividness upon a distraught mind, so that the reflection of garden flowers in the fallen girl's mirror become for us, as for her, a tragic message of lost purity. About the effects of pathos on perception Ruskin would have more to say. For the moment it is enough to note the deepening of his commitment to the Pre-Raphaelites in the period that elapsed between the publication of the first two letters and that of the last two letters (1851 to 1854). The sweeping assessments and tone of ex cathedra instruction of the former had given way to strongly felt personal responses to particular paintings in the latter.

In part this change can be accounted for by the fact that by 1854 Ruskin had come to see the Pre-Raphaelites as following in Turner's footsteps and had thus been able to assimilate their art into his aesthetic system. In some ways, then, he was repaying their earlier obedience to that system. In revising volume 1 of *Modern Painters* for its fifth edition in 1851 he entered two complimentary references to their work and continued to make frequent allusions to it in *Stones* and in *Modern Painters*, volume 3. But during this period he devoted two shorter studies explicitly to the importance of the Pre-Raphaelites, his long essay on *Pre-Raphaelitism* (1851) and the last of his Edinburgh *Lectures on Architecture and Painting* (delivered in 1853), also called *Pre-Raphaelitism*.

The first *Pre-Raphaelitism* opens with the assertion that the very nature of the painter is to observe and imitate and so convey such knowledge as cannot be conveyed otherwise than visually. Originally this function was essentially religious. But this passed away, leaving the painter without profession or purpose. The painter's instinct for naturalism, the accurate representation of historical events or natural beauty, which emerged as his traditional function was superseded by printing, was a true response that came at the right time, though it was misunderstood and misapplied. Consider, Ruskin urges, the knowledge we would now possess if painters had properly understood and obeyed their naturalistic instinct. But, and here he returns to the central question of *Modern Painters*, is there no place for imagination or invention in painting? Yes. The highest places in art can be achieved only by these. But they cannot be taught; they will show themselves naturally, if at all. Traditional academic art training taught the students to go to Raphael for perfection instead of to nature and taught also that even their own imaginative visions must obey Raphaelesque rules.

The Pre-Raphaelite Brotherhood was to be understood as a rebellion against this established authority in art by young men who wanted to recover the painter's birthright of honest observation and free imagination. Given that their paintings reflected the "temper of resistance" in which they were painted and that they represented departures from the conventional and plagiarized works to which the critics were accustomed, it is little wonder that a howl of ethical indignation went up against them and that blind assertions were made about their technique. These false assertions can be grouped under three main heads. First, they were accused of imitating the faults of the medieval painters. But, Ruskin replies, they imitated no painters; "they paint from nature only." What they rejected entirely was the Renaissance feeling, its "insolence, infidelity, sensuality, and shallow pride."[166] In Ruskin's system they were prelapsarian artists. Second, they were attacked for not drawing well, but this could be said only by those who had never studied their pictures. Finally, it was said that they had no system of chiaroscuro. "To which it may be simply replied that their system of light and shade is exactly the same as the Sun's; which is, I believe, likely to outlast that of the Renaissance, however brilliant."[167]

But these were all still essentially imitative attributes. The deeper question of how much inventive or imaginative capacity they had still remained. Here Ruskin is noncommittal, arguing simply that these faculties, if they exist, will appear in the course of time. What he does know, however, is that if these powers appear it will be all the more powerfully because of the severe training these painters have received from nature, presumably, and hostile criticism. To prove this, namely, the natural emergence of inventive power under the stern disciplines of truth and alienation, Ruskin traces the career of Turner. He emphasizes Turner's infinite sympathy with the human condition, comparable only to Shakespeare's; the mocking criticism he, like the Pre-Raphaelites, endured; his absolute reliance on *"seen facts,"* never on arbitrary "compositions"; and the development of his invention as apparent in his successive studies of the same subject. Ruskin's key point, however, is that all Turner's "infinite luxuriance of invention depends on his taking possession of everything he sees . . . on his forgetting himself and forgetting nothing else." Indeed it was chiefly to his "intense sense of fact" that the greatness of any painter must be attributed. "And thus Pre-Raphaelitism and Raphaelitism, and Turnerism, are all one and the same, so far as education can influence them."[168] If anything, the Pre-Raphaelites strive too hard to invent invention; the lesson of Turner's career is simply that if these young painters will stay with the stern discipline of recording facts, invention (composition) will come easily by itself, if at all.

The Edinburgh lecture on Pre-Raphaelitism was written two years later, in 1853. It makes some of the same points as the pamphlet but generally grasps the movement more distinctly and definitively. This is partly because Ruskin's platform style was more succinct and analytic and partly because the two additional years had enabled him better to digest the movement into his own system of artistic progress. The Pre-Raphaelite lecture is, as I have said, the last of a sequence of four lectures, all given in November 1853, that are valuable as a lucid summary of Ruskin's main positions on painting, architecture, and economics up to that point. The first of these, entitled "Architecture," opposes organic forms to Greek design in architecture and arrives at a brief definition of the Gothic. The second, also called "Architecture," concerns the relevance of Gothic art to modern life and includes some explicit suggestions for the reintroduction of Gothic architecture. Its most valuable passage, however, is this comment on the relation between education and consumption:

> By the purchase of every print which hangs on your walls, of every cup out of which you drink, and every table off which you eat your bread, you are educating a mass of men in one way or another. You are either employing them healthily or unwholesomely; you are making them lead happy or unhappy lives; you are leading them to look at Nature, and to love her—to think, to feel, to enjoy,—or you are blinding them to Nature, and keeping them bound, like beasts of burden, in mechanical and monotonous employments. We shall all be asked one day, why we did not think more of this.[169]

The "Addenda" (1854) to these first two lectures are interesting because they restate, in six brief propositions, Ruskin's basic position on architecture at this time:

1. That Gothic or Romanesque construction is nobler than Greek construction.
2. That ornamentation is the principal part of architecture.
3. That ornamentation should be visible.
4. That ornamentation should be natural.
5. That ornamentation should be thoughtful.
6. And that therefore Gothic ornamentation is nobler than Greek ornamentation, and Gothic architecture the only architecture which should now be built.[170]

The third lecture, "Turner and His Works," takes the landscape tradition through Turner and leads naturally toward the Pre-Raphaelites. There is little feeling for nature in pagan writers, except as sensual enjoyment, dread of desolate places, or superstitious "personification or deification of natural powers."[171] But the Bible is "full of expressions, not only testifying a vivid sense of the power of nature over man, but showing that *sympathy with natural things themselves*, as if they had human souls, which is the especial characteristic of true love of the works of God."[172] Thus, in Ruskin's Edinburgh view, Christianity created the love of nature and the landscape feeling—"inducing an immediate transformation of the cold and lifeless pagan ornamentation into vivid imagery of nature."[173] The technique of landscape developed gradually through the medieval period until "the return of Paganism in the shape of classical learning at once destroyed this love of nature"[174] at the moment when this early landscape was about to free itself from the last vestiges of medieval conventionalism. So the history of landscape looks, briefly, like this: "You have, first, your great ancient landscape divided into its three periods—Giottesque, Leonardesque, Titianesque. Then you have a great gap, full of nonentities and abortions; a gulf of foolishness, into the bottom of which you may throw Claude and Salvator, neither of them deserving to give a name to anything. Call it "pastoral" landscape, "guarda e passa," and then you have, lastly, the pure, wholesome, simple, modern landscape."[175] And the name for this pure modern landscape is, of course, "Turneresque." Bacon unlocked the *principles* of nature for man, but Turner first gave her *aspect*.

But now in the fourth lecture, "Pre-Raphaelitism," Ruskin points to "a certain schism" that had recently developed among British artists, and then comes directly to his focusing question: "What is the real difference between the principles on which art has been pursued before and since Raphael?"[176] The difference is fundamentally a mythic one. Modern art is not merely a more informed art than medieval; it is, he insists, altogether another art. Raphael marks the beginning of the end of believing art, and the broad fact that distinguishes all art before

Raphael's time from ours is "that all ancient art was *religious*, and all modern art is *profane*."[177] Early art received its form from the service of religion; modern art has not been brought into the service of religion and has received a distinctly different form. And this form, Ruskin insists, is distinctly "impurer" for not being religious. "When the entire purpose of art was moral teaching, it naturally took truth for its first object, and beauty, and the pleasure resulting from beauty, only for its second. But when it lost all purpose of moral teaching, it as naturally took beauty for its first object, and truth for its second."[178] Artists, that is, allowed conventions of technique to obscure the facts of the eye or of imagination. In medieval art, thought and truth are the *first* things; execution and beauty second. But in modern art execution and beauty are primary things; thought and truth secondary; hence that special power of academic conventionalism and formalism over modern art, an authority which is the destruction of lesser men.

All the truly great artists since Homer, Ruskin goes on, have painted their own world as they saw it despite the schools. Yet academic art continued to be taught despite the knowledge that every eminent modern artist has had to find his art by struggling *against* what he had been taught. And now the Pre-Raphaelites have had to struggle for truth against "that spurious beauty, whose attractiveness had tempted men to forget, or to despise, the more noble quality of sincerity."[179] Despite the calumnies of the critics, Pre-Raphaelitism has held firm to "one principle, that of absolute, uncompromising truth in all that it does, obtained by working everything, down to the most minute detail, from nature and from nature only. Every Pre-Raphaelite landscape background is painted to the last touch, in the open air, from the thing itself. Every Pre-Raphaelite figure, however studied in expression, is a true portrait of some living person. Every minute accessory is painted in the same manner."[180] But because Turner had been this way and beyond before them, he is the true founder of Pre-Raphaelitism: "Turner, the first and greatest of the Pre-Raphaelites, has done it already; he . . . would sometimes, in his foregrounds, paint the spots upon a dead trout, and the dyes upon a butterfly's wing, yet for the most part delighted to begin at that very point where the other branches of Pre-Raphaelitism become powerless."[181]

So by making the Pre-Raphaelites into followers of Turner, Ruskin incorporated them into the aesthetic of *Modern Painters*. But his criticism of them shared the weakness of his aesthetic as it stood: weak in its distinction between the mimetic as opposed to the expressive function of art. Ruskin appears to have realized this, for in "Addenda to the

Fourth Lecture" he returns to touch briefly on a subject closely tied to Pre-Raphaelitism but too difficult to deal with in a public lecture, "namely, that the principle of it seems adverse to all exertion of imaginative power."[182] Can it be argued, as the critics have, that the Pre-Raphaelite principle is anti-imaginative in its literalism? It is a crucial issue and one by which not only Pre-Raphaelitism but Ruskin's own aesthetic of truth must stand or fall. He evades the question here, first by asserting that the Pre-Raphaelites invent so easily that they despise it, and then by dodging into a remark of Carlyle's to the effect that the art of the future will be able to find its way to its proper domain of belief only by humbly recording fact. But he remembered the question and returned to the issue of truth and imagination as the central problem of volume 3 of *Modern Painters*.

CHAPTER 5

"Pathetic Fallacy" and Mythopoesis

By the completion of *The Stones of Venice* in 1853 the system of Ruskin's thought was remarkably extensive though by no means fully articulated. It included the beginnings of an aesthetic and hermeneutic of landscape, the recovery and exposition of Turner as the greatest of all poet-painters of nature and a persona of his critic, general theories of beauty and imagination, a sociology of architecture with outlines of a Gothic utopia, and a myth of the fall of art. Even the Pre-Raphaelites, the most aggressive movement in English art at the time, had been incorporated into the system as a vindication of it; they had been taught, after all, by himself or Turner. Yet the whole structure of his thought was still held together by an essentially vague concept of the relation between art and nature. This crucial weakness was felt by those of Ruskin's critics who wondered how he could find the mistiness of Turner compatible with the minuteness of the P.R.B. Ruskin's next book, *Modern Painters*, volume 3, subtitled "Part 4, 'Of Many Things' " (1856), evidences his need to answer the critics by defining once and for all the proper limits of the real and the ideal in art. Therefore the volume raises again, in much greater detail, the old central question of *Modern Painters*: Is art primarily mimetic or expressive?

The particular interest of the third volume, however, is that this line of inquiry leads Ruskin into his first extensive discussion of mythic awareness. Heretofore, excepting the last chapter, "The Superhuman Ideal," of *Modern Painters*, volume 2, there had been hardly any direct reference to myth in his work; yet there is, of course, a general sense of the mythic in which Ruskin has worked all along. For, although he shows an early interest in the naturalist's concentration upon the plain facts of nature, his world could not be the neutralized reality of modern science since this was just coming into being; instead all his thought is founded on the idea of nature as a sacred mystery, and it is in this fundamental sense always mythic. But Ruskin's conception of the sanctity of nature partakes of two essentially opposed "mythologies," the Evangelical and the Romantic. For the Romantic, nature tends to be the primary text; for the Evangelical, nature refers to Scripture. Evangelical exegetics, as

George Landow has pointed out,[1] had a shaping influence on Ruskin's thought primarily by way of its allegorical reading of nature and history as *typical* manifestations of Scripture. This typological orientation is more subdued in Ruskin's work after *Modern Painters*, volume 2, and *The Seven Lamps of Architecture*, but it is never entirely outgrown.

However, from childhood, Ruskin's thirst for the visible fact, for intricate textures and direct experience, was too great ever to be fully satisfied by the mythology of types. Therefore the other mythology, the Romantic or Wordsworthian, which had been part of his developing awareness alongside the Evangelical and scientific inputs, gradually asserted its dominance over his consciousness. This was to be expected since the Romantic mythology was itself an effort to reconcile the facts of direct experience in nature with the archetypes of spiritual truth. That is, a central aim of Romantic myth-making is to overcome the dualism implicit in the concept of *types*. For the Romantic, the *symbol* supercedes the allegorical types; the symbol, as Coleridge observed, "always partakes of the reality which it renders intelligible."[2] In its emphasis upon the symbol as a synthesis of sign and thing, the universal in the particular, Romantic mythopoesis stressed the visible fact so important to Ruskin; and its doctrine of imagination tended to raise the moment of symbolic apprehension, when the universal is perceived through the particular, to the plane of prophetic vision. In apprehending its symbols, the imagination, Coleridge thought, participates in the eternal creative act of the infinite mind. The sacred object of Romantic mythopoesis was unity; it yearned to comprehend the infinite in particular experience and at such moments to bring about a reconciliation of mind and nature which neither analytic typology nor scientific objectivity could accomplish. Ruskin's concepts of penetrative imagination and of pathetic fallacy are characteristic of the aims of Romantic mythopoesis because they are attempts to purify the fusion of spirit and nature, pure seeing, from the slag of allegory and bloodless personification.

The Romantic mythology, then, in which Ruskin's mind was nurtured, as it was by Evangelical theology and scientific geology, had as its central task the redemption of the world through the recovery of the unity of mind and nature that had been lost in the ascent of reason. In part it was an effort, strongly felt in Ruskin, to reconcile the conflicting claims of the other two "mythologies" on the individual spirit: the religious tradition with its inheritance of archetypes and the empirical ideal of pure objective fact. Romantic mythopoesis attempted to accomplish its task of reconciliation and redemption by moving from the generalized experience of religious allegory and empirical awareness to the subjective ground of the individual spirit in its quest to recover a lost primordial unity with nature, conceived as the solidarity of all life. But in its emphasis on the effort of the individual spirit to overcome its alienation in the rational self, to annihilate itself in the oneness of life, the Romantic mind employed—could not help but do so—archetypes drawn from earlier literature and from myth. The metaphors of Christian Neoplatonism and the archetype of the spiritual quest are obvious examples. Indeed the Romantic mythology is a compound of mythologies, but by this means it discloses the universal significance of subjective and individual experience and relates this to historical process.

It is unnecessary to attempt a summary here of the primary archetypal interests of Romantic poetics; these have been studied by many scholars but perhaps most comprehensively by M. H. Abrams.[3] We must simply mention three major interests that are also of particular significance to our view of Ruskin and which he could hardly have overlooked since all are present in two of his acknowledged masters, Wordsworth and Carlyle. First is a generalized interest in the mythopoeic mind, primitive or prophetic, and its presumed experience of the numinous unity of nature. Second is an interest in the literature of confession or spiritual autobiography stemming from Augustine; in the Romantic transformation, the moments of religious conversion or reconciliation characteristic of these accounts become natural epiphanies or apocalypses. Third, and perhaps most important is a predilection for the myth of the Fall.

The Romantic poet-prophets, Abrams observes, "measured their enterprise against the earlier revelation of present, past, and future things, either as presented in the Bible or as represented by Milton or other Biblical poets" and radically recast "into terms appropriate to the historical and intellectual circumstances of their own age, the Christian pattern of the fall, the redemption, and the emergence of a new earth which will constitute a restored paradise."[4] At another point he notes that in the Neoplatonized Christianity that some Romantics inherited "the fall of man is conceived to be primarily a falling-out-of and falling-away-from the One, into a position of remoteness and a condition of alienation from the source. Consonantly, the original human sin is identified as self-centeredness, or selfhood, the attempt of a part to be sufficient unto itself; while the primary consequence of the fall—death—is described as a state of division from the one Being."[5]

These three elements of Romantic mythopoesis have already made their appearance in Ruskin's work. (1) An interest in the mythopoeic or prophetic mind is evident in his theory of imagination, particularly of the "penetrative imagination." We are told, for instance, in volume 2 of *Modern Painters*, that "those painters only have the right imaginative power who can set the supernatural form before us, fleshed and boned like ourselves."[6] In volume 3 of *Modern Painters* the subject of mythic imagination as natural supernaturalism would be explored in relation to the history of landscape feeling. (2) We have seen how important the closely related device of the natural apocalypse is to the technique of *Modern Painters*. Such moments of infinite apprehension are involved in a generalized autobiographical impulse in the diaries and are refocused in the specifically autobiographical portions of *Fors Clavigera* and in *Praeterita*. (3) The importance of the myth of the Fall to *The Stones of Venice* and to Ruskin's whole conception of the pure Gothic as representing an Eden of organic unity from which we have fallen has been noted; further, he appears to see something like the ascent to Being as pure light in the progress of landscape art toward the purifying heroics of Turnerian light, but this is a mythic scheme that he perceives fully only as *Modern Painters* proceeds and his own interest in mythic symbolism deepens. Yet Harold Bloom has correctly observed that a consciousness of the myth of the Fall and the quest for a redemptive vision "was always present in his criticism, since he relied from the start on a Wordsworthian experience of paradisal intimations within a wholly natural context."[7]

In these paragraphs we have been using the word *myth* in the broad sense of primary archetypes or structures of experience characteristic of a particular cultural movement in order to point out that Ruskin has been involved in this sort of myth-making, Evangelical and Romantic, since the beginning of his work. But it is in *Modern Painters*, volume 3, that he first appears as a theorist and interpreter of myth in the explicit sense that we have in mind when we speak, for instance, of the deities in Homer. Therefore the work of this chapter must be to examine his new critical interest in the mythic mind and to consider the relevance of this interest to an evolving system of thought that already shows a predisposition to myth-making. To understand how the consciousness we have been tracing is drawn toward, is shaped by, and shapes the question of myth, we must enter again the developing dialectic of *Modern Painters*.

In the theoretical parts of volume 1 of *Modern Painters* Ruskin had been primarily concerned to show the dependence of art (particularly Turner's) on ideas of truth, truth meaning "bare, clear, downright statement of facts."[8] This was not to identify beauty with truth; he considered beauty to be another of the ideas conveyable by art. Ideas of truth are simply "pleasures taken in perceiving simple resemblance to Nature."[9] Nor was truth meant to be confused with imitation. Imitation also was a separate idea that art might convey. Truth has a moral as well as a material dimension and can be carried by symbols that have little or no likeness to the real object. Further, illusionistic imitation is the opposite of truth; therefore ideas of imitation tend to destroy art. So, in the general principle of the first volume, art appears to be essentially ideal and expressive, with its primary idea, truth, transcending and opposing imitation. And yet when Ruskin comes down to cases in the second half of the volume (truths of skies, clouds, earth, mountains, water in landscape and in Turner), ideal truth merges with techniques of representation and art appears to be more mimetic than expressive. (The distinction is between appearance and that which appears.) Only in poetic moments of the prose itself, where Ruskin attempts to recreate Turner's experience of the scene, does truth appear as communicated intuition or impression. So we are left wondering at the volume's end whether art gives the facts of the object or the truths of impression.

In *Modern Painters*, volume 2, Ruskin turns from the problem of truth in art to that of beauty; at the same time his attention moves inward from concern with the relations between a work and its subject to the conditions of mind in which "ideas" of "impressions" of beauty are received. This is one sense in which the book "sets forth the spiritual as opposed to the sensual theory of art."[10] There is another sense also. The work is organized around two great "faculties" by which we have access to beauty. The "theoretic faculty" is insistently described as being a spiritual rather than a sensual capability. It is a susceptibility to the sacred; therefore impressions of beauty are for Ruskin essentially "moral" (actually religious) rather than sensual or intellectual. Beauty is taken to have two primary modes, typical and vital: external qualities of things perceived as "types of divine attributes" and the sense of pure inherent life, and consequent nearness to ideal form, in living things, especially man. Thus his idea of beauty in its involvement with types and symbols of the divine and of life is, from the beginning, quite nearly a concept of mythic awareness as discernment of the sacred in things. And naturally in his "General Conclusions Respecting the Theoretic Faculty" the sources of beauty are closely identified with those of revelation. Although his distinction between theoretic and imaginative faculties in their relation to beauty is vague, it appears that the imaginative is the less passive faculty, modifying, penetrating, projecting, though apparently not creating, beauty. The main point is that this faculty also, especially in its penetrative and contemplative modes, is closely allied to mythic intuition, for it is variously spoken of as an unrefusable, visionary, animating, nature-fed power concerned solely with truth. What makes it clear that volume 2 of *Modern Painters* is constantly if unconsciously verging on a discussion of the interrelations of art, myth, and truth is the consummation of the volume in a final chapter, "Superhuman Ideal," in which Greek mythic figures are condemned as too human or lacking in "spirit-power," that is, too imitative to be true. Of course, what prevented Ruskin from connecting beauty with mythic as with moral awareness at this point was his absorption in the Christian mythic, *liber naturae*, in which could be read God's attributes and intentions.

In *The Seven Lamps* and *Stones*, though the subject now becomes true sculptured architecture and its social meaning, the distinction between mimetic and expressive truth-value remains unclear. An apparent self-contradiction or ambivalence seems to lie at the heart of all Ruskin's pronouncements on the aesthetics of ornamentation in these volumes. We learn that the older and purer the Gothic forms are, the less strictly they are imitated from organic forms and that, in general, "*the demand for perfection is always a sign of a misunderstanding of the ends of art.*"[11] Clear enough. However, this is but a corollary of the general axiom, variously expressed, that, beyond a very low point, "man cannot advance in the invention of beauty, without directly imitating natural form"[12] or that "all beautiful works of art must either intentionally imitate or accidentally resemble natural forms."[13] And we find that whenever Ruskin comes down to the particulars of ornamentation direct imitation of nature tends to be the explicit or implicit norm, his recurrent task being to show where the correct degree of imitation has been achieved or missed, often by direct comparison with the natural form. What degree of imitation then, if not perfect imitation, is right or "true"? From *Modern Painters*, volume 2, we would conclude that this must be the degree of imitation that conveys but does not deaden the "vital beauty," the appearance of healthy life, in the living form. But where, between symbolic gesture on the one hand and naturalistic representation on the other, are the guiding limits of imitation? How much of the artist's own impression of *his* life is permitted? Should the architectural ornament represent the natural object or the artisan's response to the vitality of that object? Doubt shrouds the inner standard to which Ruskin means to appeal in these volumes; yet the more he comes to see art as the measure and means of social vitality, the more urgent the reader's need to comprehend his basic aesthetic position, and the greater the need he felt to clarify it.

In the conclusion to *Stones*, when he came to draw a modern moral from the Renaissance "Fall" he had traced, Ruskin committed himself to an assertion that Cook takes to be the kernel of all his teaching on art; it is "that art is valuable or otherwise, only as it expresses the personality, activity, and living perception of a good and great human soul; that it may express and contain this with little help from execution, and less from science; and that if it have not this, if it show not the vigour, perception and invention of a mighty human spirit, it is worthless."[14] Art, then, *expresses* the soul of the artist; great art is the expression of a great and moral soul. But what does this mean in terms of objective qualities of works? We noticed earlier some unused passages from the manuscripts of *Stones* in which Ruskin attempted to clarify this assertion and his distinction between truth as mere imitation and truth as either expression or impression of the soul. "There is an ultimate truth," he wrote, "which only the soul perceives, and there is an ultimate expression which only the soul employs, very often the most thoughtful and expressive art must be that which is in one sense least like Nature; that is to say, symbolical or comprehensive instead of imitative."[15]

Goodness and greatness of soul, ultimate or soul-perceived truth expressed in symbols: Ruskin appears to be on the verge of correlating the highest art with mythopoesis, as he had been in discussing "penetrative" imagination in volume 2 of *Modern Painters*. One meaning is certain, at least, to the reader of *Stones*; clearly a "good and great human soul" means a believing soul, whether Christian or pagan. Ruskin is not simply expressing ethical intuitionism. But how are we to know from the art object itself that it is the expression of a believing soul? Of course Ruskin does not judge works solely on "internal" or objective grounds; his own perceptual experience (the appearance, not the thing that appears) is frequently the subject. Hence a work is believing work if he has experienced the sacred through it. Again, he is sometimes convinced a priori that the art is "faithful," or true in the convictional if not in the imitative sense, if the work was produced during a pious era or by an artist whom he believes to have been pious. But when he turns to the object itself, as he frequently does, it appears that the objective sign of belief is the primacy of symbol over technique, the "visible subordination of execution to conception."[16] The art is for the display of the symbol, not the symbol for the display of art. He wants visible indications that the artist has been addressed by a truth he cannot close by mere technique or imitative facility. There must be a knowing in the work that is beyond mere satisfaction of curiosity.

But if, going back a bit, we assume that Ruskin wishes us to think of ultimate or spiritual truth as expressible only by symbols, we are forced to pose other basic questions. Does the soul select or is it seized by symbols? Must the symbol be embedded in a mythic order or a living religion? We note only that Ruskin, in the passage quoted, associates symbolic truth with comprehensiveness. Is this meant in the archetypal or ontological sense? To what extent is the symbol generated by the artist and to what extent by tradition? If the evidence of spiritual truth is the primacy of conception over execution, how do we actually perceive this in the work itself? Surely Ruskin does not mean that any comprehensive symbol roughly handled is great art. Presumably there must be some apparent tension between conception and capability, some evidence of struggle of great technique with an overpowering symbol. But Ruskin is as yet unclear about the way this relationship shows itself in outward forms, and the problem is murkiest where the art object has a natural subject; for he is clearly demanding at this point more than a symbolic impression of nature. His praise of the Pre-Raphaelites merely articulates this confusion since it is their minuteness and technical precision that he most admires. Yet surely in these painters, if it can be said of any, conception is subordinated to execution. How can Ruskin acknowledge an ultimate expression that only the soul employs yet praise their microscopic fidelity to nature? Can both truths, the spiritual and the mechanical, be coherently present in the same picture?

1

Considering the muddled state of his aesthetics it is little wonder that, as Cook has pointed out, his critics "with one consent fell upon Ruskin for his inconsistency in admiring at once the closely manipulated foregrounds of Millais in his early works and the misty distances of Turner. What, then, was it in final analysis, in which the greatness of Turner consisted—in the truths that he recorded, or in the visions that he invented?"[17] It could hardly be satisfying to shrug off contradictions by saying, as he would in 1858, "I am never satisfied that I have handled a subject properly till I have contradicted myself at least three times."[18] The need was to resume, after a decade, as he reminded his readers in the preface, the larger problem of *Modern Painters*, which was not merely the urgent defense of Turner, but "the complete examination of the canons of art received among us."[19]

Accordingly, pursuing a method he describes as "less laboriously systematic" than that of the earlier volumes, he sets out to develop his aesthetics of painting in a sweeping comparative scheme, applied both analytically and historically. The first ten chapters of the volume attempt to set forth "the laws of right and wrong for all art" by contrasting false and true modes of the "ideal" in art; the last seven chapters focus attention on emergence of the modern "landscape-feeling" (or mode of idealization) conveyed by means of a historical survey of man's relations to nature as revealed by the successive intentions of landscape in poetry and painting since Homer. It is in this section of the volume that mythology in the explicit sense makes its first serious appearance in Ruskin's work, but mythic feeling in the larger senses of (1) emphasis on the sacred and (2) criticism organized by spiritual system (the Fall) permeates this volume as it has the earlier ones. Let us look more closely.

Ruskin has first to summarize the progress of the two earlier volumes and define the problem before him; in so doing he incorporates a shift of inquiry that marks a radical departure for the aesthetics of the last three volumes. Whereas, he reminds us, the first volume had dealt with ideas of Truth, especially the varying success of artists in representing the facts of nature; and the second had analyzed the two mental faculties, contemplative and imaginative, by which ideas of Beauty and of Relation are seized; it now remains to consider the achievements of various artists in addressing these faculties. That is, there is a general shift toward aesthetics of expression. Given this redirection, and the needs of his aesthetics, it seems natural that this opening chapter should concentrate on the problem of the degree of "enthusiasm" or pathos that is admissible in poetry and painting, and particularly its function in works of the "Grand Style."

In his *Idler* letter on "High Art" Reynolds had addressed himself to the very problem that had been troubling Ruskin's aesthetics from the beginning: the relation of literal detail to expressed emotion. Reynolds had declared that painting of the grand style and literalism of detail are as distinct as poetry and history, for literal truth and exact detail are "heavy matter which retards the progress of the imagination."[20] Ruskin, rightly, disagrees. Poetry, (written or painted) is by no means distinguished from the historical by omission of details; indeed, its power seems to consist in the expression of the singular and particular. Yet it is not the mere multiplication of details that is poetry nor the mere removal of them that is history. There must be some deeper difference. In fact, although poetic details are generally more "delicate" than those of prose, it is not the character of the details themselves that makes them poetic but their being "employed to bring out an affecting result."[21]

Poetry, for Ruskin as for Reynolds, is a quality that may exist in painting or in writing; similarly, in *The Poetry of Architecture,* the youthful Ruskin had pointed to a poetic quality also essential to architecture, a quality whose prime requisite, "unity of feeling," was being neglected. "Painting is properly to be opposed to *speaking* or *writing,* but not to *poetry.* Both painting and speaking are methods of expression. Poetry is the employment of either for the noblest purposes."[22] The important point is that Ruskin, unlike Reynolds, seeks the poetic, not in imitation, whether of literal or selective detail, but in some quality of *expression* he calls "noble." As George Landow has pointed out, Ruskin employs the neoclassical critical doctrine of the analogical relationship between painting and poetry, the *ut pictura poesis* tradition, but gives it the expressive bias of Romantic poetics whereas the eighteenth-century tradition had stressed the common dependence of the two arts upon selective imitation.[23] Whether in language or in painting, poetry, Ruskin concludes, is "the suggestion, by the imagination, of noble grounds for the noble emotions." The noble emotions, he explains, are "those four principal sacred passions—Love, Veneration, Admiration, and Joy (this latter especially, if unselfish); and their opposites—Hatred, Indignation, (or Scorn), Horror, and Grief,—this last, when unselfish, becoming Compassion."[24] But, since these emotions are not themselves poetry, the definition merely raises the problem of how the imagination suggests "noble grounds"; therefore, he must return to consider what kinds of images are introduced by painters in the "Grand Style."

Turning to the *Idler* letter again, Ruskin concludes that Reynold's comparison of great art with the Homeric style led him to believe, speaking broadly, "that a painter in the Great Style must be enthusiastic, or full of emotion, and must paint the human form in its utmost strength and beauty, and perhaps certain impossible forms besides, liable by persons not in an equally enthusiastic state of mind to be looked upon as in some degree absurd." To this requirement of feeling and its permissible expression in mythic or "impossible" forms Ruskin adds two restraining corollaries is his own: "First, that these Heroic or Impossible images are to be mingled with others very unheroic and very possible; and, secondly, that in the representation of the Heroic or Impossible forms, the greatest care must be taken in *finishing the details.*"[25] He will allow, with Reynolds, that the expression of pathos and mythos is necessary to greatness in painting, but he wants the expressive firmly grounded in the descriptively real. The great Venetians, Titian, Tintoretto, Veronese, now called the "Dutch part of the Italian genius," are introduced in defense of these strictures;

however, since these painters are also radically distinct somehow from the Dutch realists, Ruskin must now attempt to answer Reynolds's contempt for imitative art and show what are the proper limits of deceptive imitation in art. The second and third chapters in the volume, called respectively "Of Realization" and "Of the Real Nature of Greatness in Style," succeed merely in sharpening this question for those chapters of contrast which follow.

In the second chapter, "Of Realization," Ruskin again protests Reynolds's inability to express the real difference between high and low, though he allows that the painter himself intuited that difference. "It is *not* true that Poetry does not concern herself with minute details. It is *not* true that high art seeks only the Invariable. It is *not* true that imitative art is an easy thing. It is *not* true that the faithful rendering of nature is an employment in which 'the slowest intellect is likely to succeed best.' "[26] But what is the essence of great painting then? The painter is great only if, by whatever means, "he has laid open noble truths, or aroused noble emotions." Our attempt to understand is brought up short again at the word *noble*, the full meaning of which could be deduced only from a survey of all the contexts in which he uses it.

The impressive topic announced at the beginning of the brief chapter, "how far" a subject should be painted, is never fully confronted, though Reynolds is censured for speaking contemptuously of the power necessary to produce imitative art, particularly where high or spiritual subjects are involved. The problem of imitating mythic figures is instanced in connection with Dante's line in the *Purgatorio* (12. 31) on the summoning of Pallas. Isn't Dante saying, Ruskin asks, "that the perfect conception of Pallas should be so given as to look like Pallas herself, rather than merely like a picture of Pallas?" That even a mythic or visionary image should be somehow fully realized? Apparently so, but the art required is hardly the easy matter Reynolds supposed it to be. "Our actual powers of imitation are so feeble that wherever deception is attempted, a subject of comparatively low or confined order must be chosen."[27]

As if aware that his conception of the "Great Style" has been thus far largely an unsystematic treatment of what it is not, Ruskin sets out in his third chapter ("Of the Real Nature of Greatness of Style") to rewrite Reynolds's letter in explicit criteriological terms. He will "sketch out at once in this chapter, the different characters which really constitute 'greatness' of style."[28] The first of these criteria is "nobleness" of subject. The greatness of the style will be in exact proportion to the nobility of concerns and passions involved in the subject, provided only that the painter's choice of that subject is "sincere," chosen for the subject's own sake, and "wise," or consistent with his capabilities. The perfect harmony of expression, now called "the painter's main purpose," with execution is found only in old and modern Pre-Raphaelite work, culminating in Holman Hunt's *The Light of the World,* here considered "the most perfect instance of expressional purpose with technical power, which the world has yet produced."[29] Next comes love of beauty, which Ruskin is at pains to distinguish from truth. Angelico is assigned the highest rank in this respect. But beauty must not be achieved at the expense of truth. Great art dwells on the beautiful while false art omits or alters the ugly; yet it is only by the faithful representing of both aspects of experience that we can be taught to distinguish them. Thus the third criterion of greatness is sincerity. If art could give the whole truth of nature it should do it; the great artist can but hope to present the essential truths first and then those most consistent with these, so as to obtain the largest and most coherent sum of truth. Great drawing is essentially "*distinct* drawing"; yet, paradoxically, there being facts of mystery and indistinctness, "all good drawing must in some sort be *indistinct*."[30]

The final criterion, and the most important since Ruskin says he has been naming them in order of increasing importance, is that great art must be inventive, that is, produced by imagination. Here, we learn, a "great bar" appears between lower and higher art, for the lower kind "merely copies what is set before it," but the higher kind either "entirely imagines its subject" or so arranges it as to reveal complete imaginative power in the associative, penetrative, and contemplative phases as described in volume 2. He perceives, at this point, no incompatibility between expressed imaginative power and naturalistic detail (both of which are "subjects"), because the imagination does not actually create; it "never produces anything but by combination or contemplation."[31] The penetrative or visionary function that is central to the imagination theory of the second volume is unstressed for the moment. Thus, in direct opposition to Reynolds's doctrine, Hunt's *The Light of the World* can be called poetical and imaginative in "design," though the painting is grounded in minutely imitative detail. Although we are left in doubt as to just how a great imagination makes use of imitative materials, a major question has come into focus that will direct the inquiry of the following group of chapters and shape the rest of the volume. "How," Ruskin asks, "does the imagination show itself in dealing with truth?"[32]

The question by itself is both puzzling and large, especially if we have been tempted by Romantic theory of imagination generally and that of

Modern Painters, volume 2 in particular to think of imagination *as* a mode of truth. We wonder whether Ruskin is working toward some final distinction between imagined "seeing" and real perception or whether he means to take up a distinction between imagination and truth (that is, conviction) as modalities of consciousness (intention). Actually, in the next hundred pages Ruskin views the truth-imagination question in a moral (really mythic) perspective; that is, he examines it within the framework of a brief spiritual history of the uses and abuses of imagination in painting. Imagination, he dogmatizes, subserves the idealizing function of art; its duty is to create true ideal images. Its legitimate uses are religious and historical: "to call up the scenes and facts in which we are commanded to believe" and "to empower us to traverse the scenes of all other history."[33] Whenever imagination serves a false ideal, a false mythology or system of belief, or serves human vanity, it cannot produce true images. Thus the criticism of imagination becomes, for Ruskin, largely a criticism of the orders of belief, the "ideals" (in a loose sense, the myths) which imagination has served. Historically there have been two great false systems, and these become the subjects of the two following chapters, called "Of the False Ideal—First, Religious" and "Of the False Ideal—Secondly, Profane." In sketching the development of these traditions of idealist art Ruskin extends to painting the Fall myth within which he had visualized the history of architecture in *The Stones of Venice*.

The false religious ideal in painting, Ruskin holds, was cognate with the beginning of realistic technique. Earliest religious painting was liable to no abuses of the ideal because it lacked powers of realization: "It *asserted* nothing, for it could realize nothing."[34] But the progress of technique tempted some artists (he mentions Francia and Perugino) to turn all their skills to the delineation of "impossible" scenes. Such realistic fictions began to undermine the true grounds of faith. "A shadow of increasing darkness fell upon the human mind as art proceeded to still more perfect realization,"[35] realization, that is, of false or impossible ideal forms. However, among the religious painters before Raphael these false realizations were somewhat redeemed by true feeling; these early fantasies grew not so much from the painter's attempts to present facts as from his frank attempts to express his emotions with respect to the facts. Gradually, however, cool technical facility froze the spirit of sacred art. Painters of the "Raphaelite ideal" attempted to express neither religious truths nor even the ideal fallacies of religious enthusiasm and became totally absorbed in the display of their own artistic powers. And so the Fall: "A fatal change of aim took place throughout the whole world of art. In early times *art was employed for the display of religious facts*; now, *religious facts were employed for the display of art. . . .* It was passing from the paths of life to the paths of death."[36] Nature, of course, was being more accurately represented, but natural facts, like the religious, were sought for pride's sake not for their own. As religion was employed for the display of art, so art was employed for the display of wealth. Raphael sold his talent to the "impious luxury of the Vatican," and thereafter, through his influence, pure Christianity and high art part company.

Has there been any art of the "true" religious ideal? Generally not, Ruskin concludes, not insofar as this means sincere and unartificial rendering of religious "events historically recorded." He allows that work of the "passionate ideal" (the Angelican ideal, after Fra Angelico, essentially mythic in that it represents "imaginary beings of another world") is one true form of religious art; yet a "religious art" at once complete and sincere never has existed. However, he believes the era of its redemption is at hand, for "those bright Turnerian imageries" and "calm Pre-Raphaelite studies" have laid the foundation for a true sacred art.

In a sense Ruskin has dealt with the second delusive imaginative tradition in speaking of the first since, in his view, the pursuit of ideal beauty in sacred art gave birth to the "Profane Ideal." While men still cared for truth before beauty, they cared for first truths—mythic truths—first; and all art was, ipso facto, religious. But once the pursuit of beauty became primary, men were punished by being blinded to truth altogether, and the profane schools of art flourished.

Although the subjects of this false ideal were primarily what would be called "mythological," it is essential to notice that Ruskin does not condemn this art for being mythic so much as for not being *truly* such. He faults it mainly for its use of myth without belief. The heathen imagery, he complains, "could now be delighted in, without being believed; . . . its errors might be indulged, unrepressed by its awe; and those of its deities whose function was temptation might be worshipped, in scorn of those whose hands were charged with chastizement." Here, for the first time, Ruskin uses mythic symbols, as he might use Scripture, to make us feel the fullness of truth to which the Renaissance painters were blind: "that the returning Apollo bore not only his lyre, but his arrows; and that at the instant of Cytherea's resurrection to the sunshine, Persephone had reascended her throne in the deep."[37] Lacking depth of sacred vision, modern European ideal art developed into "the shadow of a shadow" in which mere "mechanism" substituted for deeper perfection, because all pursuers of ideal beauty, even later romantic pastoralists, ignore all the truths of existence that fall outside their codes of beauty.

Religious and profane pursuits of ideal beauty at the expense of truth are, then, for Ruskin, the two major perversions of imagination. But the imagination has its vital ways also, and, he notes, we have a responsibility to use "any refreshing or animating power ordained to be in us for our help."[38] There are three forms of idealism that permit healthy uses of imagination: the purist, naturalist, and grotesque modes. These become the topics of three successive chapters; their key points are those upon which he will later build.

The purist ideal, we are told, results from the unwillingness of certain tender and holy minds to contemplate evil, or the pain and imperfection of our existence. Fra Angelico is the exemplary painter in this style, which is characterized primarily by shadowless drawing, "as if the sun were everywhere at once."[39] Angelico represents a nature without evil or corruption, but his art, though "childish," is not a false ideal because it is, to Ruskin, the sincere and instinctive expression of a life devoted to the envisionment of heavenly beings. Similarly, he describes the features of purism in the Italian paintings of a modern German painter recently exhibited in London, drawing upon his own experience to show the innocence of the artist's work. Although the young painter had drawn his scenes with care and sincerity, "the volcanic horrors of Radicofani, the pestilential gloom of the Pontines, and the boundless despondency of the Campagna, became, under his hand, only various appearances of Paradise." His work, though "soothing and pathetic" could never reach sublimity or perfect beauty, because "for every sorrow that his heart turned from, he lost a consolation; for every fear which he dared not confront, he lost a portion of his hardness; the unsceptered sweep of the storm-clouds . . . sank into sweet rectitudes and decent formalisms; and, before his eyes that refused to be dazzled or darkened, the hours of sunset wreathed their rays unheeded, and the mists of the Appenines spread their blue veils in vain."[40] Purist paintings, ancient or recent, always indicate some weakness in the painter's mind. The opposers of Pre-Raphaelitism, Ruskin adds in a note, mistake it for a purist movement, whereas it is "stern naturalist."[41]

We are prepared, of course, for his judgment that the *"naturalist ideal"* is the "central and highest branch of ideal art"[42] but not for the special emphasis he places upon the imaginative seeing of what is as it is. In this chapter, a crucial one in the volume, he draws heavily upon the concepts of imagination set forth in the second volume. Homer he takes as the exemplary master of the naturalist ideal because his images are drawn from nature yet are imaginary. He touches on Thersites and Alecto as natural characters, but his most suggestive example is the scene in the *Iliad* where Achilles is shown cutting pork chops for Ulysses: "It is naturalist, because studied from nature, and ideal, because mentally arranged in a certain manner."[43] This illustration leads to one of the key passages in the volume, his assertion of the chief functional difference between major and minor artists.

> All the great men *see* what they paint before they paint it,—see it in a perfectly passive manner,—cannot help seeing it if they would; whether in their mind's eye, or in bodily fact, does not matter; very often the mental vision is, I believe, in men of imagination, clearer than the bodily one; but vision it is, of one kind or another,—the whole scene, character, or incident passing before them as in second sight, whether they will or no, and requiring them to paint it as they see it; they not daring, under the might of its presence, to alter one jot or tittle of it as they write it down or paint it down; it being to them in its own kind and degree *a true vision or Apocalypse*, and invariably accompanied in their hearts by a feeling correspondent to the words,—"Write the things *which thou hast seen*, and the things which *are*." (Rev. 1:19)[44]

Great imagination, then, is vision, apocalyptic seeing, in which the object presented is an ideal thing but is to the seer an existing thing. At this point Ruskin is near to connecting being with appearance as opposed to the objectively "real." Martin Heidegger reminds us that being and appearance were one in Greek thought, that "for the Greeks standing-in-itself was nothing other than standing-there, standing-in-the-light. Being means appearing. Appearing is not something subsequent that sometimes happens to being. Appearing is the very essence of being."[45] True imagination is appearing, for Ruskin; it is "seeing" and is, as he will frequently emphasize, "involuntary." This seems to mean that a great artist like Homer is the passive conductor of vision; "the choice, as well as the vision, is *manifested* to Homer. The vision comes to him in its chosen order. Chosen *for* him, not *by* him, yet full of visible and exquisite choice."[46] This complex of choices only *seems* to be an imposed order of human rules; actually the form is ordained by the vision. True invention is never the product of such rules; it "must be the involuntary occurrence of certain forms or fancies to the mind in the order to be portrayed."[47] Again one is reminded of Heidegger's point that the Greek word *techne* refers to art as revealed knowledge, not as artisanry.[48]

But if forms and facts are both disclosed, if great work is the product of "this awful, this inspired unconsciousness," of what use is the study of life? He whose habit is to seek the "stern facts" of existence will have them brought home to him magnified by vision; he who lives with fallacies and frivolities will dream them also. Further, the great worker in the naturalist ideal must have what sounds like Keatsian "negative capability": "The whole of his power depends upon his losing sight and feeling of his own existence, and becoming a mere witness and mirror of truth, and a scribe of visions."[49] Although never egotistical, the great naturalists accept their world, "getting always vital truth out of the vital present."[50]

Ruskin's fascination with the power of grotesque conception is apparent from long analysis of it in *Stones* and the rank he assigns it in this volume. Here the grotesque is offered as the third legitimate and vital mode of imagination. The earlier discussion had identified three valid forms of grotesque art: that arising from healthy though irrational play of the imagination at rest; that which derives from the imagination's chance contemplation of terrible or evil things; and, especially, the art that arises from "the confusion of the imagination by the presence of truths which it cannot wholly grasp."[51] It is this apocalyptic or mythopoeic grotesque that Ruskin singles out for attention in this chapter. Through the ages grotesque idealism, whether in revelation or in oracles, has been the aesthetic form "through which the most appalling and eventful truth has been wisely conveyed."[52] He stresses the profound authority of vital symbols, those which the artist truly "sees," as opposed to dead or secondhand symbols. For instance, the crucial difference between Lombard and classical griffins is, as he had shown in *Stones*, that "the Lombard workman did really see a griffin in his imagination, and carved it from life,"[53] while the classical workman merely compounded his griffin from what he knew. Among modern works, Turner's dragon in the *Garden of the Hesperides* especially reveals the prospects for grotesque symbolism in a poet-painter who will, like Dante or Spenser, fearlessly open his "immortal eyes" to the spiritual world. This mythic-apocalyptic painting is a symbol to which Ruskin will return with peculiar reverence; here it is merely introduced as marking "the dawn of a new era of art, in a true unison of the grotesque with the realistic power."[54]

This last phrase brings Ruskin to the hard practical question of just how the truths of vision are brought to stand in a work of art, the picture, especially a landscape. He labors with this difficult subject in the two chapters, called "Of Finish" and "Of the Use of Pictures," that conclude the first half of the volume. The problem of finish is, simply, "How far is this true imagination to be truly represented?"[55] What did Dante mean by saying that the perfect conception of Pallas would be so given as to look like the goddess herself and not like a picture of her? How does the artist know when he has given the final touch, that is, when the work stops being a truth and starts becoming a mere picture? Ruskin is back to the core problem of *Modern Painters* again and can give no final answer, for that answer is very likely particular to each work and has to do with the work's somehow fulfilling its own intention. What he says is that finish is wrong when it becomes finish for its own sake rather than remaining subordinate to conception. The artist must cease finishing when he has painted what he has "seen," what he truly knows. To finish without knowledge (*techne*) is really "to blacken," and this sort of blackening becomes an important image in Ruskin's later criticism.

But the problem of finish is a nagging one and he pursues it into a second "difficult" chapter. How is it that Turner, whose finish he has praised for its exquisite delicacy and who gave "exactly the highest and most consummate truth that had ever been seen in landscape,"[56] was condemned by the critics as a madman? The answer, of course is that Turner gave a resemblance deeper than deception; he gave truth. "Turner perceives at a glance the whole sum of visible truth open to human intelligence."[57] At the same time "he *gave facts* more *delicately*, more Pre-Raphaelitically, than other men."[58] But why were his truths not received as such? To answer, Ruskin must draw again upon his theory of imagination and explain how the full truth of a work is a reciprocal union of imaginative power in both painter and perceiver.

The power of any appearance over us depends upon our ability to comprehend it, upon "that penetrating, possession-taking power of the imagination, which has been long ago defined as the very life of man considered as a *seeing* creature."[59] The greater one's degree of knowledge and his "sensibility to the *pathetic* or impressive character of things known,"[60] the greater will be his imaginative delight. But the duty of the artist is not simply to awaken and address the beholding imagination but also to *guide* it, "and there is no safe guidance but that of simple concurrence with fact."[61] This precept, however, creates a difficulty because the addressed imagination has both a perceptive and a creative function. While the viewer's imagination in its penetrative function is "preeminently a beholder of things, *as they are*;" yet "it is, in its *creative* function, an eminent beholder of things *when* and *where* they are NOT; a seer, that is, in the prophetic sense . . . for ever delighting to dwell on that which is not tangibly present . . . its great function being the calling forth, or back, that which is not visible to bodily sense." In this function the viewer's imagination will be little helped by the deceptive appearance of a real object in the work of art; "reality and substance are rather in the imagination's way."[62] Because of this creative factor in the beholder's imagination, this "dislike of substance and presence," because it rejoices in having work to do, even a slight deceptive success in a picture will "insult" or "injure" the viewer's imagination.[63]

Truth is wanted in a painting, then, "but truth so presented that it will need the help of the imagination to make it real."[64] Truth now appears as something that happens as a work is viewed; the real work tends to become an imaginal correlate, not an object. The perfection of a work of art consists in "utmost *acceptable* completion," acceptable, that is, to the creative reach of the viewer's imagination. Every detail added beyond this point will actually block the creative apprehension of it; "every added touch advances the dangerous realism which makes the imagination languid." The "noble" painter wishes to "put into his work as much truth as possible, and yet to keep it looking *un*real."[65] In this suspension of deceptive reality, freeing yet guiding our imaginations by choices, arrangements, and penetrations, the work becomes the vehicle of an indwelling presence, "the expression of the power and intelligence of a companionable human soul," in which we recognize a "supernatural operation,"[66] not simply the mirroring of nature. To the great painter we thus say "come between this nature and me."[67] Turner presumably did so but reached out to creative imaginations that were, before Ruskin, incapable of completing his truths. But can the Pre-Raphaelites be said to leave the imagination some work to do? Aren't their works overrealized? Ruskin will not allow this, of course, but he does reiterate the main criticism of them he had offered in the Edinburgh lectures. If Pre-Raphaelite art is to be great it must add "the great imaginative element to all its faithfulness in transcript."[68]

2

In the volume's first ten chapters Ruskin has attempted to teach "what is generally right and wrong in all art."[69] The heart of his theory is the idea of imagination as involuntary, apocalyptic, "seeing," in which truths grounded in this world are revealed and must be set down, yet done so in such a way as to evoke and direct, not block, the beholder's imagination. Now, in the work's second section, he must explain how these laws of imagination apply to the special concern of his study, landscape painting. However, just as we have seen his interest in truth moving away from the work as object toward consideration of the painter's experience, so in this section his subject is not so much how landscape is painted as how it is experienced. This direction of inquiry must inevitably take him into myth. Accordingly, his first chapter, "Of the Novelty of Landscape," explains that feeling for landscapes is a modern phenomenon, not generally expressed in Greek or medieval times, when man did his best work "as in the presence of, or for the honour of, his gods."[70] The intimation is that our "passionate admiration for inanimate objects" replaces or impedes some more direct religious experience yet to be considered. The guiding question is whether this new sensibility has been ennobling or not. To find the answer he will examine attitudes toward landscape implicit in Greek, medieval, and modern poetry and painting. But first he must consider the psychological effect of scenery on any mind, and so we are led to the famous discussion of the pathetic fallacy.

Ruskin opens the chapter with a stern distinction between the true aspects of things in themselves in nature and the false impressions of them received by a consciousness under the influence of emotion or fancy. False here means singly "unconnected with any real power or character in the object." There is, of course, no such thing as pure or neutral consciousness of an object. Things signify. But his distinction is broad. Emotion, or pathos, causes "fallacies" of perception that can also under certain conditions be "true." At least these emotional fallacies must first be distinguished from all *deliberate* distortions by fancy because these do not involve belief, are not involuntary seeing. Fancy aside, his essential point is that all violent feelings affect perception. "They produce in us a falseness in all our impressions of external things," to which he gives the name " 'pathetic fallacy.' "[71] Already we suspect that these impressions relate in some way to unrefusable imaginative vision described in chapter 8, yet the word "pathetic" gives Ruskin positive and negative ambiguity with which to work.

Pathetic fallacy, as most students of English literature know, Ruskin finds particularly evident in the tendency of modern poets to ascribe "characters of a living creature" to inanimate objects. This animation presents an aesthetic problem since it is clearly something "untrue" in poetry, and yet, he admits, "if we think over our favourite poetry, we shall find it full of this kind of fallacy, and that we like it all the more for being so."[72] This position is consistent with his comment in "Of the Use of Pictures" on the true perceiving imagination's necessary "sensibility to the pathetic or impressive character" of what the mind knows, and consistent also with the frequency of this "fallacy" in Ruskin's own emotive prose. Pathetic fallacy, in short, is to be found in both greater and lesser poetry, yet "we shall find the greatest poets do not often admit this kind of falseness."[73] Therefore, when they do give way to it we recognize the fallacy as spiritually true.

To illustrate his point Ruskin examines several passages of poetry. Most illuminating, however, is his comparison of parallel sections from Pope and Homer on the summoning of Elpenor. The point of this comparison is that the lines from Pope "are not a *pathetic* fallacy at all"; they are not the outbursts of a mind overborne by feeling but merely by curiosity. "Therefore we see that the spirit of truth must guide us in some sort, even in our enjoyment of fallacy." The condition of mind that admits the pathetic fallacy, he continues, "is a more or less noble state, according to the force of the emotion which has induced it."[74]

He then proceeds to set up four ranks of artists according to the relationship between the strength of intellect and the threshold of emotional fallacy in them: "[1] the men who feel nothing, and therefore see truly; [2] the men who feel strongly, think weakly, and see untruly (second order of poets); [3] the men who feel strongly, think strongly, and see truly (first order of poets); [4] and the men who, strong as creatures can be, are yet submitted to influences stronger than they, and see in a sort untruly, because what they see is inconceivably above them. *This last is the usual condition of prophetic inspiration.*"[75] It is also, presumably, the condition of mythopoeic imagination.

I introduce the mythopoeic because it appears that the true subject of the chapter on pathetic fallacy is the metaphoric or mythic means by which poetry "names the holy," in Heidegger's phrase, whether by projected nature feeling or deific presence. In this way his subject is related to the earlier discussion of the religious and naturalistic uses of imagination in the creation of ideal forms. The subject is massive and Ruskin's thought shifts erratically between pathetic fallacy as a quality of style and as a subjective state. Ultimately he wishes to describe a true mythopoeic of landscape, true marriage of poetic power with the numina of nature, by using the Homeric style as a touchstone, but this intention does not become entirely clear until the following chapter.

Pathetic fallacy as a stylistic matter reduces, like Gothic imperfection, in Ruskin's thought to expressions of vital belief and true emotion over against mere technique, especially of the neoclassical sort. If a poet animates the inanimate, projects a metaphoric presence into nature, it must be in the diction of authentic emotion signified by evident restraint of it. How can we have true poetry when a poet indicates a "presence" in things that he obviously does not feel, or, as among moderns, when the feeling of presence is in excess of belief? Ruskin detects two extremes of animating fallacies, the cold personifications of neoclassical diction and the pathetic animations of the Romantics which, though emotional, were really indications of what T. E. Hulme would call "spilt religion." Geoffrey Hartman has recently suggested that these animating projections derive in the main from the classical tradition of the *genius loci*: the poet's effort to merge his genius with the spirit of a place and so make himself its prophetic voice.[76] We need note only that Ruskin has opened a question that is as deep as the connection between nature-metaphor and myth.

The poet's recourse to such animating metaphors as "raging waves," "remorseless floods," or "ravenous billows," as stylistic conventions signifies, to Ruskin, a failure of both belief and poetry, for the poet believes in no presence and feels no emotion; they are fallacy without pathos. There is, he insists, "no greater baseness in literature than the habit of using these metaphorical expressions in cool blood. . . . It is one of the signs of the highest power in a writer to check all such habits of thought, and to keep his eyes fixed firmly on the *pure fact*."[77] Homer, for instance, when he speaks of Helen's sorrow at the death of her brothers, does not give way to metaphorical excesses in speaking of the earth to which they returned: "But them, already, the life-giving earth possessed, there in Lacedaemon, in the dear fatherland."[78] This, for Ruskin, is "high poetical truth carried to the extreme. The poet has to speak of the earth in sadness, but he will not let that sadness affect or change his thoughts of it. No; though Castor and Pollux be dead, yet the earth is our mother still, fruitful, life-giving. These are the facts of the thing."[79]

There is a loose analogy between Ruskin's strictures on pathetic fallacy and the position on nature in prose fiction taken by our contemporary, the French novelist Alain Robbe-Grillet. He would have us look upon a nature that makes no sign to us, a nature that is without depth, without anthropomorphism, and without any implicit pledge of solidarity or complicity with man. Like Ruskin he is drawn by the cleansing power of sight and pure description. "Optical description," he writes, "is, in effect, the kind which most readily establishes distances: the sense of sight, if it seeks to remain simply that, leaves things in their respective places."[80] But there is only an analogy between his desire to purge the humanist tradition of its anthropomorphic assumptions about nature and Ruskin's attack on Romantic personification. Ruskin's "pure fact" is not the neutralized nature of modern science, for he uses the term to refer not merely to the data of optical sight but also to that given by the involuntary inward vision of imagination. His distinction is not between the real and the imagined but between the truly "seen" (in either sense) and the constructions of fancy or of introspective meditation. Thus when his terms are properly understood there is no fundamental inconsistency between Ruskin's concepts of imagination and of pathetic fallacy.

"The theory of the Pathetic Fallacy," Harold Bloom correctly observes, "is a searching criticism of Romanticism from within, for the sake of saving the Romantic program of humanizing nature from extinction through excessive self-indulgence."[81] When considered in relation to the chapters that follow it, "Of the Pathetic Fallacy" appears clearly as an effort to criticize Romantic personifying projections by comparing them with genuine mythopoesis. This is why Ruskin, having assessed the myth-making of his Romantic predecessors, can yet go forward, ingesting contemporary knowledge of mythopoesis, to become, as Bloom notes, "the major Romantic myth-maker of the Victorian era."[82] At this point he is simply saying, do not give the thing a life you do not believe, or at least feel, it has. If a poet's emotion is genuine we permit some projection of it; if "the *feeling* is true, we pardon, or are even pleased by, the confessed fallacy of sight which it induces,"[83] what offends us is the "adoption of these fanciful metaphorical impressions as a sort of current coin . . . insincere, deliberately wrought out with chill and studied fancy."[84]

Ruskin's position here is, of course, reminiscent of Wordsworth's attack on the mechanical personifications as against the language of live passion in his "Appendix to the *Lyrical Ballads*" (1802). At the same time his opposition of Homeric literalism to neoclassical ornamentation has some resemblance to the more contemporary view expressed by George Grote in the first volume of his *History of Greece* (1846). Grote reminds his readers that personifying fictions were "blended by the Homeric Greeks with their conception of the physical phenomena before them, not simply in the way of poetical ornament, but as a genuine portion of their every-day life. . . . It is true that these expressions . . . have passed from the ancient epic to compositions produced under very different circumstances, and have now degenerated into unmeaning forms of speech; but they gained currency originally, in their genuine and literal acceptation."[85] One can imagine Grote's (or Wordsworth's) separation of modern degenerated personifications from the once literal belief in them as having led to Ruskin's distinction between modern pathetic fallacies of presence and the mythic "classical landscape." Beyond this the resemblance to Grote is not significant at this point but will become more so as we turn to Ruskin's next chapter and his first serious thoughts on the nature of myth.

Though Ruskin does not compare pathetic fallacy and mythic style in this chapter, he is interested in extreme or visionary conditions of the fallacy. In fact, the whole concept of there being true fallacies of pathos is grounded on those apocalyptic experiences in which the fallacy is inevitable. For although "a poet is great, first in proportion to the strength of his passion, and then, that strength being granted, in proportion to his government of it", there is "always a point at which all feverish and wild fancy becomes just and true." Just as "the destruction of Assyria cannot be contemplated firmly by a prophet of Israel. . . . So, still more, the thought of the presence of Deity cannot be borne without this great astonishment. 'The mountains and the hills shall break forth before you into singing, and all the trees of the field shall clap their hands.' "[86]

This kind of apocalyptic fallacy is clearly a challenge to Ruskin's aesthetic of "pure fact." There are cases in which objective distortion is taken as a sign of inward access to truth. To keep such distortions under his general law of truth he can only insist, as he did in speaking of certain daring but morbid projections of the imagination, that pathetic fallacy is always a sign of mental aberration: "Even in the most inspired prophet it is a sign of the incapacity of his human sight or thought to bear what has been revealed to it."[87] Yet pathetic fallacy remains a paradoxical fusion of expressive and mimetic aspects of creativity; it is "powerful only so far as it is pathetic" but "feeble so far as it is fallacious."[88] Finally, Ruskin's formula leaves open the case of genuine mythopoesis where the animation of landscape, as presumably in Homer or Hesiod, is neither a conscious ornament nor a delusion induced by pathos but a matter of preconceptual belief, taken by the poet as plain fact.

3

For this reason the famous chapter on pathetic fallacy serves to introduce that entitled "Of Classical Landscape," setting up an important religio-aesthetic contrast for deeper analysis. In tracing the development of landscape feeling Ruskin must now distinguish between modern pathetic landscape and mythic landscape. Actually his argument will touch on emotional, allegorical, and mythic views of nature implicit in the preceding chapter. Most important is the point that his argument now requires him to give some serious consideration to Greek belief, a concern that will seriously affect his own spiritual and intellectual development as we shall see. For the moment, he must contrast an awareness in which presence of a power in natural forms is literally believed—resulting in restrained feelings and minimal poetic distortion of things seen—with responses to nature which, if not coldly allegorical, are sentimental and emotional ones in which pathetic projections take the place of "pure fact." We must pursue this distinction in "Of Classical Landscape" with some care.

"My reason," Ruskin continues, "for asking the reader to give so much of his time to the examination of the pathetic fallacy was, that, whether in literature or in art, he will find it eminently characteristic of the modern mind." In the modern painter-poet, imagination, it appears, either does duty for or preempts the function of belief. Where the modern artist tries to express "something which he, as a living creature, imagines in the lifeless object, . . . the classical and medieval painters were content with expressing the unimaginary and actual qualities of the object itself." Given the generally empirical and realistic development of art, this assertion conveys the essential paradox to be explored. But before going on Ruskin pauses to remind us that he intends to "use the words 'painter' and 'poet' quite indifferently, including in our inquiry the landscape of literature as well as that of painting"; perhaps this means he recognizes no discontinuity between vision and language, but chiefly here it is because "the spirit of classical landscape has hardly been in any other way than by words."[89]

Moving on, Ruskin reiterates his point that pathetic fallacy is eminently characteristic of modern art. He illustrates with a pair of lines from *Endymion*: "Down whose green back the short lived foam, all hoar,/ Bursts gradual, with a wayward indolence." Hardly representative of the modern, we suppose, but it is the contrast with Homeric style that matters. Homer could never have written or thought in such language. "He could not by any possibility have lost sight of the great fact that the wave, from the beginning to the end of it, do what it might, was still nothing else than salt water; and that salt water could not be either 'wayward' or 'indolent.' " The Greek poet, of course, had epithets for the sea: "over-roofed," "full-charged," "compact-black," "dark-clear," "violet-colored," "wine-colored," et cetera. "But every one of these epithets is descriptive of pure physical nature."[90]

Here is the pathetic paradox again. Does this literalism mean that, on the scale of pathos developed earlier, Homer had less feeling for the sea than Keats? No, Ruskin replies, as if echoing Grote and the early German mythologists, "Homer *had* some feeling about the sea; a faith in the animation of it much stronger than Keats's. . . . He never says the waves rage, or the waves are idle. But he says there is somewhat in, and greater than, the waves, which rages, and is idle, and *that* he calls a god."[91] This "great abstract image of Sea Power" is an example of the "personifying fiction" that Grote and his predecessors thought of as having degenerated into a mere ornament in modern poetry. This distinction, coupled with the necessity of demonstrating the degree of restrained feeling in Homer, draws Ruskin into his first theoretical discussion of myth.

"I do not think," he writes, "we ever enough endeavour to enter into what a Greek's real notion of a god was." We tend to think that Homer, like Pope, "was merely an ingenious fabulist; nay, more than this, that all the nations of past time were ingenious fabulists also, to whom the universe was a lyrical drama; and by whom whatsoever was said about it was merely a *witty allegory*, or a graceful lie, of which the entire upshot and consummation was a pretty statue in the middle of the court, or at the end of the garden." Similarly mistaken is the puritanical view of myth that sees the classical deity as a mere idol or else a "diabolic or betraying power, usurping the place of God."[92] It was only in its corruption that the Greek religion became empty idolatry.

We should note that Ruskin immediately takes a stand against the allegorical conception of myth: the view that myths are conscious imaginative creations rather than a primordial language or mode of knowing. This antiallegorical view is also taken by Grote in his *History* and in his own probable sources, Thomas Keightley's *Mythology of Ancient Greece and Italy* (1831) and Karl Otfried Müller's *Introduction to a Scientific System of Mythology* (1825; tr., 1844). Whatever his source, Ruskin appears to be aware of an important ideal about myth relating it to language and to a preconceptual bond of mind and nature rather than to deliberate creation. It was an idea that had been making its way into scientific mythology since the discoveries of animism and fetishism a century earlier. In his own interpretations of particular myths, Ruskin tends to read them as if they were allegories, finding his own teaching encoded there; but in speaking about myths, as opposed to reading them, he assigns them the veracity of immediate experience. This is why they are *worth* interpreting.

I have attempted elsewhere to reconstruct the stock of mythological theories upon which Ruskin might have drawn for his discussion of Greek belief in this volume.[93] Here it must suffice to quote a brief passage from Grote's first volume as being representative of the general theoretical outlook at mid century. In mythopoeic times, he writes, "the whole view of nature was purely religious and subjective, the spontaneous suggestions of an early mind. It proceeded from the instinctive tendencies of the feelings and imagination to transport, to the world without, the familiar type of free-will and conscious personal action: above all, it took deep hold of the emotions, from the evidently extended sympathy which it so perpetually called forth between man and nature."[94] Grote's discussion emphasizes the intrinsic religiousness of the mythopoeic world view and the impossibility of recreating it from a modern empirical standpoint. A relational gap like that between Martin Buber's "I-It" and "I-Thou" relations appears. Once myths ceased to be the total of man's knowledge, once he developed historical and philosophical perspectives, nature was perceived as inanimate and objective, and the mythopoeic spell, the primordial bond between mind and nature, was broken in Greece forever.

Though Ruskin and his contemporaries might dogmatize about the distinction between myth and allegory and seem generally to have been on the right track in assigning myth to a less objectifying, more immediate consciousness, their concepts reveal the need for the kind of general semiology and epistemology developed in our time by Ernst Cassirer. Allegorical conception is object-consciousness to which a signification has been superadded, but mythical consciousness does not know objects, strictly speaking. For Cassirer, "the mythical form of conception is not something superadded to certain definite *elements* of empirical existence; instead, the primary 'experience' itself is steeped in the imagery of myth and saturated with its atmosphere. Man lives with *objects* only insofar as he lives with these *forms*; he reveals reality to himself, and himself to reality, in that he lets himself and the environment enter into this plastic medium, in which the two do not merely make contact, but fuse with each other."[95]

"What, then, was actually the Greek god?" Ruskin asks, plunging into the morass of theories. "In what way were these two ideas of human form, and divine power, credibly associated in the ancient heart, so as to become a subject of truth faith irrespective equally of fable, allegory, superstitious trust in stone, and demoniacal influence?" His answer is that mythopoesis fuses the ordinary pathetic fallacy of poetry with a true and projective belief in the immortality of the soul.

"It seems to me," he continues, "that the Greeks had exactly the same instinctive feeling about the elements that we have ourselves. . . . To Homer, as much as to Keats, the sea-wave appeared idle, or whatever else it may be to the poetical passion." But the Greek, by reason, makes a faith of this fallacy. He supposes that, with the water as with his own body, "there may be a power in the water which is not water, but to which the water is as a body;—which can strike with it, move in it, suffer in it, yet not be destroyed with it. This something, this great Water Spirit, [he] must not confuse with the waves, which are only its body. *They* may flow hither and thither, increase or diminish. *That* must be indivisible—imperishable—a god.''[96]

But what about those materializations of Greek deities that shock us by their sensuous being and make us think of idolatry? This materialism, he argues, is never truly positive or complete. In every god-image "there is always some sense of exaltation in the spiritual and immortal body; and of a power proceeding from the visible form through all the infinity of the element ruled by the particular god.''[97] For instance, in the *Iliad*, when the river-god Scamander comes as a man to remonstrate with Achilles, the hero is instantly able to recognize him in terms of his element, and the god is said to speak with a voice "out of the deep whirlpools." And when the god-river is attacked by Vulcan's fire and cries out for respite, we are given the impression of "a vital part of the river-body, which acted and felt, to which, if the fire reached, it was death, just as would be the case if it touched a vital part of the human body.''[98]

Ruskin allows that it is very difficult for our minds to conceive, without inconsistencies, the spirit part of the spirit-thing relationship that is a Greek deity. The difficulty seems analogous to that of defining the relation between spiritual truth and literal imitation in the work of art that has plagued him, and even here we detect an inconsistency between the "vital part" just mentioned and the "indivisible—imperishable" power introduced in the preceding paragraph. "But," he insists, however difficult this spirit-thing relation may be to contemplate, "I do not believe that the idea ever weakens itself down to mere allegory.''[99] He is aware of Wordsworth's evocation of the mythic consciousness in book 4 of *The Excursion* and explicitly rejects it as allegorism. Diana hunting with her nymphs is not, as Wordsworth thought, simply a figurative expression for moonlight and starlight glancing through the trees (11. 861–70). The myth attests to literal belief in a "living spirit, to which the light of the moon is as a body," a spirit that might on occasion assume a "perfect human form" and hunt live beasts with real arrows.

We can see that Ruskin is anxious to show that Greek myths involved a genuinely believed spiritual, yet anthropomorphic, conception of vital power in natural forms. (Perhaps it is to emphasize the actuality of Greek belief that he avoids the word myth here; though at the same time it should be understood that his reference is to deities rather than to narratives.) He wants us to see that with the Greeks the identification of the spiritual powers of man and nature is complete, a point that will emerge more clearly in a moment. He must dispose of any notion that the Greek deity is a mere creation of fancy, on the one hand, or materialized into an idol on the other. This position will serve Ruskin in two significant ways; it will explain the apparent matter-of-factness with which Homer can name the sacred, and, more important, it will provide a deep cultural lineage for his own feeling about nature. This last is a point to which we must return.

For the moment, we should notice that Ruskin now moves to defend the consistency of his idea of an anthropomorphic yet spiritual presence by means of a rather daring analogy, considering his puritan background, between Greek deities and Christian angels. He observes that "the highest authority which governs our own faith requires us to conceive divine power clothed with a human form (a form so real that it is recognized for superhuman only by its 'doing wondrously') and retaining, nevertheless, sovereignty and omnipresence in all the world. This is precisely, as I understand it, the heathen idea of a God [*sic*]; and it is impossible to comprehend any single part of the Greek mind until we grasp this faithfully, not endeavouring to explain it away in anywise, but accepting, with frank decision and definition, the tangible existence of its deities."[100] It appears, though Ruskin does not make this point, that the mythic consciousness, or, in Homer, the mythic style is in fact a mode of the elusive and paradoxical "true ideal" he had labored to define in the first half of the volume. The Greeks actually heard Apollo's quiver rattle on his shoulder as he moved, though they knew the darts he shot did not strike as arrows but as plague.

In sum, Ruskin finds the Greek conception of deity "much more real than we usually suppose," that is, more familiarly human. Where we err in seeking deity in that which is above human comprehension, the Greek's error lay in "making hardly any effort to conceive the divine mind as above the human";[101] in consequence he felt no dread of the deity's immediate presence. But this, to us, shocking familiarity with deity is not so much a misunderstanding of divine nature as a too confident comprehension of the human. Because, as Ruskin sees it, the Greek lived a healthy, natural life, free of all morbid anxiety, he was confident of his own immortality and of the ultimate justice of existence. He found God revealed in the image of his own heroic spirit, and "did not feel that it was an appalling superiority in those gods to have bodies of water, or fire, instead of flesh, and to have various work to do among the clouds and waves, out of his human way; or sometimes, even in a sort of service to himself."[102]

Of course Ruskin's interest in Greek religion has not been entirely for its own sake. He is in the midst of a survey of landscape feeling, and so, as we might expect, the entire digression on mythology comes around into a decisive contrast between the Homeric landscape, where nature is literally god-stuff, and ours. This contrast comes to focus in a passage that is among the most powerful in the volume and at the same time makes definitive the first use of the idea of myth in Ruskin's thought: "With us, observe, the idea of Divinity is apt to get separated from the life of nature; and imagining our God upon a cloudy throne, far above the earth, and not in the flowers or waters, we approach those visible things with a theory that they are dead; governed by physical laws, and so forth." Our vital instincts defy the lethal knowledge yet cannot find expression in real belief, only in pathetic fallacy. "But coming to them, we find the theory fail; that they are not dead; that, say what we choose about them, the instinctive sense of their being alive is too strong for us. . . . And then, puzzled, and yet happy; pleased, and yet ashamed of being so; accepting sympathy from nature, which we do not believe it gives, and giving sympathy to nature, which we do not believe it receives—mixing, besides, all manner of purposeful play and conceit with these involuntary fellowships,—we fall necessarily into the curious web of hesitating sentiment, pathetic fallacy, and wandering fancy, which form a great part of our modern view of nature." But the Greek did not need to return spirit to nature in outbursts of involuntary feeling and fallacy, "the Greek never removed his god out of nature at all; never attempted for a moment to contradict his instinctive sense that God was everywhere."[103]

To understand why the human figure instead of landscape predominates in Greek art we need only follow Ruskin's analysis of Homeric consciousness a final step, bringing us back to his meaning in volume 2 of *Modern Painters* when he spoke of the Greek god as being always finite, never a spirit. In clearly defining his belief the Greek "threw it entirely into a human form, and gave his faith to nothing but the image of his own humanity."[104] Though the theory is the same, we sense that his attitude is less negative than it had been in the earlier volume where he felt obliged to warn that "all Greek conception [is] full of danger to the student in proportion of his admiration of it."[105] Here we simply learn that the humanistic bias of his religion caused the Greek to reserve his sympathy for the spirit *in* natural forms, not for the forms themselves; "always for the dryad in the wood, not for the wood." Thus he "approached the actual waves and woody fibres with no sympathy at all. The spirit that ruled them, he received as a plain fact. Them, also, ruled and material, he received as plain facts; they, without their spirit, were dead enough."[106]

The chapter on classical landscape, more than a theory of Greek belief and what might be called the mythic style in landscape, presents an awareness of nature that is, for Ruskin, the rhetorical antithesis of nature in most modern art and meant to shed redemptive light of ironic contrast on that "curious web of hesitating sentiment" into which we have fallen in our relations to nature. The chapter invokes a landscape so full of being that it conveys no mystery as landscape, no symbolic depth, no sentiment for the picturesque. Homer is the representative figure in this style, "eminently the Greek of Greeks." Some Greek writers, notably Aeschylus and Aristophanes, Ruskin considers more modern and pathetic in their nature imagery and therefore un-Greek in these respects. A final point: because the Greeks concentrated their admiration of beauty per se on the order, symmetry, and tenderness of the human form, they tended to shrink "with dread or hatred from all the ruggedness of lower nature,—from the wrinkled forest bark, the jagged hill-crest, and irregular, *inorganic storm of sky.*"[107]

4

Having brought into play the idea of a Greek awareness of nature as radically humanized, Ruskin now proceeds to invoke a sense of medieval landscape that is by contrast primarily symbolic yet suffused with evidences of the modern pathetic response to nature. However, the two chapters under the main title "Mediaeval Landscape," subtitled "The Fields" and "The Rocks" respectively, do not have the theoretical coherence of the preceding pair. They are largely a miscellany of medieval landscape symbolism of which Dante is taken as the exemplar, paralleling the use of Homer as the Greek model. Despite their lack of cohesiveness these chapters foist up a number of symbolic themes that permeate Ruskin's later work and should be brought to mind here as we pass on toward the modern idea of landscape.

Primarily we should note that Ruskin views the medieval landscape as already marked by "loss of sense of actual divine presence";[108] it follows from his general thesis of landscape feeling that "exactly in proportion as the idea of definite spiritual presence in material nature was lost, the mysterious sense of *unaccountable* life in things themselves would be increased, and the mind would instantly be laid open to all those currents of fallacious, but pensive and pathetic sympathy, which we have seen to be characteristic of modern times."[109] This loss of the numinous sense of nature coupled with the medieval preference for the garden over the farm and led to greater sentimental, as opposed to practical, contemplation of nature. This overview is modified, however, by the peculiar sanctity and terror of mountains in the medieval mind. Their special sanctity derived from the scriptural and homiletic evidence that God had manifested himself most frequently and intimately to man among the hills; terror of them stemmed from their being "voiceful of perpetual rebuke" to the vain and uncontemplative comforts of life below. The medieval, Ruskin argues, shared the Greek's admiration for the human form. This led to a relative contempt for natural beauty; "all that they admired was tender, bright, balanced, enclosed, symmetrical."[110] His greater respect for the loveliness of man meant that nature was generally seen only as subordinated to human interests, yet "mingled with curious traces of terror, piety, or superstition, and cramped by various formalisms." In sum, where the "pagan" awareness of nature was "rooted in pride, and fruited with sorrow," the Christian perception is "rooted in self-debasement, and strengthened under suffering by gladness of hope."[111]

These are the general theoretical outlines of Ruskin's account of medieval landscape. Much of his two chapters is given over to examples of those "curious traces" of terror, piety, superstition, and formalism. The replacement of golden backgrounds by blue skies marks, he declares, a critical change in the spirit of medieval art, a shift in the early fifteenth century from the symbolic to the imitative mode. In Dante, "the great prophetic exponent of the heart of the middle ages," Ruskin finds the consummate articulation of the medieval faith "that all perfect active life was 'the expression of man's delight *in God's work.*' "[112] This he takes to be the "*sealing* difference between the Greek and the medieval, in that the former sought the flower and the herb for his own uses, the latter for God's honour."[113] He finds this difference signified in their uses of color, "the most *sacred* element of all visible things."[114] Since the medieval sought the sacred in things, his color is precise; the Greek's dim and uncertain. Dante's metaphoric description of the grass of the *Inferno* as "green enamel" (*verde smalto*) becomes an example of this precision, and the idea of its hardness leads to the surprising observation that " '*Venga Medusa, si lo farem de Smalto*' ["Medusa summoned to turn Dante to enamel"] is perhaps the most awful passage of the whole *Inferno*,"[115] an impression that would serve him again.

The imagery of Dante, a massive and mythic influence on Ruskin, also dominates the second medieval chapter, "Of Rocks." Allusions become dense and tangled here, as in his late style. The idea of medieval dread-tinged reverence for mountains leads him to a consideration of Dante's treatment of the rocks in the eighth circle. Connecting medieval dislike of rocks with their monotony of color, he notes that Dante's rock color is, significantly, ashen grey streaked with iron ochre. This in turn leads to notes on Dante's references to the "brown" air of Hades and to the color of the river of oblivion, Lethe, as "brown *exceeding* brown," with no warmth in it. Both colors, grey and brown, were "hues of distress, despair, and mortification" in the medieval color vocabulary, they suggest, of course, the umber and asphaltum of the modern tenebrism that he detests. Finally, he notes, for future reference, that "the air which torments the passionate spirits is 'aer nero,' *black* air, called presently afterwards malignant air, just as the grey cliffs are called malignant cliffs."[116] The chapter concludes with an assertion of Dante's (as Ruskin's) "intense love of light" and his "equally intense detestation of all mist, rack of cloud, or dimness of rain." In the *Paradisio* "all the beauty," he insists, "depends on spheres of light, or stars, never on clouds,"[117] while the pit of the *Inferno* is sunk in clouds, and the slough in which the souls of the sad and angry are caught is obscured by fog. Therefore the clouds, which could convey benevolent messages to the Greeks, "seemed, in the heart of the Middle Ages, to be only under the dominion of the spirit of evil."[118]

Although myth is not, strictly speaking, his subject at this point, Ruskin has derived a symbolic message from medieval landscape: the tendency of the medieval mind to ascribe all indistinctness, colorlessness, and cloudiness to the influence of evil. With this emphasis on Dantean cloud symbolism his survey of nature feeling, which is really a history of nature mythology, has merged with his personal mythology of sky phenomena. By this I mean the use of sky effects to symbolize spiritual events, personal and racial, which is a major motif in his private and public writing. This convergence of two "mythologies," his history of nature feeling and his symbology of evil, is apparent in the volume's climatic chapter, "Of Modern Landscape," where Ruskin is able to speak of the modern consciousness of landscape in the language of sky effects.

The interpretive key to modern landscapes, then, is their cloudiness. Where "all the pleasure of the medieval was in *stability, definiteness,* and *luminousness,* we are expected to rejoice in darkness, and triumph in mutability."[119] This feeling is conveyed by the modern landscapist's "general delight in breeze and darkness" and by such careful attention to the real form of clouds and the effects of mist "that the appearance of objects, as seen through it, becomes a subject of science with us," the science of aerial perspective. Sunrises and sunsets, "with all their attendant phenomena of cloud and mist," so fascinate the painter that in a typical daylight landscape "the sky is considered of so much importance, that a principle mass of foliage, or a whole foreground, is unhesitatingly thrown into shade merely to bring out the form of a white cloud." So distinct is this tendency that no better name for modern landscape art could be given than " 'service of clouds.' "[120]

This "modern cloud-worship" reminds him of Aristophanes' judgment of clouds, Aristophanes being "the only Greek who studied them attentively." The judgment appropriated is that the love of mystery in much of our philosophy and art is merely " 'speaking ingeniously concerning smoke,' " a phrase he is fond of quoting. So in the subjection of foreground to cloud we have a symbolic expression that is the contrary of the medieval rage for clarity and color. "That darkening of the foreground to bring out the white cloud, is, in one aspect of it, a type of the subjection of all plain and positive fact, to what is uncertain and unintelligible." And this, for Ruskin, also signifies the crucial difference between medieval and modern landscape; for, where the early landscapist drew everything as clear as he could, "now our ingenuity is all 'concerning smoke.' "[121] Whatever else we draw is vague. "Nothing is truly drawn but that; all else is vague, slight, imperfect; got with as little pains as possible."[122] Apparently Ruskin would agree with Eric Heller's observation that *"The Invisible always steals the show of Romantic art."*[123] However, as a Romantic, he will come to new terms with the meaning of cloudiness in dealing with Turner's. At this point the rhetoric of antithesis is in control.

Under the general message of cloudiness Ruskin groups three subsidiary signs of the modern temperament in landscape. First, love of liberty; Romantic rebelliousness, we might say, is reflected in imagery of wildness, ruin, and desolation. It is nature seen as emancipated from human control. Then, correlatively, there is an evident love of mountain scenery, but this affection, he says, is untempered by any sense of solemnity or dread. This easiness among mountains he takes to be plain evidence of our "total absence of faith in the presence of any deity therein." Where "the mediaeval never painted a cloud, but with the purpose of placing an angel in it; and a Greek never entered a wood without expecting to meet a god in it; *we* should think the appearance of an angel in the cloud wholly unnatural, and should be seriously surprised by meeting a god anywhere."[124] Finally, the profane temper of modern times is conclusively signified by our "strong tendency to deny the sacredness of colour, and make our boast in blackness." The predominance of dark tones in our art and artifacts Ruskin takes to be a clear indication of modern existential despair. Where the medieval period, with its emphasis on clarity and color, has been improperly called the Dark Ages, ours must be called "the ages of umber."[125]

Clouds, mountains, desolation, gloom: these are the main lineaments of the modern landscape. Turning from objective features to subjective causes Ruskin appends to this vocabulary of symbols a diagnosis of seven symptoms of the modern temper. Much as Schlegel and Carlyle had spoken of the agony of mythlessness and the existentialists would speak of dread and meaninglessness, Ruskin points first to "despondency arising from faithlessness," not tragic sadness, but sadness in "a dim and wearied way,—the way of ennui, and jaded intellect, and uncomfortableness of soul and body."[126] He notes that Pre-Raphaelitism is an exception to this pervading "darkness of heart" as was Blake, who, though sincere, was "full of wild creeds and somewhat diseased of brain"; but he specifically charges many of the major writers of his age with being "against all religious form." Others are "anchored, indeed, but anxious or weeping."[127] Levity in modern life and art he views as a symptom arising from mythless despair. One is reminded of our own dark laughter of the absurd. Further, Renaissance detachment of beauty from truth led to beauty's being lost sight of all together and finally to the triumph of ugliness in urban culture. "To powder the hair, to patch the cheek, to hoop the body, to buckle the foot, were all part and parcel of the same system which reduced streets to brick walls, and pictures to brown stains. One desert of Ugliness was extended before the eyes of mankind."[128] The Romantic reaction to this cultural desert was to rejoice excessively in all wild inanimate beauty.

A result of this sentimental reaction, Ruskin argues, has been disdain for human beauty, a consequent loss of interest in physical health, and an increasing susceptibility to psychological disorders. The naturalist reaction against the beauty of man and his works was also coupled with a "romantic imagination of the past." With the search for beauty in the wilds and in the past Ruskin sees mingled another "more rational passion," the love of science, which, at this stage, he thinks has acted for good or evil according to the mind that received it. Finally, and most curiously, he maintains that modern fear of war has led to the neglect of the art of it and therefore has "somewhat weakened and deformed the body" while at the same time leaving man more leisure than ever before for the pursuit of science.

Because the modern mind has generally shifted its admiration "from men to mountains, and from human emotion to natural phenomena,"[129] it is to be expected that the arts will have followed suit, that the great painter of the age will necessarily be a landscapist and that painting will predominate over poetry by its greater capacity to represent nature. To document this change and to illustrate modern landscape Ruskin will take two men who are the first fruits of their age, as were Homer and Dante. These are Turner, of course, and, though "many readers may be surprised," Scott. In bringing their work to bear, however, he introduces two new tests of greatness. The first is humility, which does not mean self-doubt but "a curious under-sense of powerlessness, [the] feeling that greatness is not *in* them, but *through* them,"[130] and leads to a complete absence of affectation in their work. Mannered it may be, but mannered inevitably by sheer force of feeling. This doctrine is simply his theory of the involuntariness of true imaginative vision in new terms; the second test of greatness, clear seeing, also belongs to it. "To see clearly is poetry, prophecy, and religion,—all in one." All great writers may be divided into thinkers and seers, and "the Seers are wholly the greater race of the two."[131] Here again is the phenomenological bias of Ruskin's thought, with its emphasis on pure seeing and on the primacy of vision among the portals of perception.

Scott, for present purposes has become a landscapist, who, like Turner, is a supreme seer, set apart from metaphysical writers (though Carlyle is "in some sort a seer"[132]) and from "sentimental" writers like Byron, Keats, and Tennyson. Turner, the landscapist whose position in art compares with Bacon's in philosophy, will be taken up at length later; but now, Scott. Ruskin will not, as he says he has with Homer and Dante, attempt to give a complete analysis of the feelings implicit in Scott's landscapes. What matters is his habit of seeing nature neither with Homeric matter-of-factness nor as altered by his own emotions into pathetic fallacy. Scott, he insists, sees nature "as having an animation and pathos of *its own*, wholly irrespective of human presence or passion,—an animation which Scott loves and sympathizes with, as he would with a fellow creature, forgetting himself altogether, and subduing his own humanity before what seems to him the power of the landscape."[133]

Ruskin is convinced that Scott in his humility, as against the egotistical sentimentality of other nature-poets such as Keats and Tennyson, addresses an authentic "Thou" to nature. This he proceeds to illustrate by quotations from *Marmion* and *The Lady of the Lake*. We might wish to argue that this is simply pathetic fallacy and ventriloquism in a slightly different guise; however, Ruskin insists that the poet has not projected his own emotions. He detects in Scott's imagery a genuine mythic style, though it is powerless to bear mythic forms. "Observe, therefore, this is not *pathetic* fallacy; for there is no passion in *Scott* which alters nature." However, Scott does share with the other moderns an inherent (and cloudy) habit of thought that is "nothing else than the instinctive sense which men must have of the Divine presence, not formed into distinct belief. In the Greeks it created, as we saw, the faithfully believed gods of the elements; in Dante and the medievals, it formed the faithfully believed angelic presence: in the modern it creates no perfect form, does not apprehend distinctly any Divine being or operation; but only a dim, slightly credited animation in the natural object, accompanied with a great interest and affection for it."[134] Though he shares intensely this religious vagueness, Scott is among the seers because he does not subject nature to his own mood. Free of the Wordsworthian egotistical sublime, he subordinates himself to nature and accepts her temper as he finds it. This humility, Ruskin declares, makes Scott's "enjoyment of nature incomparably greater" than that of any other poet known to him. Yet he has a reservation. Scott has the "habit of drawing a slight *moral* from every scene, just enough to excuse to his conscience his want of definite religious feeling; and . . . this moral is almost always melancholy,"[135] presumably because it is immanent. So despite this praise of Scott's nature feeling the reader is left with significant questions. Is any distinctly religious feeling to be derived from landscape? Has the joy in it any intrinsic moral value? What would an authentically religious response to landscape, in a modern, be like? These questions become the essential subject of the volume's penultimate chapter, "The Moral of Landscape."

5

His long and meandering chapter does bring into focus two major and interinvolved questions for Ruskin. First, what qualities of mind are necessary for full experience of nature? Second, what is the moral value, if any, of total response to nature? One can see that the two questions are related insofar as the mental qualities involved in nature-feeling will have a bearing on its moral value. On the first question Ruskin's view is that true landscape feeling is by no means pure feeling. Wordsworth and Scott were wrong in assuming that their responses to landscape were devoid of any "remoter charm, by thought supplied." They believed this because their delight was composed of thought "so curiously languid and neutralized" that they were unable to trace it. However, this vagueness of thought in nature's presence was not a fault;

the copresence of discursive thought *would* dispel the feeling. Actually a delicate harmony of mental attitudes is necessary for right response to scenery. The great observer will not see with the selectivity of the painter or the engineer; "he will not altogether share the emotion of the sentimentalist, nor the trance of the idealist; but fancy, and feeling, and perception, and imagination, will all obscurely meet and balance themselves in him."[136]

Ruskin cites a passage from Wordsworth's "Yew Trees" in order to show that the capability of "fully *perceiving* any natural object depends on our being able to group and fasten all our fancies about it as a centre." However, he concludes by reminding us that this is not the only valued mode of perceiving nature. To the average man "the most useful members of society are the dissectors, not the dreamers."[137] In fact, even in Wordsworth and Scott love of nature is more or less associated with their immaturity and weakness; if it had not been combined with other qualities their love of nature, he observes, would have been comparatively worthless.

Here we are drawn into the second question: whether this nature-feeling itself is of any moral value, especially considering that it is said to belong primarily to youth. By way of answer Ruskin turns autobiographical and researches his own exceptional sensibility to nature. He recalls that his own first experiences of nature feeling were "never independent of associated thought" and that, although no distinct religious feeling was interfused, there was "a continual perception of Sanctity in the whole of nature, from the slightest thing to the vastest;—an instinctive awe, mixed with delight; an indefineable thrill, such as we sometimes imagine to indicate the presence of a disembodied spirit."[138] This, he says, is the "pure landscape instinct," and the moral value of it may be reasoned from this standard.

This innocent nature feeling, though it may die away with manhood as it had for him, is, even in simplicity, "an invariable sign of goodness of heart and justness of moral *perception*, though by no means of moral *practice*."[139] More important it has a primal mythic or religious value: "The nature-worship will be found to bring with it such a sense of the presence and power of a Great Spirit as no mere reasoning can either induce or controvert; and where that nature-worship is innocently pursued . . . it becomes the channel of certain sacred truths, which by no other means can be conveyed."[140] Love of nature reveals not only the presence but the way of life. It is a way, he notes, utterly opposed to the "great mechanical impulses of the age" in their pursuit of material wealth and speed. The living message of nature feeling, which he is

"Utopian and enthusiastic enough" to believe we will finally come to see, is this:

> To watch the corn grow, and the blossoms set; to draw hard breath over the ploughshare or spade; to read, to think, to love, to hope, to pray,—these are the things that make men happy; they have always had the power of doing these, they never *will* have power to do more. The world's prosperity or adversity depends upon our knowing and teaching these few things: but upon iron, or glass, or electricity, or steam, in no wise.[141]

The sense of animating presence and of a life to be lived by it constitute the inherent moral of landscape. It is only by accidents of education and historical moment that love of nature has become associated with escapist willfulness or sentimental faithlessness. The nature metaphors in scripture confirm the view "that the instinct which leads us thus to attribute life to the lowest forms of organic nature, does not necessarily spring from faithlessness, nor the deducing a moral out of them from an irregular and languid conscientiousness."[142] True morality of nature feeling depends upon two conditions of maturity in the beholder. "When the active life is nobly fulfilled," and because of this, "the mind is raised beyond it into clear and calm beholding of the world around us," then "the same tendency again manifests itself in the most sacred way: the simplest forms of nature are strangely animated by the sense of the Divine presence; the trees and flowers seem all, in a sort, children of God; and we ourselves their fellows, made out of the same dust . . . and all the common uses and palpably visible forms of things, become subordinate in our minds to their inner glory, to the mysterious voices in which they talk to us about God, and the changeful and typical aspects by which they witness to us of holy truth, and fill us with obedient, joyful, and thankful emotion."[143]

For true perception of this inherent moral of landscape the mind must be lifted from "morbid and inactive revery" to the higher plane of "useful thought." The accomplishment of this, Ruskin argues, is the chief value of science. Yet this is paradoxically offset by science's tendency to check this impulse to higher contemplation and for which it is chiefly to be feared. Better ignorant enjoyment of nature than informed despair. The way out of this dilemma is to consider that there is a science of the *aspects* of things as well as of their essence. In this, I believe, Ruskin wishes to distinguish existential from essential knowledge; the science of aspects reveals the "there" of man's being in relation to his capacities of visual perception. Whatever the case, this analysis brings us to Turner, who is the "master of the science of *Aspects*," just as Bacon is the "master of the science of *Essence*."[144]

The volume's last chapter, "Of the Teachers of Turner," is essentially transitional. It sketches the development of landscape-painting technique from medieval times down to the state in which Turner found it and at the same time anticipates the explicit treatment of the master to be accomplished in later volumes. The primary point, of course, is that nature herself was the chief teacher of Turner and that he was the first to paint for nature's sake rather than for the picture's. He accomplished this, we learn, only by overcoming or transcending the chief cultural influences upon him. There were, however, a few partially positive influences upon him apart from nature. Unlike Scott, Turner was not "blessed by a neglected education." Where Scott was led freely into Gothic imagination, Turner's classical education deprived him of Gothic feeling and led him into Renaissance mythological affectations; at the same time, however, his miseducation gave him a larger breadth of sympathy for scenes and moods than Scott, who "was entirely incapable of entering into the spirit of any classical scene."[145]

Among painterly impressions, he especially felt the influence of the Venetians, particularly that of Titian. Ruskin's general law of Renaissance landscape development is that "profanity of feeling, and skill in art, increased together; so that we do not find backgrounds rightly painted till the figures become irreligious and feelingless; and hence we associate necessarily the perfect landscape with want of feeling."[146] In Titian, however, there is significant, if somewhat ominous, naturalism. "We are now far from cities: the painter takes true delight in the desert; the trees grow wild and free; the sky also has lost its peace, and is writhed into folds of motion, closely impendent upon earth, and somewhat threatening, through its solemn light."[147] Yet the true wildness characteristic of Titian's backgrounds is accompanied, Ruskin concludes, by occasional "looseness" or vagueness; it is in Tintoretto that we find "Venetian love of gloom and wildness, united with perfect definition of detail."[148] The direction was vital, and Turner received almost the only healthy teaching he had from this school, but historically the development died out with Tintoretto in 1594 and nothing in the seventeenth century approached it.

Not Titian, however, but Claude Lorrain was Turner's principal master. Though his capacities were severely limited, Claude "had tenderness of perception, and sincerity of purpose, and he affected a revolution in art. This revolution consisted mainly in setting the sun in heaven."[149] As Ruskin had shown in volume 1, Turner became the disciple of Claude and his solarism. But the negative influences of Claude were equally immense; his work was generally so lifeless, mannered, and idealized that Turner "only did noble things when the immediate presence of nature had overpowered the reminiscences of his master."[150] Further, Ruskin concedes that the naturalism of certain Dutch painters, notably Cuyp and DeHooch also helped to neutralize the idealism of Claude. In sum, the dead landscape tradition that Turner inherited was "broadly divisible into northern and southern: The Dutch schools, more or less natural, but vulgar; the Italian, more or less elevated, but absurd. There was a certain foolish elegance in Claude, and a dull dignity in Gaspar [Poussin]; but then their work resembled nothing that existed in the world. On the contrary, a canal or cattle piece of Cuyp's had many veracities about it; but they were, at best, truths of the ditch and dairy." Everything important about nature remained to be painted. "The grace of Nature, or her gloom, her tender and sacred seclusions, or her reach of power and wrath,"[151]—none of this mythic life of nature had been painted because the Dutch and Italians had agreed on one thing, they painted not for the love of nature's life but for the sake of art. Some feeble modern efforts, for instance those of Robson and Fielding, were for nature's sake and had the "germ of true life" in them that grew and produced the beginnings of the first true school of landscape; but "from the last landscape of Tintoretto, if we look for *life*, we must pass at once to the first of Turner."[152]

CHAPTER 6

The Sun as God

In the third volume of *Modern Painters* Ruskin approaches the subject of mythopoesis, the religio-aesthetic vision by which invisible powers are realized, from three directions. He redefines his aesthetic of truth, under the "naturalist ideal," to emphasize "true vision or Apocalypse," which is unrefusable (involuntary) imaginative vision in which the appearing is truly seen and demands to be set down; it is a condition he compares to prophetic inspiration. Then, in undertaking a history of the feeling for nature expressed in art, he bases his survey in a distinction between "the curious web of hesitating sentiment" about nature that induces modern pathetic fallacy and genuine mythopoeic awareness in Homer, where the animation of nature is not projected sentiment but a matter of plain fact. Finally, having reached modern Romantic response to nature with its characteristic "cloudiness," he attempts to draw his survey together by deciding whether there is any inherent moral value in landscape feeling. He concludes that where the active life has been "nobly fulfilled," that is, where the sense of "Divine presence" in nature is genuinely felt and is not a mere projection of morbid sentiment, and where this feeling of presence is coupled with a deep knowledge of natural forms, then there is an inherent moral or mythic relation to nature.

At this point Turner is reintroduced into the argument of *Modern Painters* as the first great landscapist, the "master of the science of aspects," and the first modern with the capacity to read and paint the inherent though misty morality of landscape. In this way he consummates the first stage in the mythicizing of Turner, which I take to be the overriding purpose of the last three volumes. By this I mean that Turner emerges in them, not merely as the supreme literalist and technician of landscape, but as a painter-hero with something of the stature of Carlyle's *Vates*, those who can reveal the "sacred mystery" at the heart of the phenomenal world, whose seeing eye "discloses the inner harmony of things, what Nature meant."[1] By the end of the work Turner appears as the prophet or discloser of the human field of care and the full color of it through his deep reading of nature and myth.

1

Before going on to trace the evolution of his hero in volumes 4 and 5 of *Modern Painters* it would be useful to restate precisely the ideas of nature and landscape at which Ruskin has arrived by the end of the third volume, since these are the truths that Turner will be conceived as disclosing. But they resist summary because they rest on shifting imagery rather than on philosophically consistent or coherent theory.

Francis Townsend has attempted such a survey in his helpful monograph entitled *Ruskin and the Landscape Feeling*.[2] He begins with the view that nature in volume 1 of *Modern Painters* is essentially an amalgamation of the Wordsworthian landscape feeling with Ruskin's inherited Evangelical religion, one that develops into a "sacramental system" in the second volume as aspects of natural beauty become "types" of divine attributes. What Townsend records is the disappearance of the personal Evangelical Deity from Ruskin's nature feeling by the mid fifties under the impacts of his deepening awareness of social distress and the failure of the pious aesthetic of the second volume to accommodate the obvious artistic power of the worldly Venetian painters. This means that by the time Ruskin resumed *Modern Painters* in 1854, after his socioarchitectural digression, he confronted a shadowed nature which was not so distinctly a theological image as that of the first part of *Modern Painters*, volume 2, and not, therefore, so unambiguous a text for our moral improvement as the earlier work had asserted.

However, while it is broadly true that "the face of nature darkens" for Ruskin as his childhood religion begins to erode and his aesthetic and social awareness pass from innocence to experience, it is also true that nature continues to be an apocalyptic vehicle for him throughout his life. Thus Townsend, with some vagueness, concludes that "Ruskin had not abandoned the idea that nature, like the Bible, is a revelation of the Almighty. But he had come to understand that the interpretation of both revelations requires considerable effort."[3] Indeed, both modes of revelation were under attack by science and mythological theory at the time. The difficulty is that this view of what disappeared from Ruskin's concept of nature ignores what developed in it as the Evangelical Deity departed. We will see that as his idea of nature became less dogmatically moral and theological after the first part of *Modern Painters*, volume 2, it became, as is revealed by his concepts of the prophetic imagination and the Homeric landscape, more mystical and mythological. Landscape, which is to nature as world is to earth, becomes more secularized by the third volume into the place where the human world interpenetrates with the mysteries of nature, so that by the conclusion of *Modern Painters* Turner has become the master of the visible in landscape and of its relation to mystery and myth.

"By 1853," Townsend suggests, "Ruskin's use of the term 'Nature' closely resembled Carlyle's in *Past and Present*."[4] But nature is "The Sphinx" in that work; she is indifferent, riddling, obscure, not, as in Ruskin of the fifties, visible designs showing us comprehensible and essentially benevolent laws of form.[5] However, while his concept of nature is never so transcendental as Carlyle's, there are topics in *Sartor Resartus*, and especially in *On Heroes, Hero Worship, and the Heroic in History*, that bear more closely on Ruskin's altering view of nature in the fifties. One thinks of Carlyle's discussions of "organic filaments" and of symbols, of nature in the pagan mind and in poetic and prophetic "seers," and of his sweeping description of nature as the "God-written Apocalypse."

More recently, in *The Science of Aspects*,[6] Patricia Ball has related Ruskin's awareness of nature to a general shift of attention from self to object in the poetics of the period, a shift she connects with the advance of science and its techniques of description. She reminds us that in the poetics of Coleridge the object is "essentially fixed and dead" until seized by the animating power of the poet's imagination, until the external has been made internal by assimilation into the poet's subjective experience. Ruskin, on the other hand, wishes to concentrate on the visible texture of external nature and to resist the ready translation of the physical into the psychological. Under the influence of descriptive classifiers of natural phenomena such as the botanists and geologists, some of whom had a quasi-theological bent, Ruskin was drawn to the exposition of the structure of natural forms, a tendency visible in the contrast between the attempts at Romantic nature ecstasy in his early poems and the scientific descriptions in his concurrent contributions to Loudon's *Magazine of Natural History*. In consequence of these influences, Ball argues, it is "the pure fact" of nature that the Ruskin of *Modern Painters* desires to convey, not the humanizing of it. For Ruskin, "any discovery of 'laws' in the universe was only arrived at by the development of close study of natural detail."[7] And, finally, " 'pathetic fallacy' is the term in which he sums up his point of view."[8] Pathetic fallacy, that is, epitomizes Ruskin's hostility to Romantic psychologizing of natural phenomena.

While this opposition of the pure fact to pathetic fallacy appears to be a neat distinction, and one based on Ruskin's own assertions, it does not convey the complex meaning of nature that emerges from his other comments on the subject and from the nature epiphanies described in his prose. A glance at the index to the Library Edition reveals that nature, for Ruskin, is not merely visible fact, but also indistinct, mysterious, inimitable, evanescent, infinite, irregular, and mystically bonded to the human spirit. The visible fact often simply mediates the invisible fact; as we have seen, there is a strong component of "natural supernaturalism" in Ruskin. Indeed, Patricia Ball goes on to qualify the pure fact versus pathetic fallacy distinction in various ways that indicate that she perceives its limitations. She observes, for instance, that although he stresses the primacy of visible fact, "Ruskin is following Romantic tradition in taking the view that 'nature could be read like a holy book,' "[9] and that "being able to see the facts of nature is for Ruskin not in the least a routine or automatic activity, but rather, a rare gift and hence a mark of genius."[10]

We would go on to argue that Ruskin's "pure fact" does not mean an object that is merely "there," as in the dehumanized descriptions attempted by Robbe-Grillet, but an object met by consciousness in a particular way. We, of course, cannot meet Ruskin's objects directly but only through the medium of the acts of consciousness represented in his prose. And these are characteristically, as we have seen, apocalyptic moments, in which the object is not perceived in "simple location" but within "entwined prehensive unities" (to use A. N. Whitehead's phrase for Wordsworthian nature).[11] We can agree with Patricia Ball, then, when she says that Ruskin "never reduces nature to simplicity."[12] He sees complexities—and unities—everywhere.

However, Ruskin's self-avowed fondness for "all sorts of filigree and embroidery, from hoarfrost to the high clouds,"[13] his tendency to concentrate on localities of texture when describing nature or works of art, need not lead us to conclude, as Kristine Garrigan does, that he has a "tendency to perceive the world about him as two-dimensional."[14] Many of his preferences—for Turner and Turnerian aerial effects, for sweeping sublimities in mountain scenery, cloud forms, and transitions of sunset colors—militate against this view. Again, we do not have Ruskin's direct perceptions but only, his drawings excepted, those perceptions as they are recreated in the medium of his prose; and the prose, in turn, is partly determined by Romantic poetics. Rather than to argue that Ruskin saw the world as patches of surface texture, which implies that he saw things as merely "there" in simple location, it seems more nearly true to observe that, in the Romantic-Platonic tradition, Ruskin tends to see the whole in the part.

Like Blake, he sees through the eye and not with it; he believes he can "see" concrete universals. But within the limits of prose description, if he is to cleanse the doors of perception with regard to the particular he cannot describe the whole with the same intensity of vision; indeed, the whole, the infinite, appears through or in the particular; it seizes perception at a given point in the texture of things. He agreed that his friend George Richmond had made a "clever guess" in pointing out that his aim in art was "infinity."[15] In pursuing infinity in nature Ruskin was generally drawn in either of two directions: toward perspectives of ascent to the distant purity of snowlit peaks and complex, evanescent interfusions of color and cloud; or toward intricacies of plant forms or rock textures, toward infinity in gradation of light and color or infinity in organic variation. For Ruskin nature was, implicitly or explicitly, always organized infinity; therefore he thought he could see, for instance, that Turner was "the only painter who has ever drawn a mountain or a stone," because not only had he recorded their visible surfaces, he had "learned their organization, . . . possessed himself of their spirit."[16]

This organized infinity always implied an organizer to Ruskin, a "Forming Power" as he later called it. While this power does not long remain the personal Evangelical Deity for him, we have seen that in volume 3 of *Modern Painters* he continues to refer to a "Divine presence" perceived by responsive minds as being immanent in nature. While Ruskin opposes "the pure fact" of nature to the sentimental personifying of pathetic fallacy he allows at the same time for the true fallacies of vision in the strongest prophetic and mythopoeic minds, and he constantly admits an element of personification to his own descriptions of nature. As Ball observes, "The fallacy, banished from one door, comes back through another in its most sentimental guizes."[17] If there is one constant in Ruskin's work it is his sense of an organizing power in or evidenced by natural forms. This is a fundamental quality of his consciousness, like his love of light; his objection to the pathetic fallacy means only that he resists the projection of powers upon nature which, in his view, derive from need in the self as opposed to direct and intimate observation of natural forms. "Because he finds that the 'Divine mind is . . . visible in its full energy of operation on every lowly bank and mouldering stone,' " Ball continues, "he is roused to exert all his literary energies in characterizing the bank and the stone, the clouds and the lichens. The vitality which distinguishes his descriptive presentation of the object, so that it lives in the words, is an attempt to convey the sense of that creative imprint with which every living form is stamped and which makes it so intensely itself."[18]

Martin Foss has observed that "only when objects lose their independent character and turn into aspects of an indivisible process is personification in the making."[19] In this elemental sense of objects freely
drawn into the drive of an organizing process Ruskin's natural facts are
constantly colored by personification, even where the "Divine presence"
or "inner glory" are not involved. If we assume, with Foss and many
others, that personification (in this sense) is the essential element of
metaphorical thinking and that metaphor is the essential element of
mythic thinking, we have a sense in which Ruskin's language of natural
description is always radically mythopoeic; even when no personal
deific presence is specifically infused, his "pure facts" point beyond
themselves to an organizing power.

The same ambiguity that enters Ruskin's opposition of "pure fact" to
Romantic pathetic fallacy extends to the more inclusive problem of
nature as fact and symbol. Ball concludes vaguely that although he
attacks the Romantics for transforming natural aspects into psychological symbols, "there remains the irony that the concept of identity, so beloved by his foes, attracts him just as strongly. Ruskin's art is
indeed inspired by it. He merely shifts the ground of the research from
the psychic to the physical world."[20] I can agree that Ruskin insists on
the object's being known in itself, if not entirely for itself; he will even
call upon science to assist in this knowledge. His attention is primarily
on the surface textures, on the immediate visibility of things as they are
seen; natural forms do not stand forth for him as mere "appearances" to
be penetrated, as with Carlyle, nor are they, except in the repudiated
argument of the first part of *Modern Painters*, volume 2, conceived as
rationalized "types" that point toward a theological system. Yet even his
"palpable and visible forms of things" retain a symbolic function in his
writing since symbolism is present in a fundamental way when the part
signifies the whole. Very often in Ruskin's descriptions the part, the
natural object clearly seen in its intricacy of organization, is meant to
stand for, just as it participates in, those qualities of organization
possessed by the whole.

Looking back in *Praeterita* he chose to recall that as he languidly set
out to draw an aspen at Fontainbleau in 1842 he was drawn into a
revelational experience, a kind of nature epiphany, in which "the
languor passed away: the beautiful lines insisted on being traced," and
he saw "that they 'composed' themselves, by finer laws than any known
of men." It was an experience of identity; he felt "the bond between the
human mind and all visible things." But it was also an experience of the
symbolic participation of the vital part in an organized whole; where

before he had seen woods simply as "wilderness," he now "saw, in their beauty, the same laws which guided the clouds, divided the light, and balanced the wave."[21] These same formative laws Ruskin would also see at work in vital Gothic, in crystallization, and in the shaping of any truly cohesive social order. But these universal "laws" would be seen as working in the concrete forms, "pure facts," of nature. This emphasis on the formative laws represents a different view of nature than the natural theology of "types" of divine attributes. His attention is on the manifested "laws" rather than on the ideas of deity they may reveal. This proved to be a more useful and enduring view of nature for Ruskin since it could be opposed to all rational and mechanical systems. It is rooted, however, in the organic model of experience, in which the whole has symbolic "presence" in the part.

Ruskin's view of nature is not a fixed conception, then, but a shifting and inconsistent mixture of at least three modes of experiencing it: the apocalyptic or mythopoeic (like the "seer's" nature in Carlyle, nature as the "God-written Apocalypse"); the phenomenological (emphasizing the "pure fact" of immediate experience), and the organicist (in which the natural object signifies organic laws of form in itself and in the whole of nature). This last, of course, is essentially the Romantic concept of nature as "one life." As Albert S. Gérard has observed, "the romantic perception of nature consists essentially in an intuition (which need not be mystical) of the unity that underlies the intrinsic diversity of things. Coleridge defined life as '*the principle of individuation*, or the power which unites a given *all* into a *whole* that is presupposed by all its parts.' "[22]

Landscape, in Ruskin's conception of it as a subject for painting, ought to be distinguished from nature, which may be represented by a single organic form like his famous aspen. Landscape, in his view, represents nature as the human abode; as with the particular natural object, it is a part, itself a unification of parts, that signifies and participates in the whole, but with landscape the part is not simply a unified form but a "world" that includes or implies the human presence. Ruskin's ideal landscape (and consequently his Turner's) is not a complex of empirical objects (mere things); nor a scene upon which I project my mood; nor is it the focal point of "theoretic" contemplation of formal properties; nor, finally, a metaphor or counter in a theological allegory. Landscape, for Ruskin, appears to be no less than a symbol of Being, the living, emerging, and enduring unity of things illumined into meaning by the soul of man.

"Turner perceives at a glance the whole sum of visible truth open to human intelligence."[23] The aim of great landscape painting, it will appear, is not merely to preserve a scene but to make visible the truth of what *is*, or to make visible the *mysterium tremendum et fascinosum* through the imagery of nature. Landscape, as Heidegger has said of art work in general, "sets up a world. The work holds open the Open of the world."[24] This "Open," suggesting the world as a place of care, dread, and indeterminacy, is made visible by the "foggy choice," the Turnerian mystery Ruskin dwells on in volume 4 of *Modern Painters* and by his concentration on "ruin" and on the "labour, sorrow, and death" of men, Turnerian themes with which Ruskin concludes the fifth volume. He has noticed that the presence of the sacred in modern landscape, unlike the Greek or medieval, is signified by indistinctness, cloudiness, mystery. The sacred is made visible by the painter's attempt to illuminate the infinity of the actual. The presence of this illuminated mystery in Turner's landscapes, he will say, gives him the experience of the sacred in contemplating them.

In concluding *Modern Painters* Ruskin will discuss both nature and myth in Turner, and I shall be concerned here mainly with the relations he discovers between these two forms of symbolism (the one "intrinsic," the other "extrinsic" in Carlyle's terms),[25] and with their special message to him. Light, skies, clouds, mists, and mountain forms are given special attention. Turnerian light, particularly, comes under Ruskin's scrutiny. Solar light in Ruskin's Turner is the visible manifestation of the forming power; the source of purity and energy, it is the image of the godhead in landscape. In a recent study of the ontological presuppositions underlying various modes of illumination in the history of painting, W. M. Zucker observes that "light plays in art a role comparable to that which Being-as-such plays in metaphysics."[26] Darkness, of course, is analogous to nonbeing. He goes on to assert that Turner's great innovation in the history of illumination in art was the attempt to paint the source of light itself, marking a break with the Renaissance convention by which only the illuminated, not the source of illumination itself (in metaphysical terms, only beings not Being-as-such) might be painted. He remarks that Ruskin was unaware of the radical nature of this departure, but we will see that this is not the case, and that Ruskin takes note of Turner's attempt to paint the sun and of his reputed deathbed remark that "the sun is God." In fact it will appear that Ruskin himself came near to sharing this view as the Evangelical Deity disappeared from his skies and his mind opened to the meaning of myth.

However, in Turner's work solar light is generally veiled by atmospheric effects and expressed as color; therefore his work, and Ruskin's accounts of it, might be regarded as participating in the general Romantic reverence for translucent symbols, those Platonic counterfeits of infinity in which the eternal is veiled by the temporal as clouds and mists veil the sun. Yet when these symbols occur in living landscape they become what Carlyle called symbols with "intrinsic meaning" as opposed to those symbols, like mythic figures, for which the meaning is "extrinsic" or culturally supplied.

It follows that in speaking of symbolism in Ruskin's idea of Turnerian landscape we cannot always think in terms of a separation between the symbolic and symbolized or of some meaning expressed through the symbol. Light does not stand for being or life; it *is* these. Ruskin does, of course, frequently separate signifier and signified (especially as he comes to speak of Turner's mythological subjects), but the predominant urge is to keep his eye fixed upon the real and to look for natural bond between signifiers and signifieds. It is Turner's mastery of aspects, of the visibility of things, that concerns him. For in nature what the thing is, how it is seen, and what it symbolizes are one. This is why "to see clearly is poetry, prophecy, and religion—all in one."[27] Mircea Eliade points to the identity of the real and the sacred in the mind of archaic man, for whom "the World is at once 'open' and mysterious."[28] Ernst Cassirer has argued that the mythic consciousness is characterized by the feeling of the "solidarity of life" and the "sympathy of the Whole";[29] he observes that the separation of *image* and *thing* is alien to the mythic consciousness, for there "the whole does not 'have' parts and does not break down into them; the part is immediately the whole and functions as such."[30] Similarly, for Ruskin the sacred is in the infinite texture of nature and every leaf and stone names the holy. Hence it is only in the choice of what he represents and in utter limit of his capacity to finish that he will allow the landscapist to separate the expressed from the seen. The painted landscape, like the actual, *is* what it intends. Nature is inherently mythic and symbolic, just as, in the view of his time all myths are about nature.

Karl Jaspers has written about symbols, or "cyphers," in a way that conveys this identity of symbol and symbolized in the revelation of Being. "If I interpret the soul of Nature, of the elements, of the landscape," he observes, "then I find no empirical meaning for expression . . . but rather the presence of a being which appeals to us only in itself and through itself." Cyphers are the same, he tells us; "they do not permit interpretations in regard to an 'other,' but are the presentness of their content. I become aware of them in a consciousness of their suspension in respect to empirical reality. They speak through the very presence of an essential reality in their own language."[31] Authentic symbols are not interpreted but contemplated; they *are* reality. "Reality itself is immediately present in the symbols. In them appearance and being are unseparated."[32] But the essential reality in symbols depends upon the mind's openness to it and is easily lost. Symbols dissolve when seen as things of use, or when they are interpreted, conceptualized, viewed with aesthetic detachment, or imprinted with a desired meaning. But to him who can perceive them anything objective can be a cypher. Since all being is bound up with Being, to the one who dwells in awareness of Being "everything becomes a cypher, illuminated by the ray of light out of the ground of Being, and every content becomes pale when this ray is extinguished. Then only the slag of matter-of-factness, conceptuality, and of endless and indifferent determinations remains."[33]

This is not Ruskin's language to be sure, yet Jaspers's "world of Cyphers" approximates his conception of the sacredness and self-givenness of truth in pure seeing, truth that is slipped when nature is utilized, analyzed, imitated, dissected, allegorized, or sentimentalized. What else can be the meaning of his insistence that Turner was the first to paint for nature's sake? Similarly we noted that imagination in his view is irresistible, passive seeing of the truths of things in themselves, not a creative function in the ordinary sense. Mythologized, this means that a great imagination is simply the instrument of a higher power or, in mundane language, it means that imagination achieves truth through surrender or self-awareness to the self-givenness of things and so becomes a form of pure seeing.

However, the essential point here is simply that the mythologizing of Turner, for which groundwork was laid in volume 3, passes now through two final stages. In volume 4 of *Modern Painters* Turner emerges as the great imaginative and impressionistic landscapist where pure vision reveals being through "the cypher-script of things themselves."[34] Through his pursuit of the visible mysteries of mists and mountains Turner conveys the inherent mythology, the boundaries of known and unknown, of landscape. Four years later, however, in volume 5, a new element enters. It appears that Ruskin has come to know something of the German philological nature-mythologists, especially of the work of the famous Sanskrit scholar and solar mythologist F. Max Müller. This leads him to new insights into the meaning of Turnerian solar phenomena, and, in the chapters entitled "The Lance of Pallas" and "The Hesperid Aeglé," to deeper appreciation of Turner's treatment of mythological subjects. These works, which had previously seemed mere concessions to the painter's classical education, now reveal archetypes of his vision—and Ruskin's own. Solarist interpretations of actual mythic images in the paintings connect now with the inherent mythology of the landscape cyphers, and he is able to perceive a unifying apocalyptic truth permeating Turner's landscape art. The task of this chapter, then, is to trace the evolution of Ruskin's thought from the moral of landscape to the Turnerian apocalypse.

2

E. T. Cook has pointed out that Ruskin apparently worked on volumes 3 and 4 of *Modern Painters* together. He argues that the two volumes were originally conceived as one. Among the manuscripts a first-draft list of proposed contents shows a unified work proceeding in twenty-five chapters from true and false modes of the ideal in general to parallel chapters on the purist, naturalist, and grotesque ideals in landscape; then to the drawing of Turner; and finally to the materials, the moral, and the forms of mountains. However, the chapters on pathetic fallacy, classical landscape, and moral of landscape are not indicated, nor are the mountain gloom and glory chapters of volume 4, although an intended chapter on the "meaning" of landscape is indicated.[35] From this draft list it appears that thoughts on the emotional or psycho-spiritual implications of landscape in general and of mountains in particular entered the scheme at a later stage and demanded its expansion into two volumes. The many revisions in the manuscripts also show how much effort Ruskin expended in working up his more poetic passages, for instance the famous Calais Tower passage, which is quoted below.

Taking the two volumes as an intended unit, Cook proposes that the first five chapters of volume 4 actually continue the early chapter of volume 3, and that the last eight chapters of the third volume and the last two of the fourth are intended to form a separate treatise on the moral influence of landscape. This is a useful classification of their contents, but it implies a more systematic blocking out of the two volumes than one is aware of in reading them. The mountain gloom-mountain glory chapters cannot be fitted coherently to the scheme of the landscape feeling survey of volume 3 and do not refer back to it; rather, they are yoked together as antithetical evocations of mountain influences in a different tone from that of the survey, because they do not deal with landscape or nature as generalities but with mountain cyphers in particular, and because these are juxtaposed as negative and positive presences. Similarly, the early chapters of volume 4 do not take up the argument or the conceptual language of the early part of volume 3 but in general they push on to new concepts or reshape earlier ones in order to come to terms anew with the major features of Turner's landscape style. In reading, one has the sense of the work's compulsive growth and its search for more adequate language or more essential truth rather than of the careful articulation in it of a critical scheme.

Taking up the concluding promise of volume 3 to examine the peculiarities of Turner's landscape system, Ruskin begins the new work by introducing a subject he had merely alluded to in sketching the main feature of the modern temper. Perhaps the strangest feature of the master's work is the concession he makes to the modern delight in ruin, an aspect of the "picturesque," a term he had defined in *The Seven Lamps of Architecture* as being "sublimity not inherent in the nature of the thing, etc."[36] This delight in ruin he now takes to be the most suspicious and curious of all the aspects of the modern landscape feeling, though little is made of it in the preceding volume. To illustrate ruin as a mode of the picturesque outline Ruskin draws a famous prose image of the tower of Calais church.

> The large neglect, the noble unsightliness of it; the record of its years written so visibly, yet without sign of weakness or decay; its stern wasteness and gloom, eaten away by the Channel winds, and overgrown with the bitter sea grasses; its slates and tiles all shaken and rent, and yet not falling; its desert of brickwork full of bolts, and holes, and ugly fissures, and yet strong, like a bare brown rock; its carelessness of what any one thinks or feels about it, putting forth no claim, having no beauty or desirableness, pride, nor grace; yet neither asking for pity; not, as ruins are, useless and piteous, feebly or fondly garrulous of better days; but useful still, going through its own daily work,—as some old fisherman beaten grey by storm, yet drawing his daily nets: so it stands, with no complaint about its past youth, in blanched and meagre massiveness and serviceableness, gathering human souls together underneath it; the sound of its bells for prayer still rolling through its rents; and the grey peak of it seen far across the sea, principal of the three that rise above the waste of surfy sand and hillocked shore,—the lighthouse for life, and the belfry for labour, and this for patience and praise.[37]

Here, as we have noted, is landscape as an image of the "there" of human existence; the described ruin is made to be instinct with being or presence so that it becomes a kind of mythic or tragic image of human destiny and of the regeneration of life from decay. The ruin symbolizes its faithful social function yet illuminates the strife of the human "world" with "earth" as it descends toward nature. Ruskin's feeling for the sacred in infinite organic texture is evident. The tower, he notes, has "infinite symbolism in it" and expresses to society "that agedness in the midst of active life which binds the old and new into harmony";[38] it is not only a cypher of providence but of social coherence.

Socially, the small-scale regularity and "trimness" of English genteel dwellings and the removal of all ruin efface evidence of the fateful and tragic continuity of human labor; but the picturesque can be an environmental expression "of *suffering*, of *poverty*, or *decay*, nobly endured by unpretending strength of heart."[39] In fact, by their conditions of maintenance, buildings can express at least three social attitudes toward the human condition; "there are the two extremes, the *consciousness* of pathos in the confessed ruin, which may or may not be beautiful according to the kind of it; and the *entire denial* of human calamity and care in the swept properties and neatnesses of English modernism: and, between these, there is the *unconscious* confession of the facts of distress and decay."[40] True picturesque exists only when the building is an authentic expression of "unconscious suffering," like the careworn body of an old laborer; then the symbol truly participates in the whole of nature, and in its infinite texture of decay it is like an organic form. However, Ruskin insists that where this sublimity of care is only superficial, a pathetic fallacy impressed on the object turning it into a sentimental symbol, we have only "surface picturesque." True picturesque is revealed only by true sympathy with the inner pathos of a real object; the chief difference between high and low picturesque is that the low is "heartless" picturesque. As such its social influence is perverse because, unlike the higher picturesque, it permits innocence of or indifference to evil. Turner is the first artist to be "the entire *type*" of the higher picturesque, for in him is "a range of *feeling* which no other painter . . . can equal."[41]

Having defined under "Turnerian Picturesque" the communion of heart that the great painter will have with his subject, Ruskin moves in the second chapter, "Of Turnerian Topography" to consider what these subjects themselves ought to be. Noble picturesque appears to mean sympathy with a real object or scene as a cypher of Being; in its ruggedness or ruin the visible object holds open the Openness, the fatefulness, struggle, suffering of the lived world if the painter will commune with it. The comparison made between windmills painted by Turner and by Standfield as well as his own description of Calais Tower makes clear that the object must be truly "seen." But this again brings up the question of the place of imagination or impression, as against pure mimesis, in art. In this chapter Ruskin must once more attempt to make clear where he stands on the function of imagination in landscape art.

He begins by reminding us of the distinction made earlier in volume 3 between "historical" and "political" painting. Historical, or "narrative" art, has its own value but it is never great art until touched by "poetical or imaginative power." For imagination or "invention" is the great bar between higher and lower art. Now in landscape the equivalent of historical art is mere "topography," but imaginative ("Poetical") landscape he will call "Turnerian Topography." Since great art requires invention, "great landscape art can never be a mere copy of any given scene." But, the law of unmediated vision still applies: "It is always wrong to draw what you don't see."[42] If the painter sees only topography then he must paint this. But if he sees mythography he must paint this too: "If, going to the place, we see something quite different from what is there, then we are to paint that—nay, we *must* paint that, whether we will or not. . . . But let us beware of pretending to see this unreality if we do not." If a painter really has these "visions of unreal things" and they are truly ungovernable, then he has invention or imagination. The cyphers, we might say, are seen not expressed; if the painter "only sees the commonly visible facts," empirical reality, and, wishing to alter these facts, "finds that he must think of a rule whereby to do so, he has no invention. All the rules in the world will do him no good"; rules without vision will "produce nothing but *scientific absurdities*."[43] Imagination, true vision, is irresistible; if nature intends you to see more than topography "she will force you to it; but never *try* to be a prophet."[44]

It follows, for Ruskin, that if a landscape is to be plain topography, no alteration of the scene is permissible; it must be "as far as possible, the reflection of the place in a mirror."[45] However, the topographer still has his choice of scene to represent and should choose worthy scenery. The Pre-Raphaelites have been at fault in this respect; they have tended to "morbid indulgence of their own impressions."Though they have respected nature their reputations have been based mainly on "duck-pond delineation."[46] If, on the other hand, a painter is imaginative he will treat a scene in quite another way, "giving not the actual facts of it, but the impression it made on his mind."[47]

This impressionism is not to mean a "piece of manufacture," some ingenious composition derived from this or that formula, which is what is generally meant by invention. It means the painter gives accurately the appearance, for him, of that which appears. In Turner's picture of the *Pass of Faido*, for instance, "the confused stones . . . become exponents of the fury of the river by which he has journeyed all day long" and which has left a deep and irresistible impression of its power on his mind. The general law is that "the aim of the great inventive landscape painter must be to give the far higher and deeper truth of mental vision,

rather than that of physical facts, and to reach a representation . . . capable of producing on the far-away beholder's mind
precisely the impression which the reality would have produced, and
putting his heart into the same state."[48] Art communicates the cyphers of
Being in landscape; it does not express them or interpret them; it does
not compose them by rule, it conducts them, just as they appear in the
poet's consciousness. As revelations of Being, the power of the place,
they are in a sense sacred. Hence Ruskin speaks of the "sacredness of the
truth of *Impression*" not to be revealed by any composition and likely to
be impaired by mere mechanical accuracies of technique. Turner erred
when he tried to compose; he did right only in "passive obedience" to his
first vision. The imaginative artist paints "not so much the image of the
place itself, as the spirit of the place," so "let him yield to such fancies,
and follow them wherever they lead."[49] He compares the imaginative
experience to the mental chemistry of "dream vision," where there is
"just this kind of confused remembrance of the forms of things which we
have seen long ago, associated by new and strange laws."[50] He refers back
with renewed approval to his discussion "Imagination Associative" in
volume 2, which, in turn, has its roots in eighteenth-century associa-
tionist views of imagination.

Again, there is an attempt to convey the real nature of the imaginative
mind, filled with an "unindexed and immeasurable mass" of visual
energy, "brooding and wandering, but dream-gifted, so as to summon at
any moment exactly such groups of ideas as shall justly fit each other."[51]
Yet this is not strictly the property of a finite mind, some deceptive
faculty arranging fantasies according to its private will. No, he is more
convinced than ever that imagination is the "most accurate truth-telling
faculty which the human mind possesses."[52] Imagination conveys not
individual self-conscious truths; on the contrary, "in *its* work, the vanity
and individualism of the man himself are crushed, and he becomes a
mere instrument or mirror, used by a higher power for the reflection to
others of a truth which no effort of his could ever have ascertained; so
that all mathematical, and arithmetical, and generally scientific truth,
is, in comparison, truth of the husk and surface, hard and shallow; and
only the imaginative truth is precious."[53] In contemporary language we
might say that true imagination is superior to empirical and rational
modes of knowing because it communicates Being in the pure self-
givenness of things. Imagination, in Romantic theory, is the power by
which our rationalistic estrangement from Being is to be overcome.

Since Turnerian imagination appears to be that unconscious or
preconceptual communion with Being which is the condition of purest

seeing, and since light is its chief medium and message, it is appropriate that this chapter on the supreme truth-telling faculty by followed by a discussion of "Turnerian Light." The imagery of light, natural or supernatural, projected or reflected, is deeply interfused with the Romantic concept of imagination. Meyer Abrams has pointed to such ultimate sources of this central image as the Plotinian symbol of the One as a fountain of light.[54] Similarly important as root-images of light are Plato's sun as symbol of the highest good in his parable of the cave and also the whole identification of God with light in the New Testament, images that have their sources or equivalents in the solar myths. While the archetypal meaning of light is particularly important to Ruskin, his immediate purpose here is to show that Turner's imagination does not work with mystical or symbolic light ("the light that never was, on sea or land") but with the light that *is*, the light of life infusing sacred color.

Turner's colors look false to those who do not understand the deeper truth of them. This truth is that he has chosen closeness to natural color over coherence within the picture; he has painted for the sake of nature rather than for pictorial contrasts. Appreciation of the fact that only Turner, "of all men, *ever painted Nature in her own colours*"[55] begins with an understanding of the real brightness of landscape in relation to the painter's limited means for expressing it. This, in turn, leads to a comprehension of the choices the painter must make and that Turner has made. Because the true contrasts of nature such as the "blue fire" of heaven, "white fire" of cloud, and dead earth-darkness can never be painted, it is essentially a question of whether the painter will be false to the light side or to the dark side of the life-scale, "whether you will lose yourself in light or in darkness."[56] That is, with a range of contrasts between zero and forty, say, the painter must represent nature's full scale from zero to one hundred. If he wants full contrasts he can set his forty against nature's one hundred and lose everything below her sixty in darkness, or he can set his zero against nature's zero and lose everything above forty in whiteness.

But, a vital consideration bears on this choice. The problem of chiaroscuro is intervolved with the problem of color. If the painter chooses fidelity to the dark end of the scale with all its symbolic implications, his contrasts will be more nearly true but his local colors will be false for there will be no light in them. (This, to Ruskin, is essentially the Rembrandtean system, in which "*not one colour* is absolutely true, from one side of the scale to the other; only the contrasts are true at the top of the scale.")[57] On the other hand, if the painter makes the choice of light his colors will have the light of life in them but his contrasts will be defective. Thus a great dichotomy of painters appears in Ruskin's view: the chiaroscurists like Leonardo, Rembrandt, and Raphael who painted principally with reference to light and shade; and, opposing them, the colorists, like Veronese, Titian, and Turner, who painted primarily with respect to local color. With the former, vast areas of the picture are likely to be lost in dead shadow, for they begin with the lights and go down into blackness; with the latter, however, "the whole picture is like the rose,—glowing with colour in the shadows, and rising into paler and more delicate hues, or masses of whiteness, in the lights; they having *begun* with the *shadows,* and gone up *to* whiteness."[58]

The moral implicit in this polarity of schools becomes clear in Ruskin's concluding evaluation of them. The colorists have taken the way of life; the chiaroscurists have fallen into deadly material knowledge. First, of course, the colorists give the greater proportion of visible truth. "With the colourists the shadows are right; the lights untrue: but with the chiaroscurists lights and shadows are both untrue."[59] The chiaroscurists favor "abstract shade," because it is philosophical and scientific. *"Pride is at the bottom of all great mistakes."* Behind the errors of the chiaroscurists is pride of style; "endeavours, much fostered by the metaphysical Germans, to see things without colour, as if colour were a vulgar thing,"[60] have resulted in most art students' being unable to see at all.

Among the colorists, however, the nobility and sacredness of their pictures is increased in direct proportion to the amount of light and color that they are able to introduce into their shadows, where the chiaroscurists are reduced to black and grey. Ruskin again insists on the sacredness of color. This sanctity of color is explicitly stated in scripture. Scarlet in particular stands apart symbolically as "absolute *colour*"; it is used primarily in scripture as an emblem of purification and only incidentally, he argues, to indicate the stain of sin. But colors are sacred in a more intrinsic sense as cyphers of life itself, "associated with *life* in the human body, with *light* in the sky, with *purity* and hardness in the earth,—death, night, and pollution of all kinds being colourless."[61] So in the colorist-chiaroscurist opposition we have a version of the vital-lethal antithesis that is the center of Ruskin's thought. Look around broadly, he proposes, at the relation of color language to the helpfulness or deadliness of things in the world, "compare generally rainbows, sunrises, roses, violets, butterflies, birds, goldfish, rubies, opals and corals, with alligators, hippopotami, lions, wolves, bears, swine, sharks, slugs, bones, fungi, fogs, and corrupting, stinging, destroying things in general, and you will feel then how the question stands between the colourists and chiaroscurists,—which of them have nature and life on their side, and which have sin and death."⁶²

The chapter ends, however, with an important reservation about this apparently decisive opposition. (Ruskin will later class himself among the chiaroscurists, and his respect for their work generally increases as his own life darkens and as he comes to appreciate Greek art.) What if one had to choose between a master of form (like Dürer) without color and a formless colorist? He is able to make a distinct choice between form and color: "Form is beyond all comparison the more precious of the two."⁶³ Turner is among the colorists, has the light of life in his color, but proof of this greatness still depends upon showing his mastery of form, of delineation. This is problematic because his style is marked by a "mysterious and apparently uncertain execution"⁶⁴ that distinguishes him from most other painters. Turner, Ruskin agrees, is the very painter most of us would think of as the paragon of that indistinctness, the " 'ingenious speaking concerning smoke' "⁶⁵ that he had defined in the preceeding volume as the central characteristic of nineteenth-century landscape feeling. In fact, Turner is "the head of modern mystery"⁶⁶ with all the ranks of distinct and placid painters ranged against him. Now Ruskin, "long a cloud worshipper" himself, must undertake to explain and defend this mysteriousness. This he does in the two following chapters dealing respectively with "Essential" and "Wilful" Turnerian mystery.

These two modes of indistinctness in Turner might be said to represent mystery of perception and mystery of knowledge, the full mystery of Being expressed in landscape. Under the first head, "Essential" mystery, Ruskin defends Turner by pointing out that "the clouds are there"; a "universal law of obscurity" governs our existence. In nature we have not only the "partial and variable mystery" of real clouds and mists, but also "there is a continual mystery caused throughout *all* spaces, caused by the absolute infinity of things. WE NEVER SEE ANYTHING CLEARLY."⁶⁷ If the painter is to paint what he sees instead of what he knows is there, then Ruskin's general law that all great drawing is distinct drawing must be understood as the distinct obscurity of things; it now appears "that all *distinct* drawing must be *bad* drawing, and that nothing can be right, till it is unintelligible."⁶⁸ Since all subjects have a mystery of infinity in them, all true drawing must have this mystery in it. Indeed, it is an inviolable law that "EXCELLENCE OF THE HIGHEST KIND, WITHOUT OBSCURITY, CANNOT EXIST."⁶⁹

Pre-Raphaelite works are full of this mystery, and those of Turner, of course, as "true head" of Pre-Raphaelitism.⁷⁰ But in men like Turner,

Tintoretto, and Veronese there is such intensity of perception and subtlety of execution that an indistinctness, a sense of infinity, is produced, with the result, Ruskin concludes, that he always feels "in the presence of their pictures just as other people would in that of a supernatural being." In fact, he says there would be danger of offending his reader if he described the degree of awe with which he has encountered certain works. "They mean a great truth."[71]

But in Turner there is more than the essential perceptual mystery caused by the deep infinity of things as such, there is his deliberate "foggy choice" of clouds and mists as subjects, "Wilful" mystery. How can this be justified? Ruskin argues that these vapors have impressed themselves upon our consciousness as natural symbols for the necessary acceptance of indefinite knowledge in this world. "Mist and all its phenomena have been made delightful to us, since our happiness as thinking beings must depend on our being content to accept only partial knowledge, even in those matters which chiefly concern us. If we insist upon perfect intelligibility and complete declaration in every moral subject, we shall instantly fall into misery of unbelief."[72] Just as organic life depends upon mists and clouds, some mental mysteries are vital, life giving. "Our whole happiness and power of energetic action depend upon our being able to breathe and live in the cloud,"[73] the cloud of noble unknowing. For there is ignoble as well as noble mystery; where noble mystery is "a veil thrown between us and something definite, known, and substantial; ignoble mystery is a veil cast before chaos, the studious concealment of Nothing."[74] Noble mystery can be reached only by intense labor; the greatest artists will work through clarity into obscurity; becoming dark with excess of light. So with Turner, the very comprehensiveness of his natural knowledge, for instance, his understanding of the intricacies of mists and shadows, adds to the mystery of his pictures. There can, of course, also be mystery in the clarity of Purist art, but it is not the mystery of worldly being; clouds and mists are cyphers of the "imperfect knowledge granted to the earthly life, while serene and cloudless mysteries set forth that belonging to the redeemed life."[75] We should think of clouds "not as concealing the truth of other things, but as themselves true and separate creations" mysterious in their forms and motions.[76]

3

At the sixth chapter there is a major structural division in *Modern Painters* and a change of approach. Following roughly the scheme of the "General Truths" in the second section of volume 1, Ruskin has attempted to define the overriding features of Turner's landscape style: sympathy with ruin, impressionistic topography, living light, infinity, and cloudy mystery. He now explains that the next phase of the volume (and most of the following one, as it turned out) will be given to "the ascertaining as far as possible what the proper effect of the natural beauty of different objects *ought* to be on the human mind, and the degree in which this nature of theirs, and true influence, have been understood and transmitted by Turner."[77] At bottom this is no less than a mythic, or at least prophetic task that Ruskin undertakes, for he means to explain how the major aspects of nature should be perceived, how we are intended to read them, and how far Turner succeeded in this.

The pattern of the second half of volume 1 of *Modern Painters* is to be carried out, he says, "with more observant patience." However, the scheme of that volume called for the truths of skies, earth, water, and vegetation to be taken up in that order. The morphology and meaning of clouds should begin the new section. As it happens, Ruskin's interest in geology strangely asserts itself. He apparently has his geology notes already worked up; therefore, the study of earth forms preempts the place of clouds and their study is set aside for the next volume. Yet there are a few truths of skies that will not wait because they are so intimately bound up with what has just been said about the meaning of Turnerian mystery. These truths are presented in a pivotal chapter called "The Firmament," which is at once the first chapter of a new survey of natural truth, the intrinsic symbolism of natural forms, and the final comment on the meaning of Turnerian mystery. This chapter, in which Ruskin conveys a distinctly mythopoeic view of skies based on his reading of Scripture, is not only central to this volume but is also a kind of prologue to his reading of Greek myths of cloud and storm that begins in volume 5 of *Modern Painters* and culminates a decade later in *The Queen of the Air*. He thought the statement important enough to reprint in 1885 (the year after his *Storm-Cloud* lectures) as the first chapter of *Coeli Enarrent*.

In turning to the sky myth set forth here we should recall what he has been saying about the Turnerian mystery of mists and clouds. They stand for (and *are*) sustaining mysteries of life in this world, representing the adequacy of indistinct knowledge, the necessity of myth, it could be said, as well as of mystery. Perhaps the major such sustaining mystery is the idea of heaven. How should we in the natural world think of the Biblical "heaven" or the "firmament"? Are we to think of the atmospheric skies, the astral sky, or of some luminous theological locus beyond the stars? In this chapter Ruskin simply argues that for us on earth the clouds in their mysteriousness and beauty are intended cyphers for the idea of heaven, *are* heaven for us. Passages of Scripture are cited to show that the clouds are generally spoken of there as God's dwelling. They are, in effect, natural myths. Possibly some reading in nature mythology has influenced Ruskin here, but Greek cloud myths and their meaning are not directly introduced until volume 5. At this point we merely find scriptural language, mysteriousness of cloud, and the idea of actual deific presence brought together. By taking the biblical words in their literal sense, he declares, "we are thus led to apprehend the immediate presence of the Deity, and His purpose of manifesting Himself as near to us whenever the storm-cloud stoops upon its course; while by our vague and inaccurate acceptance of the words we remove the idea of His presence far from us, into a region which we can neither see nor know."[78]

Ruskin is not only stressing the idea of numinous presence in nature but advocating the primacy of visible, existential mystery (noble mystery) over abstract or theological (ignoble) mystery that removes God from the nature of ordinary experience. "I reject at once all idea of the term 'Heavens' being intended to signify the infinity of space inhabited by countless worlds. . . . But I suppose the heavens to mean that part of creation which holds equal companionship with our globe . . . and I understand the making of the firmament to signify that, so far as man is concerned, most magnificent ordinance of the clouds."[79] It would follow, of course, though Ruskin does not say so at this point, that if we pollute the clouds we pollute our heaven, and our punishment will come from there.

"The Firmament" does not proceed entirely by discursive analysis. Fortunately for the student of literature Ruskin has no need to rely entirely on argument and exegesis to set forth the symbolic power and mystery of clouds. In this chapter we have another of those apocalyptic sky passages in which prose of statement gives way to the poetically recreated experience of immediate revelation in the imagery of the sky. We see and feel the "magnificent ordinance of the clouds" in his description.

> As the great plain of waters was formed on the face of the earth, so also a plain of waters should be stretched along the height of air, and the face of the cloud answer the face of the ocean; and that this upper and heavenly plain should be of waters, as it were, glorified in their nature, no longer quenching the fire, but now bearing fire in their own bosoms; no longer murmuring only when the winds raise them or rocks divide, but answering each other with their own voices from pole to pole; no longer restrained by established shores, and guided through unchanging channels, but going forth at their pleasure like the armies of the angels, and choosing their encampments upon the heights of the hills; no longer hurried downwards for ever, moving but to fall, nor lost in the lightless

accumulation of the abyss, but covering the east and west with the waving of their wings, and robing the gloom of the farther infinite with a vesture of divers colours, of which the threads are purple and scarlet, and the embroideries flame.[80]

If heaven means the clouds, does God mean the sun? Ruskin concludes his chapter with a passage in which he seems to be on the verge of turning the text "In them hath He set a *tabernacle* for the sun" into solar mythology as he explains that "by the firmament of clouds the golden pavement is spread for his chariot wheels at morning; by the firmament of clouds the temple is built for his presence to fill with light at noon; by the firmament of clouds the purple veil is closed at evening round the sanctuary of his rest; by the mists of the firmament his implacable light is divided, and its separated fierceness appeased."[81] But if the clouds are his temple, who then is the charioteer? Or is this mere pathetic fallacy? He is not God, it appears, but *as* God; he will not echo Turner's "The sun is God." However, he is certain that this implacable light and cloud-shielded heat are the manifestation to us of the justice and power of "the Inhabiter of Eternity" whose abstract image we cannot behold; yet, "as the Judge of the earth and Preserver of men, those heavens are indeed His dwelling-place." The sun may not be God, but as the light of our being it is our judge and preserver; and, as a cypher, it will be less susceptible to the neutralization by science that was affecting its theological counterpart. A disappearing "Inhabiter of Eternity" had little power of chastisement left in him, but the skies and the sun might yet punish.

Although "The Firmament" is a key chapter for the access it gives to the meaning of Ruskin's studies in sky phenomena in the diaries, *Modern Painters*, volume 5, *The Queen of the Air*, *Fors Clavigera*, his *Storm-Cloud* lectures, *Coeli Enarrent*, and elsewhere, it is, as he says, an interruption in the general scheme of the fourth volume. But the fact of its inclusion and its placement are significant in showing his need to ground what had been said about Turnerian light and mystery in a general sky myth before going on to the basic mountain business of the book. As Ruskin moves into mountain geology his tone becomes generally analytic and expositional until the gloom and glory chapters at the end, where once again prophetic mode is adopted along with archetypal light-darkness contrasts and apocalyptic skies. These mountain chapters, which make up the remaining three-fourths of the volume (some 340 pages) are, in terms of bulk, its major content. They constitute a single treatise in two major sections; twelve chapters are devoted to mountain form and two to mountain effect.

The chapters on mountain form and its visible causes, showing "the

J. M. W. Turner. *The Angel Standing in the Sun*. Courtesy of the Tate Gallery, London.

depth of the wisdom and love which are manifested in the ordinances of the hills,"[82] can be treated summarily here; for, although they reveal the empirical and ecological side of his mind, they are not the Ruskin who is the chief concern of this book. Much of this section could hardly be called literature if literature means emphasis on emotive as opposed to cognitive content. Yet it could be argued that even these chapters are in a vague sense mythic. They are intended to be a unified system that will show how mountains should be "seen" (and painted) in their full relation to the "there" of man's being. Even the geological Ruskin does not generally speak of rock formations as abstract entities; they evidence the purpose and design of the mythic builder. They are rocks but also God-stuff. The analogy with architecture is recurrent in these chapters; high mountains are "cathedrals of the earth" with approaches, foundations, buttresses, and spires, the organically unified structures and sculptures of the divine architect.

It should be observed again that Ruskin's treatment of mountain forms and other features of the earth's crust in this section (Pt. 5), like his treatment of cloud forms in part 7, opposes the view that he studied nature only in a "microscopic manner"[83] or only in patches of surface texture. It is true, however, that in his exposition of the earth's "architecture" Ruskin comes closer to dealing with structure than he generally does in his treatment of Gothic architecture. This is because, taught by his reading in geology, he is looking at crust formations primarily as empirical objects rather than as aesthetic objects or as exponents of human feeling and labor. Yet the mountains are recurrently addressed as cyphers. They are houses of life, intended by their builder to fit the earth for habitation and to quench the heart's thirst for beauty. At the strictly ecological level, as houses of life, the essential function of mountains is to give motion to water, to air, and to the earth itself.

These general ideas of a mountain's purpose are developed in an introductory chapter called "The Dry Land," most of which Ruskin reprinted in 1885 as part of *In Montibus Sanctis*. Then follow eleven comparatively dry chapters on mountain building. Four chapters are given to the "Materials of Mountains" ("Compact Crystallines," "Slaty Crystallines," "Slaty Coherents," and "Compact Coherents"); two to the "Sculpture of Mountains" ("Lateral Ranges," "Central Peaks"); and five to "Resulting Forms" ("Aiguilles," "Crests," "Precipices," "Banks," "Stones"). Ruskin's chief technical guide in geological study was the work of the Swiss physicist H. B. de Saussure (1740–99). His father had given him a copy of Saussure's *Voyages dans les Alpes* (1779–

96) for his fifteenth birthday, and in diaries he frequently compares his own observations of rock formations with those in this work. There are references in these chapters to Saussure ("My first master in geology")[84] and to other more contemporary geological literature as Ruskin touches on controversial technical matters of glacial action and peak formation. These materials indicate that he was in touch with the geological theory of his day; yet to determine the precise extent to which his classifications are personal would be beyond the scope of this study. What is clear is that though his immediate observations are in the objective language of academic geology, they are ultimately referred to a divine architectural intuition or to general laws of natural design that could hardly have been acknowledged by the scientific geologist.

In this long geological treatise, which Ruskin placed among the most valuable of his works, painting and Turner are largely forgotten. But the divine building and sculpturing "presence" is still frequently invoked. Here, for instance, in one of the more poetic passages in these chapters Ruskin summons the mysterious unifying power by which the solitary drifting mica flake became part of an imperishable Alpine spire.

> If one of those little flakes of mica-sand, hurried in tremulous spangling along the bottom of the ancient river, too light to sink, too faint to float, almost too small for sight, could have had a mind given to it as it was at last borne down with its kindred dust into the abysses of the stream, and laid, (would it not have thought?) for a hopeless eternity, in the dark ooze, the most despised, forgotten, and feeble of all earth's atoms; incapable of any use or change; not fit, down there in the diluvial darkness, so much as to help an earth-wasp to build its nest, or feed the first fibre of a lichen;—what would it have thought, had it been told that one day, knitted into a strength as of imperishable iron, rustless by the air, infusible by the flame, out of the substance of it, with its fellows, the axe of God should hew that Alpine tower; that against *it*—poor, helpless mica flake!—the wild north winds should rage in vain; beneath *it*—low-fallen mica flake!—the snowy hills should lie bowed like flocks of sheep, and the kingdoms of the earth fade away in unregarded blue; and around it—weak, wave-drifted mica flake!—the great war of the firmament should burst in thunder, and yet stir it not; and fiery arrows and angry meteors of the night fall blunted back from it into the air; and all the stars in the clear heaven should light, one by one as they rose, new cressets upon the points of snow that fringed its abiding place on the imperishable spire?[85]

And here in his description of the Zmutt Glacier (near Monte Rosa), which he called the "Red glacier" ostensibly to distinguish it from the Zermatt glacier, the apocalyptic element in his prose again makes its appearance.

> Higher up, the ice opens into broad white fields and furrows, hard and dry, scarcely fissured at all, except just under the Cervin, and forming a silent

and solemn causeway, paved, as it seems, with white marble from side to side; broad enough for the march of an army in line of battle, but quiet as a street of tombs in a buried city, and bordered on each hand by ghostly cliffs of that faint granite purple which seems, in its far-away height, as unsubstantial as the dark blue that bounds it;—the whole scene so changeless and soundless; so removed, not merely from the presence of men, but even from their thoughts; so destitute of all life of tree or herb, and so immeasurable in its lonely brightness of majestic death, that it looks like a world from which not only the human, but the spiritual, presences had perished, and the last of its archangels, building the great mountains for their monuments, had laid themselves down in the sunlight to an eternal rest, each in his white shroud.[86]

Turner, of course, is not altogether forgotten among the mountains. In the chapter on banks, for instance, Ruskin delineates four primary systems of mountain lines: lines of fall, lines of projection, lines of escape, and lines of rest, all of which belong to the "infinite redundance" of natural lines. The line of escape of debris hurled down by mountain torrents, for example, shows the same lines of curvature found in bird's feathers; therefore all the apparent cruelty of such torrents "is overruled by the law of loveliness: the hand of God, leading the wrath of the torrent to minister to the life of mankind, guides also its grim surges by the laws of their delight; and bridles the bounding rocks, and appeases the flying foam, till they lie down in the same lines that lead forth the fibres of the down on a cygnet's breast."[87] From such examples we understand what is meant farther on when he declares that although we may find invention and grace of arrangement in the scenery of Tintoretto and Veronese, expression of the "infinite redundance of natural landscape had never been attempted until Turner's time; and the treatment of the masses of mountain in the 'Daphne and Leucippus,' 'Golden Bough,' and 'Modern Italy' is wholly without precursorship in art."[88] Turner, it seems, perceives the deep structures of mountain form in terms of their concurrence with general laws of natural form, whether benevolent or threatening.

Ruskin concludes his treatise on mountain structures with a discussion of the catastrophic stonefalls in *The Goldau*, which Turner had painted for Ruskin in 1843. The example is important because here Turnerian earth symbols and sky symbols are dealt with as one meaning in such a way as to anticipate the tone of the following chapter on mountain gloom and at the same time convey the idea of landscape as symbol of Being. In his picture, we are told, Turner felt the connection between the background masses of mountain and the ominous ruin of fallen stones among which he stood, and he imaged the threat in the painting's sky, "brought the long lines of danger clear against the sunset, and straight as its own retiring rays."[89] But in the color also there is the scarlet shadow of death, for Turner was "very definitely in the habit of indicating the association of any subject with circumstances of death, especially the death of multitudes by placing it under one of his most deeply *crimsoned* sunset skies. The colour of blood is thus plainly taken for the leading tone in the storm-clouds above the 'Slave-Ship.' " But the sky of *The Goldau*, the *last* drawing Turner made in his full strength, Ruskin holds, is "scarlet and crimson," deeper in tone than any other he knows of among the drawings. The feeling in this sky reflects "an acute sense of the contrast between the careless interest and idle pleasures of daily life, and the state of those whose time for labour, or knowledge, or delight, is passed for ever."[90] So in the picture Turner has set idle beings against looming nothingness, "two figures fishing, leaning against these shattered flanks of rock,—the sepulchral stones of the great mountain Field of Death."[91] These shattered rocks "are the type of all that humanity which, suffering under no sudden punishment or sorrow, remains 'stony ground,' afflicted, indeed, continually by minor and vexing cares, but only broken by them into fruitless ruin of fatigued life."[92]

4

This description of Turner's *Goldau* rockfalls as types or cyphers of human futility sets the mood for the first of the two justly famous chapters on the human effects of mountains that close the fourth volume. Ruskin has prepared us to receive the gloom and glory here as referring not to objective features of mountains but to the state of soul induced or sustained by them. The subject shifts from mountains as earth's architecture to conditions of life and belief among them. Accordingly the style alters, in the main, from prose of statement to prose of suggestion. Indeed, these chapters are such complex aggregates of argument, allusion, explicit description, and prophetic metaphor that only the major tones and themes can be gathered up here. The major vital-lethal, light-darkness archetypes in his work become dominant again, and the symbolic vocabulary of sky phenomena is now involved with a new social concern. "Every day here," Ruskin told his diary one day at Chamonix in 1854, "I seem to see farther into nature, and into myself, and into futurity." These chapters seem to exemplify that deep seeing, for now the fallen nature of experience is opposed to the Alpine Edens of innocence; and the vision is his own, not offered as if through Turner's eyes, for the painter hardly appears here.

"The Mountain Gloom" is developed out of immediate personal

experience. So that the reader may not think of this gloom as something unreal or merely allegorical, Ruskin begins by taking him down into the actual there of the Savoyard peasant. Following a mountain path through a deep glen, under a sky "thin with excess of light" and below mountains "flushed in that strange, faint silence of possession by the sunshine which has in it so deep a melancholy" we come at last, through so much pure beauty, to a secluded village where one would expect to find "at least innocence and peace, and fellowship of the human soul with nature." But no:

> Enter the street of one of those villages, and you will find it foul with that gloomy foulness that is suffered only by torpor, or anguish of soul. Here it is torpor—not absolute suffering—not starvation or disease, but darkness of calm enduring. . . . They do not understand so much as the name of beauty, or of knowledge. They understand dimly that of virtue. . . . For them, there is neither hope nor passion of spirit; for them there is neither advance nor exultation. Black bread, rude roof, dark night, laborious day, weary arm at sunset; and life ebbs away. No books, no thoughts, no attainments, no rest.[93]

What are the causes of these conditions? Religious, it appears, or mythic, ultimately. Although Ruskin urges his English readers to bring real material help and not poetic fancies to these Alpine villages, the causes of the misery are seen as rooted in their belief. He describes a kind of morbid interaction between threatening landscape and fatalistic otherworldly religion in such a way that all healthy communion with the living forms of nature is blocked. The mythology of death among them so supervenes upon the mythology of life, which depends upon the feeling of divine presence in beautiful organic forms, that these people can read only dread and martyrdom in their landscape. Their religion comforts them little in this life and brings only a dim vision of another. It is a deadly condition, possibly reflecting Ruskin's own religious doubts, and to the description of it he brings the apocalyptic sky language with which we are familiar. These villagers leave their churches with "the cloud upon them still unbroken—that cloud of rocky gloom, born out of wild torrents and ruinous stones, and un-lightened, even in their religion, except by the vague promise of some better thing unknown, mingled with threatening, and obscured by an unspeakable horror, a smoke, as it were, of martyrdom, coiling up with the incense, and, amidst the images of tortured bodies and lamenting spirits in hurtling flames, the very cross, for them, dashed more deeply than for others, with gouts of blood."[94]

To bring home to his readers the actuality of the life he describes and the crying need for change, Ruskin moves within the village to the cottage. By contrast with the wholesome serenity of its English counter-part, the Savoyard's cottage is a symbol of despair and resignation of this world, "itself a dark and plaguelike stain in the midst of the gentle landscape. Within a certain distance of its threshold the ground is foul and cattle-trampled; its timbers are black with smoke, its garden choked with weeds and nameless refuse, its chambers empty and joyless, the light and wind gleaming and filtering through crannies of their stones. All testifies that to its inhabitant the world is labour and vanity . . . that his soul hardly differs from the grey cloud that coils and dies upon his hills, except in having no fold of it touched by the sunbeams."[95]

The mountain gloom is sometimes worldly and heroic. Ruskin in-stances the "noble" gloom of the Lucernois, their ancient bridges adorn-ed with pictures of Swiss battles and victories, "a gloomy lesson frow-ning in the shadow."[96] But even the Swiss gloom is not always noble. "As we penetrate farther among the hills we shall find it becoming very painful. . . . We see, a little way off, a small white chapel, sheltered behind one of the flowery hillocks of mountain turf; and we approach its little window, thinking to look through it into some quiet home of prayer; but the window is grated with iron, and open to the winds, and when we look through it, behold—a heap of white human bones mouldering into whiter dust!"[97]

As Ruskin conveys his reader southward toward Italy and Romanism he finds that the gloom deepens still further; the pervasive religious symbolism of death, now coupled with constant signs of suffering and disease in the human form. Again he supposes it is the religion of dread and despair of this life, the death orientation, that leads to "insensibility to ugliness and imperfection in other things; so that ruined wall, neglected garden, and uncleansed chamber, seem to unite in an ex-pressing a gloom of spirit possessing the inhabitants of the whole land."[98] To convey his sense of a spiritual infection that is essentially religious yet entwined with adverse, especially asthmatic, environmen-tal conditions, Ruskin takes up the plague symbol, an atmospheric cypher (the plague is real) that will gradually assume something like mythic significance in his writing and pathological significance in his life. Here we are simply reminded that this gloom cannot be attributed merely to poverty or indolence; rather "there seems a settled obscurity in the soul,—a chill and plague, as if risen out of a sepulchre, which partly deadens, partly darkens, the eyes and hearts of men, and breathes a leprosy of decay through every breeze, and every stone."[99]

In a strangely vituperative digression Ruskin singles out the engraving of Martin Shöngauer (or his workman) as a central instance of this "plague of the heart." There he finds first "perpetual tampering with death" coupled with delight in dismemberment and dislocation of the human body. He notes, significantly, that this dissective tendency "is one of the eminent conditions of a mind leading to vice and ugliness."[100] In Shöngauer, he believes, this tendency is abetted by ignorance of the truths of form, Romanist attachment to blood symbolism, and complete absence of imaginative power. Yet in the end he is dumbfounded by the "pure mortiferousness" of such work; "this horrible apathy of brain, which cannot ascend so high as insanity, but is capable only of putrefaction, saves us the task of all analysis, and leaves us only that of examining how this black aqua Tophana mingles with other conditions of mind."[101]

Apologizing for this vehement digression, he comes back to a final attempt to sort out the cause of this psychoreligious gloom. He cites intelligence and imagination (the gloom cannot occur among stupid people), unwholesome environment (especially "black" or impure air), rudeness of life, ugly and disordered conditions caused by violence of the elements—and Romanism. This, we sense, is the most significant cause for Ruskin at this stage, because it is carefully broken down into subinfluences: bad art put to religious uses; meditation on penances, tortures, martyrdoms; idleness induced by frequent religious holidays; "superstitious indignation," "an indefinable pensiveness leading to great severity of precept, mercilessness in punishment, and dark or discouraging thoughts of God and man." This religious gloom is also connected with a more distinct belief in the "presence and power of evil spirits" than is common among Protestants, except, he notes, among "the more enthusiastic, and *also gloomy* sects of Puritans."[102] (There is a hint here, then, of the relationship between the peculiar religious emphasis of this mountain gloom chapter and the waning of his own strict Evangelicalism.)

This strange interaction between malignant natural forces and the spiritual influences of Romanism is fully orchestrated in the long description of the Valais town of Sion with which the chapter ends. Sion is "quite the center of Romanism in Switzerland," where its beliefs are sincerely held, and there religiosity has combined in such a way with an unhealthy environment, to produce a plague-city in which every feature, human or architectural, shows signs of disease and despair. The curiously detailed description, based on the long diary entries of 5 and 10 September 1854, suggests that, for Ruskin, Sion, with its ironically appropriate name, has become a natural cypher for the mountain gloom. The symbol, again, is real; the plague is there.

> It is in the midst of a marshy valley, pregnant with various disease; the water either stagnant, or disgorged in wild torrents charged with earth; the air, in the morning, stagnant also, hot, close, and infected; in the after-noon, rushing up from the outlet at Martigny in fitful and fierce whirlwind; one side of the valley in almost continual shade, the other (it running east and west) scorched by southern sun, and sending streams of heat into the air all night long from its torrid limestones; while less traceable plagues than any of these bring on the inhabitants, at a certain time of life, violent affections of goitre, and often, in infancy, cretinism.[103]

These natural influences have infected even the walls and weeds of the place; there is dolor in its very dust.

> The plaster, with its fresco, has in most instances dropped away, leaving the houses peeled and scarred; daubed into uncertain restoration with new mortar, and in the best cases thus left; but commonly fallen also, more or less, into ruin, and either roofed over at the first story when the second has fallen, or hopelessly abandoned;—not pulled down, but left in white and ghastly shells to crumble into heaps of limestone and dust, a pauper or two still inhabiting where inhabitation is possible. The lanes wind among these ruins; the blue sky and mountain grass are seen through the windows of their rooms and over their partitions, on which old gaudy papers flaunt in rags: the weeds gather, and the dogs scratch about their foundations; yet there are no luxuriant weeds, for their ragged leaves are blanched with lime, crushed under perpetually falling fragments, and worn away by listless standing of idle feet. There is always mason's work doing, always some fresh patching and whitening; a dull smell of mortar, mixed with that of stale foulness of every kind, rises with the dust, and defiles every current of air; the corners are filled with accumulations of stones, partly broken, with crusts of cement sticking to them, and blotches of nitre oozing out of their pores.[104]

Ruskin opens "The Mountain Glory" with the explanation that he has dwelt on mountain sadness with "greater insistence" out of fear that his personal love of mountains would lead him into a too favorable account of their spiritual effects. He succeeded too well in avoiding this bias, for he has made the gloom much more immediate and poetically forceful than the glory. Perhaps by this time it was in fact more real to him. Whatever the case, the glory is presented, except in the chapter's peroration, more indirectly, analytically, and less passionately than its infernal counterpart. He divides the benign effects of the hills into three categories of influences: religious, artistic, and literary. A further section on the influences of mountains, on "domestic and military character," is deferred for later treatment as belonging to the general effects of rural life.

Most interesting here is the distinction Ruskin makes, under religious influences, between religious imagination and religious purity. Mountains, we are told, have the power of both "exciting religious enthusiasm" and "purifying religious faith"; however, these two spiritual effects are somewhat opposed to each other. On the one hand mountains have excited the mythic imagination, sometimes morbidly or falsely. But "we are not to deny the nobleness of the imagination because its direction is illegitimate, nor the pathos of the legend because its circumstances are groundless; the ardour and abstraction of the spiritual life are to be honoured in themselves, though the one may be misguided and the other deceived." This distinction allows him to see the mountains of Greece and Italy as "forming all the loveliest dreams, first of Pagan, then of Christian mythology."[105] (This appears to be his first use of the word mythology in this general religious sense.) But by enforcing simplicity of life mountains have fostered religious austerity and purity as well as religious enthusiasm. We find, in general, that "formalism, respectability, orthodoxy, caution and propriety live by the slow stream that encircles the low-land abbey or cathedral; and that enthusiasm, poverty, vital faith, and audacity of conduct, characterize the pastor dwelling by the torrent side."[106]

Under artistic and literary influences of mountains, the two other categories of discussion in this chapter, Ruskin offers us little that bears his thought forward or little in the way of valuable insight into the subject. Turner, strangely, does not appear in the discussion of the influence of mountains on the development of painting. As for literature, we learn that the scenery of "mingled" hill and plain has been most productive of literary greatness. Shakespeare, for instance, had no mountain passions; "cast upon him but one cloud of the mountain gloom; and his serenity had been gone forever—his equity—his infinity."[107] A digression on Shakespeare's general inability to enter into the medieval spirit, leads by contrast to Browning ("unerring in every sentence he writes of the Middle Ages") and the famous praise of "The Bishop Orders His Tomb at Saint Praxed's Church" as the epitome of the Renaissance spirit, "its worldliness, inconsistency, pride, hypocrisy, ignorance of itself, love of art, of luxury, and of good Latin," which was nearly all he had said about the central Renaissance in thirty pages of *Stones* compressed into as many lines.[108]

In a conservationist's protest against the corrupting influence of the rise of tourism in the mountains, he points to the general danger that Europe twenty years hence—having removed all the memorials of its past—may be reduced to "the likeness of America."[109] He pleads that the mountain temples (and their peoples) may at least be saved from the money changers.

The allusion to Christ draws him, in the volume's peroration, toward a deeper spiritual meaning of the "glory" than he has yet evoked. To the monastic mind the mountains meant "refuges from Judgment, signs of Redemption, and altars of Sanctification and Obedience; and they saw them afterwards connected, in the manner the most touching and gracious, with the death . . . of the first anointed Priest; the death, in like manner, of the first inspired Lawgiver; and, lastly, with the assumption of his office by the Eternal Priest, Lawgiver, and Savior."[110] Ruskin explores these various significations in order, coming at last to Christ's Transfiguration—"the first definite preparation for His death"[111]—on the slopes, he believes, of Mt. Hermon. There, while His feet are dashed in the mountain's dew, a great light exalts Him, "the full glory falls upon him from heaven, and the testimony is borne to His everlasting Sonship and power."[112] Although, from the meaning of "heaven" in his chapter called "The Firmament," this transfiguring light would have to be the sun's, mountains in their snowlit peace are memorials of eternal glory, "of that Light of His Mercy, that fell, snow-like, on the Mount c Transfiguration."[113]

CHAPTER 7

A Religion of Humanity: 1858–1874

The last two chapters of *Modern Painters*, volume 4, (1856), "The Mountain Gloom," and "The Mountain Glory," are about something quite other than mountain scenery and mountain art, the volume's subtitle (part 5, "Of Mountain Beauty") notwithstanding. Actually they enunciate a deep religious conflict that had been maturing in Ruskin's mind since 1842 when, near Naples, he had heard the voice of the "birdless lake" and read the cyphers of the "spasmodic ground": "There *were* such places then, and Sibyls *did* live in them!—but is this all?"[1] This spiritual conflict, intimated by the "gloom" and "glory," reached a climax and temporary resolution during the four years between the publication of the fourth volume and the appearance of the fifth in 1860. If we judge by what Ruskin says of it, this crisis of faith was the central event of his mental life during this period. Objectively, this experience not only alters the tone, style, and purpose of the last volume but also shifts the main focus of his work for more than a decade beyond it; and, although there will be another religious change in the mid seventies, the earlier crisis will lend a tragic and existential cast even to his last writings.

Because we have to speak of a new phase rather than simply of a new volume, it will be necessary to devote this chapter to thematic materials that look forward to and yet through and beyond *Modern Painters*, volume 5. For the same reason we must concentrate on the religioaesthetic crisis here—on the radical transformation of his faith, aesthetic, and sense of mission, and on the symbolic language in which he expressed this change. This means we must overlook for the time the many lesser biographical events and creative enterprises of these very busy years, some of which may have helped to precipitate the crisis: attempting to gothicize the Oxford Museum, cataloging the massive Turner bequest, teaching at the Working Men's College, lecturing in the manufacturing towns, touring, writing, and drawing. To chronicle these labors in detail would be to digress at length from the effort to trace the development of the controlling symbols or mythic core in Ruskin's work. This interest directs us to the waning and end of his Evangelicalism, to the religion that replaced it, to the connections he now felt between nature (especially light) and belief, and to the sense of vital-lethal conflict in existence that polarized his awareness and his figurative language.

1

"The Mountain Gloom" and "The Mountain Glory" point to two essentially antithetical religious developments involved with the perverse and beneficent influences of mountains on human consciousness. The religion of the gloom is severe in precept, despairing of this world, oriented toward martyrdom and death and the obscure hope of a better world beyond death; its acceptance of suffering has been reinforced by the objective hostility of certain environments, so that faith and nature interacted adversely to cause indifference to ugliness and disease, a torpid state that Ruskin describes as a plague of the soul. The glory expresses fundamentally a religion of hope that looks to the mountains as symbolizing the expectation of eternal life ("Refuges from Judgment, signs of Redemption, altars of Sanctification and Obedience"), the mountain light, especially, signifying the light of Christ's Transfiguration as "He takes upon Him the ministry of death." Within the religious conflict two other factors are emphasized. First, certain natural environments are spoken of as intrinsically deadly; polluted, miasmatic places (generally subjected to bad air) are there as cyphers of permitted evil, the plague presence, opposing the purity of the peaks. Second, the religious outlooks Ruskin describes, as the titles *gloom* and *glory* themselves imply, are inextricably bound up with the language and real effects of light. If we follow the meaning of "heaven" set forth in the chapter called "The Firmament," we must suppose that the glory that is shed from heaven on "The Light of the World" must be sunlight. We have, therefore, a complex of interrelated aspects of his consciousness to pursue before going on with the development of Ruskin's thought in volume 5 of *Modern Painters* and the socioeconomic works: his emergent recognition of a malevolent power in nature and the human spirit; the religious conflict in himself between life-oriented and death-oriented belief that reached a temporary resolution in what he would call his "unconversion" from Protestantism in 1858; the Greek-influenced "religion of Humanity" that he said sustained him during the period of his apostasy that lasted until 1874 or 1875; the religioerotic involvement with Rose La Touche that spanned this same phase; and finally, as we pick up volume 5 of *Modern Painters* in the following chapter, the influence of Max Müller and solar mythology on his deepening awareness of the connections between language, myth, and natural phenomena (especially solar light).

Something has already been said about the emergence of Ruskin's plague symbolism in connection with "The Mountain Gloom," where it first appears. It is necessary only to elaborate slightly here. In *Modern Painters*, volume 3, the chapters on classical and modern feeling for landscape, Ruskin speaks seriously of the necessity for distinct belief in a divine presence animating the forms and forces of nature. He wants, like Wordsworth, "authentic tidings of invisible things," numinous glimpses that would make us less forlorn; yet this must be true mythic vision, not nostalgic paganism (in 1856), which sees the old gods through an imaginary eye. Of course, his readers might wonder whether the apocalyptic presence is to be thought of as wholly vital and benevolent, or whether we must believe also in an antipresence, demonic and malevolent, animating the ugly and malignant aspects of nature, the aspects of which are abetted by human apathy, ignorance, and greed. If we look into Ruskin's diaries, his later writings, and *Praeterita*, we see increasing intimations of such a malevolent presence as we are made to feel in the landscape of Sion in "The Mountain Gloom." Most commonly this presence is associated with adverse atmospheric effects (like Jarndyce's East Wind in *Bleak House*); dark fogs, storms, plague winds, polluted skies.

We will observe the development of these cyphers of evil in Ruskin's writing as we look into *Modern Painters*, volume 5, and beyond. For the moment it may be sufficient to cite a comment or two of his own on this developing awareness of a malevolent presence. A passage in *Praeterita* referring to the state of his nature feeling in 1841 bears closely on this; however, *Praeterita* views the experience of the year in distant retrospect and in terms of the providential plot of his life; the revelation of evil described is not nearly so distinct in the diaries of the time, yet it does become so over the next thirty years. "The first sight of the Alps had been to me as a direct revelation of the benevolent will in creation," he recalls in the passage quoted earlier. He had been taught long before by Homer and his own reason to see in the destructive forces of the volcano "if not the personality of an Evil Spirit, at all events the permitted symbol of evil, unredeemed." Therefore, "in the same literal way in which the snows and Alpine roses of Lanterbrunnen were visible Paradise, here, in the valley of ashes and throat of lava, were visible Hell."[2] Again, the cyphers *are* what they represent. We notice also, in passing, that this is a religious awareness taught him, in part at least, by mythic Homer. In connected passages on the "birdless" Avernus and Sibylline grotto it is, as we have noticed, the sulphurous place that is prophetic, "a warning law of future life." Myth, nature, and experience merge in the ominous sense of a malevolent *genius loci*: "The legends became true,—*began* to come true, I should have said,—trains of thought now first rising which did not take clear current till forty years afterwards; and in this first trickling, sorrowful in disappointment. 'There *were* such places then, and Sibyls *did* live in them!—but is this all?' "[3]

More ordinary and familiar places might also intimate the presence of deforming spirits. One thinks especially of Ruskin's comments on the Rhone valley with its peculiar "noon-wind" causing organic and spiritual degeneration in the district, a condition he detected in other northern Alpine valleys as well. Here, from *Praeterita*, is a passage based on his diary entry for 11 July 1849, in which he describes the "malignant wind" of the Sallanches-Martigny area, a phenomenon that appears to have influenced his later obsessional symbolism of plague wind. "It arises, too fatally, punctual to the noon, in the brightest days of spring all over western Savoy . . . this noon wind, associated with inundation, is one of the chief agents in producing the character of the whole scene, and informing the tempers of the inhabitants. Very early my mind fixed on this their physical distress, issuing finally, not in the distortion of growing trees only, but in abortion of human form and mind."[4] The description leads to a brief account of his efforts, much later, to explore the causes of and find some means to alleviate this mountain evil by working land in the district; however, he was unable to purchase any suitable property.

Ruskin's allusion to his practical attempts to combat the plague presence leads us to two final points about his revelation of it. First, the sense of it is obscurely bound up with all his quasi-scientific and mythic interests: the daily meteorological entries in his later diaries (his weather watch for signs of storm cloud and plague wind), his observations of peculiarities of cloud formation, readings of sunsets, plant forms, et cetera; and in *Fors Clavigera* his search for indications of fateful or morbid patterns in human events. Most important, however, is the religious implication for the period under discussion, 1854 to 1858. Because these various cyphers of evil are what they mean, the forms of life here are seen as the arena of final, apocalyptic conflict of vital and lethal forces. The religious duty of man is to perceive the forces of evil in the world and to struggle with them here, not to resign from the struggle in the hope of a comfortable hereafter. Such religious resignation is itself perverse in its neglect of the human present which is the only ascertainable place of redemption, the only image we have of heavenly peace. Such is the essential cause of Ruskin's "unconversion" from Evangelicalism in 1858 and the primary theme of that "religion of Humanity" which he said was his faith until the mid seventies.

The religious conflict in him at this time, the mid fifties, which is implicit in "The Mountain Gloom" and "The Mountain Glory," is described in a chapter of *Praeterita* as are the circumstances of his "unconversion," though they are viewed from beyond another religious change that he underwent in the mid seventies. Another account, written at the end of this phase just after he had undergone a reconversion to something near Catholicism, appears in the *Fors Clavigera* letters. This *Fors* version, though closer to the spiritual events described, is more didactic in intent and more concerned to deduce a social and aesthetic significance from these changes; therefore, it ascribes a controlling unity to the sixteen-year period that is valuable for us to have in mind as we take up this period of his work. On the other hand a situational immediacy is given to narrative in *Praeterita*; it is less rationalized and more suggestive and at the same time focuses attention on experiences leading up to the moment of Ruskin's final apostasy from Protestantism rather than on what followed. For these reasons we do well to look first at the *Praeterita* version first, though it was written a decade after the *Fors* account and based on it.

It may be noticed in passing that while the *Diaries* are by no means silent about the religious crisis through which, in his later view, he had been passing in the fifties, it would be difficult to interpret his religious condition from the concurrent diaries alone. Although *Praeterita* ties the moment of his final departure from Protestantism to the incidents of a particular Sunday in 1858, there is no account of this in the diary. In general the diaries are not self-analytical or confessional but are mainly comments on things seen or read. Yet, like his observations of "plague" symptoms in the landscape and people of the Valaise in 1854, his notes on Bible readings at the time suggest a hidden coherence that a close reading of them might disclose. For instance, at Geneva in June 1854 he ponders the meaning of the ultimate purge, especially the fire-Baptism ("like Carlyle in its irony and intensity") prophesied in Matthew 3:7–12. Similarly, an entry in July of the same year, written at plagued Saint Martin, studies the meaning of the first words of the Sermon on the Mount, "Blessed are the poor in spirit, for theirs is the kingdom of heaven." He questions both the meaning of "poor in spirit" and the heaven to be inherited and concludes, significantly, that "the 'Poorness in Spirit' seems truly to describe the broken hearted and fear struck state of mind of a man before conversion."[5]

The chapter of *Praeterita* that Ruskin devotes to the disappearance of his Christian faith is called "The Grand Chartreuse," and it opens with a brief account of his visit to the monastery with his parents in 1849. There, he recalls, "a word was said, of significance enough to alter the course of religious thought in me, afterwards for ever."[6] In the chapter the word gathers significance from the situation in which it is said as well as from its function as the theme of a religious rejection. Hence the relevance of the title. In the diary entries, curiously, the significant remark is not recorded, no description of the monastery appears; yet the "steep, dark, fiery precipices of Chartreuse hills" give "infinite pleasure." However, in the diary only he does record a chat with an old man at nearby Chambery "who complained bitterly that the priests and the revenue seized everything, and that nothing but *black bread* was left for the peasant."[7] In the chapter both the monastery and its setting are remembered as having been a disappointment; the mountains were dull and "commonplace", the buildings "meanly designed and confusedly grouped"; and the monk who guided them "had no cowl worth the wearing, no beard worth the wagging, no expression but of superciliousness without sagacity."[8]

As the Ruskins tour the building they are shown nothing of beauty, "not a picture, or well-wrought vestment; nor any architectural feature in the least ingenious or lovely." At last John, evidently supposing that the mountains alone must be beauty enough for these monks, offers a comment, "in the style of *Modern Painters*," on the benefits of mountain scenery to religious minds, and receives an acid rebuke: " 'We do not come here to look at the mountains.' "[9]

For Ruskin these words gradually come to epitomize everything perverse in monasticism, Catholicism, and eventually in his native Protestantism. They suggest, one might say, the religion of gloom. Why come to the mountains at all, he asks, if one's purpose is rejection of the world? Why not solitary confinement on the plain? And, once among the mountains, how can these monks "pass their days in meditation without getting interested in plants and stones, whether they would or no"?[10]

The experience of the Grand Chartreuse is partly countered in the chapter by the contrasting account of an "eager and beautiful little sermon" delivered to him and his father in 1840 by their hostess-sister at the Convent of Saint Michael, which is located "on the summit of an isolated peak of lava at LePuy, in Auvergne." Despite her seclusion she appears to have caught some of the glory of the Transfiguration; at least this appears to be the implication of his description of her cheerful and charitable behavior, as opposed to that of the gloomy monk, and also the meaning of her modest criticism of their Protestant faith. "The one flaw in our faith which at last her charity fastened on, was that we were not *sure* of our salvation in Christ, but only hoped to get into heaven,—and were not at all, by that dim hope, relieved from terror of death, when at anytime it should come."

Yet, though he had been touched by the sister's personal grace and simple faith and found her exhortation "to be *sure* of our safety in Christ" unforgettable, he concludes that for himself "there was no entering into that rest of hers but by living on the top of some St. Michael's rock too," which it never seemed he was meant to do.[11] Consequently, several pages later, we find him setting forth the general doctrine that all deliberate withdrawal from the human community, whatever its purpose, is in disobedience of Divine Law. By the writing of *Stones* he had understood that all men, "whether in seeking for Divine perfection, or earthly pleasure, were alike disobeying the laws of God where they withdrew from their direct and familiar duties, and ceased, whether in ascetic or self-indulgent lives, to honor and love their neighbor as themselves." He makes it clear, however, that this view was to become something more than a Protestant's repudiation of Catholic monasticism or even the Evangelical gospel of work invoked against the pursuit of self-indulgence. A few sentences later he defines a conviction, growing in him in the mid fifties, that points toward a religion of self-sacrifice for social good and rejection of sectarian exclusiveness or all notion of a saved elite. "I grew daily," he writes, "more sure that the peace of God rested on all the dutiful and kindly hearts of the laborious poor; and that the only constant form of pure religion was in useful work, faithful love, and stintless charity."[12]

But here, in the retrospect of thirty years, Ruskin is getting somewhat ahead of events and anticipating what he calls "the inevitable discovery of the falseness of the religious doctrines in which I had been educated."[13] He must now return and trace more sequentially his spiritual progress in the fifties through to this "sorrowful end." He begins with a brisk chronological account of his public activities in a decade "for the most part wasted in useless work," useless, that is, in the light of the religious transfiguration just described, because it was largely self-interested work or dreaming dilettantism, as Carlyle might have said.

Then the decade is reviewed again, this time in terms of a number of religious discoveries that revealed to him, in their sum, that his own spiritual life, fusing religion and religion of art, transcended the limits of his "old Scotch shepherd Puritanism." He seems to be saying here that this religion was not actually false but confining. "I had again and again proof enough of its truth, within limits, to have served me for all my own need, either in this world or the next. But my ordained business, and mental gifts, were outside of those limits."[14] In Catholicism he found beauty, but not belief: "And then followed, of course, the discovery that all beautiful prayers were Catholic,—all wise interpretations of the Bible Catholic;—and every manner of Protestant written services whatsoever either insolently altered corruptions, or washed out and ground-down rags and debris of the great Catholic collects, litanies, and songs of praise."[15] Still "I no more believed in the living Pope than I did in the living Khan of Tartary." For Ruskin, unlike Newman, there was no question of reasoning his way to some intellectual grammar of assent. His emphasis was on being caught in an involuntary imaginative or spiritual current: "I *could* become nothing, but what I was, or was growing into." What he had to become is not discussed directly in "The Grand Chartreuse." There are hints of more eclectic and mythic needs, a desire for more open access to the holy than the old code allowed: "But I had never read the Koran, nor Confucius, nor Plato, nor Hesiod, and was only just beginning to understand my Virgil and Horace. How I ever came to understand *them* is a new story, which must be for the next chapter" (but these are not the subjects of the following chapter). This chapter, however, is brought to its climax and conclusion with the tale of his "final apostacy from Puritan doctrine."[16]

The crucial year was 1858, the first since 1845, he says, in which he had complete self-guidance. Thus the throwing off of Protestant and parental influence are brought together; this suggests that the "useless work" of the decade might refer not merely to selfish work done in the old faith, but to Oedipal striving, especially the completion of *Modern Painters* under paternal pressure. This is also the year of his first meeting Rose La Touche. What Ruskin actually gives here in *Praeterita* is a narrative full of complicated biographical, mythic, and aesthetic suggestions. He begins by identifying his own rebellion with "Christ's first article of teaching"; this was "to unbind the yoke of the Sabbath," since "the Day of the Sun, the first of the week, was only by misunderstanding, and much wilful obstinacy, confused with the Sabbath of the Jew."[17] The moment of his final apostasy is tied, in his recollection, to his breaking or attempting to break, "the inveterate habit of being unhappy all day Sunday" and to set himself free on the "Day of the Sun."

He recalls a happy Sunday walk at Rheinfelden that year, gathering spring flowers "in which the dark-purple orchis was chief," studying their structure in the afternoon sunlight, and, conscious of its being a new fact of his existence, drawing on Sunday. Yet, though he continues to draw on the Sabbath, his drawing is strangely affected, as if by guilt or openness to new existential weight; his memory is that the drawing "did not prosper that year, and, in the deepest sense, never prospered again."[18] Vignettes done at Rheinfelden please him well enough; however, some time after, at Bellinzona, he attempts at first to draw "the entire town, three fortresses and surrounding mountains, "but finds this beyond his capacity and is gradually reduced to an obstinate study of the stones in one of the vineyard towers, a structure his guide, Couttet, calls "cette baraque." In the meantime, we are told, he has read the *Plutus* of Aristophanes through three or four times in two months, but feels his Greek is not up to the translation of it. Finally, "general desolation" and discouragement with his work causes him, in a fit of hunger for city life, to set out suddenly for Turin.

It is at Turin on a particular Sunday in 1858 that the moment of decisive unconversion occurs. The situation is narrated in considerable detail. The excitements and luxuries of the city are a vital relief after the gloomy austerities of Bellinzona: the Veroneses of the Royal Gallery, the comforts of the Hotel de Europe, decent opera, troops maneuvering, military bands with beautifully tossing plumes, "and pretty ladies looking on." However, on the climactic Sunday he has left the city and made his way to a small protestant chapel in the south suburb. There the preacher's message is denunciation of the entire fallen world outside of that tiny chapel and its Waldensian congregation of some two dozen persons, mostly old women:

> Their solitary clerkless preacher, a somewhat stunted figure in a plain black coat, with a cracked voice, after leading them through the languid forms of prayer which are all that in truth are possible to people whose present life is dull and its terrestrial future unchangeable, put his utmost zeal into a consolatory discourse on the wickedness of the wide world, more especially of the plain of Piedmont and city of Turin, and on the exclusive favour with God, enjoyed by the between nineteen and twenty-four elect members of his congregation, in the streets of Admah and Zeboim.[19]

Having listened to this doctrine with indifference Ruskin walks back into the "condemned city' and seeks out Veronese's *Solomon and the Queen of Sheba* where it "glowed in the full afternoon light" and he could hear the strains of martial music from the courtyard below, sounds that seemed to him then "more devotional in their perfect art, tune, and discipline" than anything he could recall of the old Evangelical hymns. The experience is another service, now in the larger worldly religion of art and life, in utter opposition to the confined and grotesque experience of the Waldensian chapel that morning. Its message was "the old article of Jewish faith, that things done delightfully and rightly, were always done in the Spirit of God." No sudden conversion *to* anything was possible to him then, he tells us, but an hour's meditation in the Turin gallery brought to a climax the currents of thought that had been leading him to that moment, and "that day, my evangelical beliefs were put away, to be debated no more."[20] It is, then, not a conversion but an unconversion, that the "Grand Chartreuse" chapter describes, a forced emergence, like Carlyle's "Everlasting No," from religious garment that could no longer contain the religious experiences of art, nature, and the human field of care that he was having. And, like the mentality of Arnold's poem, he is left between two spiritual worlds, one dead and the other powerless to be born. Somehow also, we should note, this whole worldly religious experience became symbolically associated with the art of Veronese's *Solomon and the Queen of Sheba* so distinctly that he could refer to the event in the following chapter simply as "the Queen of Sheba crash."[21] (Thereby the Queen of Sheba takes on an equivalent significance with that elsewhere assigned to Ilaria de Caretto, Athena, Carpaccio's Saint Ursula, Lady Poverty in the fresco then attributed to Giotto, and other feminine art symbols that become his spiritual guides.) Finally, despite the crash of his old faith Ruskin remained religious; yet he felt the antagonism between the limits of that faith and his own "ordained business, and mental gifts." Like Blake, he had to create a system of symbols to express his enlarging religious experience, or be enslaved by a received one.

2

"Gods should be iridescent, like the rainbow in the storm. Man creates a God in his own image, and the gods grow old along with the men that made them. But storms sway in heaven, and the god-stuff sways high and angry over our heads." So intoned D. H. Lawrence with a music much like Ruskin's, decrying also the neutralization of nature and the automatism of modern man. But he could insist more blatantly on the same need for new mystery, new myth, much as Carlyle had. "Gods die with men who have conceived them. But the god-stuff roars eternally, with too vast a sound to be heard. Like the sea in storm, that beats against the rocks of living, stiffened men, slowly to destroy them. . . . Ye must

Paolo Veronese. *Solomon and the Queen of Sheba.* Galleria Sabauda, Turin. (Alinari Editorial Photocolor Archives)

be born again. Even the gods must be born again."[22] Yet it was essentially this way with Ruskin when, by 1858, the flow of his Evangelicalism
had frozen and had nearly receded: though his nursery faith had aged
and died within him, he still could not shut out the "god-stuff." He
continued to hear it and see it as he had since his youth, not only in the
morning light and in the high, bright snows of Chamonix, but also in J.
M. W. Turner's radiant landscapes and cloudscapes, in the "Turnerian
Mystery" and the "Turnerian Light."

But while he continued to receive natural revelations of paradisal
glory and purity ("The Mountain Glory") there were other messages of
an opposing kind that came with increasing frequency throughout his
middle years. These would be climaxed by his first distinct observation
of the "Plague Wind" in the Spring of 1871. We have noticed Ruskin's
own retrospective declaration in *Praeterita* that the "pure childish love
of nature which Wordsworth so idly takes for an intimation of immortality" was no longer possible to him after 1837, that he dated his
awareness of malefic influences in nature from his "volcanic" experiences at Naples in 1841, and that in the diaries of 1849 he began to
take notice of certain malignant atmospheric conditions and their effects
upon the inhabitants of the lower Alpine valleys. These observations
enter the "Mountain Gloom" chapter of volume 4 of *Modern Painters*
and the eleventh chapter of *Praeterita*, volume 2. It appears that by the
mid fifties nature had changed considerably for Ruskin, becoming less
often pure and paradisal in its intimations and more frequently the
scene of conflict between vital and lethal powers.

Coupled with this tragedifying of nature, and to some extent cor-
relative with it, were recurrent periods of religious despondency that he
began to discuss in his letters as early as 1850 and which culminated in
the crisis of his "unconversion" in 1858. Within this religious transition
one theme appears dominant: the relation between the promise of
futurity and service to humanity. To Henry Acland in 1850 he confesses
plainly the weakening fabric of his faith and his feeling that both the
scientists and the churchmen were neglecting the needs of humanity:

> You speak of the Flimsiness of your own faith. Mine, which was never
> strong, is being beaten into mere gold leaf, and flutters in weak rags from
> the letter of its old forms; but the only letters it can hold by at all are the old
> Evangelical formulae. If only the Geologists would let me alone, I could
> do very well, but those dreadful Hammers! I hear the clink of them at the
> end of every cadence of the Bible verses—and on the other side, these
> unhappy, blinking Puseyisms; men trying to do right and losing their very
> Humanity.[23]

Writing to his father in 1852 he returns to the theme of the erosion of doctrine and the necessity of serving in the human present. "The higher class of thinkers," he notes, ". . . for the most part have given up the peculiarly Christian doctrines, and indeed nearly all thought of a future life. . . . Carlyle, for instance, is continually enforcing the necessity of being virtuous and enduring all pain and self-denial, without any hope of reward." But this is a direction that Ruskin believes himself to be incapable of taking: "I do not find myself in the least able to do this," he continues, "I am too mean, or too selfish; and I find that vexations and labours would break me down, unless I could look forward to a 'crown of rejoicing.' "[24] Besides, he has recently experienced a moment of spiritual confirmation, believes he has been "appointed" to go forward in the way of faith, and intends to continue on that road without ever looking back. But, despite the pious protestations of 1852, he did look back and took the other road in 1858. The symbol of his change becomes not the "crown of rejoicing" but the "crown of wild olive," the humble reward of those who help in the human present without promise of futurity. And the doctrine of Carlyle's that he felt himself incapable of accepting in 1852 becomes the essence of the "religion of Humanity," in which, as he recalls, he sojourned for sixteen full years.

Though nature became less paradisal and more tragic in its revelations to him as his faith failed and as he became more aware of evil, uncertainty, and conflict in the daily world, it still remained sacred and could never become for him the neutralized objectivity of materialism and science. In the mid forties the still-pious Ruskin could systematize the "god-stuff" of his experience into a traditional natural theology of "types" of the one Deity, types centering on the idea of Purity. But the "unconverted" Ruskin, who was now turning "from the study of art to the study of life," needed sacred symbols that could transcend sectarian narrowness and convey a more primordial spiritual bond to nature; moreover, he wanted, his later work shows, humanized images (not abstract "types") that could at the same time express his deepened awareness of division and tragic conflict in nature and the human landscape.

To find them he turned again in these years to volume 5 of *Modern Painters*, *The Queen of the Air*, and the Oxford *Lectures on Art*, mainly, to the Greek myths, which he thought he had slighted in earlier writings. And now under the joint influences of his intense personal need to rebuild a religion out of the inescapable "god-stuff" of his painter's eye; his readings in the classics, especially Homer, Hesiod and

Pindar; his attentive study of Turner's mythological subjects; and, finally, his interest in the blossoming science of comparative mythology (represented to him mainly in the person and works of his friend, and colleague of his Oxford years, Max Müller) he built within what were ostensibly interpretations of Greek myths a foetal private mythlogy of the formative influence of light and sky, an ethic and a dependent aesthetic of solar and atmospheric purity expressed in Greek god-symbols. These mysteries of light and air became, in the end when the pagan phase was over, his apocalyptic obsessions: the storm cloud and plague wind. This private religion of solar purity expressed in the terms of Greek mythology is what Ruskin alludes to when he writes in 1862 that "if ever I get better I mean to be religious again too, but my religion is to be old Greek. It will do quite as well as his [Aubrey de Vere's], and is entirely 'certain' also, which is an immense comfort."[25] There was considerable irony in that expression of certainty and associated comfort, for the Greek religion meant also, to Ruskin, living without heaven. Hence in a depressed moment in 1864 he would write to Dr. Brown, "*I* have no future in ANY world."[26]

Whatever may have been the precise chronology of Ruskin's rejection of the Evangelical indoctrinations of his childhood, we know that a famous letter of 1842 is thought to show this faith beginning to wane,[27] that he spoke of himself (in 1877) as having been "conclusively unconverted" in 1858, and that he felt *Fors* had become again "much more distinctly Christian in its tone" after 1875. The particular interests of this chapter are not in the total pattern of Ruskin's circuitous quest for a viable faith but in the place the Greek religion assumed in his mind during the period of his apostasy. Of course it will be obvious in the following chapters that, despite his private doubts about crucial mutters of Christian doctrine and the interest in the spiritual truth of myth that derived from these doubts, Ruskin never ceases to employ in his prose quotations, cadences, parables, images, and archetypes drawn from Scripture. It is simply true that by 1858 Greek myths had joined nature, Scripture, and "true" art as homologous texts of the sacred in his thought.

Ruskin uses the terms "Greek religion" and "Greek mythology" interchangeably to signify the total system of Greek belief. However, his phrase "Greek religion" conveys in Ruskin's attempts to penetrate the sources and implications of a faith rather than the details of his analyses of particular myths. He thought that "all great myths are founded, partly on physical, partly on moral fact";[28] it is the moral fact that

Ruskin saw behind the physical particulars in Greek myths and systems of myths that most interests us.

The broader aspects of Ruskin's mythological studies, his interests in myths as religious rather than fictive, are of the greater interest because he was not a "scientific" mythologist. Greek myths, as will be plain, were "revealed" to Ruskin like a religion; he was more nearly a *mythographer*, one attempting to reveal myths by writing in the mythic idiom, than a mythologist. As we will see, this accounts for the Joycean obscurity of much of *The Queen of the Air* and *Fors Clavigera*. He felt that his peculiar sensibility to the connection between natural and spiritual life enabled him actually to see nature through Greek eyes, to recreate the ancient state of mind, and thus to give a more vital reading of the myths than was available to the comparative philologists of his day. What he did was unfold his *own* faith in the shell of the Greek; and this, because of his own (and Turner's) empathic involvement with skies and because of the special bias of mythological theory in his day, was bound to be a private solar mythology.

Ruskin alluded to his special sympathy with the Greek mythopoesis in its relation to nature when he planned a little preface for *The Queen of the Air* in 1874: "I knew ten times less Latin and Greek than the philologists; a thousandfold more about the morning and its breeze. Also, I knew something of Greek art, and had a little, in my own mind, of actual Greek faith."[29] And in 1860 he put his position more broadly: "I believe no interpretations of Greek religion have ever been so affectionate, none of the Roman religion so reverent, as those which will be found at the base of my art teaching, and current through the entire body of my works."[30]

It is not Ruskin as a mythologist in the technical sense that concerns us here, but rather the "actual Greek faith" of his own that he wrote into his studies of Greek mythology and art. We are looking for Ruskin's own Greek religion. The framework of our search, therefore, is mainly chronological, following as best we can Ruskin's assimilative and bifurcative processes, unraveling a thread of intellectual biography, trying to show the ways in which psychological, meteorological, mythological, and philological circumstances combine to inform the testaments of his "Greek faith."

3

It is, then, his religious condition between the Turin "*un*conversion" of 1858 and his reconversion in 1874–75, probably under the combined effects of his work in the church of Saint Francis at Assisi (1874) and the death of Rose La Touche (1875), that must be considered before we return to the works themselves. Here we will rely mainly on his autobiographical account in *Fors Clavigera*, since it assesses from a nearer perspective the crisis just reviewed from *Praeterita* and yet looks through and beyond that crisis to seek the meaning of this phase as a whole. During this interim, as he tells us in *Fors*, Letter 76, he "lived sixteen full years with 'the religion of Humanity,' " the central testament of which is the Preface to *The Crown of Wild Olive* (1866).[31] This preface, which he retitled "Introduction" in 1873, is among the most affecting of all his writings.

During this humanistic interlude Ruskin turned to Greek myths, particularly those of Apollo, Athena, and Demeter, to sustain on the one hand his continued sense of divine presence in nature and on the other his new conviction that one must serve life in the world—through personal virtue, integrity of work, and love—though without hope of heaven other than its pure skies. He alludes to something like this in that same *Fors* letter of April 1877 when, continuing the passage just quoted from it, he tells us that upon the "rough and strong and sure foundation" of "the religion of Humanity" he went on to build a "Greek and Arabian superstructure taught me at Venice, full of sacred colour and melancholy shade. Which is the under meaning of my answer to the Capuchin that I was 'more a Turk than a Christian.' "[32]

He thought of his religion in the sixties, then, as founded on something he called a "religion of Humanity," upon which he built a (visible) "superstructure" of Greek and Arabian beliefs. However, it will be apparent that this "Greek and Arabian superstructure" is more like the fusion of Ruskinian nature mysticism with then-current solar theories of mythology than anything now understood to be essentially Greek or Arabian. But the substructure, too, Ruskin's religion of "Worldly visible Truth,"[33] is also tied to his studies in Greek mythology; and it seems best to clear some ground around this foundation before asking what he must have meant by saying that the superstructure of this belief was both Greek and Arabian.

"You cannot but have noticed—any of you who read attentively—that *Fors* has become much more distinctly Christian in its tone, during the last two years," he wrote in *Fors*, Letter 76 (April 1877), "and those of you who know with any care my former works, must feel yet more vivid contrast between the spirit in which the preface to the *Crown of Wild Olive* was written, and that in which I am now collating for you the mother laws of the Trades of Venice." From this he proceeds to give the

reader a brief account of what appeared, from the perspective of 1877, to
have been a religioaesthetic fallacy, "a fallacy which had underlain all
my art teaching (and the teaching of Art, as I understand it, is the
teaching of all things) since 1858."[34] This is "the fallacy under which I
had been tormented for sixteen years,—the fallacy that Religious artists
were weaker than Irreligious."[35] Ruskin is at some pains to explain how
he fell into that fallacy. Here we see a structure of aesthetic and humanist
values not directly apparent in the *Praeterita* version. As an aesthetic
crisis, it had emerged during his study of Venetian painters in 1858.

> My works on the Venetians in that year not only convinced me of their
> consummate power, but showed me that there was a great *worldly* har-
> mony running through all they did—opposing itself to the fanaticism of
> the Papacy; and in this worldly harmony of human and artistic power, my
> own special idol, Turner, stood side by side with Tintoret; so also Velas-
> quez, Sir Joshua, and Gainsborough, stood with Titian and Veronese; and
> those seven men—quite demonstrably and indisputably giants in the
> domain of Art, of whom in the words of Velasquez himself, *"Tizian z'e
> quel che porta la Bandiera,"*—stood as heads of a great Worldly Army,
> worshippers of Worldly visible Truth, *against* . . . worshippers not of a
> worldly and visible truth, but of a visionary one, which they asserted to be
> higher; yet under the (as they asserted—supernatural) teaching of the
> Spirit of this Truth, doing less perfect work than their unassisted op-
> posites![36]

But the actual difficulty posed by this apparent superiority of humanist
painters lay in the spiritual state of the beholder. Still biased by his
youthful Evangelicalism, Ruskin had expected superiority of the painters of supernatural truth. But doubts, seeded as far back as the Vesu-
vian encounter of 1841, were leading him toward his own "Everlasting
No." The moment of revelation that was to dissolve all doubts of
Venetian power and enlist the critic himself into the "Worldly Army" of
humanity came in that same year in which the Venetian harmony had
been discovered. He narrates this moment of apostasy in the same *Fors*,
but in this, unlike the *Praeterita* account, he remembers going from the
"Queen" to the Waldensian chapel and is, more ironically, unconverted
there instead of in the gallery.

> I was still in the bonds of my old Evangelical faith; and, in 1858, it was,
> with me, Protestantism or nothing: the crisis of the whole turn of my
> thoughts being one Sunday morning, at Turin, when, from before Paul
> Veronese's Queen of Sheba, and under quite overwhelmed sense of his
> God-given power, I went away to a Waldensian chapel, where a little
> squeaking idiot was preaching to an audience of seventeen old women and
> three louts, that they were the only children of God in Turin; and that all
> the people in Turin outside the chapel, and all the people in the world out

> of sight of Monte Viso, would be damned. I came out of the chapel in sum
> of twenty years of thought, a conclusively *unconverted* man. . . . You
> will find what was left, as, in much darkness and sorrow of heart I gathered
> it, variously taught in my books written between 1858 and 1874. It is all
> sound and good, as far as it goes: whereas all that went before was so mixed
> with Protestant egotism and insolence, that, as you have probably heard, I
> won't republish in their first form, any of those former books.[37]

He thought, and goes on to say, that the most significant spiritual theme
in his works between 1858 and 1874 is that "religion of Humanity" with
its "Greek and Arabian superstructure" that describes the periphery of
our present subject.

In *Fors*, Letter 76, Ruskin contrasts the religious equanimity of that
present writing (1877) with the spirit of the preface to *The Crown of
Wild Olive* (1866). The reason for the allusion is plain when the central
tenet of his "religion of Humanity" is brought to mind. In *Fors*, Letter
86, he points out that his writings on political economy previous to 1875
pleaded not the English Bible as the rule of faith but "for honesty
without praise, and for charity without reward;—that they entirely
rejected, as any motive of moral action, the fear of future judgement."[38]
He goes on to reiterate the "assertion, so often made in my former works,
[Ruskin's note here is, "Most carefully wrought out in the preface to *The
Crown of Wild Olive*"] that human probity and virtue are indeed
entirely independent of any hope in futurity; and that it is precisely in
accepting death as the end of all, and in laying down, on that sorrowful
condition, his life for his friends, that the hero and patriot of all time has
become the glory and safety of his country."[39]

This "human probity and virtue . . . independent of any hope in
futurity" is the existential core of his "religion of Humanity" and in the
preface to *The Crown of Wild Olive* (which E. T. Cook calls "a
characteristic expression of the religious phase through which he was
passing at the time")[40] we find him insisting that man's "fate may be
bravely met, and conduct wisely ordered" whether there is hope of
futurity or not. The crown for which the brave nobly expire need not be
the halo of heavenly grace, but simply it may be a crown of wild olive
"mixed with grey leaf and thorn-set stem." Thus the crown of wild olive
is the symbolic hope of his "religion of Humanity"; it is the crown
toward which aspired that "Worldly Army" of "worshippers of Worldly
visible Truth," at the head of which the Venetian masters stood, a crown
"serviceable for the life that now is; nor, it may be, without promise of
that which is to come."[41]

Within all this, the humanism of 1858 to 1874, the aesthetics of light in

Aratra Pentelici (1871), and the dark obsessions after 1871, lay that "Greek faith" to which, as has been noted, Ruskin occasionally alluded. But the significance of this "Greek faith" cannot be understood without knowing what he understood myth to be, what he made of it and out of it. We will see that he read Greek mythology as figurative of the moral power he had long felt in nature, and that, as scholarly solar mythologists of his day would have done, he saw in sky phenomena the chief psychological source of this moral and mythological power.

In the solarist doctrine that myth and, ultimately, religion derived linguistically from the phenomena of the sky such as sun, dawn, sunset, blue light, air, cloudscape, or snow-bright peak, Ruskin saw an obvious ethnic lineage of his own instinctive belief in the moral influence of skies. The chief document of this belief is *The Queen of the Air* (1869), that mythography of air and inspiration which he once characterized as "the best I ever wrote, the last which I took thorough loving pains with, and the first which I did with full knowledge of sorrow.[42] As we will see, the solarist view of myth is also reflected in his interpretations of two central Turnerian myths in volume 5 of *Modern Painters*. However, the matter at hand is to indicate that both what he alluded to as the "foundation" and also the "superstructure" of his religious position in this period of apostasy were involved with his interest in Greek belief. This is the broadest avenue by which his Greek religion may be approached, and the one which will show his studies in Greek mythology and art and his own observations of black aerial effusions in most meaningful relation and perspective.

4

Turning first to the "foundation," his existential idea of a religion of the human present, we recall that his central symbol for it, the worldly reward of wild olive, is ultimately Greek. He had alluded to the mythological suggestions of the olive tree while discussing, in *The Stones of Venice*, volume 3, the symbolic representation of it in the mosaic of the central cupola of Saint Mark's. His concern there was chiefly with the practical achievements of the mosaicist, but he called attention to the significance of the olive tree in the spiritual and physical landscape of northern Italy, the Holy Land, and Greece. English painters, he thought, ought to have loved the olive tree "for Christ's sake, partly also for the helmed Wisdom's [Athena's] sake which was to the heathen in some sort as that nobler Wisdom which stood at God's right hand, when he founded the earth and established the heavens."[43]

Similarly, the motto on the title page of *The Crown of Wild Olive* itself, taken from the *Plutus* of Aristophanes, reminds us that this crown was Jupiter's prize, showing the god's poverty. With it he mocked the Greeks for seeking a better crown in wealth and tyranny, which is why, as Ruskin understood it, the crown was to be of *wild* olive merely, "the tree that grows carelessly, tufting the rocks with no vivid bloom, no verdure of branch; only with soft snow of blossom, and scarcely fulfilled fruit, mixed with grey leaf and thorn-set stem," for "such as it is, you may win, while yet you live; type of grey honour, and sweet rest."[44]

Later, in *The Queen of the Air*, he invokes the triple symbolism of the olive tree: "the use of its oil for sacred anointing, for strength in the gymnazium, and for light," but particularly, for us, he connected it with the powers of Hercules and Athena; the crown of Hercules standing for "consummate honour and rest"; the oil, the prize at the Panathenaic games, standing for "encouragement to continuance of effort."[45] Here, as in the passage quoted from *The Stones of Venice* and in the last sentence of the preface to *The Crown of Wild Olive* ("serviceable for the life that now is; nor, it may be, without promise of that which is to come"), Ruskin genuflects also to the Christian association of the olive tree with Mount Olivet and "the chief Agonia of humanity, and chief giving of strength from heaven for its fulfillment."[46] But in the passages intended for the third volume of *Dilecta* (1886-1900) it was the Greek associations that he remembered: "The fable of Apollo and Daphne, is chief of those founded on the humanity of trees, and the resultant acceptance [is] of the laurel crown as the purest reward of moral and intellectual power used nobly in the service of man."[47]

"To commemorate Apollo's own chief victory over death—over Python, the corrupter," he wrote in *Proserpina*, chapter 3 (1875–86), "the laurel leaf became the reward or crown of all beneficent and enduring work of man—work of inspiration, born of the strength of the earth, and of the dew of heaven, and which can never pass away."[48]

This olive crown, then, symbolic of Ruskin's humanistic reaction against his early Puritanism and all religion of gloom, was mainly Greek for him, though it had Christian overtones. In both respects it stood for the worldly *agonia*, not hopeless of another life but laboring for the good of this one, and finding in that contest "grey honour and sweet rest." And very likely it signified also a still deeper aspect of his humanism: his continuing concern for that part of the beneficent works of man in the service of man that tended toward the physical preservation of *this* world, toward devotion to the "moral power" in nature, and toward realization that landscapes of the spirit ultimately derive from those of the eye.

Apart from this symbolic reward of wild olive, the living crown, there is another feature of Ruskin's "religion of Humanity" that appears to be connected independently with his Greek studies: its heroic creed that "human probity and virtue are indeed independent of any hope in futurity."

Referring, in the main, to Homeric subjects, he observes in the chapter "Lance of Pallas" in volume 5 of *Modern Painters* that

> The Greeks never shrink from horror; down to its uttermost depth, to its most appalling physical detail, they strive to sound the secrets of sorrow. For them there is no passing by on the other side, no turning away the eyes to vanity from pain. . . . Whether there be consolation for them or not, neither apathy nor blindness shall be their saviour; if, for them, thus knowing the facts of the grief of earth, any hope, relief, or triumph may hereafter seem possible,—well; but if not, still hopeless, reliefless, eternal, the sorrow shall be met face to face.[49]

In the scene of the death of Hector in the *Iliad* Ruskin sees a mythic expression of the central irony of all supernal dependence. Assuming the form of Hector's brother, Deiphobus, Athena encourages him to fight, but in that fight she not only disappears, leaving Hector to call upon Deiphobus without hope, she hands Hector's vainly thrown spear to Achilles; thus Hector is slain by the lance of Pallas. Then, foreshadowing that quality in *The Queen of the Air*, Ruskin's own mythopoesis merges with the Greek; the interpretation becomes double-faced in form and thought, for it is the meaning of the meaning that Ruskin is after.

> We trusted in the Gods;—we thought that wisdom and courage would save us. . . . Athena had the aspect of Deiphobus—terror of the enemy. She has not terrified him [Achilles], but left us in, our mortal need.
>
> And beyond that mortality, what hope have we? Nothing is clear to us on that horizon, nor comforting. Funeral honours; perhaps also rest; perhaps a shadowy life—artless, joyless, loveless. No devices in that darkness of the grave, nor daring, nor delight. . . .
>
> Be it so. With no better reward, no brighter hope, we will be men while we may; men, just, and strong, and fearless, and up to our power, perfect. Athena herself, our wisdom and our strength, may betray us:—Phoebus, our sun, smite us with plague, or hide his face from us helpless;—Jove and all the powers of fate oppress us, or give us up to destruction. While we live, we will hold fast our integrity; no weak tears shall blind us, no untimely tremors abate our strength of arm nor swiftness of limb. The gods have given us at least this glorious body and this righteous conscience; these will we keep bright and pure to the end. So may we fall to misery, but not to baseness; so may we sink to sleep, but not to shame.[50]

Perhaps enough has been quoted here to suggest the connection between Ruskin's idea of Greek faith as he expressed it in the last volume of

Modern Painters, near 1860, and the foundational religion of the preface
to *The Crown of Wild Olive* of 1866, which he said sustained him from
1858 to 1874.

Before moving on to its superstructure we should consider several
other points about Ruskin's "religion of Humanity." Notice first that he
thought of this religion as a necessary mean between two extremes of
error: religion of the soul's otherworldly destination, on the one hand,
which ignores the vital mystery of man's existential being, and science,
on the other, which postulates no soul at all, "caring for the universe
only; for man, not at all." Both neglect the mystery of organic being, the
soul of man as the dark but only mirror of deity bound in relation to
landscape, the soul's organic vestment and our only image of possible
rest. This is the point of the famous "Dark Mirror" chapter of volume 5
of *Modern Painters*, which clears the ground for "The Lance of Pallas"
immediately following. For Ruskin of 1858, then, "that flesh-bound
volume," the human being, is the only revelation. But revelation nonetheless. Not a gleam in isolation but in an organic globe. Shadowy
image though the soul may be, it is the true sun of creation. Man is not
the creation but the light of it, yet the light he casts must be that of
relational awareness by which everything that lives takes on mystery and
holiness through its relation to that central mystery, the human soul.

> Let him stand in due relation to other creatures, and to inanimate things—
> know them all and love them, as made for him, and he for them;—and he
> becomes himself the greatest and holiest of them. But let him cast off this
> relation, despise and forget the less creation round him, and instead of
> being the light of the world, he is a sun in space—a fiery ball, spotted with
> storm.[51]

Considering its mixture of antiscientism and anti-Puritanism it is
easy to understand why Ruskin's "religion of Humanity" would be
deliberately antagonistic toward that other, more famous, Religion of
Humanity of which Auguste Comte was founder and first high priest.
This positivist Religion of Humanity (Ruskin's use of the lowercase *r*
not only differentiates his but contains an implicit criticism of the other)
was being advocated in England during this period by such figures as
John Stuart Mill, G. H. Lewes, George Eliot, Harriet Martineau, and
others, but particularly by his friend and critic Frederic Harrison.[52] The
chief labor of Harrison's life was his attempt to introduce Comtian
humanist sociology into England. He led the positivist front in England
from about 1870 until his death, and he was president of the English
Positivist Committee from 1880, shortly after its inception, to 1905.

Harrison regarded Comte as "undoubtedly the first who ever showed a uniform and continuous evolution; *as the law of being of the physical and social world alike.*" His "Religion of Humanity" was, therefore, "simply the Evolution of Man idealized and revealed."[53] And he set out to idealize and reveal it. "It was the great idea of our master, August Comte," he wrote, "that when the conception of Humanity and of the relation of our lives to the life of Humanity, had attained to its fullness, each of the great acts in the life of each of us should be formally dedicated by a fitting religious expressions to the service of Humanity."[54] It is not difficult to understand why Harrison saw in Ruskin's famous dictum "There is no wealth but life," the key to his political economy, a "central and saving truth" that "had never been illustrated with more incisive eloquence, nor enforced with a more intense conviction."[55]

For Ruskin's thoughts on Harrison's humanism, and these in the light of his own on Hellenism, one turns first to *Fors*, Letter 66, (1876) where Ruskin begins by dropping the remark that he has been reading, "by Fors' order," E. B. Tylor's *Researches into the Early History of Mankind* (1865) and "Humanity: a Dialogue," a "gushing article" by Harrison in the *Contemporary Review* (May 1876). Taking first a lead from Tylor's "idea of the Greek faith in Apollo," Ruskin sprints away into a brief homily on "the practical connection between physical and spiritual light," a theme, he says, that can be found "all up and down my later books, from *Unto this Last* to *Eagle's Nest* and again and again throughout *Fors*," and obviously a subject to which we must return. The point made here, connectible as has been suggested with his studies in myth and with solarist theories of myth, is simply that physical gloom conditions the spiritual, a part of his broader view that "the powers of Nature are depressed or perverted together with the Spirit of Man."[56]

To Harrison, Ruskin addressed, in this same *Fors*, a somewhat condescending letter which the former took, rightly, as a "rebuke."[57] Harrison's positivist of the article (the dialogue is between "Positivist" and a "Critic") suggests that the Critic direct his gaze to the "sweet landscape, with its myriad blossoms and foliage, its meadows in their sudden glory" and see there evidence of "the collective evolution of the human race," the consensus of human capability. "These flowers and plants, which we can see between the cloisters and trellised around the grey traceries, what races of men in China, Japan, India, Mexico, South America, Austral-asia, first developed their glory out of some wild bloom?"[58] There was more to the argument, but these particular phrases caught Ruskin's eye, and he rounded upon them with such pyrotechnics of indignation that Harrison was apparently rather stunned by it all.[59]

Essentially, Ruskin bombarded Harrison with a number of ludicrous comparisons developed from items supposedly pictured in their modern and classical "type"—Ruskin himself (in a current derogatory caricature) with the Elgin Theseus, Mrs. Frances Power Cobbe and her "sauce pan" with the "Amazonian Virgin," et cetera. He then queries Harrison (who was professor of jurisprudence and international law to the Inns of Court from 1877 to 1889) on the evolution of the law with four questions "of vital importance to Humanity" which, he says, if Harrison will indeed answer clearly, he will in so doing perform "more service to Humanity than by writing any quantity of papers either on its Collective Development or its Abstract Being."[60] Ruskin concludes by imploring Harrison to, "by all that's positive, and all that's progressive, all that's spiral, all that's conchoidal, and all that's evolute—great Human son of Holothurian Harries, answer me."[61] This last phrase is a neat bit of wordplay in which Ruskin, as Harrison acknowledged in his own reply, traces "my birth to a species of slug."[62]

In sum, then, Harrison's "Religion of Humanity," insofar as it depended upon the "Evolution of Man idealized and revealed," could not satisfy Ruskin. He condemned Harrison for saying that he (Harrison) would listen only to the judgments of those "who have patiently weighed the *whole*" of both thought and life,[63] and Harrison attacked Ruskin for "indiscriminate abuse of all that the human race has now become."[64] But Ruskin's need creed—founded, he said, in Greek belief (though a letter of 1852 quoted earlier suggests Carlyle's influence also)—pointed to the moral predicament of particular man, to the imperative of humanity in him, and not to the abstract idea of the development of humanity in the aggregate sense. "An aggregate of men is a mob, and not 'Humanity,' " he declared.[65]

In *Fors*, Letter 76, (1877) Ruskin reasserverates the humanism he had read out of Homer: "I set myself to work out that problem thoroughly in 1858, and arrived at the conclusion—which is an entirely sound one, and which did alter, from that time forward, the tone and method of my teaching,—that human work must be done honourably and thoroughly, because we are now Men;—whether we expect to be angels, or ever were slugs, being practically no matter. We *are* now Human creatures, and must at our peril, do Human—that is to say, affectionate, honest, and earnest work"[66] To this he appends a note that at once suggests both his view of Harrison's positivist faith and the derivation of his own in this period: "This is essentially what my friend Mr. Harrison means (if he knew it) by his *Religion of Humanity*—one which he will find, when he is slightly more advanced in the knowledge of all life and thought, was known and acted on in epochs antecedent to that of modern Evolution."[67] How near an ally in his forays against the plutonomists Ruskin actually had in the Comtists, he apparently never knew.[68]

5

The major thesis of the present chapter is that Ruskin's "religion of Humanity," especially in the olive crown, its controlling symbol, and the assertion of the independence of human bravery and virtue from belief in a hereafter, derived from his studies in Greek belief pursuant, especially, to the writing of volume 5 of *Modern Painters*. This is the basis of belief he specified at the time, whatever his private debt to Carlyle's work. He also remarked that upon this religion as a sure foundation he built a "Greek and Arabian superstructure" that he had learned at Venice, and which was "full of sacred colour and melancholy shade." Having related that foundation, in part at least, to his idea of Greek religion, we must take a moment to see in what way the superstructure was also Greek.

What, in the first place, *was* that superstructure, and why was it learned at Venice? I think it is plain that by the superstructure of his "religion of Humanity" Ruskin signifies chiefly the aesthetic implications of that belief ("The fallacy under which I had been tormented for sixteen years,—the fallacy that Religious artists were weaker than Irreligious"). But in what way is this connected with Venice? ("My work on the Venetians in that year [1858] not only convinced me of their consummate power, but showed me that there was a great *worldly* harmony running through all they did.") More important still, why was this superstructure Greek *and* Arabian? Why "full of sacred colour and melancholy shade"? And why does he say that this was the "under-meaning" of his telling the Capuchin (in 1858) that he was "more of a Turk than a Christian"?[69]

Since the broadest answers to these questions will, in fact, form a large part of the following discussion, they are merely sketched in at this point by way of showing that the current of Ruskin's religion of the human present as field of care had several Greek tributaries. First to be remembered, of course, is the fact that in the *Fors* passages just referred to Ruskin was writing in 1877, out of the perspective of his later years, and looking back through his own religious and aesthetic development to 1858. Therefore, considering the date and the need to trace the avowed Greek lineage of that aesthetic superstructure learned at Venice, the essential document is the chapter in the fifth volume of *Modern Painters*, entitled "The Wings of the Lion," in which Ruskin connects Venetian art with the Greek.

There he begins by reminding us, and one immediately relates this to what has been said of the idea of Greek humanism in his "religion of Humanity," that "all the nobleness, as well as the faults of the Greek art were dependent on its making the most of this present life . . . ; its dominion was in this world."[70] Going on in this vein, Ruskin observes that while "Florentine art was essentially Christian, ascetic, expectant of a better world, and antagonistic, therefore to the Greek temper," Venetian art, on the other hand, "began . . .with asceticism; always, however, delighting in more massive and deep colour than other religious painters. . . . They were, also . . . always quarrelling with the Pope. Their religious liberty came, like their bodily health, from . . . wave training; for it is one notable effect of a life passed on shipboard to destroy weak beliefs in appointed forms of religion."[71]

The influences of the sea and sky, then, opposed the development of conventional Christianity in the Venetians and, consequently, of hypocrisy in their metaphors: "This ocean-work is wholly adverse to any morbid conditions of sentiment. Reverie, above all things, is forbidden by Scylla and Charybdis. By the dogs and the depths, no dreaming! The first thing required of us is presence of mind."[72] Thus in the physical influences at work upon them, the Greeks and the Venetians were similarly productive of a kind of sea realism of the spirit: "Whereas, God and the sea are with us, and we must even trust them both, and take what they shall send."[73] To be sure "the Greek Sea was indeed less bleak, and the Greek hills were less grand; but the difference was in degree rather than in the nature of their power."[74] Both were, like Stevens's Crispin, "washed away by magnitude."

The "ocean-work" of the Venetians, like that of the Greeks, was adverse to *ubi sunt* and *memento mori* and tended, moreover, to induce "a great respect for the whole human body, . . . from the sweeping glory of the sea we learn to love another kind of beauty; broad-breasted, level-browed, like the horizon;—thighed and shouldered like the billows; footed like their stealing foam;—bathed in cloud of golden hair like their sunsets."[75]

Though the physical inspirations of the Greeks and Venetians were similarly humanistic and realistic, the religious influences on each were very different. "Evil, as we saw, had been fronted by the Greek, and thrust out of his path. Once conquered, if he thought of it more, it was involuntarily, as we remember a painful dream, yet with a secret dread that the dream might return and continue forever."[76] The Venetian, however, as a Christian painter, had his faith, which, while promising him a future life, invited also speculations upon the morbid aspects of this one. "The Venetian was, therefore, in his inner mind, less serious than the Greek: in his superficial temper, sadder. In his heart there was none of the deep horror which vexed the soul of Aeschylus or Homer. His Pallas-shield was the shield of Faith, not the shield of the Gorgon. All was at last to issue happily; in sweetest harpings and seven-fold circles of light. But for the present he had to dwell with the maimed and the blind, and to revere Lazarus more than Achilles."[77] If the tone is not sufficient here to indicate Ruskin's preference at that time for the Greek over Christian influences on Venetian art, the next step of his argument will do so. "This reference to a future world," he wrote, "has a morbid influence on all their conclusions. For the earth and all its natural elements are despised . . . Man, the immortal, is alone revered."[78]

Though, for Ruskin, the Venetian landscapes were too little of this world and hence fallacious, they were peopled with figures in which the Venetian had tempered a sincere piety with the humanizing influences of the sky and sea. "Throughout the rest of Italy, piety had become abstract, and opposed theoretically to worldly life; hence the Florentine and Umbrian painters generally separated their saints from living men."[79] But "the Venetian mind . . . and Titian's especially, as the central type of it, was wholly realist, universal, and manly."[80] Thus in the Venetians, particularly Giorgione and Titian, the female form, painted "fearlessly, with all right and natural qualities," can become the principal subject. This realism is possible because "in the greatest studies of the female body by the Venetians, all other characters are overborne by majesty, and the form becomes as pure as that of a Greek statue."[81]

Along these lines, then, Ruskin had been thinking in 1858 concerning the similarities between Greek faith and the best influences upon the Venetian painters. But the aesthetic superstructure of his "religion of Humanity" was, he said, both "Greek and Arabian." This, of course, refers to the Byzantine aspects of his Venetian experience. Venice learned her art, he later wrote, out of Greece by way of Byzantium. When we recall this Byzantine influence upon Venetian art, and when we remember that Ruskin would say that "a Byzantine *was* nothing else than a Greek—recognizing Christ for Zeus"[82] we perceive yet another Greek tributary to the Ruskinian humanist aesthetic of 1858 to 1874. In his respect for the Greek in the Byzantine and both in the Venetian he was, as he thought, "more of a Turk than a Christian."

So much for the Greek and Byzantine influences upon the aesthetic or critical "superstructure" he built upon his "religion of Humanity." But why should this edifice be "full of sacred colour and melancholy shade?"

The answer touches upon Ruskin's deep empathic and spiritual involvement with light and the light-darkness archetype; it must necessarily be incomplete at this point.

In his Oxford *Lectures on Art* (1870) Ruskin formulates most clearly his distinction between what he thought of as the "Greek School," the "school of light" (dependent on "Greek sorrow and Greek religion" and "founded in the Doric worship of Apollo") and the Gothic "Christian" school, the "school of colour."[83] The "Gothic school" is always cheerful, but the Greek school, the chiaroscurist school of line and light, is "full of sorrow," its lights and darks symbolizing, especially in the Greeks, the contest of light with spiritual darkness.[84]

This chiaroscurist school, then, depends upon Greek religion and its concept of spiritual darkness; its great modern masters are Holbein, Leonardo, Dürer, Correggio, and Turner; their concern is with "the representation of light, and the effects it produces on material form—beginning practically for us with Greek vase paintings, and closing practically for us with Turner's sunset on the *Téméraire*; [is] throughout a school of captivity and sadness, but of intense power; and which in its technical method of shadow on material form, as well as in its essential temper, is centrally represented . . . by Dürer's two great engravings of the 'Melancholia' and the 'Knight and Death.' " By the "Gothic School" Ruskin says he means "the entire and much more extensive range of schools extending from the earliest art in Central Asia and Egypt down to our own day in India and China:—schools which have been content to obtain beautiful harmonies of colour without any representation of light."[85]

But the highest achievements of art, he believes, have had something to learn from each school: "the consummate art of Europe has only been accomplished by the union of both."[86] In this the worldly Venetians alone achieved perfection. "Titian deepens the hues of his Assumption, as of his Entombment, into a solemn twilight; Tintoret involves his earth in coils of volcanic cloud, and withdraws,through circle flaming above circle, the distant light of Paradise."[87] Such is the meaning of Ruskin's "sacred colour and melancholy shade"; the Venetian aesthetic united them. Thus, under the solemn if remote influence of Greek faith, Correggio, whose frescoes he had characterized in 1845 as beating "all vulgar, coarse, obscene, paltry decorators of sacred subject I ever cast eyes on,"[88] became fully transvalued in 1870 to a union of "the sensual element of the Greek schools with their gloom, and their light with their beauty, and all these with the Lombardic colour, became, as since I think it has been admitted without question, the captain of the painter's art as such."[89]

6

"Who *giveth* peace?" Ruskin asked in the last chapter of *Modern Painters*, separated from the first by several years and a fallen world. "Many a peace we have made and named for ourselves, but the falsest is in the marvelous thought that we of all generations of the earth, only know the right; and that to us at last,—to us alone,—all the scheme of God, about the salvation of men, as been shown."[90] God loves the world, and Christ, we are in the habit of saying, is the light of it, moving over the face of this chaos; "but chaos, on the face of which, moving, the Spirit of God yet causes men to hope that a world will come. The better one, they call it; perhaps they might, more wisely, call it the real one. Also, I hear them speak continually of going to it, rather than of its coming to them."[91]

Thinking that the only better world must be another, England, "by her goodly gardening," had left the "festering work of the worm . . . to infect her earth-flowers." Thus, "so far as in it lay, this century has caused every one of its great men, whose hearts were kindest, and whose spirits most perceptive of the work of God, to die without hope:—Scott, Keats, Byron, Shelley, Turner." "Perhaps," Ruskin had written, "some day, people will again begin to remember that sin cannot be judged by us."[92] Then the better world might be understood to be this one; its peace, the Greek peace of earth, dependent upon preservation of the earth; peace, receptive of what may come, yet joyous in the beauty of this human world, the dark but only mirror of Deity, and in its only true reward, the wild olive crown.

CHAPTER 8

The Medusa Cloud

The spiritual vacuum created in Ruskin by his un-conversion from Evangelicalism in 1858 was largely filled by two new quasi-religious involvements that would become major determinants of his thought and style. He felt an increasingly urgent sense of social responsibility, a direction of concern that had both aesthetic and political-economic aspects; and at the same time he reached a deeper comprehension of the relation between nature and myth, giving him a new sense of the authority of myth as a vehicle of nature's truth. This latter line of assent would lead by 1874 to his assertion against the scientists that "the feeblest myth is better than the strongest theory,"[1] while the vector of social concern would lead to quixotic assaults on the dismal science of Manchester-school economics into which he poured his main energies in the sixties. But since both the social and the mythic interests had begun to appear in earlier writings, notably in *The Stones of Venice*, it might be more accurate to say that these two (apparently contradictory) impulses gradually displaced the religion in which he had been nurtured and drew together into a belief he would look back on as a "religion of Humanity" vitally opposed to the religions of death: dissective science, divisive greed, supernal reward.

Other primary beliefs continued, of course. Nature remained for him the root of art and a source of apocalyptic cyphers; Turner remained the great seer of landscape whose soul and sight were one; the forces of existence that are locked in vital-lethal conflict became more clearly defined to him; and there was still that special interest in the messages of sky effects and light. All these major themes are orchestrated in the fifth volume of *Modern Painters*. In its prophetic solemnity of tone and thematic breadth it is the climactic work of his first period. Here the "ocular and passionate study of nature" is joined to a nature mythology and a tragic humanism learned from the Greeks; these, in turn, lead to a new depth of appreciation of Turner's work in mythological subjects and a new understanding of his skies and light.

We will wish to look closely at this major work of Ruskin's first or essentially aesthetic phase. But, just as no proper understanding of the book can be reached without some conception of its relation to those preceding it and to his personal religious crisis, so also the controlling consciousness of the work cannot be understood without placing what has already been said here about his religious, mythic, and sky interests against certain developments in the theory of nature mythology, especially the mythology of the sky and of light, which were taking place at the time.[2] Yet it is not my aim to attempt a precise specification of influence; I wish to trace the evolution rather than the sources of Ruskin's thought. Consequently, in chapter 10 the solar mythology of Max Müller is to be juxtaposed briefly with the sky mythology of *Modern Painters*, volume 5, and some of Ruskin's later remarks on the spiritual significance of light in order that the central meaning of that volume, not a distinct pattern of influence, may emerge. It will merely be necessary to view philological nature mythology as a concept in its relation to the directions of his thought and art in this phase, and to bear that concept in mind as we proceed to trace his mythic interests forward within his social thought of the sixties until they culminate, at the end of the decade, in his major "mythbook," *The Queen of the Air*.

It should be remembered also that this interim between the last two volumes of *Modern Painters* was a period of near-frenetic public activity for Ruskin, a fact evidenced by the numerous "by-works" of these years that have been collected in volumes 13 through 16 of the Library Edition. These include the Turner Catalogues (vol. 13); the *Notes on the Principal Pictures in the Royal Academy* (1855–59, vol. 14); the *Elements of Drawing* (1857) and *Elements of Perspective* (1859, vol. 15); and the various lectures, speeches, remarks, and letters on the Oxford Museum, twenty-one items in all, collected in volume 16. Of these writings the most important to us are the two lectures delivered at Manchester in 1857 and first published as *The Political Economy of Art*, and also *The Two Paths* (1859), five lectures "On Art and Its Application to Decoration and Manufacture" that Ruskin delivered in manufacturing towns during 1858 and 1859. Insofar as these subsidiary works offer something new in the development of his thought, particularly on the relation between art and political economics, they will be touched on in the following chapter as I take up the main lines of socioeconomic thought in his work of the sixties. However, there is nothing in these works of such significance as to delay us from a reading of this great and pivotal final volume of *Modern Painters*. In it, as the following three chapters will show, Ruskin perceives the main message of Turner's symbolism in terms of his own emergent social prophecy; both are universalized in mythic metaphors at three levels: organic form as a mythic paradigm of all vital order; the mythic-historical scheme of the fall and death of landscape painting and its redemption by Turner; Greek nature myths of cloud, storm, and solar light as a continuity of apocalyptic symbolism in which, Ruskin will attempt to show, both he and Turner participate.

1

In turning to volume 5 of *Modern Painters* we should be conscious of the immensity of the task that lay before Ruskin in 1858 if he meant to make this volume into a literal completion of the whole projected *Modern Painters.* The first volume had defined the major topics of the work in terms of the chief "Ideas" conveyable by art (those of truth, beauty, and relation) and had gone forward to set forth generic and specific concepts of truth in painting. That is, general truths of technique in paintings were separated from particular truths of visibility or representation in the primary categories of landscape form, forms of clouds, earth, water, and vegetation. The second volume had taken up ideas of beauty, really impressions of beauty, as received by those receptive faculties he called "Theoretic" and "Imaginative." The third volume, after a decade's intermission, had redefined his view of Turner's art in such a way as to reconcile it with the second volume's expressive concept of imagination and free it from the first volume's essentially mimetic aesthetic of truth; at the same time he interpolated into this volume a history of the development of landscape feeling from mythic animation in classical poetry to the Turnerian vision. The fourth volume, published concurrently, after having explored the paradoxical fusion of light and mystery in Turner, had resumed "with more observant patience" the phenomenological task of determining the "real effect of things painted on men's minds" following the plan of the last part of the first volume.

But the analysis of "Mountain Beauty" alone had required nearly four hundred pages in this volume, and completion of the scheme meant clarifying the "proper effect" on the human mind also of the beauty of skies, water, and vegetation and then assessing "the degree in which this nature of theirs, and true influence, have been understood and transmitted by Turner." All this, essentially a phenomenology of landscape, would, if accomplished, still leave the third major topic of the work, ideas of relation, or thoughts conveyable by art, yet to be dealt with.

It is clear that, even if Ruskin's aesthetics and his other concerns had remained somehow static in time, it is unlikely that the original scheme of *Modern Painters* could have been completed in a fifth volume. But of course this assumption would mean that the critic, now entering his forties, would be effectively imprisoned in an analytic structure or "intrinsic genre" he had conceived in his twenties. However, Ruskin allowed his view of art to evolve, and with it the generic conception of *Modern Painters*, even at the expense of argumentative inconsistency and structural incompleteness as more profound truths were revealed to him. As the volumes progress he moves, in general, farther from confident analytic and descriptive discourse and becomes increasingly dependent upon symbolic, mythic, or apocalyptic modes of rhetoric appropriate to more urgent truths.

"I am at work upon it," he told Norton as he struggled with the fifth volume, "in a careless, listless way—but it won't be the worse for the different tempers it will be written in. There will be little or no bombast in it, I hope, and some deeper truths than I knew—even a year ago."[3] There is doubt as to whether Ruskin would have completed the work at all had it not been for the strong pressure of entreaty from his father, considering especially that this was for him a period of crucial redirection of interest. He had by no means reached any point of mental equilibrium. Hence if the last volume of *Modern Painters* were to be more than a stillborn monument to filial piety or a perfunctory completion of the old scheme, it would have to be a vital synthesis of the old structure and new truths and concerns.

The old scheme required him to deal now with the visual influences and aspects of skies, water, and vegetation (as he had with mountains) and then take up "Ideas of Relation" as defined in the first volume. This project would have to be accommodated to an expressionistic aesthetic built on the concepts of imagination and pathetic animation of nature developed in the third volume, to a deepening interest in nature mythology (especially of skies) that was replacing the aesthetic function of his Puritanism, and, most important, to his emergent "religion of Humanity" from which he saw a tragic "worldly harmony" uniting the greatest of painters. We have noted that all three of these new directions were deeply influenced by his thoughts on Greek literature and belief, abetted by readings in contemporary mythological theory. In short, nature had changed for him, taking on a new tragic and mythic depth projected from the human mind, making it less possible to speak confidently of the "proper effect" of visible forms: "all the power of nature," he would now conclude, "depends on subjection to the human soul."[4] Nature is visible only in the light of man's being. Art changed also in the sense that the highest art must now, for him, express the tragic truths of the life-world, the field of care, rather than intimations of immortality. Consequently, in this final volume, under ideas of relation, the message of Turner would have to be revalued in terms of the new mythic and humanistic perspective of his "religion of Humanity." But, as Cook points out, not all of the volume was written in 1859 after his "unconversion"; some of the materials for it seem to have been written at the time of the fourth volume. These too would have to be fitted to the new perspectives.

In a preface that is strangely silent about the essential message of the book, Ruskin speaks of his predicament in 1859 as he set himself "to arrange materials of which it was not easy, after so much interruption, to recover the command;—which also were now not reducible to a single volume." As if his study turned on certain pieces of factual knowledge, he goes on to mention two primary questions, crucial to his planned sections on the forms of water and of vegetation, one question "respecting the origin of wood," the other having to do with the laws of wave curvature, "to neither of which, from botanists or mathematicians, any sufficient answer seemed obtainable."[5] More explicitly, however, concerning the intended sea section, he concludes that Turner's "pathetic interest in the sea and his inexhaustible knowledge of shipping" required a depth of treatment for which the analysis of wave forms would merely have been a foundation; therefore, since he was determined to handle the subject well or not at all, the proposed division on the forms of water had to be abandoned altogether. It is also possible, as will be evident from the following discussion, that Ruskin simply could not adapt sea forms to his current mythic and social interests as readily as he could the tree and cloud forms and the mythological Turners which are his essential subjects in the finished volume.

The vegetation section of the volume, Ruskin's preface explains, had to be put together from the knowledge then available to him. Cook suggests that some of this material may have been written at the same time as his analyses of earth forms for the fourth volume. There is, of course, a generic resemblance; Ruskin's analytic categories are simple (comparatively reified) in both and are built out of ordinary language and the everyday visibility of things; both are infused with the sense of purposive, systemic interrelations of parts; and in each discussion there are analogies with architecture and there are emotive descriptions. On the other hand, his intentional glance is not the same in these vegetation chapters; it is more animistic, more pathetic in his own sense; the view is less objective and scientific than in the chapters on earth forms and richer in social or moral implications; yet the vegetation section does not reach the overt mythologizing of the following section on cloud forms. Contrasts with other divisions of this part of *Modern Painters* are comparatively easy to see. Ruskin's altering eye alters the meaning of natural forms (here the internal purposiveness and life struggle of the plant is emphasized as opposed to evidences of divine design among the mountains), but the actual method or intrinsic genre of this section on vegetation is not itself easy to define.

On 19 April 1861 he delivered a lecture entitled "Tree Twigs" at the Royal Institution. From an account of it and Ruskin's own abstract, both printed in the Library Edition, it is apparent that his method in the lecture was much the same as that of the first section of the fifth volume of *Modern Painters*. Carlyle, who was present, wrote to his brother that he had not liked any neat lecture he had heard there so well as this "chaotic" one in which the lecturer dealt with "Tree Leaves as physiological, pictorial, moral, symbolical objects."[6] Froude connected the lecture's power with Ruskin's ability to convert detailed observation of natural phenomena into poetry. In Cook's view, both the lecture and the vegetation chapters show "the same close study of natural aspects combined with poetical fancy, and the same imaginative connection of those aspects with ideas of morality and mythology."[7]

Whatever this last phrase may mean, there is clearly more to the ten chapters on leaf beauty than an analysis of plant forms touched with "felicities of poetical observation." Despite the exigencies of their composition and Ruskin's protestations of the tentativeness of their conclusions, these chapters have a distinct function in a work that shows remarkable coherence of intention and is, read for itself, a masterpiece of apocalyptic prose and the culminating effort of the first phase of his work. The four sections of the volume, "Leaf Beauty," "Cloud Beauty," "Invention Formal," and "Invention Spiritual," are not separate treatises in aesthetic topics as the titles imply; they betray an inherent unity of purpose that binds ethical, ecological, and mythical concerns together with the aesthetic. His observations on trees are indeed poetical in that there are occasional emotive descriptions and many places where botanical analysis takes on social and political implications; but they are poetical also in the deeper sense of belonging to a whole work that moves from delineation of the life force and its meaning in simple organic forms through mythic presentation of the life of clouds to study finally the intimations of a global prophecy in certain mythical subjects of Turner. The plot of structure of *Modern Painters* volume 5, as Cook suggests, ties the close study of natural aspects to ideas of morality and mythology. But the relationship is extremely complex. The subtly animated analysis of tree growth makes the tree into a redemptive natural myth[8] of social coherence.

The studies of clouds, apparently written later, become explicitly mythological at points, as Ruskin attempts to recreate the Greek awareness of clouds as mysterious messengers of fate. Man's dependence on the two life-giving veils of earth is declared in a section enunciating the laws of life in form, especially in art form; then the artist is introduced as "spiritual inventor" or prophet in form. The culminating example is a solar mythic painting of Turner's that blazons his vision of the death mode of the nineteenth century, and it is Ruskin's task to interpret it. In this way the work moves rhetorically from simple pathetic animation of plant forms, really an existential study of the tree's being, to apocalyptic mythology that owes something to the solarism of Max Müller.

The first chapter, "The Earth Veil," quickly intimates the socioecological sub-theme of the volume: "How have we ravaged the garden instead of kept it." The garden, however, is neither a biblical symbol nor an objective complex of ecosystems. It is a veil of animate being "which breathes, but has no voice; moves, but cannot leave its appointed place; passes through life without consciousness to death without bitterness"; it is "an imperfect soul, given to meet the soul of man."[9] Thus the subtle process of mythic animation begins as Ruskin sets his task of exploring the meanings of the forms of this vital underveil, "this mystery of intermediate being . . . link between the Earth and man," just as the following sequence of chapters will study the equally mysterious and sustaining overveil of cloud forms.

After a restrained yet moving invocation of the adaptive and preparatory action of plant life on the earth, and of its multifold immediate utility to man, Ruskin concludes that our relation to trees is "a nearly perfect test of our being in the right temper of mind and way of life."[10] He then touches on the counterinfluence of urban life and concludes the chapter with a prophetic assertion that the influence of country environment on man is "a grave question, more than most we contend about . . . The day will assuredly come when men will see that it *is* a grave question; at which period, also, I doubt not, there will arise persons able to investigate it."[11]

In the following chapter, "Leaf Orders," Ruskin introduces his "childish" classification of plants. There are tented plants, or flowers, which "pass as the tented Arab passes," leaving "*no memorials of themselves*, except the seed, or bulb, or root which is to perpetuate the race." Of the more enduring races, the trees or building plants, there are two distinct types of organization, "builders with the shield," the broad-leaved, deciduous trees; and "builders with the sword," the evergreens.[12] He will devote most of his attention to the shield builders since theirs is the "chief mystery of vegetation" in its external form. Of course his scheme of classification is not simply poetical in the fanciful sense; it is relational and animating yet at the same time ethical and political since the three classifications suggest social orders and a moral preference. These implications enlarge as he proceeds to analyze the being of shield builders.

Six chapters are devoted to shield builders and one each to the sword builders and tented plants. Ruskin's recurrent themes are, first, that the infinite subtleties and complexities of organic form are not to be caught in art either by niggling mechanical imitation or in any conventions of representation but rather by intimate knowledge of plant aspects coupled with imaginative penetration of the being-there of the particular living form. Further, the subtleties of organic form manifest an inherent ordering and unifying will that we call life; its relation to the particular form in a plant is to be understood only by entering the lived world, the *Dasein* as it were, of the plant. Of course Ruskin does not literally prescribe this kind of existential analysis of plants; this is what his own approach implies. Finally, the tree as a study in organic order, coherence, and existential growth suggests crucial analogies with the human social tree in much the same way that certain organic forms, lines, and vital elasticities disclose the true nature of Gothic building.

Thus in "The Bud" we are reminded that every mature leaf "has assuredly an infant bud to take care of, laid tenderly, as in a cradle, just where the leaf-stalk forms a safe niche between it and the main stem"; at the season's end this "boy bud is put out to rough winter schooling, by which he is prepared for personal entrance into public life in the spring."[13] This nurturing of a budded rod is the essential annual work of the building plant at this point in its structure. In its relation to the whole as the tree-tower develops, each budded rod "has the power and disposition to make a pinnacle of himself, but he has not always the opportunity."[14] What most interests Ruskin in this chapter, however, is the intricate placement of buds and the delicate twist each imparts to the stem, so that "every shoot is affected by a subtle (in nature *infinitely* subtle) change of contour between bud and bud."[15] The budded stem, whose essential business has been "to get every pair of buds set at right angles to the one below," gradually takes on a form that is much like that of the resiliently twisted tower of a Gothic cathedral.

Again in "The Leaf" Ruskin is most anxious to discern the principles that govern the positions leaves assume with respect to others on the same shoot, though he is constantly aware of the infinite complexity of these arrangements. By some inherent "Law of Deflection" leaves of a stem, he notes, are made to fall gradually away from the uppermost leaf or leaf group; however, as in human communities, "when the community is small, people fall more readily into their places. . . . The members of a vast community are separately weaker, as an aspen or elm leaf is thin, tremulous, and directionless, compared with the spear-like setting and firm substance of a rhododendron or laurel leaf."[16] The "Law of Succession" determines that each leaf must be stronger or weaker than that above or below it in an order of succession determined by its position on the twisted spire. Members of a leaf community, unlike sections of dead crystalline forms, do not grow side by side but above and below one another, though they dislike it; and they are, by the law of nature, unequal in size and strength. Further, they are compelled to fall into subcommunities or formal clusters, quatrefoil or cinquefoil for example, taking direction "given them by the uppermost cycle or spiral of the buds."[17] But, though the relative positions and strengths of leaves are fixed by the structure of the whole, they are given a mode of uniqueness by the "Law of Resilience" that determines that each leaf will, in seeking the light, find its own peculiar twist on its stalk, taking up a tensive position with respect to others: "You must note the resulting characters on *every* leaf; namely, that not one leaf in a thousand grows without a fixed turn in its stalk, warping and varying the whole of the curve on the two edges throughout its length, and thus producing the loveliest conditions of its form."[18]

The language by which Ruskin carefully animates the structure he describes is the most significant feature of his discussion, especially in the light of the movement into myth that unifies the whole volume. We are reminded, for instance, that in their clustering and twisting into the community of the stem the leaves reveal an "exquisite sensibility." "They do not grow each to his own liking, till they run against one another, and then turn back sulkily; but by a watchful instinct, far apart, they anticipate their companions' courses, as ships at sea, and in every new unfolding of their edged tissue, guide themselves by the sense of each other's remote presence, and by a watchful penetration of leafy purpose in the far future."[19] The leaf relationships thus developed, unlike crystalline or mechanical structures, "are always visibly the result of a volition on the part of the leaf, meeting an external force or fate, to which it is never passively subjected." External natural forces affect the communal structure, of course, altering its whole life. "But it is *life* which they affect;—a life of progress and will,—not a merely passive accumulation of substance. . . . The leaf, full of fears and affections, shrinks and seeks, as it obeys."[20]

Having in this way invoked the vital mysteries of interrelationship that determine the infinite subtleties of form in "The Leaf," Ruskin has laid the groundwork for an aesthetic digression at this point, the chapter "Leaf Aspects," in which the massive difficulties of leaf drawing can be conveyed. Of course to draw a living leaf in the sense in which he has described it, with due regard for the existentials that have determined the leaf's particular form, is only a barely conceivable task for art. He is asking the painter to bring all the dynamic truths of a leaf's being to stand in the representation of it. We understand his contempt for those who think it might be a simple matter to paint the leaves as they grow: "Alas! My innocent young friend. 'Paint the leaves as they grow!' If you can paint *one* leaf, you can paint the world."[21]

No method for such painting can be given. It is simply clear that the leaf cannot be caught in its life by any "niggling," the word with which he sweeps away most Dutch leaf painting as "disorganized and mechanical work, applied on a scale which may deceive a vulgar or ignorant person into the idea of its being true."[22] No work that is mean or merely minute, no dead-handed conventionalism of approach, can capture the tensive relation among leaves that expresses their life. Only a free touch like Turner's, itself vital, can convey this. As Ruskin had declared in the first volume, "A single dusty roll of Turner's brush is more truly expressive of the infinitude of foliage than the niggling of Hobbima could have rendered his canvas, if he had worked on it till doomsday."[23] Turner is the master of the infinity or mystery of landscape; this we have learned, but we must now be made to see that this quality is a function not only of complexity of texture but also of dexterity of touch. Turner's brushwork is itself a vital mystery, "at once so dexterous and so keenly cunning, swiftest play of hand being applied with concentrated attention on every movement, that no care in facsimile will render it."[24] It appears that in both his understanding and his execution Turner participates in the life of his foliage, so long at least as his subject is shield builders. "Into the spirit of the pine he cannot enter."[25]

In the three remaining chapters on shield builders, "The Branch," "The Stem," and "The Leaf Monuments," Ruskin becomes more explicit about the social and moral implications of tree growth as a cypher of communal life. As with the leaf, the subtle and responsive curvature of the branch is stressed; the branch, for instance, is curved, "not merely as the edge or lip of the wine glass is curved, . . . but as the edge of a lip or an eyebrow is curved, partly upwards, and partly forwards, so that in no possible perspective can it be seen as a straight line."[26] But the core of the discussion of the larger elements of tree structure is an answer to what might be a child's question: How does the tree make its trunk? The study of botany, Ruskin thinks, is heavy with dehumanized nomenclature of ramification. But in the world of ordinary language, the ethical world, the question is simply how it is that a tree's stem "grows straight and true, while its branches, constructed by the same process as the mother trunk, and under the mother trunk's careful inspection and direction, nevertheless have lost all their manners, and go forking and flashing about, more like the cracklings of spitefullest lightning than gentle branches of trees that dip green leaves in dew?"[27] Interpretation of the causes of these modes of seeking in the tree constitutes, he argues, the "true natural history of trees;—or, more accurately, their moral history."[28] This is the central subject of his chapter "The Stem," and in fact of the whole section on vegetation.

What the tree has to teach the state cannot be better expressed than by the tree itself, but Ruskin's language suggests that he reads in the tree something like the givenness of growth, a diverse unity of *elans*, initial equality of upward seeking or moral will in each member, leadership of the fittest, and the tendency to autonomy in branches or colonies. "A tree," he tells us, "is born without a head. It has got to make its own head. It is born like a little family from which a great nation is to spring; and at a certain time, under peculiar circumstances, this nation, every individual of which remains the same in nature and temper, yet gives itself a new political constitution, and sends out branch colonies, which enforce forms of law and life entirely different from those of the parent state. That is the history of the state. It is also the history of a tree."[29]

But more emotive, for Ruskin, is the meaning that the formal beauty of the tree, its ordered disorder, depends not only upon the successful striving of the topmost members but equally upon the free waywardness and struggle, even the failure and early death, of others. Given three first buds of a branch, each, as Ruskin sees it, will desire the same degree of upward development, the same viability of connection with the earth. Their beauty will not result from their achievement of this equality, but only from their maintained purpose and resolve to do so. "They will fail—certainly two, perhaps all three of them: fail egregiously;— ridiculously;—it may be, agonizingly. Instead of growing up, they may be wholly sacrificed to happier buds above, and have to grow *down*, sideways, roundabout ways, all sorts of ways."[30] And now, in one of the most effective passages in this section, the tree is seen as a cypher of the quantity of sacrifice which sustains any social structure and is necessarily generated by such a structure. "Yet out of such sacrifice, gracefully made—such misfortune, gloriously sustained—all their true beauty is to arise. Yes, and from more than sacrifice—more than misfortune: from *death*. Yes, and more than death: from the worst kind of death: not natural, coming to each in its due time; but premature, oppressed, unnatural, misguided—or so it would seem—to the poor dying sprays. Yet, without such death, no strong trunk were ever possible; no grace of glorious limb or glittering leaf; no companionship with the rest of nature or with man."[31]

This theme of the tree as a vital structure, like a society, in which the beauty of the whole including the topmost rise of a few depends upon the shadowy sacrifice and premature death of many "leaf-workers" lower down, suggests to Ruskin ultimately, in the closing paragraph of the chapter, a probable grim meaning of certain peculiarly pear-shaped trees in Turner's *Mercury and Argus*. This theme of leaf-sacrifice and death leads also into the message of his final chapter on shield builders, "The Leaf Monuments." Here he considers the ways in which the visible aspects of branches memorialize the endurance and sacrifice of leaf life. Here also the animating, humanizing, protomythic quality of Ruskin's intentional glance is most apparent: "Here is a birch-bud, farther advanced. . . . Who shall say how many humours the little thing has in its mind already; or how many adventures it has passed through?"[32] The same quality is suggested also by the title and expressive form in his carefully finished branch drawing called *The Dryad's Waywardness*.

Ruskin discerns "three great conditions of branch aspect," that is, three primary qualities of appearance in branches. By "Spring" he refers to the elasticity and "progressive power" of the branch, wholly unlike the limp curvature of a bent rope. "This follows partly on the poise of the bough, partly on its action in seeking or shunning."[33] He insists that the balance of a bough is as subtle a thing as that of a girl dancing. "All these proportionate strengths and measured efforts of the bough produce its loveliness, and ought to be felt, in looking at it, not by any mathematical evidence, but by the same fine instinct which enables us to perceive, when a girl dances rightly, that she moves easily and with delight to herself; that her limbs are strong enough, and her body tender enough, to move precisely as she wills them to move."[34]

A bough's "Caprice" is the visible record of its being in its world; it is "in reality the written story of all the branch's life,—of the theories it

John Ruskin. *The Dryad's Toil.* An illustration to *Modern Painters*, volume 5, reproduced from *Works* (Library Edition), vol. 7.

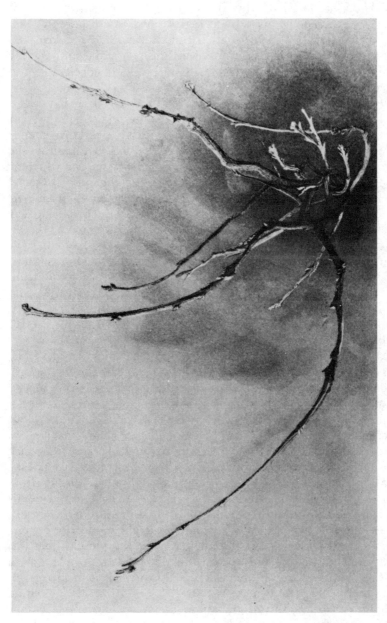

John Ruskin. *The Dryad's Waywardness.* An illustration to *Modern Painters*, volume 5, reproduced from *Works* (Library Edition), vol. 7.

formed, the accidents it suffered, the fits of enthusiasm to which it yielded in certain delicious warm springs; disgusts at weeks of east wind, the mortifications of itself for its friends' sakes; or the sudden and successful inventions of new ways of getting out to the sun."[35] Only Turner, we are told, foreshortens his branches with sufficient care to render the full being of the branch in this sense.

"Fellowship," the final aspect of branch form, is that which reveals "the mode of their association in masses."[36] At this point, in the last part of his concluding chapter on shield builders, Ruskin sets down what he takes to be the self-regulating laws of any organic structure, from the microorganisms to human societies. It is a conception upon which he will elaborate later in the volume and that will be at the core of his social thought, because it is the plainest social meaning of natural form as he sees it. The organic loveliness of a tree, he argues, would be destroyed by the disobedient or discordant behavior of any member, or by the indulgent overprotection of any, or by the tendency to slavish symmetry of behavior among the members. This illustrates a truth that holds "down to the smallest atom and beginning of life: so soon as there is life at all, there are these conditions of it;—harmony, obedience, distress, and delightsome inequality." So at the other extreme of life, in the social organism, "help, submission, sorrow, dissimilarity, are the sources of all good;—war, disobedience, luxury, equality, the sources of all evil."[37]

Although Ruskin devotes six chapters to his "shield-builders," he gives only one each to his other two orders of vegetative life, the "sword-builders" and "tented plants." He excuses this imbalance by offering, on the one hand, that sword builders, because of their definiteness, cannot be so readily generalized about (they are really shield builders "put under severest military restraint")[38] and, on the other hand, that flowers, tented plants, are generally avoided by painters because they lack "sublimity"—"impressions of awe and sorrow being at the root of the sensation of sublimity."[39] But, if we may judge his intentions here from what is developed later in the work, it is clear that he has made his essential point about vegetation in discussing shield builders: Turner's ability (and his own) to penetrate and convey the mystery of organic being, at least with respect to deciduous trees, and the idea that this penetration means not only perceiving the subtleties of contour in branches but reading the tree's "moral history" as a cypher of all communal being. The general laws of life set forth in the preceding paragraph would, of course, hold true for evergreens and flowers, but the specific moral message of each leaf order as living myth would be different.

These vegetative myths are not pursued at length in the two chapters, called "The Leaf Shadows" and "Leaves Motionless." But the myths are intimated here and there in moments of poetic penetration. The evergreens speak to him of restrained, brooding force; of pride and discipline. "All comfortless they stand, between two eternities of the Vacancy and the Rock: yet with such iron will, that the rock itself looks bent and shattered beside them—fragile, weak, inconsistent, compared to their dark energy of delicate life, and monotony of enchanted pride:—unnumbered, unconquerable."[40] The flowering plants (which "seem intended for the solace of ordinary humanity")[41] suggest luxuriance, disorder, transience, but also humble and patient service. The motionless lichen and mosses, especially, evoke pathos and its "fallacy": "Meek creatures! The first mercy of the earth, veiling with hushed softness its dintless rocks; creatures full of pity, covering with strange and tender honour the scarred disgrace of ruin,—laying quiet finger on the trembling stones, to teach them rest. No words that I know of will say what these mosses are."[42] And here, finally, in what may be the most astonishing piece of scene painting in this portion of the volume, Ruskin attempts to penetrate, as he says Turner cannot do, the solemn mysteries of the pine.

> Far in the blue of evening, like a great cathedral pavement, lies the lake in its darkness; and you may hear the whisper of innumerable falling waters return from the hollows of the cliff, like the voices of a multitude praying under their breath. From time to time the beat of a wave, slow lifted, where the rocks lean over the black depth, dies heavily as the last note of a requiem. Opposite, green with steep grass, and set with chalet villages, the Frohnalp rises in one solemn glow of pastoral light and peace; and above, against the clouds of twilight, ghostly on the gray precipice, stand, myriad by myriad, the shadowy armies of the Unterwalden pine.[43]

2

The second section of the volume consists of four chapters on the nature of clouds; the unit is part 7 of *Modern Painters* and is entitled "Of Cloud Beauty," though the aesthetics of clouds is not its essential subject. The first of these chapters, "The Cloud-Balancings," makes clear that Ruskin regards the clouds, like the leaves, as a veil of "intermediate being" upon which we are physically and spiritually dependent. This veil also has two functions, adaptative (to "appease the unendurable glory" of the sun) and symbolic (to "sign the changeless motion of the heavens with a semblance of human vicissitude"). The clouds and leaves, then, are the protective and interpretive shelters of man's being and are themselves zones of being. "Between the earth and man arose the leaf. Between heaven and man came the cloud. His life being partly as the falling leaf, and partly as the flying vapour."[44]

Despite this parallel Ruskin approaches the cloud forms with a greater sense of their mystery than he does the leaves. He had already made clear in the fourth volume that clouds are the sign of mystery itself for him. There clouds are spoken of as types of the soul, as manifestations of God's *"immediate* presence" (the literal meaning of the biblical "heaven"), and as signs of unpaintable mystery or infinity in Turner. In the present chapter, taking an empirical stance, he points out that, although he cannot claim to be fully in touch with the advances of science, he finds "no book which fairly states the difficulties of accounting for even the ordinary aspects of the sky."[45] His task is to evoke these difficulties as mysteries of cloud being.

The mysteries of clouds are of two kinds essentially, mysteries of substance and of form. While both aspects interest him, we sense that the mystery of cloud form is of a different order not only from questions of volatility, visibility, and hue in clouds, but different even from the problem of form in vegetation, where form is to be accounted for partly in terms of the evident life–struggle of the plant. But what forces have shaped the fearful assymmetry of the storm cloud? "On what anvils and wheels is the vapour pointed, twisted, hammered, whirled, as the potter's clay? By what hands is the incense of the sea built up into domes of marble?"[46] Ruskin's animating diction sometimes begins to intimate the higher order of mystery he wishes to invoke: "Or those war-clouds that gather on the horizon, dragon-crested, tongued with fire;—how is their barbed strength bridled? . . . Fierce murmurers, answering each other from morning until evening—what rebuke is this which has awed them into peace? What hand has reined them back by the way by which they came?"[47] Nor does he aim to dissipate the mystery of clouds, though he will describe certain forms with care and reduce them to broad categories. He enjoys their mystery and expects his reader to do likewise, for theirs is a necessary mystery and of a kind that will ultimately require him to have recourse to the speech of myth. He refers to a passage from *Sartor Resartus* in which the glowing clouds are said to be "still a Hebrew speech" to the young Teufelsdröckh, though he is attracted already by "the fair illuminated letters" and has an eye for their gilding.[48] It is clear even in this opening chapter that skies are prophetic speech for Ruskin and clear that his concern is not simply with the forms of the letters and their gilding but also with what they are meant to communicate to us. Unlike the leaves, the clouds do not appear to him to express their own purposes but the mysterious will of some higher power.

In the chapters on clouds that follow ("The Cloud-Flocks," "The Cloud-Chariots," "The Angel of the Sea"), considered as a group, Ruskin's interests in clouds appear as essentially threefold. He wishes to consider whether any special laws of form govern them as with mountains and trees, a meteorological interest paralleling his uses of geology and botany as shaping perspectives. Then he must discern Turner's peculiarities in painting clouds. But most of all he must assert the numinous power of clouds, power implying a wholly different order of life and volition than could be discerned in mountains and trees. This sense of indwelling presence he conveys specifically in "The Angel of the Sea," a chapter that contains the most significant effort at myth-making thus far in his work. As such the chapter is, or at least aims at, poetry of a higher kind than poignant description, it attempts poetry that names the holy. "We never get to know a mystery by unveiling or analyzing it," Heidegger observed; "we only get to know it by carefully guarding the mystery *as* mystery."[49] In "The Angel of the Sea" Ruskin attempts to perform the poetic function of guarding the god–stuff by veiling the mystery of cloud in myth, though at the same time he claims to be acting merely as interpreter or mediator of Turner's mythic awareness of cloud presences. Finally, it will be clear that this chapter on rain and storm clouds is naturally central to this group of chapters because in this numinous zone of "intermediate being" these particular beings are most significant in their ministering and punitive power with respect to our own being.

In organizing his study of clouds Ruskin adheres to the same regional divisions of them he had used in volume 1 of *Modern Painters*, clouds of the upper region, central clouds, and lower or rain clouds. Clouds of each layer are given a chapter in which their formal characteristics are described in a relatively objective way; at the same time, in contrast with this analytic I-It glance, Ruskin's imagery projects here and there a kind of voluntary power into the cloud forms, suggesting a meaning in them that is unapproachable by analysis. This I-Thou relational glance culminates in the overt mythologizing or mythopoesis of the rain-cloud chapter, but it is evident even in the title metaphors by which Ruskin identifies the characteristic clouds of each region: cloud-flocks, cloud-chariots, angel of the sea.

He proceeds first, then, to the uppermost clouds, those which, "owing to their quietness and multitude, we may perhaps conveniently think of as the 'cloud-flocks.' "[50] Immediately there is that curious fusion of analytic and mythic apprehension of these phenomena. Smoke denies Londoners two out of three sunrises, he notes, but given a particularly clear morning he is able to estimate the number of clouds in something like an average flock. In this day's configuration, not extraordinary, he counts five or six ranks of clouds, each of about 150 oblique, close-set rows, each row containing an average of some 60 clouds. So we have "150 x 60, that is, 9,000, separate clouds in this one rank, or about 50,000 in the field of sight. Flocks of Admetus under Apollo's keeping. Who else could shepherd such? He by day, dog Sirius by night; or huntress Diana herself—her bright arrows driving away the clouds of prey that would ravage her fair flocks."[51]

But this mythologizing tendency gives way shortly to awed questioning concerning the infinity, complexity, and harmony of forms represented by this stratified multitude of clouds, "all obedient to one ruling law, gone forth through their companies;—each marshalled to their white standards, in great unity of warlike march, unarrested, unconfused."[52] Perhaps, Ruskin suggests, answers to problems of order and form among the clouds will be provided by the science of electricity, once that science has become more perfectly systematized; his concern is merely that we should have clear questions ready for the scientists. Some of these questions he poses implicitly by showing what intricacies of form the artist must attempt to capture in drawing these highest clouds. These multitudinous ranks of altocumulus clouds present a massive problem in rectilinear perspective of the kind he had discussed in his *Elements of Perspective*; however, the academic problem is rendered staggeringly complex in living skies where the perspective is subjected to subtle curvature or to distortion through the interpenetration of feathery cirrus forms. The presentation of these complexities of form not only poses implicit questions to the scientists about the forces that shaped them, but at the same time it serves to disclose the achievement of Turner. We are told that he "stands more absolutely alone in his gift of cloud-drawing than in any other of his great powers. Observe, I say cloud-*drawing*; other great men coloured clouds beautifully; none but he ever drew them truly: this power coming from his constant habit of drawing skies, like everything else, with the pencil point."[53]

Having little more than asserted Turner's sole penetration of the mystery of cloud form, he concludes the chapter with a few observations on the mystery of cloud color. Could a person, he asks, who knew clouds only as low mists or fog ever conceive that these vapors at high altitudes could become heavy with purple, crimson, scarlet, or gold? These powers of color in the cloud-flocks depend, he concludes, jointly on their peculiar opacity and on their "sponge-like power of gathering light into their bodies."[54] The ultimate question, of course, is what meaning these regal cloud colors ought to have for the human mind; but, since the answer depends upon our knowing certain facts about the mythic meaning of colors, he reserves his conclusions for another place and moves on to consider the clouds of the central region of his quasi-mythic sky.

Here also with the cumulus or cloud-chariots the ideas of mystery, infinity, and the suggestion of inherent, now vaguely threatening, will are the salient features of Ruskin's discussion of them. Again, however, this language is that of comparatively disinterested scientific or aesthetic curiosity. But from both standpoints the cumulus remains incomprehensible to him. He cannot draw or paint it. "Its divisions of surface are grotesque and endless, as those of a mountain; perfectly defined, brilliant beyond all power of colour, and transitory as a dream. Even Turner never attempted to paint them, any more than he did the snows of the high Alps."[55] Nor can he understand their purely physical being. What force prevents this aqueous vapor from diffusing itself in the air like smoke? "What should make it bind itself in those solid mounds, and stay so:—positive, fantastic, defiant, determined?" He hints that if ever he can comprehend this binding of vapors he will then be drawn further "to trace the connection of the threatening and terrible outlines of thunder-cloud with the increased action of electric power."[56] For the present, however, he will pass over these mysteries in all humility, because in the sixteen years since the first volume of *Modern Painters* he has, he says, learned to say little where he had said much and to see difficulties where he had once seen none.

As an instance of such difficulties formerly unperceived he pauses to reconsider the first volume's discussion of clouds that form in close connection with mountain peaks, particularly the "cap-cloud" phenomenon he (following his master Saussure) had once assigned simply to the relation between water vapor and the cold snow of the peak. The difficulty he now perceives is that cap-clouds form on both cold and warm summits. There are two other problems: "First, why it should form only at a certain distance above the snow, showing blue sky between it and the summit. Secondly, why, so forming, it should always show as an arch, not as a concave cup."[57] This mystery of the hovering helmet cloud appears to exert curious power over Ruskin's mind if we judge by the space he gives to it and his recurrent determination to penetrate it or at least make clear that others have not.[58]

3

The fourth and last of these chapters on cloud aspects is called "The Angel of the Sea," and its ostensible subject is the visible beauty of the lower or rain cloud. Actually the chapter contains the deepest penetration thus far in his work of the symbolic and mythic significance of sky phenomena. Its importance to us here lies primarily in the fact that this chapter contains Ruskin's first attempt to disclose the living nature meaning of a particular Greek myth (and at the same time the mythic meaning of a particular natural form), though his discussion depends in part on what he has already said about the Greek landscape feeling in volume 3. Further, while this chapter also resumes the interpretation of the biblical meaning of "the heavens" (the *Coeli Enarrent* theme) begun in the chapter called "The Firmament" in volume 4, this pious but rather abstract reading is now juxtaposed with an imagined Greek viewpoint in which the clouds, particularly the forms of storm, are seen as instinct with personal mythic powers. This mythopoesis of storm phenomena will lead, gradually gathering social implications, to *The Queen of The Air* and *The Storm-Cloud of the Nineteenth Century*. Hence "The Angel of the Sea" marks a significant stage in the development of a major, perhaps the dominant, symbolic and apocalyptic theme in Ruskin's work. Finally, in this chapter his interpretations of Greek mythic figures first combine his own immediate observations of nature with the then authoritative hermeneutics of the philological nature-mythologists led by Max Müller. The visible truth of a natural form is now attested by its mythic significance, which, in turn, is revealed by the root meaning of epithets. Therefore, this chapter is central also in marking the beginning of Ruskin's appeals to the authority of Greek etymology.

The chapter opens with a word of praise for his own first description of the rain cloud as being "perhaps the best and truest piece of work" in the first volume.[59] However, the question now ostensibly before him is not who has painted the rain best, but whether rain can be beautiful at all, whether art has any duty to perpetuate wet weather. An affirmative answer had already been given, of course, in the fourth volume where he had explained that any true landscapist would have to paint the effects of visible mystery and mist. But there are one or two as yet unnoticed reasons for this answer that he will consider in this chapter.

There follows a general discussion of the climatic zones of the globe with respect to their fitness for intellect and art. We learn that the "vine-lands" have nurtured the highest forms of creativity and that they represent a climatic mean between two extremes. The "moss-lands," with their "too diminutive vegetation under bleakest heaven" are opposed to the "wood-lands," with vegetation "too colossal under sultriest heaven." Both are productive of shrewd intellect yet barren of art while in the zones producing grapes and wheat "the perfect ministry of the elements, represented by bread and wine, produces the perfect soul of man."[60]

Yet of the two climatic extremes the moss-lands have an "infinite" advantage in their exposure to the "continual play and change of sun and cloud." Change, Ruskin notes, is the operative word here; because of their openness to elemental action the moss-lands are "the freest ground in all the world."[61] It is severe climatic discipline, "but it is a discipline compelling to action"; whipped by ragged cloud and swept by light, the moss-lands are "the rough schools of the world, in which its strongest human frames are knit and tried, and so sent down, like the northern winds, to brace and brighten the languor into which the repose of more favored districts may degenerate." So the ultimate work of moss-land weather is not bread or wine or art but social regeneration through the rough schooling of prophets like himself, presumably, or Carlyle. And this "great renovating and *purifying* work" for man is done by the symbolic and physical action of the angel of the sea, "the Angel, observe, the messenger sent to a special place on a special errand."[62]

The central meaning of the angel of the sea, the spiritually and physically regenerative action of light and rain over the moss-lands, is its "intermittence," like moments of social renovation sent down from the north. There follow two exquisite passages in which the gentle, animating, but intermittent presence of this *genius loci*, the sea messenger of the north, is invoked as a prelude to the heavier mythic interpretation to follow:

> All turns upon that intermittence. Soft moss on stone and rock;—cave fern of tangled glen;—wayside well—perennial, patient, silent, clear; stealing through its square font of rough-hewn stone; ever thus deep, no more; which the winter wreck sullies not, the summer thirst wastes not, incapable of stain as of decline;—where the fallen leaf floats undecayed, and the insect darts undefiling: cressed brook and ever-eddying river, lifted even in flood scarcely over its stepping stones,—but through all sweet summer keeping tremulous music with harp-strings of dark water among the silver fingering of the pebbles. Far away in the south the strong river Gods [*sic*] have all hasted, and gone down to the sea. Wasted and burning, white furnaces of blasting sand, their broad beds lie ghastly and bare; but here in the moss-lands, the soft wings of the Sea Angel droop still with dew, and the shadows of their plumes falter on the hills: strange laughings and glitterings of silver streamlets, born suddenly, and twined about the mossy heights in trickling tinsel, answering to them as they wave.[63]

Mindful of the painter's work, he insists that these sea angel wings, far from being drab and grey, are frequently infused with light and inimitable color.

> Often in our English mornings, the rain-clouds in the dawn form soft, level fields, which melt imperceptibly into the blue; or, when of less extent, gather into apparent bars, crossing the sheets of broader cloud above; and all these bathed throughout in an unspeakable light of pure rose-colour, and purple, and amber, and blue; not shining, but misty-soft; the barred masses, when seen nearer, composed of clusters or *tresses* of cloud, like floss silk; looking as if each knot were a little swathe or sheaf of lighted rain. No clouds form such skies, none are so tender, various, inimitable. Turner himself never caught them. Correggio, putting out his whole strength, could have painted them, no other man.[64]

With the aid of some passages from Job (36:33–31) Ruskin can now interpret the mythic meaning of "those strange golden lights and purple flushes before the morning rain," which are the sea angel's "robes of love." Their meaning is that "the rain is sent to judge, and feed us; but the light is the possession of the friends of God, and they may ascend thereto,—where the tabernacle veil will cross and part its rays no more."[65]

But the sea angel of social regeneration has also another message for us, a storm message, a "rain of trial, sweeping away ill-set foundations." When he comes to scourge, the sea angel's robe "is not spread softly over the whole heaven, as a veil, but sweeps back from his shoulders, ponderous, oblique, terrible—leaving his sword-arm free." It is curious and yet apparently coherent with his personal religious state that Ruskin invokes the storm-self of the angel now as if seeing it through Greek rather than Evangelical eyes. First, however, we are given a general image of his watchful approach:

> Not slow nor horizontal, but swift and steep: swift with passion of ravenous winds; steep as slope of some dark, hollowed hill. The fronting clouds come leaning forward, one thrusting the other aside, or on; impatient, ponderous, impendent, like globes of rock tossed of Titans—Ossa on Olympus—but hurled forward all, in one wave of cloud-lava—cloud whose throat is as a sepulchre. Fierce behind them rages the oblique wrath of the rain, white as ashes, dense as showers of driven steel; the pillars of it full of ghastly life; Rain-Furies, shrieking as they fly;—scourging, as with whips of scorpions;—the earth ringing and trembling under them, heaven wailing, the trees stooped blindly down, covering their faces, quivering in every leaf with horror, ruin of their branches flying by them like black stubble.[66]

The pillars of the rain can be filled, then, with the "ghastly life" of the rain furies, shrieking and scourging as they fly, punishing the open heath, and yet disciplining the northern character into an occasional instrument for the moral regeneration of society. But instead of furies, Ruskin continues, "I ought to have written Gorgons." For the Gorgons do live. "Perhaps the reader does not know that the Gorgons are not dead, are ever undying. We shall have to take our chance of being turned into stones by looking them in the face, presently. Meantime, I gather what part of the great Greek story of the Sea Angels has meaning for us here."[67]

With this nonexplanation he plunges into a thematic and stylistic strategy that is in one sense new and in another sense part of a deep continuity in his work. The new sense is that this is his first attempt at "interpretation" of a specific myth group, the Nereids, from the then-current standpoint of the etymological nature-mythologist. But interpretation of myth hardly means to Ruskin the detached decoding of a nature allegory or etymological exploration of mythic names for its own sake; the interpretation is used as part of the broader interpretive work with skies that he has in hand. Further, interpretation means sympathetic penetration into, participation in, and translation of the myth; Ruskin preserves where he can the mystery of the myth by reactivating it through imagination in the poetry of his prose, as he claims Turner had done in the poetry of his drawing.

At the same time, myths are providing him with symbols of archetypal universality and authority that serve to polarize his feelings for storm phenomena and to express the meaning he perceives in the immediate experience of nature. For Ruskin, the very existence of myth expresses the presence of volitional powers in nature and is therefore an assertion of the mystery of life; further, it asserts the "solidarity of life"[68] and the moral imperatives of that solidarity to man. Though interpretation of specific myths is something new rhetorically and thematically for Ruskin, it is also continuous with the discussion of Greek landscape feeling in volume 3 and with the interpretation of the biblical "Firmament" undertaken in volume 4. At a deeper level mythic interpretation is tied to the whole apocalyptic or revelational view of nature present in his writing from the beginning and anticipates the more involved and personal mythology of *The Queen of The Air* and *The Storm-Cloud of the Nineteenth Century* and other late works. With these continuities in mind we should look rather closely at his remarks on the Greek sea angels.

Among the children of Nereus, the prophetic old sea god who could change his shape, are Phorcys and Ceto, "the malignant angel of the sea and the spirit of its deep rocky place."[69] The children of this pair of sea beings include the Graiae and the Gorgons. The Graiae, the grey ones, according to Ruskin, are the gentle rain clouds. The Gorgons are the "true storm-clouds." He builds his interpretation toward these ominous forms, considering the benevolent Graiae first. He reminds us that the Greeks had a "greater dislike for storm than we have," hence they represented even the rain's violent action by "harsher types" than we would choose. He cites Aristophanes' lines mocking the poets' use of such images for the rain cloud as "coiled and glittering . . . locks of the hundred-headed Typhon . . . bent clawed birds." But this last expression conveys he thinks two primary aspects of the Graiae clouds: their coiling form and their ability to claw down earth from the hillsides. Theirs is the power to open trenches in the hillsides as if with a pickax; hence the Greek notion that the three Graiae have but one eye and beak between them. He cannot find any precise significance in their names but supposes merely that Hesiod's epithets, "Pephredo, the well-robed; Enuo, the crocus-robed," refer to the beautiful morning colors of these clouds. Finally, he is convinced that the Greeks looked upon the rain cloud as primarily beneficent, despite certain harsh features of the mythic image, and quotes another passage from *The Clouds* for support:

> "O eternal Clouds! let us raise into open sight our dewy existence, from the deep-sounding Sea, our Father, up to the crests of the wooded hills, whence we look down over the sacred land, nourishing its fruits, and over the rippling of the divine rivers, and over the low murmuring bays of the deep."[70]

But the Greek storm figures, the Gorgons, are to Ruskin much more menacing and complex in form and meaning. Where the Graiae have but one beak or tooth between, "all the Gorgons have tusks like boars; brazen hands (brass being the word used for the metal of which the Greeks made their spears), and golden wings."[71] The Gorgons are Steino (Stheno), whose name ("straitened") signifies compact storms; Euryale ("having wide threshing-floor"), signifying widespread storms; and Medusa, "(the dominant), the most terrible." Of the three, only Medusa is discussed; but the connection he supposes in the Greek mind between the Medusa symbols and certain storm clouds gives Ruskin the most important metaphor of the whole section on clouds, a metaphor for the most dangerous meaning and iciest mystery of the clouds. "She is essentially the highest storm-cloud; therefore the hail-cloud or cloud of cold, her countenance turning all who behold it to stone."[72] This same storm power, Ruskin implies, was alluded to by the Psalmist in the words "He casteth forth His ice like morsels. Who can stand before His cold?"[73] We are to understand that the serpents of her head are *partly* an expression of the storm cloud's fringes of hail, because the Greeks connected coldness with the bite of the serpent as well as with the effect of hemlock.

This storm-serpent-stony-cold connection is curious enough as a Ruskinian nature metaphor. However, the fact that this metaphor is assigned mythic authenticity is itself a metaphor, or, more properly, a metamyth. That is, the interpreted Greek myth is not offered for literal belief or for its anthropological interest but as a vehicle for Ruskin's own meaning, his myth. This larger whole begins to show itself as he goes on to read in the Gorgoneum on Athena's shield, an even more vital nucleus of meaning: the connection of storm cloud with unwise knowledge. As the antitype of Athena, Medusa stands for "the cloudy coldness of knowledge, and its venomous character."[74] This idea of the mystery's vengeance on its violators he will develop in greater detail in *The Queen of the Air*.

But for the present, however, the connection between serpents and the storm cloud needs further clarification. This identification, Ruskin continues, arose not only from the visibly serpentine fringes of hail but also from the kind of modification the cloud must undergo before it releases its torrents, for this cloud does not break into "full storm until cloven by the cirrus." This storm meaning is revealed by the myth of Perseus, whose curved adamantine sword or sickle is the cirrus.[75]

Perseus was conceived when Zeus came to Danae, who had been imprisoned by her father, Acrisius, in a brazen tower or perhaps a tower with brazen doors, in a shower of gold. The tower, Ruskin thinks, is simply "another expression for the cumulus or Medusa cloud; and the golden rain for the rays of the sun striking it." The hints in the myth of Perseus ("the destroyer") that enabled Ruskin to interpret him as a cloud cleaver, releasing the cataracts, are read in this way:

> And again note, that when the father of Danae, Acrisius, is detained in Seriphos by storms, a disk thrown by Perseus is carried *by the wind against his head*, and kills him; and lastly, when Perseus cuts off the head of Medusa, from her blood springs Chrysaor, "wielder of the golden sword," the Angel of the lightening, and Pegasus the Angel of the "Wild Fountains," that is to say, the fastest flying or lower rain-cloud; winged, but racing as upon the earth.[76]

This latter storm power, springing from the blood of Medusa, is specifically the "wild" fountains, the "fountains of the great deep" mentioned in Genesis.[77] Pegasus, we are told, is named for the "sudden and furious" torrents released by the thunder storms or for the geyserous jetting forth of water. Hence this power means the "deep and full source of streams"; however, the same imagery of lightning and fountain is also used, he notes, for both "the source of evils, or of passions" and for the signs of true poetic power.[78] To return the reader to the living truth of the myth, Ruskin shifts suddenly now from depersonifying Greek mythic names to an act of poetic animation of his own. This ability to couple interpretation with illustrative mythopoesis, to become the mythopoeic mind, is, as he would explain elsewhere, his chief gift as a student of myth.[79] Here he invokes the "English Pegasus," for us, a swifter rain cloud than the Greek.

> On the Yorkshire and Derbyshire hills, when the rain-cloud is low and much broken, and the steady west wind fills all space with its strength, the sun-gleams fly like golden vultures: they are flashes rather than shinings; the dark spaces and the dazzling race and skim along the acclivities, and dart and dip from crag to dell, swallow-like;—no Graiae these,—gray and withered: Grey Hounds rather, following the Cerinthian stag with the golden antlers.[80]

But the central mythic image that Ruskin is in pursuit of in this section is not the darting Pegasean rain cloud but the cumulus storm head with locks of hair or serpents, locks of Typhon or Medusa. The vital truth of these monsters of storm is attested to by the art of Turner, who read nature like a Greek and could, like Ruskin, interpret the storm meanings of their myths. To illustrate this he provides an engraving that reproduces, over the title "Locks of the Typhon," a "careful facsimile" of the advancing storm head in Turner's *The Slave Ship*, so that we may observe "the witch-like look of drifted or erected locks of hair at its left side."[81] He reminds us also that Turner's description of the picture in the Academy catalogue is, "Slavers throwing overboard the Dead and Dying. *Typhoon* [*Typhon*] coming on." Ruskin says nothing explicit here about the relation between the storm imagery and the human event in the picture; he is clearly saying, however, that the mythic perception of such clouds as a monster's tossing locks is a true presentation of the immediate experience of such clouds, that Typhon lives and Turner perceived this truth and meant to convey it.

Turner also knew that the Greeks saw the locks of storm not merely as drifted hair but as coiling serpents and, particularly, that furious rain lit by solar glow represented the "dissolving of the Medusa cloud in blood."[82] But Ruskin will not speak of this red weather here, for it is connected with other more tragic mythic symbols to be explored later in the volume. "Of that sanguine rain, or of its meaning, I cannot yet speak. It is connected with other and higher types, which must be traced in another place."[83] Yet he must give examples here to show at least

Turner's familiarity with the unbloodied Medusa cloud. First, he refers to a drawing of his own, entitled *Venga Medusa* after Dante's phrase,[84] showing the violent action of the Medusa cloud around an Alpine peak. His descriptive remarks on the drawing show a peculiarly forced connection between the cloud coilings and the chill of knowledge. The drawing, of course, shows "the Medusa serpents writhing about the central peak," and more:

> In this instance, they take nearly the forms of flame; but when the storm is more violent, they are torn into fragments, and magnificent revolving wheels of vapour are formed, broken, and tossed into the air, as the grass is tossed in the hayfield from the toothed wheels of the raking-machine; (perhaps, in common with all other inventions of the kind, likely to bring more evil upon man than ever the Medusa cloud did, and turn them more effectually into stone.)[85]

Now Turner, he continues, was fully aware "of most of the great Greek traditions," and what is more, his mind, as had been shown in volume 3, was affected by natural phenomena in much the same way as the Homeric mind had been. "To him as to the Greek, the storm-clouds seemed messengers of fate. He feared them, while he reverenced; nor does he ever introduce them without some hidden purpose, bearing upon the expression of the scene he is painting."[86] This might be a fair statement of Ruskin's own position, of course, but the immediate subject is four paintings of Turner's that, he believes, contain hidden storm meanings, combining Greek with biblical implications. Most revealing of Ruskin's interests are his interpretations of the contrasting sky messages in Turner's drawings of Salisbury and Stonehenge.

In the *Salisbury* "the cathedral occupies the centre of the picture, towering high over the city, of which the houses (made on purpose smaller than they really are) are scattered about it like a flock of sheep. The cathedral is surrounded by a great light. The storm gives way at first in a subdued gleam over a distant parish church, then bursts down again, breaks away into full light about the cathedral, and passes over the city, in various sun and shade." While this storm action is taking place, the shepherd and his flock in the foreground are a study in pastoral care and peace, and the rain that falls on the scene "is the rain of blessing—abundant but full of brightness."[87] In the *Stonehenge*, forbidden knowledge, "also, stands in a great light; *but it is the Gorgon light*—the sword of Chrysaor is bared against it. The cloud of judgment hangs above. The rock pillars seem to reel before its slope, pale beneath the lightning. And nearer, in the darkness, the shepherd lies dead, his flock scattered."[88]

John Ruskin. *The Graiae.* An illustration to *Modern Painters*, volume 5, reproduced from *Works* (Library Edition), vol. 7.

John Ruskin. *"Venga Medusa."* An illustration to *Modern Painters*, volume 5, reproduced from *Works* (Library Edition), vol. 7.

With the evocation of "these secret meanings of Turner's" (and more are promised for the second half of the volume) the whole section of *Modern Painters* devoted to aspects of visible beauty in nature is drawing to a close, and it is time for Ruskin to point a moral that will both summarize the general significance of nature cyphers and conclude for the moment his analysis of cloud beauty. Perhaps, he continues, the reader had hoped for "more pleasure and freedom" from these investigations of visible beauty and has been surprised to find himself "always under a sterner dominion of mysterious law." But this is a necessary truth, for, as he had shown in the second volume, both the powers and modes of appeal of natural phenomena are determined by the fact that they are expressions of divine attributes and laws. The beauty of nature is always mythic; everything that lives is sacred. Therefore, in this whole section on natural beauty the reader had to be shown "not a pleasure to be snatched but a law to be learned."[89]

In order to show that the essential mode of appeal of natural forms, particularly clouds, to the human mind is as a type or symbol of human obedience to merciful Law, Ruskin proposes a natural reading of the nineteenth psalm, to be the "last message from the Angel of the Sea."[90] What *is*, then, the experiential meaning of this psalm? "The heavens declare the glory of God." But what is meant by "heavens"? Ruskin concludes, substantially as he had in the chapter entitled "The Firmament" in volume 4, that the term "the heavens," used plurally by the sacred writers, "stood naturally for the entire system of cloud, and of space beyond it, conceived by them as a vault set with stars." But by "the firmament" and *heaven* used in the singular they meant "the system of clouds as spreading the power of water over the earth."[91] This meaning is revealed by the constant use of such expressions as "the rain of heaven" or "the dew of heaven." *Heavens,* then, stands "for the great vault or void, with all its planets, and stars, and ceaseless march of orbs innumerable," which the great Greeks had truly called "the Rolling"; *firmament*, "for the ordinance of the clouds."[92]

While the heavens express "the *glory* of God," His light, stability and infinity, "the firmament," on the other hand, "sheweth His *handywork*"; that is, veiling his infinite and eternal light they reveal his "daily handiwork." Thus the biblical mythic sky as Ruskin interprets it has two modes of meaning, "two divisions of declaration": abstract and relational. "The heavens . . . declare the eternal glory of God *before* men, and the firmament the daily mercy of God *towards* men."[93] This is the deeper meaning of the idea of clouds as a veil of intermediate being, signing the eternal motion of the heavens "with a semblance of human vicissitude," the general idea with which the section on clouds opened. But Ruskin makes this relational message of the clouds clearer.

The heavenly dichotomy of the psalm is broken down in Ruskin's reading into three primary aspects of spiritual opposition in the matter of human obedience to divine law. First, "Between law and commandment." Where law is fixed, unitary, and eternal; commandment is particular, relational, and existential, "given momentarily to each man, according to the need." Clouds symbolize the transient existential mystery of personal commandment against the light of universal, supratemporal law. "The Law is, 'Do this always'; the commandment 'Do *thou* this *now*': often mysterious enough, and through the cloud; chilling, and with strange rain of tears; yet always pure (the law converting, but the commandment cleansing)." There is spiritual opposition also "Between testimony and fear." Testimony, the true eternal promise of salvation, is bright as the sun and beyond all cloud, the focus of all wisdom; but the fear of God is now given and now withdrawn like the interposition of earth-cloud; yet this fear cleans, purges, and casts out all other fears. The third opposition is "Between statute and judgment." The statutes of eternal justice are essential, fixed as the stars in their courses, but the judgments are particular, existential; "the judgments are special judgments of given acts of men," as sudden and mysterious as the darting flight of the angel of the sea.[94]

CHAPTER 9

That Old Greek Question

Having concluded his remarks on form and meaning in the clouds, Ruskin had, by his own account, completed two of the three major divisions of *Modern Painters*. He had, in the first division of his subject, shown "how far art may be, and has been, consistent with physical or material facts," and in the second had "examined how far [art] may be and has been obedient to the laws of physical beauty." In reality, of course, he had not dealt conclusively with facts, laws, or even with works, considered objectively; rather he had generally dealt with his own experience, objectified, of natural forms (in and out of art) as cyphers of a purposive unity in things. He had readily accepted the truth of myth because it validated his own experience of nature. His experience, which was essentially Romantic "natural supernaturalism," though closely bound to the phenomenology of organic form, had constantly verged on mythic and apocalyptic awareness. It was climaxed by personifying and revelational penetrations into the life of things. Therefore, it fused readily with the nature of myth as then understood, since this conception was itself based on Romantic organicism and animism. But with new insight into the teaching of nature conveyed by myth and the teaching of myth to be conveyed by art, he was now ready for the "most important" task of *Modern Painters*, which remained for the third division (parts 8 and 9) of the work; this was "to consider the relations of art to God and man: its work in the help of human beings, and service of their Creator."[1]

Ruskin correctly calls what is to come the most important task of *Modern Painters*. Clearly, if the first two sections had dealt, as he thought, with what *is* in nature, with material facts and laws, this final section must now consider what those facts and laws *mean*. Nor could this section be written in mere obedience to the aesthetic category "Ideas of Relation" vaguely announced in the first volume as having to do with ideas conveyable by art "which are the subject of distinct intellectual perception."[2] Here he had been thinking particularly of historical or religious art's ability to relate narrative messages. His whole spiritual outlook had altered since then and with it his notion of what art has to communicate. The term *relation* now refers more deeply to the power of art to mediate, by form and symbol, between man's being and that of other forms. Art is to express man's "due relation" to other creatures, both animate and inanimate, in his lived-in world, not to relate pious impressions of another life or of worlds without disorder, decay, or death.

On the other hand, this final section of *Modern Painters* is by no means discontinuous with what precedes it. We have just seen in his studies of leaves and clouds that Ruskin's own function as artist-critic has been relational, or mediational, between natural cyphers and human experience. The task he sees before him is apparently to cast this fluid activity into general truths about the responsibility of art to God and man. We have also seen, notably in his interpretation of the Medusa cloud, how myth has recently come to his aid in this relational function, because myths by their nature signify ideas of relation between the human soul and natural powers. There is reason to expect that this concluding section of the work will be, as it should be, a summation and consummation of the hermeneutic and myth-making tendency of his thought. We expect that some conclusive mediation of natural and human meaning (or being) will be attempted, probably by way of myth, and that Ruskin's own mediation will be focused through the art of Turner so that the painter's work will stand in light as the supreme prophetic or relational message of his age, and Turner will appear as the ultimate interpreter of the century's spiritual condition.

In taking up conclusively the social and spiritual functions of art as he now sees them, Ruskin also forms an important bridge in his interests, bearing him in mid career from primarily aesthetic to primarily social and prophetic concerns. This section formulates the aesthetic of his new Greek-based "religion of Humanity." At the very center of his thought is the organic "Law of Help," re-enunciated here following the first brief formulation of it in the earlier chapter called "The Leaf Monuments"; however, the idea is now so universalized that it becomes virtually the myth of help in his work. I say myth because the organic concept first personified in leaf-being now becomes his controlling and essentially religious image for the meaning of life in nature, art, and society. It is a myth of redemption.

Myth, as the awareness of presences and as symbols in certain Greek myths, is vital to Ruskin's thought at this juncture. For myth, to him, is the reverent attribution of a conscious and moral life to things, an assertion of the interdependence and inherent purposiveness of natural forms. All myths, again, are symbols of relation, in the sense with which he is now concerned. Art, society, and myth have a common basis in the idea of living form; all can be read as life metaphors. In each mode, however, vital-lethal conflicts are detectable, and in each the meaning of this conflict is the same: any violation of the law of help, of coherence or consistency, is corruption and death. The opposite of help and harmony is death. With his own focal meaning, or personal myth, clearly seen, Ruskin is better able to integrate certain Greek sky myths with his own than he had been in working out cloud-myth interpretations. He will even be able to integrate the strange symbolism of the dissolving of the Medusa cloud in blood which he had simply alluded to in the cloud section. But the great relational meaning of the law of help and its opposite, that of competition, he finds most fully declared to us in two solar myths, the conflict of Apollo with Python and that of Hercules with the Hesperidian dragon Ladon; both represent heroes of purity opposing modes of pollution.

His choice of two solar myths for their archetypal expression of the nineteenth century's spiritual crisis (the assumption of the dragon signifying the ascendency of materialistic competition over the organic law of help) is compatible with the contemporary prestige of solar mythology stemming from the influential solar interpretations of Max Müller. More important, however, is the deep coherence of these solarist interpretations with Ruskin's own long-standing interest (one that he shared with Turner) in light and sky effects, particularly in apocalyptic sunsets. By bringing together in a complex way the law of help, two solar myths of conflict as interpreted by himself and Turner, and Turnerian sunset light, Ruskin is able to accomplish his conclusive critical apotheosis of Turner as the great master of spiritual invention in modern art, who expressed in myth and light the soul crisis of modern times, life as help against wealth as competition. In this chapter I shall follow him more closely as he develops and interprets the ideas, relationships, and symbols just touched on and give these materials, very briefly, their setting in contemporary mythological theory.

1

Showing the penchant for classification that opposes his interests in particularity and uniqueness, Ruskin opens the subject of relation in art by dividing it into two subtopics: "material or formal invention" to be dealt with in part 8 and "expressional or spiritual invention" to be taken up in the ninth and last division of *Modern Painters*. In this division the hopelessly ambiguous term *relation* is effectively abandoned as an operative term in favor of *invention*, which in turn comes to mean structural composition or arrangement in the first section and imagination or vision in the second. The general topic "Invention Formal" (composition or arrangement) is itself subclassified into four topics, each devoted to a supposed law of composition. These laws, each given a chapter, are called "The Law of Help," "The Task of the Least," "The Rule of the Greatest," and "The Law of Perfectness." In fact, however, only one principle is set forth, that of a vital or organic harmony.

He begins his discussion of formal invention rather defensively by explaining that, although he is often accused of neglecting the structural factor in pictures, it is this very element that actually gives him the greatest delight in them. He has slighted composition in earlier discussions only because he considered the subject "too great and wonderful" for him to deal with; yet he rejoices in it, and it is clear to him that "expression, sentiment, truth to nature are essential: *but all these are not enough.*"[3] Does this mean, then, that there has been a deep inconsistency in his thought all along over this matter of form? Is he about to retract his earlier repudiation of Renaissance formalism and urge us now to judge pictures by their obedience to rules of composition? Quite the opposite, he insists. "Every great work stands alone." It is composed as only the particular being who made it could have composed it. His gift of arrangement is a law unto itself, it appears; or else we are to understand that every great composition is an autonomous structure with its own self-regulating principles. Ruskin is ambiguous here; while it is plain that, in his view, there are no rules of composition that can be successfully imposed from without (he calls this composition by rule "false composition"); "Yet there are certain elementary laws of arrangement traceable a little way."[4] So he will now set himself to consider what meaning the idea of technical composition ought to have in his scheme of things.

"Composition," he explains, "may be best defined as the help of everything in the picture by everything else." This is essentially aesthetic organicism. Parts of so-called inanimate or inorganic forms do cohere with each other, he notes, but they do not *help* each other in such a way that the removal of any element injures the rest. Whenever any part of a plant or animal enters into the "helpless" state, we call that part "dead." And "the power which causes the several portions of the plant to help each other, we call life." Life is help, then; "intensity of life is also intensity of helpfulness";[5] when help ceases we call it corruption, and the loss by corruption, Ruskin believes, is dreadful in proportion to the intensity or perfection of the help.

He does perceive, however, that inanimate substances are not always mere aggregates of lesser parts; they have structural laws equivalent to that of help which may cause the elements of inorganic structure to be consistent with each other. In inorganic matter the equivalent of life or help is "consistence." "Thus the parts of a crystal are consistent, but of dust, inconsistent."[6] Yet Ruskin has no real wish to distinguish here between animate and inanimate modes of being, and they are eventually joined in a single moral idea: life or help is purity and sacredness in everything. Matter that is either consistent or living, he continues, we think of as being either pure or clean; thus both life and consistency express the same moral characteristic: helpfulness. Whatever lives is helpful, holy. Stain, pollution, taint, corruption, decay are all cyphers of the same mode of evil: competition or inconsistency of parts. A mythical, or at least religious, element has entered Ruskin's concept of help. Whatever lives, or is consistent, is composed of helpful parts; the sacredness of help, evident in life, is sustained by scripture, where holy often means helpful. "You will find," he suggests, "a wonderful clearness come into many texts by reading, habitually, 'helpful' and 'helpfulness' for 'holy' and 'holiness' or else 'living,' as in Rom. xi. 16."[7] The "Holy One" is then the "Helpful One," the "Lord of Life," as is the sun. And the Devil, it follows, is the defiler, polluter, corrupter, Lord of Death, whose laws are inconsistency and competition among parts.

With these ideas we have arrived at something like the transept of Ruskin's thought, from which as much of his "total view" of things as we are likely to have at any one point becomes visible, though in fact his thought is not a fixed structure that one might enter fully at this point but a processional experience of meaning to be recovered. "A pure or holy state of anything," he continues, reformulating as a general law an observation he had made about leaf communities, "is that in which all its parts are helpful or consistent. They may or may not be homogeneous. The highest or organic purities are composed of many elements in an entirely helpful state. The highest and first law of the universe—and the other name of life is, therefore, 'help.' The other name of death is 'separation.' Government and cooperation are in all things and eternally the laws of life. Anarchy and competition, eternally, and in all things, the laws of death."[8]

In "help," the "highest and first law of the universe," Ruskin has come at a global and systemic view of the major aspects of his experience. He has found a principle that appears to underlie everything that lives or expresses life, from composition in a great painting to the perfect organization of imperfect forms in the Gothic building, from creative societies to the natural environment as a system of systems. "Consistence" links organicism to "purity" as vital energy (light) and spotlessness. But in the life principle of "help" he has also perceived its lethal antithesis: competition.

The concept of "help" also serves well as the first principle of that Greek-tragic religion of Humanity that, according to Ruskin's own account, had replaced his evangelical Protestantism between 1858 and 1874. "Help," like Carlyle's "work," (or our "care") belongs to this world, is the redemptive imperative of life *here* and is not directed by the promise of another life. First discussed in reference to leaf builders, the law of help derives from the direct perception of the existential forms of the life-world; it is a principle at work deep down in things themselves, not a precept whispered by the infinite.

But, though not derived from other worldly or transcendental perspectives, Ruskin's "help" is ethical and mythical in its implications. He can apply its ethic of purity, judging degrees of supportive interaction of parts, to a range of entities from a handful of dust to the highest work of art, from tree twigs to social systems. Its mythic, or at least sacred, implications Ruskin himself suggests by equating the helpful with the holy, the Holy One with the Helpful One. We will take note shortly of the symbolic use he makes of the Greek solar Apollo in this connection as lord of purity, harmony, and life; the source of "help" whose cosmic antagonist is Python the corrupter. More deeply, "help" is simply conceived mythically as the animating, synthesizing, and purposive power in things, the "forming power" operating everywhere in nature.

The obvious human analogue of this vital power is the synthetic capacity of the artistic imagination or invention that, like Coleridge's "esemplastic power," gives the law of life or help to what it conceives.[9] This, of course, is Ruskin's proper subject at this point in the volume and he will return to it. Less obvious, but crucial as a bridge to his later thought, is the analogous working of the law of help in social systems as "government and cooperation" against "anarchy and competition," laws of social life against those of social death. Much remained to be defined in this direction, yet Ruskin noted later on that the passage just quoted summed up his principles of political economy. Most important, however, is his clear belief that he was pointing very simply to a sacred, self-purifying principle at work in things, a principle whose operation is detectable at the most elemental level, an ethic of the dust in fact. This law, he continues, discloses itself in the "instinct for unity" that must operate, say, even in the polluted and heterogeneous materials that are trodden underfoot in the roads of a modern industrial town;

"take merely," he observes, "an ounce or two of the blackest slime of a beaten footpath on a rainy day, near a large manufacturing town."[10]

We could not have a more "absolute type of impurity" than this manufacturing mud or slime, composed of clay or brick dust mixed with soot, sand, and water. "All these elements are at helpless war with each other, and destroy reciprocally each other's nature and power, competing and fighting for place at every tread of your foot;—sand squeezing out clay, and clay squeezing out water, and soot meddling everywhere and defiling the whole." Yet if we will leave these materials peace enough and time, each will follow its own self-purifying "instinct of unity," the clay becoming first white earth and ultimately sapphire. The sand "also becomes, first, a white earth, then proceeds to grow clear and hard, and at last arranges itself in mysterious, infinitely fine, parallel lines, which have the power of reflecting not merely the blue rays, but the blue, green, purple, and red rays in the greatest beauty in which they can be seen through any hard material whatsoever. We call it then an opal." Most miraculous, of course, is the consummation of the soot. "It cannot make itself white at first, but instead of being discouraged, tries harder and harder, and comes out clear at last, and the hardest thing in the world; and for the blackness that it had, obtains in exchange the power of reflecting all the rays of the sun at once in the vividest blaze that any solid thing can shoot. We call it then a diamond." And then the water, finally, is imagined taking its form of most perfect consistence, the snow crystal. The sum meaning of this apocalyptic transformation of the dust is a lesson for us in aesthetics, environmental ethics, and social economics: "for the ounce of slime which we had by political economy of competition, we have by political economy of cooperation, a sapphire, an opal, and a diamond, set in the midst of a star of snow."[11] The importance, to Ruskin, of this illustration of the instinct for purity and unity in the dust is suggested by the fact that he takes it up again later in *The Ethics of the Dust* and the *Lectures on Architecture and Painting*.

At this point, however, the crystallization example serves to illustrate by analogy his definition of an aesthetic "invention" as "an arrangement, in which everything in the work is thus consistent with all things else, and helpful to all else." But there are at least two important distinctions to be made. First, the art work is conceived more nearly on the organic than on the crystalline model; the parts of a great work are not so much consistent as helpful, for "in a true composition, if one [element] be taken away, all the rest are helpless and valueless." The composition dies, in effect. Further, "in true composition, everything not only helps everything else a *little*, but helps with its utmost power. Every atom is in full energy; and *all* that energy is kind."[12]

A second difficulty in his analogy, is that, in speaking of purity in natural forms, he seemed content to speak of the "instinct of unity," of help, as if it were a quality of the things themselves, a view somewhat qualified by his mythic identification of the Holy One as the Helpful One. In turning to art, however, his attention is ambivalently divided between ideas of invention as a quality of the art work and as a quality of the creating mind. Inventive power, that of creating totally helpful or vital arrangements of parts, is, we are told, an inexplicable, even unconscious power. His language comes close to suggesting that in true invention a higher power uses the artist's mind as its vehicle.

Invention "is not only the highest quality of art, but is simply the most wonderful act or power of humanity. It is pre-eminently the deed of human creation; ποίησις, otherwise poetry."[13] But what is a deed? What is creation? If an act is to be a true deed, Ruskin continues, the effect of it must be foreseen, and such an act cannot be performed "but by a person who knows, and in his deed obeys, the laws of the universe, and of its Maker." The true doer or maker is a believer, then, and in his faith obeys the laws of cosmic composition; he is at the same time a seer and a knower. And the creator? From the model of primal creation we perceive that to create anything is to give it life, inherent help. "A poet, or creator, is therefore a person who puts things together, not as a watchmaker steel, or a shoemaker leather, but who puts life into them." His act "is the gathering and arranging of material by imagination, so as to have in it at last the harmony or helpfulness of life, and the passion or emotion of life. Mere fitting and adjusting of material is nothing; that is watchmaking."[14]

Of course the actual nature of this creative act, assuming we are not to consider the creator as the mere vehicle of the universal laws of help, still remains hidden in the terms "imagination" and "harmony." The mode of imagination referred to here, Ruskin suggests, is essentially that inexplicable associative imagination he had attempted to describe in the second volume. The idea of "helpful and passionate harmony" he now characteristically ties to Greek etymology and myth. This harmony of life is "essentially choral harmony, so called from the Greek word 'rejoicing,' " and, he continues, falling into doubtful etymology, it belongs mythically to Apollo and the Muses, "the word Muse and Mother being derived from the same root, meaning 'passionate seeking,' or love, of which the issue is passionate finding, or sacred INVENTION."[15]

Such, then, is Ruskin's attempt to apply his general "Law of Help" to the creative act. True invention is totally helpful (mutually implicative) or organic arrangement; it is composition that has the harmony of life, a harmony that is the result only of love or passionate seeking. The assertion of this law, with its mythic implications and its integration of artistic composition with social and natural structures, is the most significant point in the whole section devoted to invention formal. But the chapter given to the law of help is complemented by three others in which Ruskin attempts to deal in a more practical and specific way with the coherence of texture, structure, and finish in painting.

In the second chapter, called "The Task of the Least," Ruskin insists, as would obviously follow from the law of help, that "the *minutest* portion of a great composition is helpful to the whole."[16] He then proceeds to describe closely two engravings of Turner's in order to demonstrate that the minor details of texture support, in each case, the "main motives" of the whole composition; that texture and structure are organically coherent, as it were. His readings of these engravings are affectionate and explicit, but they are hardly astute critical demonstrations of the law of help in composition. His avowed subject is *formal* coherence, but in discussing these engravings he drifts away from the question of form into emotional content; his position becomes essentially that, given the primary emotional meaning (main motive) of the work, every detail can be shown to be expressive also of that controlling mood. Of course the difficulties of the hermeneutic circle are apparent in this view: How can the mood of the whole be determined apart from that of the parts and vice versa? Ruskin is at least aware that he has been distracted from his "proper subject here, invention formal" into questions of emotive content; the reason for this drift, he notes, "is that the emotional power can be explained, but the perfection of formative arrangement . . . cannot be explained, any more than that of melody in music."[17]

In the following brief chapter, "The Rule of the Greatest," he considers the "nature and influence of magnitude" in compositions. Again he is drawn into the content as opposed to the structures of pictures. In fact, the central point of the chapter concerns no painting in particular, but rather a limiting characteristic of the intentional glance or characteristic awareness in painters of "the modern pathetic school," the Pre-Raphaelites, whom he had attacked in the fourth volume for their "duck-pond delineations" at the expense of nobler scenery.[18] He had noticed in the first and succeeding efforts of these painters "that they were almost destitute of the power of feeling vastness, or enjoying the forms which expressed it." They generally "fastened on confined, broken, and sharp forms; liking furze, fern, reeds, straw, stubble, dead leaves, and such like, better than strong stones, broad-flowing leaves, or rounded hills," and "missed the main and mighty lines" of such masses as they were forced to paint. These metaphoric choices imply a deep spiritual limitation in these moderns, a lack of feeling for global energies, large systems, or apocalyptic powers; their works betray "a petulant sympathy with local and immediately visible interests or sorrows, not regarding their large consequences, nor capable of understanding more massive view or more deeply deliberate mercifulness;—but peevish and horror-struck, and often incapable of self-control, though not of self-sacrifice."[19] We are, of course, a long way from the laws of formal invention here, and Ruskin merely surrenders the little chapter with the general principle that "the greatest treatment is always that which gives conception the widest range, and most harmonious guidance."[20]

The final chapter of the group on formal invention sets forth the "Law of Perfectness." This is simply that "partial conception is no conception," and follows directly from what has been said about the mental limitations of the Pre-Raphaelites. The painter must seize his entire picture in one unified imaginative act or he has lost all of it. He can not piece it together from separate partial truths of vision. But this total grasp, seeing the composition steadily and whole in the imagination, implies moral qualities in the artist that are "very strange and sublime," far beyond mere cleverness and dexterity. "It is only perfectness of mind, unity, depth, decision,—the highest qualities, in fine, of the intellect, which will form the imagination." Only a mind that is naturally calm, not resolved to be calm, can paint; only a mind that is itself whole and perfectly sincere can perceive the organic wholes that are true inventions; "no false person can paint."[21] Finally, invention that proceeds from such authenticity of self is rightly called "sacred," Ruskin insists; such invention, or "passionate seeking," finds and paints what *is*. It does not form, it finds, truths of being; it can find no lie. "False things may be imagined, and false things composed; but only truth can be invented."[22]

2

The heart of Ruskin's theory of formal, as opposed to spiritual, invention is, then, his "Law of Help." This comes near to being a doctrine of coherence as an aesthetic norm; however, his concept is based on organic forms in which it appears that the parts actively support the whole and are not simply arranged in passive conformity to some governing principle. Yet the "law of help" is not simply an organic metaphor drawn into art criticism; it is expressed in anthropopathic terms to convey its social and mythic implications. Help composes societies as well as tree twigs; *helpful* is another name for *holy*. Taking help as the law of life in all vital structures, Ruskin rejects as deadly all abstract laws of composition imposed by the schools. And the implicit personification of this concept, supported by such expressions as "The Task of the Least" and "The Role of the Greatest," indicates that he is using art theory again as a vehicle for his social and spiritual concerns; or it may be more accurate to say that Ruskin sought to define aesthetic composition, not as a system unto itself, but in terms of a universal law or myth of form.

With "Ideas of Relation: Second, Of Invention Spiritual," the last and, at moments, most distinctly apocalyptic, section of *Modern Painters*, Ruskin leaves the theory of composition and returns to the question of the sacred content of art, a subject more compatible with his genius. The main topic of this group of twelve chapters is "the moral of landscape"; it is a problem he had approached again and again in volume 3 and is one of the several most pervasive interests of his work. He will make another attempt here, as he had in the third volume and in *The Stones of Venice*, to study the secularization of Western art. But at this point his particular interest is to trace the degenerating relationship between the mythic and the mundane in landscape art in order to herald the redemptive appearance of Turner, whose genuinely mythic landscapes oppose the process by which landscape had lost its moral significance.

Again, as in the preceding sections of this volume and the closing chapters of the fourth, the increasingly urgent note of social concern can be heard, making these chapters resonant with a meaning broader than the aesthetic issues. But now the infusion of his new tragic humanism into the survey of the sacred history of landscape gives this section, of all the divisions of *Modern Painters*, the most moving prophetic and apocalyptic tone. I have already examined two chapters of this group, "The Dark Mirror" and "The Lance of Pallas," for their relation to his personal "religion of Humanity" and its sources in what he understood to be the Greek religion. We are now concerned with the function of these chapters within this section of the volume, their relation to its aesthetic, social, and spiritual message. Briefly, this message is that spiritual invention, like formal invention, must be existential, bound to the lived world of man, not to some imagined model. Spiritual invention has its own equivalent of the "law of help." Just as aesthetic composition projects help, the one law of organic and social form, so spiritual invention is a projection of the existential relation of spiritual powers to man, powers that are expressions of his living passions and hopes.

"The Dark Mirror," which opens this final part of *Modern Painters*, confronts the Why? of landscape painting. Since we are likely to receive religious lessons more willingly when they come directly from external nature, it is in fact, Ruskin agrees, a waste of effort "to draw landscape mere and solitary, however beautiful." Yet there *is* a kind of landscape that is worth drawing. A brief historical survey of the content of landscape reveals that "all true landscape . . . depends primarily for its interest on connection with humanity, or with spiritual powers,"[23] which may be thought of as symbolic projections of human powers and needs. Landscape is by its nature apocalyptic: "Fragrant tissue of flowers, golden circlets of clouds, are only fair when they meet the fondness of human thoughts, and glorify human visions of heaven." An emphasis on this truth, he asserts, "has been the distinctive character of all my own past work." Noting that the definitive character of a man's work is often the very point his critics deny him, Ruskin insists that his own past work has been distinctively humanist in emphasis: "In these books of mine, their distinctive character, as essays on art, is their bringing everything to root in *human passion or human hope*."[24]

He seems particularly anxious here, as he opens the discussion of spiritual invention, to repudiate the idea that his work has been neglectful of immediate human concerns. His writings, he affirms, have been "continually altered in shape, and even warped and broken, by digressions respecting social questions, which had for me an interest tenfold greater than the work I had been forced into undertaking."[25] He has traced each principle of painting he has set forth to its root in some "vital or spiritual fact"; and his writing on architecture, he points out, has been unique in discussing architectural styles in terms of their influence on the life of the workman. Now, in taking up spiritual invention, he presupposes that there is an "essential connection of the power of landscape with human emotion,"[26] though this connection may be slight or confined to a single point in the picture.

He illustrates the relation between man's being and nature by analogy: nature is to his being as dress is to the body; a relation, he says, that "may be carried out into the extremest parallelism." That the garment is worn by a figure, that nature is seen as the vesture of human existence, makes all the difference in our perception of it. (And, of course, the fact that Ruskin speaks of nature as a human rather than divine garment suggests the change in religion he has undergone.) Consider, he suggests, drapery in Tintoretto's *The Crucifixion* as an illustration of this analogy. In this painting one of the swooning Marys has thrown her mantle over her head so that her face is hidden in its shade, and the whole of her figure is shrouded in folds of gray. But what a difference there is "between that gray woof, that gathers round her as she falls, and the same folds cast in a heap upon the ground"; just such a difference "exists between the power of Nature through which humanity is seen, and her power in the desert." For a true desert "is not in the want of leaves, but of life." Where human being, is not, the tissue of nature is "as an embroidered shroud hiding a skeleton."[27] Man's being, then, is the true life and light of landscape. This view is partly consistent with his notion of clouds and vegetation as veils of intermediate being. The subject of landscape art is not, for Ruskin, neutral nature but mythic nature, nature perceived as the physical and spiritual "there" of man, as a unity of interdependent zones of being.

Men have been liable, he continues, to two extremes of error with respect to this interdependence of human being and nature. They have cared for man only and little or nothing for the universe, which was the tendency of the Greeks and Florentines; or they have cared for the physical universe only and little for the human presence, which is the tendency of the modern scientific world view and of the art that shares that view. But the power of any landscapist will depend ultimately on his perception of the interacting influences of the human presence and nature. "If he has to paint the desert, its awfulness . . . will arise simply and only from his sensibility to the story of life." Without this knowledge "he is nothing but a scientific mechanist."[28]

Landscape is dead, then, unless it is illuminated by the "true presence of sympathy with the spirit of man." This might be called his spiritual law of help in landscape art; or one might think of it as Ruskin's new "religion of Humanity" expressed as an aesthetic tenet. We have humanity and nature interfused, but what of deity? Will the landscape not reveal spiritual presence or presences higher than humanity, those true pathetic fallacies of passion and piety spoken of in volume 3? His answer at this point is that deity is revealed to us only through the "Dark Mirror" of humanity; without this sympathy with the human condition, "sympathy with any higher spirit is impossible."[29]

The mythical support for this view is in Genesis; the words "In His own image. After His likeness" contain a truth that is "at the foundation of our knowledge both of God and man."[30] (Here we have passed beyond landscape to inscape, of course.) What, Ruskin asks, is the plain meaning of this verse? It cannot be supposed that man resembles the Deity in his bodily shape. The resemblance must be in the soul and still there, unchanged, for death only was our punishment, not change. The divine image is still there; defiled, broken, all but effaced but essentially unaltered. Of course the soul may be conceived as having pure and impure, heavenly and earthly, states; yet "the soul of man is still a mirror, wherein may be seen, darkly, the image of the mind of God."[31] Though these are "daring words" he reiterates them: the soul of man is a "true mirror" and the only means by which we may know the Deity.

But what of those who say God is known by "revelation" only, not by inward looking? Consider, he argues, *to* what and *by* what the revelation is. Revelation can be only *to* a mind that is capable of receiving truth, and insofar as it possesses this capability it is already an image of the divine mind. Further, if revelation is by sight, it is only to eyes that see justly and are therefore an image of God's sight; and if the revelation is *by* words like "God is love" or "God is just" it is only to souls that already discern the nature of love and justice and are therefore already reflectors of God's powers. Hence the true precept "know thyself; for through thyself only can'st thou know God." In the "flesh-bound volume" of the soul "is the only revelation that is, that was, or that can be."[32]

And now, with a change of image, we come to the powerful peroration of the chapter, a passage that may be the most remembered of Ruskin's words. "*Through* the glass, darkly. But, except *through* the glass, in no wise."[33] The metaphor is problematic. The biblical "*in* a mirror, darkly," which he has taken to mean the human soul, our only image of deity, is shifted now so as to place the soul in nature and it becomes now a glass seen "through." This is not the ordinary silvered looking glass but a deep and fluid glass backed by earth and taking in the sky. "A tremulous crystal, waved as water, poured out upon the ground;—you may defile it, despise it, pollute it, at your pleasure and at your peril; for on the peace of those weak waves must all the heaven you shall ever gain be first seen; and through such purity as you can win for those dark waves, must all the light of the risen Sun of Righteousness be bent down, by faint refraction." Through or in the tremulous and corruptible living glass of his soul, then, man must see all he is to see here of divinity or heaven. But this glass has yet another function which is to transmit or reflect the holy light of life to nature. To clarify this Ruskin shifts, in his concluding paragraph, to a solar metaphor. "Therefore it is that all the power of nature depends on subjection to the human soul. Man is the sun of the world; more than the real sun. The fire of his wonderful heart is the only light and heat worth gauge or measure. Where he is, are the tropics; where he is not, the ice world."[34]

Ruskin examines the meaning of this assertion at the outset of his second chapter, "The Lance of Pallas." I have already discussed portions of this key chapter in connection with his personal religious development; we have now to consider it in its argumentative context. He begins by considering the apparent inconsistency between the near narcissism of what he has just said and the repeated assertion in his earlier work that all great art expresses man's delight in God's work not in his own. His present view is that man alienated from himself, whether through asceticism or scientism, cannot rejoice in God's work. For man "cannot, in a right state of thought, take delight in anything else, otherwise than through himself."[35] He cannot rightly perceive the power of creation unless through the best of it—himself. Man is the "sun of creation" as he perceives himself as the culmination of its law of help. However, he is merely the "light of creation," not *the* creation. Only if he perceives *through* himself his due relation to the rest of creation, animate and inanimate, does he become the light and life of it; otherwise he is "a sun in space—a fiery ball, spotted with storm."[36]

All the most destructive diseases of modern minds stem from the isolation, or alienation, as we would say, of man from the "there" of his being. "They are the concentration of man upon himself, whether his heavenly interests or his worldly interests matters not; it is the being *his own* interests which makes the regard of them so mortal."[37] Asceticism, or isolation of soul, and sensualism, or isolation of body, are each modes of the same error. But healthy individuals or nations can exist only in the "unselfish presence of the human spirit everywhere, energizing over all things; speaking and living through all things." All man's best art speaks of himself as "the soul of things, and ruler of creatures"; that art is in error which denies either man's animal or his spiritual nature. The so-called Christian art, which (following Lindsay and Rio) he had admired in the second volume, he now sees as having been weakened by pride through its denial of the animal nature of man. By looking always toward another world it wasted its strength in visions and so was easily swept away by the "naturalist art" of the sixteenth century. However, this new art erred ultimately by denying man's spiritual nature and so "perished in corruption." But Ruskin sees a "contemplative reaction" taking place in his own time from which, he hopes, a new spiritual art will develop; hence his concern to define the true nature of spiritual invention.[38]

The immediate question is what, considering these "Christian" and

"Naturalist" polarities of error, are the signs of an art, particularly a
landscape art, that is properly suffused with the human presence? How
is nature, since landscape is the preeminent modern genre, to be depicted
as the physical and spiritual "there" of man? Ruskin has already given
his answer in the chapter "Mountain Gloom" in volume 4, but it is
developed again here as a criticism of the Christian "landscape." (His
ulterior subjects are the Evangelical mythology and the crisis of faith
through which he was passing.) There is no true Christian school of
landscape, because in this art landscape is always subordinated to the
conception of saintly or divine presence. Such feeble landscape
conventions as existed were merely decorations or types rather than
attempts to paint true relations between man and nature.

Moreover, such Christian art can never constitute "a real school," it
cannot be existentially real, "because its first assumption is false,
namely, that the natural world can be represented without the element of
death." Indeed, it seems generally to have been true of art, Ruskin
continues, "that when the immortality of the soul was practically and
completely believed, the elements of decay, danger, and grief in visible
things were always disregarded." To the painters of the early Christian
or "Purist" schools, as described in volume 2 of *Modern Painters*, "ideas
of danger or decay seem not merely repugnant, but inconceivable to
them;" they can express only ideas of "immortality and perpetuity."[39]
They take note of the fact of corruption, but "this external fact of
corruption is separated in their minds from the main conditions of their
work"; these facts appeared to be irrelevant to the essential dealings of
the Diety with his creation. To these painters, "death, pain, and decay
were simply momentary accidents in the course of immortality, which
never ought to exercise any depressing influence over the hearts of men,
or in the life of Nature."[40]

This state of religious distraction is not simply a mental phenomenon
confined historically to the "Purist epoch." It is also a frequent condition of the modern mind, a characteristic of "persons whom either
narrowness of circumstance or education, or vigorous moral efforts,
have guarded from the troubling of the world, so as to give them a firm
and childlike trust in the power and presence of God, together with
peace of conscience, and a belief in the passing of all evil into some form
of good." Persons so disciplined (like his own mother), the purists,
medieval or modern, are unable to feel "in any of its more acute phases,
the sorrow for any phenomena of nature, or terror in any material
danger which would occur to another."[41] This absence of direct sympathy with the lived-in world and consequent loss of the sense of oneness

with nature and humanity explains, for Ruskin, the apparent fact that no painting or literature of the highest kind has ever been produced "by minds in the pure religious temper." In fact such religious purism constitutes, in his view, a misuse of faith.

As Ruskin moves forward now to consider the proper relation between faith and being-in-the-world, he has drifted far from his avowed subject of spiritual invention in landscape. Yet this digression can be viewed as a necessary expression of his own religious crisis together with the urgent pull of social concern in him. The aesthetic discussion reflects, or becomes the vehicle of, the conflict then coming into focus in his life, of two partially antagonistic "myths of concern" (in Frye's terminology),[42] the Christian Puritan and the socialist-humanitarian. There has been no great purist art, he continues, because "the right faith of man is not intended to give him repose, but to enable him to do his work." Man's faith is not intended to direct his attention away from the lived world toward another, but to enable him to "look stoutly into this world, in faith that if he does his work thoroughly here, some good to others or himself, with which however he is not at present concerned, will come of it hereafter." Such a "brave, but not very hopeful or cheerful faith" is "always rewarded by clear practical success and splendid intellectual power; while the faith which dwells on the future fades away into rosy mist, and emptiness of musical air."[43]

3

True greatness in landscape, therefore, depends upon the expression in it of nature as the place of man's being: his labor, passion, and death. The only manifestation of heaven is through the human spirit; but this is ideally the heroic spirit confronting the pain and corruption, the "deep colours," of earth. For "all great and beautiful work has come of first gazing without shrinking into darkness," as Ruskin perceives he must now do at this turning point in his work. But if, having faced this way, "the human spirit can, by its courage and faith, conquer the evil, it rises to conceptions of victorious and consummated beauty." Such is the spirit of the greatest Greek and Venetian art. If the spirit is unable to conquer evil yet remains "in strong though melancholy war with it, not rising into supreme beauty," we have the spiritual condition of the best Northern art, represented by Holbein and Dürer. However, if the spirit is conquered by evil, is "infected by the dragon breath of it," so that it takes delight in evil forever, we have at best the "spirit of the dark, but still powerful sensualistic art, represented by Salvator."[44] Ruskin has now to give evidence for the pattern of degeneration he has sketched by constructing a moral, a mythic, history of art. He will examine the concerns implicit in Greek, Venetian, Düreresque, and later art to show ultimately that the decline of art came from ignoring the facts of evil and seeking to give aesthetic pleasure only.

Turning first to Greek art, his thesis is that "the ruling purpose of Greek poetry is the assertion of victory, by heroism, over fate, sin, and death."[45] This victory he believes to be typified by the "Homeric temper," which is tender, practical, and cheerful by comparison with that of the tragedians, and "bent chiefly on present things and giving victory now, and here, rather than hope in the hereafter."[46] The enemies of man are "more distinctly conquerable" in Homer than in the tragic writers; these enemies are "ungoverned passions, especially anger, and unreasonable impulse generally (ἀτή)." The "wild powers and mysteries of Nature"[47] are also, in Homer, among the enemies of man; so that "all the labours of Ulysses are expression of the contest of manhood, not only with its own passions or with the folly of others, but with the merciless and mysterious powers of the natural world."[48]

Whatever the enemy, inner or outer, "the Greeks never shrink from horror; down to its uttermost depth, to its most appalling physical detail, they strive to sound the secrets of sorrow."[49] Ruskin, as we noted earlier, appears to be expressing in the guise of this insubstantial analysis of Greek belief the "trial hour" of his own faith, his personal awakening to the inherent danger of Christian belief in futurity with its consequent disbelief in the human here and now. For the Greeks, meaning ourselves, "neither apathy nor blindness shall be their saviour; if, for them, thus knowing the facts of grief of earth, any hope, relief, or triumph may hereafter seem possible,—well; but if not, still hopeless, reliefless, eternal, the sorrow shall be met face to face."[50] It is in this context that he cites the paradoxical mythic incident that gives the chapter its focus and title. We have already discussed this passage at some length in attempting to explain what Ruskin meant by his personal "religion of Humanity." Here he uses the mythic action of Hector's being slain by the lance of Pallas as a "paradigmatic action," in Mircea Eliade's phrase,[51] to express the "highly ambiguous" nature of existence. Athena in the form of his brother Deiphobus betrays the heroic Hector in his mortal need.

Ruskin sees in this mythic event something nearly as desolating as our sense of absurdity. "We trusted in the gods;—we thought that wisdom and courage would save us. Our wisdom and courage themselves deceive us to our death." We Greeks have the certainty only of our mortality and the question it poses. "Beyond that mortality, what hope have we?

Nothing is clear to us on that horizon, nor comforting. Funeral honors; perhaps also rest; perhaps a shadowy life—artless, joyless, loveless. No devices in that darkness of the grave, nor daring, nor delight."[52] Though Athena, our wisdom, and all the powers of nature or of our own that we project, may betray us; yet "we will be men while we may," though certain only of our humanity. "While we live, we will hold fast to our integrity; no weak tears shall blind, no untimely tremors abate our strength of arm nor swiftness of limb."[53]

In the Greek's rejection of the "better reward" or "higher hope" beyond the natural world there was nonetheless a conquest of that world. "So defied, the betraying and accusing shadows shrank back; the mysterious horror subdued itself to majestic sorrow. Death was swallowed up in victory."[54] Having defied death and meaninglessness, for them nature was no longer filled with shadow and terror; they were able to respond to the beauty of earth and its powers became, as gods, their helpmates. "All nature round them became divine,—one harmony of power and peace. The sun hurt them not by day, nor the moon by night; the earth opened no more her jaws into the pit; the sea whitened no more against them the teeth of his devouring waves. Sun, and moon, and earth, and sea,—all melted into grace and love; the fatal arrows rang not now at the shoulders of Apollo, the healer; lord of life, and of the three great spirits of life—Care, Memory and Melody."[55] So, in Ruskin's fanciful interpretation of Greek belief, the law of help, anthropomorphized, could rule the earth for those who rejected both the hope and the dread of futurity.

He spends most of his chapter in the effort to convey the "heroic spirit" of the Greek religion and the "trial hour" through which that faith had to pass in order to become an existential polytheism, a religion of man in nature, in which the Greeks found their courage to be. He elucidates the Greek faith at length because, as we have seen, this allowed him to express in a veiled way his own spiritual crisis and new "religion of Humanity." However, perhaps for the same reason, he has few specific things to say about his avowed subject, Greek art. This is a defect he would remedy to some extent a decade later in his Oxford lectures. At this point he offers us simply the generalization that "all the nobleness, as well as the faults, of the Greek art were dependent on its making the most of this present life." Despite the mythic basis of that art, "its dominion was in this world."[56]

Having characterized Greek art in this general way as worldly, heroic, and naturalistic, Ruskin is now ready to extend his spiritual history of Western art to the Florentines and Venetians, using the Greek spirit as a ground for contrast. In "The Wings of the Lion," the third chapter of this section, the Florentine art he had so much admired in the second volume is now quickly dismissed as "essentially Christian, ascetic, expectant of a better world, and antagonistic, therefore, to the Greek temper." His present view that Greek art, eventually forced on the Florentine, destroyed it because of its "absolute incompatability" with the ascetic mode, would be modified in his later thought to see certain Florentines, notably Botticelli, as true continuators of the pure Greek spirit. But here his interest is mainly in landscape, not in figures, and he concludes that Florentine painting could produce no landscape because it had no use for the living world. "It despised the rock, the tree, the vital air itself, aspiring to breathe the empyreal air."[57]

Venetian art, we learn, began under the same ascetic restraints as the Florentine, but these were washed away by magnitude, for the Venetian "had his free horizon, his salt breeze, and sandy Lido-shore; sloped far and flat,—ridged sometimes under the Tramontane winds with half a mile's breadth of rollers; sea and sand shriveled up together in one yellow careering field of fall and roar." Their sea of faith was broader, it appears, for the presence of such horizons, and both religious liberty and respect for the body-self derived from the Venetians' "wave training"; "for it is one notable effect of life passed on shipboard to destroy weak beliefs in appointed forms of religion."[58] Not only this but, in Ruskin's thesis, the vigilance demanded of the sailor was averse to all morbid introspection. "Reverie, above all things, is forbidden by Scylla and Charybdis. By the dogs and the depths, no dreaming! The first thing required of us is presence of mind."[59]

This necessity for vigilant attention to his physical surroundings and enforced respect for his bodily existence brought the Venetian into a temper comparable to the Greek. Yet his religious training worked against this. The Greek had confronted evil, thrust it aside, and thought of it thereafter only involuntarily. But the teaching of the medieval church made the contemplation and confession of evil a chief duty of man. Further, medieval man "had been taught a faith which put an end to restless questioning and discouragement." All was to be well in eternity, but "though suffering was to cease in heaven, it was to be not only endured, but honoured upon earth." Therefore, the Venetian was "in his inner mind, less serious than the Greek: in his superficial temper, sadder."[60] As with the Florentines, "this reference to a future world has a morbid influence on all their conclusions. For the earth and all its natural elements are despised. They are to pass away like a scroll."[61] Man, the immortal, is alone revered; his work and presence are all that

can be noble or desirable. But the worst fault Ruskin has to find with
Venetian landscape feeling is its pride. The Venetian had no interest in
the human abode, in field or farm, in birds, beasts, seasonal transfor-
mations or intricacies of foliage. "No simple joy was possible to him.
Only stateliness and power; high intercourse with kingly and beautiful
humanity, proud thoughts, or splendid pleasures, throned sensualities,
and ennobled appetites."[62]

His essential point is that the Venetians had no interest in landscape
that was particularized, intricate, or defined by humble human use.
Their landscape backgrounds are merely decorative and stereotypical;
"the customary Venetian background is without sign of laborious rural
life." The typical background consists of "mountainous land with wild
but graceful forest, and rolling or horizontal clouds." Yet this conventionalized "heroic" landscape "was peopled by spiritual beings of the
highest order." This ability to embody mythic figures was the vital core
of Venetian artistic power and was, in Ruskin's view, the result of two
seemingly antagonistic forces, their faith and their worldliness. Venetian Catholicism down to Tintoretto's time was, he supposes, entirely
"real and sincere." "They were the *last believing* school of Italy."[63]
Nonetheless, they took a delight in mortal flesh, glowing color, and the
pomp of power, which, to the uninitiated observer of their pictures,
looks like pure sensualism and religious hypocrisy.

To Ruskin, however, the Venetian religion was at once sincere and
worldly, and this gave the power of concreteness to the spiritual inventions of their art. By comparison, elsewhere in Italy "piety had become
abstract," otherworldly. Florentine and Umbrian painters "delighted in
imagining scenes of spiritual perfectness;—Paradises, and companies of
the redeemed at the judgment;—glorified meetings of martyrs;—
madonnas surrounded by circles of angels. If, which was rare, definite
portraitures of living men were introduced, these real characters formed
a kind of chorus or attendant company, taking no part in the action."[64]
With the Venetians, however, sacred figures are not abstract or conventionalized forms; they are given real bodies and are introduced into our
daily world. "They are on our own plain ground . . . our own friends
and respected acquaintances, with all their mortal faults, and in their
mortal flesh, looking at them face to face unalarmed: nay, our dearest
children playing with their pet dogs at Christ's very feet."[65] As with the
mythic figures in the Greek poetic landscapes he had discussed in
volume 3, the evidence of literal belief is the absence of emotional
distortion, pathetic fallacy, in the image. Ruskin's illustrative instances

at this point are Veronese's *Madonna and Child, with the Cuccina Family* and his *Solomon and the Queen of Sheba.* In both he points to the fusion of the sacred or mythic element with details drawn from mundane experience. "Throughout these designs," he concludes, "I want the reader to notice the purpose of representing things as they were likely to have occurred, down to trivial, or even ludicrous detail—the nobleness of all that was intended to be noble being so great that nothing could detract from it."[66] Though Veronese was capable of the utmost tragic power, his habitual preference, we learn, was for "sweet, every-day incident" with the deep tragic meaning hidden beneath it.[67]

Titian's *Magdalen* of the Pitti Palace, which Ruskin had called "the disgusting Magdalen" in volume 2, is now introduced in order to emphasize, by contrast with the lovely "received types of the Magdalen," the solid ordinariness of this sacred figure: "A stout, red-faced woman, dull, and coarse of feature, with much of the animal in even her expression of repentance—her eyes strained, and inflamed with weeping."[68] Ruskin takes Titian for the "central type" of the Venetian mind, a spirit "wholly realist, universal and manly." In this connection, however, he must account for two superficially profane aspects of Titian's work: his "alternation of . . . great religious pictures with others devoted wholly to the sensual qualities" and his "exulting and bright representation of heathen deities."[69] The first of these qualities he can explain by the view that Titian rightly had to see his Deity in the dark mirror of human being; for him "sensual passion in man was, not only a fact, but a Divine fact; the human creature, though the highest of animals, was, nevertheless, a perfect animal, and his happiness, health, and nobleness, depended on the due power of every animal passion, as well as the cultivation of every spiritual tendency. He thought that every feeling of the mind and heart, as well as every form of the body, deserved painting."[70] As for Titian's "fond introduction of the heathen gods," Ruskin has no convincing explanation; he can only conclude, inconsistently, that they are merely introduced symbolically and without heartfelt reverence, yet they are "always conceived with deep imaginative truth, much resembling Keats's conception."[71]

The ultimate question of the chapter is simply this: If the Venetian mind was "in its belief, its breadth, and its judgment . . . perfect," why did it perish so quickly? It had, Ruskin asserts, one deadly fault: "recklessness in aim."[72] The social uses to which the Venetians put their art were entirely unworthy of their creative capacities; their paintings were not made or used for moral enlightenment but for delight. "The

Venetian gave the most earnest faith, and the lordliest faculty, to gild the shadows of an antechamber, or heighten the splendours of a holiday."[73] The life of its art was destroyed by its wealth.

With the essential relations between myth and reality in Greek and Italian Renaissance art delineated for background, Ruskin is now ready for the third phase of his proposed survey: an examination of the spirit of Northern, especially Düreresque, art. Accordingly, the fourth chapter of this section, "Dürer and Salvator," opens with a summary of his developing argument. We have studied that art which, whether through heroic defiance (Greek) or sincere faith (Venetian), was able to conquer evil. In these styles, as opposed to Florentine purism, sacred invention appears in a real or worldly context, yet is dominant; they have not banished reality to assert faith or vice versa; however, "we have next to examine the art which cannot conquer the evil, but remains at war with, or in captivity to it."[74] The former condition is represented by Holbein and Dürer, the latter by Salvator Rosa.

Ruskin sees the Reformation as the spiritual watershed in European art; before it, faith dominated art; after it, doubt. Before the Reformation "it was possible for men even of the highest powers of intellect, to obtain a tranquillity of faith, in the highest degree favourable to the pursuit of any particular art."[75] For himself, he is "unable to understand how it was so," because such faith involved the belief in Papal infallability, and "the acceptance of the doctrine of eternal punishment as dependent on accident of birth, or momentary excitement of devotional feeling," and acquiescence to the "system which condemned guiltless persons to the loss of heaven because they lived before Christ." Nevertheless, he considers it an unquestionable fact that intelligent faith was possible before the Reformation and ended with it. "Thenceforward human life became a school of debate, troubled and fearful." Fifteen centuries of faith were called into question. This dark time for man he compares with the "trial-hour of the Greek," symbolized by Athena's betrayal of Hector, when "the heavens themselves seemed to have deceived those who had trusted in them."[76]

And now the fact of death, the specter of meaninglessness, which the Greeks had overcome with their heroic acceptance of the lived world and early Christians with their rejection of it, came to life again. "Then came the Resurrection of Death. Never since man first saw him face to face, had his terror been so great."[77] In their existential despair men reveled in the flesh, attempting to flee death in pleasure; so in this sense death became a new Dionysus; the dance of death became the new Dionysiac revel. In place of the Greek Pan-Athenaic Triumph, and the Christian Feast of the Jubilee, "there came up, through the fields of spring, the Dance of Death. The brood of weak men fled from the face of him. A new Bacchus and his crew this, with worm for snake and gall for wine."[78] In Ruskin's view only three artists looked steadily at this new Dionysiad of death to see what it meant: Holbein and Dürer in the North and Salvator in the South.

Therefore, in "Dürer and Salvator" he undertakes to characterize the lives and spiritual tempers of these two artists in order to show how their situations determined the differing answers they could give to the resurrected fact of death, that is, to the disintegration of the old unified mythic scheme of redemption. The milieus of Dürer and Salvator differed almost totally, Ruskin explains. Dürer, at Nuremberg, lived "amidst the formal delights, the tender religions, and practical science, of domestic life and honest commerce."[79] In his world "things were for the most part as they ought to be. Men did their work in his city and in the fields round it. The clergy were sincere. Great social questions unagitated; great social evils either non-existent, or seemingly a part of the nature of things, and inevitable."[80]

As a result of his life-world, which, in Ruskin's account, included the domestic life-patterns, the landscape, and even the rough but restrained and contented architecture of Nuremberg, Dürer's answer to death "was that of patient hope."[81] This answer was given twofold and conclusively in two great designs of his, the *Fortitude* or the *Knight and Death* and the *Melancholia*, which Ruskin takes to be "the history of the sorrowful toil of the earth, as the 'Knight and Death' is of its sorrowful patience under temptation."[82] He interprets the allegories of both works rather closely, and it is possible to give only suggestive elements of his reading here. The knight, first, as a symbol of fortitude,

> rides quietly, his bridle firm in his hand, and his lips set close in a slight sorrowful smile, for he hears what Death is saying; and hears it as the word of a messenger who brings pleasant tidings, thinking to bring evil ones. A little branch of delicate heath is twisted round his helmet. His horse trots proudly and straight; its head held high, and with a cluster of oak on the brow where on the fiend's brow is the sea-shell horn. But the horse of Death stoops its head; and its rein catches the little bell which hangs form the knight's horse-bridle, making it toll as a passing-bell.[83]

In the *Melancholia*, Ruskin observes, the labor symbolized is the ordinary daily work of men. "Not the inspired or gifted labour of the few (it is labor connected with the sciences, not with the arts), shown in its four chief functions: thoughtful, faithful, calculating, and executing."[84] Though he is certain about the general meaning of the symbolism, he is in doubt about "how far Dürer intended to show that labour, in many of its most earnest forms, is closely connected with the morbid sadness or 'dark anger' of the northern nations."[85] However, Melancholia's work is, clearly:

> thoughtful, first: all true power coming of that resolved, resistless calm of melancholy thought. This is the first and last message of the whole design. Faithful, the right arm of the spirit resting on the book. Calculating (chiefly in the sense of self-command), the compasses in her right hand. Executive—roughest instruments of labour at her feet: a crucible, and geometrical solids, indicating her work in the sciences. . . . In the distance a comet (the disorder and threatening of the universe) setting, the rainbow dominant over it. Her strong body is close girdled for work; at her waist hang the keys of wealth; but the coin is cast aside contemptuously under her feet. She has eagle's wings, and is crowned with fair leafage of spring.[86]

Dürer's mythic image of labor, Ruskin concludes, with a prophetic glance toward his own nation and Turner, is a noble answer to death but an imperfect one compared with the definitive answer of the knight, for "it was reserved for another country to prove, for another hand to portray, the labour which is crowned with fire, and has the wings of the bat."[87]

Salvator Rosa's world was antithetical to Dürer's and so also was his answer to death. Ruskin speaks of his youth at Naples, spent "amidst the pride of lascivious wealth, and the outlawed distress of impious poverty."[88] From this corrupt society he fled to the stark landscape of the Calabrian hills. Here, in one of the volume's more impressive virtuosic passages, Ruskin invokes that landscape apocalyptically from his own experience of it:

> Its forests are sombre-leaved, labyrinth-stemmed; the carubbe, the olive, laurel, and ilex, are alike in that strange feverish twisting of their branches, as if in spasms of half human pain:—Avernus forests; one fears to break their boughs, lest they should cry to us from the rents; the rocks they shade are of ashes, or thrice-molten lava; iron sponge whose every pore has been filled with fire. Silent villages, earthquake shaken, without commerce, without industry, without knowledge, without hope, gleam in white ruin from hillside to hillside; far-winding wrecks of immemorial walls surround the dust of cities long forsaken: the mountain streams moan through the cold arches of their foundations, green with weed, and rage over the heaps of their fallen towers. Far above, in thunder-blue serration, stand the eternal edges of the angry Apennine, dark with rolling impendence of volcanic cloud.[89]

Yet Salvator might have been "calmed and exalted" even by this landscape with its intimations of unredeemable evil (though Ruskin himself was not) had his early life conditioned him to such feelings. Instead his infected mind saw only the wasteland, "saw only what was gross and terrible,—the jagged peak, the splintered tree, the flowerless bank of grass, and wandering weed, prickly and pale." Receiving only signs of a malignant presence in nature, "his temper confirmed itself in evil, and became more and more fierce and morose; though not . . . cruel, ungenerous, or lascivious." Ruskin confesses that, of all the artists he has studied, Salvator gives him the most distinct impression of being a "lost spirit." Yet the violent morbidity of the painter's reaction to his experience convinces him that Salvator's was a mind "capable of pensiveness, of faith, and of fear." In the embittered works he sees vestiges of a mythic mind, "the last traces of spiritual life in the art of Europe." Salvator "was the last man to whom the thought of a spiritual existence presented itself as a conceivable reality. All succeeding men, however, powerful,—Rembrandt, Rubens, Vandyck, Reynolds—would have mocked at the idea of a spirit."[90]

Strangely, however, Ruskin interprets no particular painting for us in the way he strengthens his impressions of Dürer by explicit objective reference. This fact suggests that he may be projecting his own religious rage at that moment, his sense of betrayal by his inherited doctrines, into his Salvator Rosa: "The religion of the earth is a horror to him."[91] Without the consolations of a benign landscape, sincere religion, or a coherent society, Salvator's answer to absurdity is utterly opposed to Dürer's: "Desolation, without hope, throughout the fields of nature he had to explore; hypocrisy and sensuality, triumphant and shameless, in the cities from which he derived his support. His life, so far as any nobility remained in it, could only pass in horror, disdain, or despair."[92]

The last painter with any trace of the old faith in him, Salvator Rosa stands utterly apart from his contemporaries in Ruskin's scheme of the disappearance of the sacred in Western art. "The whole body of painters around him, but chiefly those of landscape, had cast aside all regard for the faith of their fathers, or for any other; and founded a school of art properly called 'classical.' " The definition and total repudiation of this school is the essential thrust of the fifth chapter of this section, "Claude and Poussin." Ruskin's hostility to the irreverent uses of myth in these painters reflects his own special sympathy with Greek belief at that moment and his deepening interest in the meaning of myth. The spiritual condition of these painters, characterized by hedonistic aestheticism, is described in this brisk and vitriolic passage:

> The belief in a supreme benevolent Being having ceased, and the sense of spiritual destitution fastening on the mind, together with the hopeless

perception of ruin and decay in the existing world, the imagination
sought to quit itself from the oppression of these ideas by realizing a
perfect worldly felicity, in which the inevitable ruin should at least be
lovely, and the necessarily short life entirely happy and refined. Labour
must be banished, since it was to be unrewarded. Humiliation and
degradation of body must be prevented, since there could be no compensa-
tion for them by preparation of the soul for another world. Let us eat and
drink (refinedly), for to-morrow we die, and attain the highest possible
dignity as men in this world, since we shall have none as spirits in the
next.[93]

The term *classical* is therefore charged with irony for Ruskin, since
that mentality is so antithetical to the Greek spirit as he has already
defined it. "Neither Claude nor Poussin," he continues, "nor any other
writer, properly termed 'classical,' ever could enter the Greek or Roman
heart, which was as full, in many cases fuller, of the hope of immortality
than our own." This despiritualized condition of the neoclassical universe had two important implications for the history of art. First, there
was the habit of looking to the self for both judgment and government.
Hence this school elevated taste and restraint to ideals of value and
became, in the first instance, a school of condescension. "As the school of
taste, everything is, in its estimation, beneath it, so as to be tasted or
tested; not above it, to be thankfully received." This attitude, in Ruskin's
view, "has destroyed art since the close of the sixteenth century, and
nearly destroyed French literature, our English literature being at the
same time severely depressed, and our education (except in bodily
strength) rendered nearly nugatory by it, so far as it affects commonplace
minds." No mind of the highest quality could ever succumb to this
spirit. Pope, he declares, is "the greatest man who ever fell strongly
under its influence; and though it spoiled half his work, he broke
through it continually into true enthusiasm and tender thought."[94] This
reference to enthusiasm and tenderness brings him to the second aspect
of the "classical" school's perverse influence: its emphasis on reserve or
restraint is such that "it refuses to allow itself any violent or 'spasmodic'
passion."[95] Although he thinks this contemporary critical term is
"ugly," he allows that it is quite accurate to express the spiritual pathos
characteristic of such "spasmodic" books as Solomon's Song, Job, or
Isaiah.

The codes of taste and restraint, restricting spiritual and emotional
expression, determined, in Ruskin's view, that neoclassical landscapes
would be sterile, devoid of both the mundane and sacred truths he
demands. Lacking the existential realities suggested by images of humble life and labor, the natural supernaturalism of wild landscape, or the

awe of dreadful presences, their landscapes are "representative of perfectly trained and civilized human life, associated with perfect natural scenery and with decorative spiritual powers."[96] Their world, though ornamented with minor mythic figures, is essentially demythologized; there are no apocalyptic implications; "ornamental gods, not governing gods" appear, "for the presence of any great god would at once destroy the whole theory of classical life."[97] Taking the two leading masters of this school, Claude and Poussin, Ruskin predictably accuses the former of expressing no other feeling than "weak dislike to entertain the conception of toil or suffering"[98] and the latter of an absence of sensibility that "permits him to paint frightful subjects without feeling any true horror," so that certain of his pictures are "ghastly in incident, sometimes disgusting, but never impressive."[99] Both of these accusations, though central to this brief chapter, are more expressive of the rising urgency of social concern in Ruskin with his "religion of Humanity," than of cautious analysis of an aesthetic.

Although his disapproval of the "classical" landscape, typified by Claude and Poussin, is almost total, Ruskin has yet another stage to trace in the spiritual degeneration of European art. The following three chapters, numbers 6, 7, and 8 in this section, describe what he considers to be the nadir of spiritual invention in landscape. Entitled "Rubens and Cuyp," "Of Vulgarity," and "Wouvermans and Angelico," respectively, their essential subject is the utter neutralization of nature together with the human spirit, signified for him by the Dutch and Flemish pastoral landscapes. Rhetorically, of course, the purpose of these chapters is to set the spiritual scene for the triumphant appearance of Turner as the truly sacred and mythic landscapist of the modern era. Hence their meaning in terms of this study can be summarized briefly.

While the school of "taste and restraint" had contempt for the despair and death of ordinary men and introduced its deities in a purely decorative capacity, it had not forgotten the religious experience entirely, being simply devoid of spiritual pathos. But in the Dutch pastoral landscapes, Ruskin concludes, "we lose, not only all faith in religion, but all remembrance of it. Absolutely now at last we find ourselves without sight of God in all the world." There has, so far as he knows, been nothing like this utter mythlessness in human history. "The human being never got wholly quit of the terror of spiritual being before. Persian, Egyptian, Assyrian, Hindoo, Chinese, all kept some dim, appalling record of what they called 'gods.' " Even savage minds had their spirits and idols, "but here in Holland we have at last got utterly done with it all."[100] These painters seem to be saying, "Of deities or virtues, angels, principalities, or powers, in the name of our ditches, no more. Let us have cattle and market vegetables."[101] While Ruskin does have some praise for the love of animals and respect for rustic life evident in these landscapes, his attitude toward their spiritual value is summed up in the irony of his phrase "Dutch cattle-pieces."[102]

The chapter called "Vulgarity" has the ostensible purpose of enabling the observer to comprehend these Dutch faults, but it is indicative primarily of the social anxiety that is the weft of this volume. Gentlemen, we are told, have neither the duty nor the privilege of living by the sweat of others. They must learn that it is no degradation to perform the humblest or most servile work; no sort of work is of itself vulgar. Deep degradation lies rather in "extravagance, in bribery, in indolence, in pride, in taking places they are not fit for, or in coining places for which there is no need."[103] Vulgarity is not lowliness of life but deadness of spirit, insensibility as opposed to human sympathy; it is "a deadness of the heart and body, resulting from prolonged and especially from inherited conditions of 'degeneracy,' or literally, 'unracing';—gentlemanliness, being another word for an intense humanity." Vulgarity appears primarily as "dulness of heart, not in rage or cruelty, but in inability to feel or conceive noble character or emotion."[104] As such, vulgarity is a mode of death; yet "death itself is not vulgar, but only death mingled with life." For this mingling of death and life in vulgarity Ruskin proposes that "the term 'deathful selfishness' will embrace all the most fatal and essential forms of mental vulgarity."[105]

Coming back to the Dutch in the chapter contrasting Wouvermans and Angelico, who are polar opposites in the spirit of art, Ruskin insists that he is as wholly unable to enter into the Dutch landscape feeling as he is to enter into the feelings of lower animals. "I cannot see why they painted,—what they are aiming at,—what they liked or disliked. All their life and work is the same sort of mystery to me as the mind of my dog when he rolls on carrion."[106] The chapter concludes with a spiritual scaling of five painters, enabling him to resurvey quickly the contrasts in mythic invention he has been tracing down to this point, except, however, for the unannounced apotheosis of Giorgione's painting as the ultimate achievement in spiritual art. Wouvermans, the Dutch representative, signifies the "carnal mind," wholly versed in materialism but "incapable of conceiving any goodness or greatness whatever." At the opposite extreme there is Angelico, "the entirely spiritual mind," full of heavenly knowledge, but "incapable of conceiving any wickedness or vileness whatsoever." Between these extremes we have Salvator, who contends with evil and despair but is captured by them, and Dürer, whose spirit is purer, but whose intellect shows "some defect" and whose victory over evil is not so complete as to conquer his sadness. And then, in unexpected resolution, we have, suddenly, Giorgione: "with entirely perfect intellect, contending with evil; conquering it utterly, casting it away for ever, and rising beyond it into magnificence of rest."[107]

CHAPTER 10

The Assumption of the Dragon

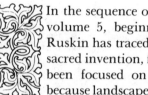In the sequence of seven chapters of *Modern Painters,* volume 5, beginning with "The Lance of Pallas," Ruskin has traced the disappearance of believed myth, sacred invention, from European art. His attention has been focused on the poetics of landscape. This is because landscape is, for him, symbolic of Being, of that which contains the mysterious unity of man and nature; and landscape painting is the highest statement of this relation that nature calls upon the artist to make. As such its fall into mere objective representation reveals completely our loss of relation to nature, loss of feeling for what nature means as opposed to what it is. True landscape, he holds, depends for its power on the interfusion of scenery with humanity, or with spiritual powers, visible or invisible, that are projections of human visions. To Ruskin, features of landscape can never have alien objectivity without promise of solidarity beyond mere utility. Architecture, in a parallel way, is never mere structure but is the poetic expression of the character of a people and their region, in *The Poetry of Architecture,* or of the life of the workman, in the Gothic studies. This assertion of the essential humanism of both landscape and architecture, he insists, has been the "distinctive character" of his past work. Man is "the sun of creation"; not the creation, but the soul of it. And the deadliest errors of art have consisted in isolating this soul from its world-body, in the withdrawal of man into his own interests, whether ascetic, sensual, or scientific.

Christian art, we were told, erred by caring for the soul only; it produced no landscape because it assumed that the natural world could be represented without the elements of decay, danger, and death. Greek poetic landscape, on the other hand, had faced the human present and had asserted the victory here and now of heroism over the forces of fate, sin, and death. But the Greek found no love in physical nature, found its powers hostile, and defied them by deifying them so that they shrank back into companionable beings. The Venetian painters, with Titian as the central type, achieved a momentary perfection by bringing their Christian piety down to earth, without losing its spirituality or losing sight of the lived world. With the Reformation and its religious antagonisms, Ruskin argues, the possibility of tranquil faith was lost, and faith went through a "trial hour" again as it had in the Greek mind when Hector was betrayed by Pallas. Religion could no longer give repose; consequently, death was resurrected in "Düreresque" art; yet that art was still capable of true, if melancholy, spiritual vision. Finally, in the so-called classical landscapes of Claude and Poussin the world is mere elegant decor in which the realities of ruin and decay together with believed spiritual presences have simply been idealized out of existence, and in the Dutch "cattle-pieces" the idea of the sacred is forgotten entirely and man is replaced by his beasts. His myth of the fall of landscape is complete.

1

In a sense Ruskin's survey of the disappearance of authentic spiritual invention from landscape is merely preparatory, because it is within this fallen world of idealized and spiritually neutralized landscapes, devoid of humanity and deity and murky with brown shadow, that Turner begins to paint and to which he will bring both truth and light. In a group of four chapters, which are at once the climax and conclusion of *Modern Painters*, he will attempt to show how Turner recovered for modern landscape not only vital color but also the sacred and heroic tradition of the Greeks and that he is the great modern naturalist, humanist, yet mythic painter-poet. But in order to make his reader fully aware of the heroic achievement of Turner, Ruskin needs another strong antithesis (now a strained similarity in difference) of the kind he has been developing thus far in this section and on which the glow of his prose depends; therefore, in the moving chapter "The Two Boyhoods," the first of this final group, he contrasts the worlds in which Giorgione and Turner were schooled in their art.

"The Two Boyhoods" opens with a poetic evocation of Giorgione's Venice, an unfallen world of light, beauty, faith, and hope, a mythic world, to Ruskin, of noble men who were mostly pure and incorruptible in their use of power. "Deep-hearted, majestic, terrible as the sea,— the men of Venice moved in sway of power and war; pure as pillars of alabaster, stood her mothers and maidens; from foot to brow, all noble, walked her knights, the low bronzed gleaming of sea-rusted armor shot angrily under their blood-red mantle-folds."[1] In daily life it was "a world from which all ignoble care and petty thoughts were banished, with all the common and poor elements of life." Most of all, it was a world encompassed by natural scenes that were a constant apocalypse of heaven: "Ethereal strength of Alps, dreamlike, vanishing in high procession beyond the Torcellan shore; blue islands of Paduan hills, poised in the golden west."[2]

By contrast, however, Turner's boyhood world of Maiden Lane is sunken and shadowy, and its sacred places are the confusion and mystery of market and dock. "Near the southwest corner of Covent Garden a square brick pit or well is formed by a close set block of houses, to the back windows of which it admits a few rays of light."[3] Impressions of figures and produce drawn from nearby Covent Garden are recurrent in his work to the last, as is the continuous imagery of docks and shipping that derives from his early fascination with "that mysterious forest below London bridge." The fact that he sought wherever he looked for visible confirmations of these youthful haunts sustained Turner in a way, Ruskin believes, and enabled him to "endure ugliness which no one else, of the same sensibility, would have borne with for an instant."[4]

At the same time these early scenes of alley, market, and dock determined the intentional glance of his work. "Dead brick walls, blank square windows, old clothes, market-womanly types of humanity— anything fishy and muddy, like Billingsgate or Hungerford Market, had great attraction for him; black barges, patched sails, and every possible condition of fog." These became his guiding "tolerations and affections," with the result that, where "no Venetian ever draws anything foul," Turner "devoted picture after picture to the illustration of effects of dinginess, smoke, soot, dust, and dusty texture; old sides of boats, weedy roadside vegetation, dung-hills, straw-yards, and all the soilings and stains of every common labour."[5] Furthermore, he seemed to take a particular interest in the litter and débris of man and nature; his "foregrounds differ from all others in the natural way things have of lying about in them. Even his richest vegetation, in ideal work, is confused; and he delights in shingle, debris, and heaps of fallen stones."[6] This tendency, Ruskin assumes, is again a residue of his boyhood experience, the world reminding him of "Covent Garden wreck after the market." This theory of Turner's work as wreck after market is important for its coherence, at the level of local detail, with the central myths of Turner's art that Ruskin will interpret in the following chapters.

Another result of the painter's boyhood explorations of Covent Garden and also of Wapping, where he spent much time as well, was an understanding of and affection for the poor, an awareness of them in their relations with the rich, and familiarity with the conditions of humble labor, especially labor connected with the life of the river. Ships, particularly, are "the only quite beautiful things he can see in all the world, except the sky; but these, when the sun is on their sails, filling or falling, endlessly disordered by sway of tide and stress of anchorage, beautiful unspeakably; which ships also are inhabited by glorious creatures—red-faced sailors, with pipes, appearing over gunwales, true knights over their castle parapets—the most angelic beings in the whole compass of London world."[7] But ships, beautiful as they are to him, are no exception to the rule of ruin in Turner's work. As Ruskin had explained earlier in his suggestive introduction to Turner's *The Harbours of England*, once having seen shipwreck with his own eyes in 1818, Turner *"never afterwards painted a ship quite in fair order.* There is invariably a feeling about his vessels of strange awe and danger."[8]

As for the original makeup of Turner's mind, Ruskin thinks of the combined intellects of Keats and Dante, a mind "joining capricious waywardness, and intense openness to every fine pleasure of sense, and hot defiance of formal precedent, with a quite infinite tenderness, generosity, and desire of justice and truth," a mind that never became vulgar, though deeply enough infected by vulgarity for its nobility to be hidden from superficial view. "It was as if a cable had been woven of blood-crimson silk, and then tarred on the outside. People handled it, and the tar came off on their hands; red gleams were seen through the black underneath, at the places where it had been strained. Was it ochre?—said the world—or red lead?"[9]

For his spiritual training, Giorgione had the benefit of a secure and sincere religion, a mythology that was powerful in worldly affairs and beautiful in its effects; "gorgeous, harmonious, mysterious;—a thing which had either to be obeyed or combatted, but could not be scorned. A religion towering over all the city—many buttressed—luminous in marble stateliness, as the dome of our Lady of Safety shines over the sea."[10] But Turner at London had no such spiritual repose. "Some honesty, indeed, and English industry, and kindliness of heart, and general idea of justice; but faith of any national kind, shut up from one Sunday to the next, not artistically beautiful even in those Sabbatical exhibitions; its paraphernalia being chiefly of high pews, heavy elocution, and cold grimness of behaviour."[11] In his early London years, Ruskin concludes, Turner saw a religion (much like that he himself had just left) that lacked both authentic piety and worldly authority, a religion "discreditable—discredited—not believing in itself: putting forth its authority in a cowardly way, watching how far it might be tolerated, continually shrinking, disclaiming, fencing, finessing; divided against itself, not by stormy rents, but by thin fissures, and splittings of plaster from the walls."[12] This disintegrating sheepfold was a system the youthful Turner felt he need not obey or combat but merely scorn.

Later on, when he was about ten years old, Turner went to live with an aunt at Brentford where he had some experience of the elegance and dignity of life in the great country house and received some rudimentary schooling, particularly in the "more picturesque classical authors," an encounter with myth and symbol he later put to use in ways that Ruskin considers in the two following chapters. Still later, in his early twenties, Turner's spiritual life was further deepened by visits to the north, where he felt for the first time the peace, freedom, and divinity of unspoiled nature. "Those pale, poverty-struck, or cruel faces;—that multitudinous, marred humanity—are not the only things that God has made. Here is something He has made which no one has marred. Pride of purple rocks, and river pools of blue, and tender wilderness of glittering trees, and misty lights of evening on immeasurable hills." But there were dark clues for the youth here also; coupled with his first teachings from the vernal wood, came also, Ruskin points out, clear lessons in mortality: "sound preaching at last here, in Kirkstall crypt, concerning fate and life."[13]

By these components, then, of his early life Turner's message was determined; his was a littered world in which the law of help had given way. Where Giorgione had been exposed to vital faith, noble men, perfect architecture, and was sheltered largely from the sight of ruin, "he conceived the form of man as deathless, calm with power, and fiery with life." But Turner's awareness was the antithesis of this and he saw only "meanness, aimlessness, unsightliness," in the lived world of man. "As the strength of men to Giorgione, to Turner their weakness and vileness, were alone visible. They themselves, unworthy or ephemeral; their work, despicable, or decayed. In the Venetian's eyes, all beauty depended on man's presence and pride; in Turner's, on the solitude he had left, and the humiliation he had suffered."[14] Seeing this he could have but two subjects, Ruskin argues, first the power of nature, for he had known no other beauty, and secondly "he must paint also the labour and sorrow and passing away of men: this was the great human truth visible to him."[15] Labor, sorrow, and death: these aspects of the human condition in Turner's mind are signified by the title of his manuscript poems, *The Fallacies of Hope*, from which he quoted the epigraphs for many of his pictures.

Most important to Ruskin here is the point that in his vision of human absurdity Turner had raised "*that old Greek question again*; yet unanswered."[16] And now in a series of apocalyptic passages, forecasting his own *Storm-Cloud* lectures, Ruskin attempts to convey a sense of the mythic death-presence that troubled Turner's sight. "The unconquerable spectre still flitting among the forest trees at twilight; rising ribbed out of the sea-sand;—white, a strange Aphrodite,—out of the sea-foam; stretching its gray, cloven wings among the clouds; turning the light of their sunsets into blood." This malignant specter assumes a shape more terrible and vast for him than the domestic or even national modes of death that could have been contemplated by Dürer or Salvator. "The wreck of one guilty country does not infer the ruin of all countries, and need not cause terror respecting the laws of the universe."[17] But the soul plague that Turner knew, "the English death—the European death of the nineteenth century—was of another range and power; more terrible a thousandfold in its merely physical grasp and grief; more terrible, incalculably, in its mystery and shame."[18]

Ruskin does allude at this point to the possible influence on Turner of the lethal sweep of the Napoleonic wars ("he was eighteen years old when Napoleon came down on Arcola"), but this is merely to point the contrast between the soldier's death, mourned and possibly meaningful, with the spreading "English death" that he knew at first hand. This was the uncelebrated, forgotten, daily dying of alienated multitudes, of men cut off from each other, as from God and nature, by the indifferent laws of greed: "the life trampled out in the slime of the street, crushed to dust amidst the roaring of the wheel, tossed countlessly away into howling winter wind along five hundred leagues of rock-fanged shore. Or, worst of all, rotted down to forgotten graves through years of ignorant patience, and vain seeking for help from man, for hope in God—infirm, imperfect yearning, as of motherless infants starving at the dawn; oppressed royalties of captive thought, vague ague-fits of bleak, amazed despair."[19] Finally, in one of the most awesome apocalyptic passages in his work, Ruskin envisions (for the young Turner) the final global implications of this English death: the total failure of the law of help seen now in the image of a glaring, burned-out, ashen planet:

> A goodly landscape this, for the lad to paint, and under a goodly light. Wide enough the light was, and clear; no more Salvator's lurid clasm on jagged horizon, nor Dürer's spotted rest of sunny gleam on hedgerow and field; but light over all the world. Full shone now its awful globe, one pallid charnel-house,—a ball strewn bright with human ashes, glaring in poised sway beneath the sun, all blinding-white with death from pole to pole,—death, not of myriads of poor bodies only, but of will, and mercy, and conscience; death, not once inflicted on the flesh, but daily fastening on the spirit; death, not silent or patient, waiting his appointed hour, but voiceful, venomous; death with the taunting word, and burning grasp, and in fixed sting.[20]

2

"A ball strewn bright with human ashes, glaring in poised sway beneath the sun, all blinding-white with death from pole to pole."

Ruskin must now go on to show that this ashen apocalypse of nature just placed in the mind of Turner does in fact appear in his crucial paintings. This he attempts to do in two very difficult chapters that are the culmination of his seventeen-year study of Turner and the poetics of landscape. These chapters have a privileged place in the whole body of *Modern Painters*. They are not simply the last two but one (the peroration, "Peace") of that seventeen-year conceptual evolution. They are also the substantive resolution of the work's ninth and last section, that concerning "Invention Spiritual." We recall that in the preceding nine chapters of this section, Ruskin has been tracing the demise of authentic genuine spiritual vision in art, through the Greeks, the Florentines, the Venetians, the Germans, the Flemings, and the French classicists. He has arrived, through the vagaries of his analysis, at two painters who epitomize diametrically opposed spiritual truths in painting. Giorgione, reared in the milieu of perfect faith, the triumphs of Venetian art, and the beauty of nature, paints man in his strength, triumphing over evil and death. But Turner, reared amid the detritus of modern greed, sees an opposed spiritual truth. He sees "that old Greek question; yet unanswered. The unconquerable spectre still flitting among the forest trees at twilight." What Turner's truth has to look upon "in a more terrible shape than ever Salvator or Dürer saw it," with their eyes of faith, is "the European death of the nineteenth century . . . more terrible a thousand-fold in its merely physical grasp and grief."[21]

Returning to "that old Greek question" (What hope have we?) in these two chapters, "The Nereid's Guard" and "The Hesperid Aeglé," Ruskin shows not only that Turner is the great modern apocalyptist of landscape but also that his central message is embodied in two great mythic subjects and is therefore rooted in the authority of an archetypal tradition. He has fully characterized Turner's knowledge of nature and sympathy with man in preceding volumes; now he will show the painter's deep understanding of mythic symbolism. Interpretation of Turner seems to have waited for an appropriate hermeneutic, and now Ruskin has it from his study of myth.

I have mentioned that these are difficult chapters. They are so in a double sense. Few chapters in his work combine the descriptive evocation of paintings with passages of such allusive density; they are among the most symbolically resonant in his work. Some later chapters, the second lecture of *The Queen of The Air* or the "Patience" lecture of *The Cestus of Aglaia*, for example, have the same allusiveness but lack the coherence. Further, these chapters are mythic on three levels; Greek

myths are being interpreted by way of illustrating Turner's interpretation of them and their coherence with natural forms in his landscapes,
but Turner's vision is, of course, being incorporated into Ruskin's own
evolving symbology. What he has to say about Turner may indeed be of
little value to the student of the painter, but it is central to the student of
Ruskin's prophetic mythology. Turner is his mythic hero here, a
purifying solar hero, England's unacknowledged Apollo in combat
with the plague of greed in the nineteenth century; and this is a mythic
role that Ruskin will assume himself in the latter half of his creative life
when he must attack directly the vision of death he assigns here to
Turner. Finally, in a sense these chapters are conclusive not only of this
his major work, but of his work as a whole. Ruskin has already told us
that the whole of his political economy is summed up in the redemptive
life-law of help, the organic core of the volume's theory of composition.
He had, as we will see, much more to say and do. But in all that follows
two tasks are dominant: first, to describe and criticize in socioeconomic
and symbolic terms the death worm at the root of nineteenth-century
culture (the plague cloud of the century), and second, to convey the still
vital prophetic message of certain Greek myths of cloud and storm
centered on the powers of Athena. But both of these tasks, the social and
the mythological, are really explications and extensions of the
Turnerian prophecies elucidated in these two chapters.

Before we turn to these chapters it is necessary to summarize, however
briefly, the various influences that appear to have been acting on Ruskin
at this point to form the personal myth in which the forces defined in this
series of chapters (the disappearance of deity from landscape, the rule of
ruin in Turner's world, the meaning of the two myths about to be
analyzed) are incorporated.

First, there is Ruskin's own deepening social concern, evident as early
as *The Seven Lamps of Architecture*. This reaches a crisis during the
years from 1856 to 1860 when he takes to the medium of the lecture in
order "to secure more immediate effect." The two major byworks of this
period, *The Political Economy of Art* (1857) and *The Two Paths* (1859),
are collections of lectures, most of them delivered in the manufacturing
towns, on the relationship between art and socioeconomic policy. The
scheme of his economic criticism is quite fully worked out in these, as we
shall see, but their tone (as Ruskin first tests the authority of his critical
reputation on the practical question of the relation between art training
and industrial design) is hopeful. These lectures have neither the high
tragic color of these last chapters of *Modern Painters* nor the bitterness of
disappointment that mars his later economic essays.

Second, there is the hidden current of his religious development. We find Ruskin earnestly questioning the tenets of his Evangelical faith as early as 1842 in *Letters to a College Friend,* where he uses botanical arguments to prove that if there were plants in Eden there had to have been death before Adam fell. Geology, he also notes, "has but expanded before us the vast unity of system, the *one* great plan of progressive existence, of which we form, probably, the last link."[22] This questioning grows in a submerged way, surfacing here and there—in his diaries, his letters to his father, in his critical repudiation of the purist painters, and in the moderating of the arrogant orthodoxy of his own early style—until it reaches the crisis of his "unconversion" in 1858 and the replacement of his old faith by a kind of Greek tragic humanism that he called his "religion of Humanity." We have already suggested connections between this "Greek religion," centrally stated in the preface to *The Crown of Wild Olive* and the "Dark Mirror" and "Lance of Pallas" chapters of the work before us. It must only be noted here that the same tragic humanism underlies this present exploration of "that old Greek question," not only in the mythic subject and tragic tone of these chapters but in their conclusive attack on the world's three forms of asceticism (culminating in ours, the asceticism of money) to which Ruskin's humanism is antagonistic.

Finally, among his many activities during the period from 1856 to 1860 Ruskin produced a body of writing (itself worthy of separate treatment) that involved more specific study of the particular works of Turner than had been required by the scope of *Modern Painters.* The writing of *The Harbours of England* (1856), involved detailed evaluation and interpretation of twelve harbor drawings by Turner. Although the discussions can be correlated with certain principles laid down in *Modern Painters* (for example, "Of Turnerian Topography," vol. 4, ch. 2), the approach is more directly interpretive of particular drawings than the vast scheme of his great work permitted. Much more important in this connection are the catalogues Ruskin wrote in connection with the massive effort he expended during 1857 and 1858 in arranging, cataloguing, and mounting the drawings that Turner had bequeathed to the nation on his death in 1851. At this time the trustees and directors of the National Gallery arranged a selective exhibition of thirty-four oil paintings from the Turner bequest, and Ruskin prepared a descriptive and explanatory catalogue of them, working so furiously that, as he notes in his diary, he felt the symptoms of nervous breakdown. His *Notes on the Turner Gallery at Marlborough House, 1856* (1857) is important as a background for these final chapters of *Modern Painters* because here he had to perceive Turner's career as a coherent whole marked by certain phases of development. These are reflected in the chapters that I am about to treat. He had also to state briefly and forcefully the painter's distinguishing characteristics without reference to aesthetic categories. These characteristics are his "mysticism," "his human sympathy," his tendency to "express an extreme beauty where he *meant* that there was most threatening and ultimate sorrow," and "the association in his mind of sunset color with blood."[23] Finally, in this catalogue, as in the lesser following catalogues on the sketches and drawings, he had to decide which pictures were crucial to Turner's development and suggest why.

It would be an unreasonable digression at this point to attempt anything like a summary of Ruskin's positions on particular oils exhibited in 1856. But a few points are inescapable for their direct bearings on the "Nereid's Guard" and "Hesperid Aeglé" chapters. Most of the paintings he regards as major are mythical in subject and tragic or apocalyptic in tone and conception; even the great *Téméraire*, hardly a mythic subject in the literal sense, is no real exception, as Ruskin views the scene as a funeral procession of a more than human, heroic being, "her organized perfectness, giving her the look, and partly the character of a living creature."[24] Of the explicitly mythic pictures, the two that are the subjects of complete analysis in the chapters before us are singled out here for partial praise. *The Goddess of Discord Choosing the Apple of Contention in the Garden of the Hesperides*, while it is noticed as the first composition in which Turner attempted to introduce his Alpine experience, is found wholly deficient in true Alpine feeling because the painter was still laboring under the influence of Poussin's idealism. Yet the guardian dragon in the painting (as yet given no mythic interpretation) is given measured praise as a naturalistic example of the terrible grotesque, particularly because Turner's monster accurately predicts the latest paleozoological model of the Iguanodon, "now guardian of the Hesperidian Gardens of the Crystal Palace."[25] We are told, in sum, that "no serpent or dragon was ever conceived before, either so vast, or so *probable*" as those in three paintings exhibited here: *Jason, The Garden of the Hesperides*, and *Apollo and Python*.[26] This last, the second of the two great mythic subjects to be interpreted in the final chapters of *Modern Painters*, already has its hold on Ruskin in 1856: "I do not scruple to say," he exclaims, that this is "one of the noblest pictures in the world." Yet it is the serpent, not the figures, that is to be praised, especially the "way in which the structure of the writhed coil of the dragon's tail distinctly expresses mortal agony—not mere serpentine convolution."[27]

Neither of these mythic subjects is given an interpretive (as opposed to a technical) analysis at this point, but three other paintings in the catalogue, which are all deeply involved with solar symbolism, as the two just mentioned will be found to be, are subjected to interpretations centering on their mythic symbols. In discussing *The Bay of Baiae* Ruskin reminds his readers that the beautiful desolation of its landscape will be better understood if it is remembered that Deiphobe, the Cumaean sibyl, was beloved by Apollo, and that she accepted his gift of longevity while rejecting his love and so was allowed to waste away through epochs of history until nothing but her voice remained. We are led to think of her in this picture "as the type of the ruined beauty of Italy; foreshowing, so long ago, her low murmurings of melancholy prophecy." The myth made such a deep impression on Turner that he painted *The Golden Bough* as a sequel to this, with Deiphobe, bearing the golden bough, guiding Aeneas to the netherworld. Further, Turner has placed a snake among the lovely leafage in the foreground of each of these two pictures, "a type of the terror, or temptation, which is associated with the lovely landscapes."[28] *Apollo and Daphne,* a much later work, is praised, unlike *The Garden of the Hesperides,* for the *"naturalism"* of its mountain drawing and, as in *The Bay of Baiae,* the mythic figures are interpreted so that we may see how their symbolic meaning is continued in the physical aspects of the landscape. Here the myth tells us that "the whole picture is to be illustrative of the union of the rivers and the earth; and of the perpetual help and delight granted by the streams, in their dew, to the earth's foliage." Turner has answered his mythic figures naturalistically by throwing "his whole strength into the expression of the roundings of the hills under the influence of the torrents."[29]

In discussing these two mythic subjects Ruskin has read the symbolism in order to show the subtle coherence between the mythic event and the physical landscape. But with the third mythic picture I must mention, the interpretation goes beyond this, making his discussion of *Ulysses Deriding Polyphemus* (Plate III) the key analysis of the catalogue. Here Ruskin moves into something much closer to the kind of hermeneutic we will meet in the concluding chapters of *Modern Painters.* Not only is the Homeric symbolism shown to be coherent with the representation of nature in the landscape, but the whole painting, myth and setting, is read as an allegory of Turner's struggle with the one-eyed aesthetic idealism of his age. The Greek Turnerian mythopoesis is now incorporated in a Ruskinian myth of Turner.

In this picture, we are told, the painter "first asserts his perfect power." It is therefore "the *central picture* in Turner's career," but what is more "it is in some sort a type of his own destiny."[30] He had himself been shut up in the dark cave of traditionalism by the one-eyed people, but when his dawning came he thrust "the rugged pine trunk—all ablaze" of his luminism full in the faces of the people of single vision and "left them tearing their hair in the cloud banks."[31] The episode, in the Turnerian-Ruskinian reading, is another solar myth; Ulysses' escape (Turner's assertion of full natural light in his art) is celebrated in the dawning skies; its mists and colors are shown to be a coherent part of the symbolic action.

> The somewhat gloomy and deeply coloured tones of the lower crimson clouds, and of the stormy blue bars underneath them, are always given by Turner to skies which rise over any scene of death, or one connected with any deathful memories. But the morning light is unmistakably indicated by the pure whiteness of the mists, and upper mountain snows, above Polyphemus; at evening they would have been in an orange glow; and, for more complete assurance still, if the reader will examine the sky close to the sun, on the right of it, he will find the horses of Apollo drawn in fiery outline, leaping into the sky and shaking their crests out into flashes of scarlet cloud. The god himself is formless, he *is* the sun.[32]

Ruskin had come this far, then, in analyzing Turnerian "Invention Spiritual" during the years when *Modern Painters*, volume 5, was beginning to take shape in his mind. We should note again, in passing on, that the myths briefly analyzed in these *Notes on the Turner Gallery* have a common basis in the solar archetype: each involves the figure of Apollo. The two mythic interpretations that conclude *Modern Painters* are again solar but with the important difference that these emphasize solar tragedy or struggle. The three additional background determinants that must be mentioned before we look at these chapters in detail all relate to the recurrence of the solar archetype in the mythopoesis of both Turner and Ruskin.

Surely the deepest basis of Ruskin's sympathy with Turner is his recognition of their mutual adoration of the mysteries of natural light. For both, it appeared to him, the condition of living light, its purity, whether in the open sky or on the mountain snows, in its daily struggle with clouds, mists, and forms of smoke, provided a continuous symbology of the contest of moral forces for the life of man. Ruskin prepared himself very early for the sympathy. We think of him on the first Continental tours with his parents, measuring the blueness of the sky with his homemade "cyanometer" and capturing sunrises and sunsets in his diaries. The best moments of his collection entitled *Poems* (1850) are the Alpine sky effects with apocalyptic intimations; these answering skies were the "Alpine ecstasy" of his own in the derivative folktale *The King of the Golden River*. In his earliest estimate of Turner, the manuscript intended as a reply to the *Blackwoods* reviewer, the most promising passage is the evocation of the play of uncertain light in Turner's *Juliet and Her Nurse*. We have seen how in the chapter "The Firmament" in *Modern Painters*, volume 4, the biblical assertion that "the heavens declare the glory of God" is interpreted as a solar myth referring to the interaction of sun and cloud. And we have noted that in the chapter "The Angel of the Sea" of this last volume he has explained certain Turnerian cloud forms by reference to the natural meanings of particular Greek mythic symbols that both he and Turner understood. Particular reference is made to the ominous form of the Medusa cloud and to the "dissolving of the Medusa cloud in blood." But the interpretation of this sanguine rain is deferred to another place, because it is connected with yet "higher types" of mythic symbolism. Therefore, we are led to expect that the function of these last mythic interpretations in *Modern Painters* will be to give ultimate coherence of meaning to the Turnerian skies.

But, although Ruskin is about to deal with two of Turner's compositions in which myth, mist, organic form, and solar color are seen as coherent and definitive symbolic wholes communicating Turner's development as the landscape poet of modern times, their full meaning *for Ruskin* is not really to be found simply in the argument of these two chapters. These compositions are not, for him, simply ingenious correlations of myth and landscape or even visions central to Turner's development; their full meaning to Ruskin could never be expressed in terms of an aesthetic of internal coherence or by relating them to Turner's career. To matter as they evidently do to Ruskin these landscapes would have to be *true* revelations of nature's message to man in the nineteenth century; the full meaning of these Turnerian myths to him is only fully revealed against the whole body of Ruskin's work, public and private. The relevance of these interpretations of Turner to his later work in social theory and Greek myth will be evident as we proceed. But the private truth to Ruskin of these mythic landscapes is suggested in a more obscure way by the tragic animation of nature in his diaries. We have noticed elsewhere that the successive meteorological entries reveal, beginning as early as the late forties, recurrent emotional responses to a malignant, antagonistic presence he felt and described, especially in states of weather and forms of cloud. These impressions break into his public writing only in the later *Fors* and *The Storm–Cloud of the Nineteenth Century*.

So the tragic opposition of vital and lethal forces in the world that Ruskin is about to read in Turner's solar colors and to see as epitomized in the painter's *Apollo and Python* was a sky struggle in which, his diaries show, Ruskin himself participated psychologically and recorded almost daily in animistic terms. His experience, like the painter's, appears to have been generally polarized around a nature mythology of cloud and light—a solar mythology. I say mythology because the sky drama of phenomenal nature is given archetypal significance by being interpreted in terms of Greek mythic or biblical apocalyptic symbolism; however, because the mythic resonance surrounds visible skies, its function is not the backward historical glance of scholarship but the suprahistorical authority of poetry or prophecy. The struggle of vital and lethal forces for the sky is continual; the solar archetype still generates metaphor and myth.

Turner and Giorgione are linked in this last section of *Modern Painters* not only by the Greek subject of the Hesperides, but by what they represent for Ruskin: these painters' love of *translucent*, particularly rose, color. Giorgione, because his world permitted purity of faith, achieved the pure translucent rose, like the solar color Ruskin adored on the high Alpine snows; but Turner's rose, while true and lovely, was always shadowed by his tragic vision. Further, both men were, it appears, linked symbolically in Ruskin's mind to Saint George, Giorgione by his name, "George of Georges," and Turner by his birth on Saint George's day. Saint George's victory is not possible to Turner, we are told; yet the painter appears in the following interpretations, not only as the great draftsman of dragons, but as a poet-prophet locked in tragic conflict with the dragon of our age, his color perpetually struggling with serpentine exhalations of mist and smoke. Pythian Apollo, not Saint George, is the dominant symbol in these chapters; and all the figures mentioned, Perseus and Medusa, Hercules and Ladon, the Hesperids, are interpreted as sky phenomena and drawn into the aura of the solar archetype. Given this predominant solarism it is natural to suppose that Ruskin was influenced in this glowing conclusion to *Modern Painters* by the work of Friedrich Max Müller, Taylorian Professor of Modern Languages at Oxford and the great mythographer of the solar archetype in the third quarter of the century.

Müller's "Comparative Mythology" had appeared in *Oxford Essays* for 1856. This gracefully phrased and suggestive essay defined Müller's theoretical position as a mythologist. It became celebrated among both scholars and litterateurs because it combined the authority of philological scholarship with a distinct, if derivative, theory of the genisis of myth and colorful evocations of the mythopoeic mind at work. However, there is no definite evidence that Ruskin had read Müller until *The Ethics of the Dust*, where the professor's *Lectures on the Science of Language* are recommended to the girls as a reliable guide to the roots of words. In his writings after 1860 Ruskin gives increasing attention to the truths revealed by tracing the derivations of words, and, as Cook points out, this tendency was just beginning to reveal itself in the last volume of *Modern Painters*. But nothing in the interpretations of these myths shows the explicit influence of Müller's theory.

In the pair of chapters to be considered, Ruskin analyzes his Greek mythic elements into two distinct levels, their "natural meaning" and their "moral significance." This reading of a "natural meaning" behind the myth, the general tendency to read myths as allegorical descriptions of natural phenomena, is, of course, to be found in Max Müller, but it is the most common element in all mythological theory of the period. (Ruskin, however, had distinguished between myth and allegory in *Modern Painters*, volume 3, and would enlarge upon this in *The Queen of the Air*.) The "moral significance" level is, I believe, peculiar to Ruskin's view and is important because it represents his incorporation of the myth into his own moral vision and because it removes the myth for him from the realm of mere aesthetic or historical interest, drawing it into immediate and continuous truth. After volume 2 of *Modern Painters* Ruskin never trivialized myth. However, his interest, he would say, was in the highest cultural development of a myth, not in its rude beginnings.[33] He would argue also that even a natural thing can contain in its structure the lineaments of living myth:[34] myths have the same level of significance as natural form. The tendency to trace most myths to sky phenomena, especially to the passage of the sun and, particularly, to the dawn, was a trademark of Müller's, of course; but it was by no means original with him, Ruskin would not have needed the professor's arguments to show him the solar element in myth, though he might have been encouraged by the scholarly support of Müller's famous essay.

What does appear in "Comparative Mythology" as the central (though not original) factor in his analysis and yet does *not* appear in Ruskin's theory of myth at this point is the link between myth and language. Myth, for Müller, was a "disease of language." The hypothesized primal language of the Aryans, Müller held, was not capable of abstraction. They expressed the real phenomena of nature not in ideal symbols but in fundamental metaphors and instinctive poetry, projecting human life and will into the external operations of nature that held them in awe, the weak and dreamy sun embracing the dawn, for instance. This was the mythopoeic age when every account of nature was necessarily mythic. But after this period, when the Aryan tribes dispersed and their language became the basis of new languages, the original meanings of their root metaphors for natural events were forgotten, and the ingenious and sometimes grotesque narratives, the myths of later people, were invented to explain these metaphoric roots. The task of the comparative mythologist was to trace the myths of historical peoples back to their Aryan roots. This, in Müller's usual practice, meant tracing Greek and Latin god names back, following the laws of linguistic change, to their forms in the Vedas.

Ruskin shows no knowledge of the comparative philological approach at this point. Of course this strategy, because it tended to diminish the great myths, to divest them of deep religious emotion and moral significance, would not have served Ruskin's purposes with myth. This is why, later on in *The Queen of the Air*, Ruskin would nod politely to the "splendid investigations of recent philologists" but would disclaim interest in the primitive origins of myth and insist that the great power of myth is not in its root but in its blossom. Nevertheless, his later studies in myth were more linguistic in emphasis; he would tend to document the "natural meanings" of Greek mythic epithets by reference to Greek roots, and this could reflect the technique of Max Müller, who would eventually be one of Ruskin's colleagues at Oxford. Already, in parts of the fifth volume, especially in the "Law of Help" chapter, the interest in root meanings makes its appearance, as for instance when Ruskin derives (erroneously) the words *muse* and *mother* from "the same root, meaning 'passionate seeking,' or love, of which the issue is passionate finding, or sacred INVENTION."[35] More significantly Müller's general view that language is itself a mythic process may have drawn Ruskin toward that etymological interest which is a recurrent feature of his work from here on. Müller's view that mythology "is simply the power exercised by language or thought,"[36] and that thought must wage a constant battle against this mythologizing tendency inherent in language, is compatible with Ruskin's frequent concern to show how far words have wandered and branched from their root meanings, the implication being that the root contains the enduring truth.

Supposing that Ruskin was not in fact influenced by the theoretical matter of Müller's celebrated essay, it is still possible that he was impressed, as many were, by the sympathy of its manner. Therefore, in turning now to Ruskin's own solar mythography it seems appropriate to listen for a moment to Max Müller in 1856 as he recreates the nature of the mythopoeic mind. Remembering, for instance, the themes of "The Lance of Pallas" and its ancillary chapter "The Dark Mirror"—the dark mirror of the living soul, the tragic struggle in the Greek's vision of nature, the defiance by deification, the symbolic rose of the sun's combat—one might see them faintly prefigured in Müller's language. Elucidating a Vedic solar myth, for instance, that of Urvasi and Pururavas, the dawn and the sun, Müller concludes by reminding his reader that

> it was the simple story of nature which inspired the early poet, and held before his mind that *deep mirror* in which he might see reflected the passions of his own soul . . . it is the sympathy with the grief of others which first gives utterance to the poet's grief, and opens the lips of a silent despair. And if his pain was too deep and too sacred, if he could not compare it with the suffering of any other human heart, the ancient poet had still the heart of nature to commune with and in *her silent suffering* he saw a noble likeness of what he felt and suffered within himself.[37]

In the mythopoeic mind, Müller suggested, "the whole of nature was divided into two realms—the one dark, cold, windy and deathlike, the other bright, warm, vernal, and full of life." In mythic nature the conflict of the solar hero with the gloomy coils of his antagonist is symbolic not only of the struggle of physical light and heat with darkness and cold but also of the opposition of everything vital and pure with everything lethal and impure. It would naturally be in the solemn dramas of dawn and sunset (which Müller generally regards as more erotic than tragic) that the primitive poet found the physical correlatives of his deepest aspirations.

> And when the Dawn trembled, and grew pale, and departed, and when the Sun seemed to look for her, and to lose her the more his brilliant eye sought her, an image would rise in his mind, and he would remember his own fate and yet forget it, while telling in measured words the love and loss of the Sun. . . . And when, at the end of a dreary day, the Sun seemed to die away in the far West, still looking for his Eastern bride, and suddenly the heavens opened, and the image of the Dawn rose again, her beauty deepened by a gleaming sadness—would not the poet gaze till the last ray had vanished, and would not the last vanishing ray linger in his heart, and kindle there a hope of another life, where he would find again what he had loved and lost?[38]

Very likely Ruskin, had he read this with his Turner work in mind, would have disagreed with the hope of another life in that sunset, but surely he would have shared the flight and flow of Müller's prose and felt the grip of recognition in his purple assertion of cosmic pathos. He might have agreed with the philologist that "there is much suffering in nature for those who have eyes for silent grief"[39] but not that "it is this tragedy—the tragedy of nature—which is the lifespring of all the tragedy of the ancient world,"[40] because he held that all tragic sense in landscape, as in Turner's, depends upon the reference of nature to the human presence. "Man is the sun of the world; more than the real sun." But he would certainly have noticed Müller's observation that the great solar tragedies had a color of their own: *rose*. The name of the Vedic solar hero, Pururavas, for instance, has in it, we are told, *rava*, from the root *ru*, which means "cry" but "is also applied to colour, in the sense of loud or crying color, i.e. red."[41]

The fullness of meaning he finds, in closing *Modern Painters*, for the mythopoeic rose color he associates with Turner's solar hero makes this shade the climactic symbol of the first phase of Ruskin's work. This is appropriate also in terms of the preeminence of the rose among apocalyptic flower symbols. His interest in the tragic rose of purifying solar struggle is, of course, part of the broader meaning we have seen him attaching to the whole idea of the sun as a spiritual power and to the, in his view, direct and metaphorical connections between physical and spiritual light. From the Alpine poems to *Praeterita*, the rose appears in his work in a tangle of private and traditional associations of immeasurable intensity and complexity, enveloping even the person of his lady-soul, Rose La Touche. Had he read Müller, Ruskin would have met the living Rose and the solarist's mythic one at about the same time. Their conjunction could, in an undemonstrable way, account for the immense significance of the "rose shade" in the two chapters we are about to examine.

3

The first of these chapters, "The Nereid's Guard," centers on Turner's *The Garden of the Hesperides*. Ruskin had already discussed the technique of this picture in his *Notes on the Turner Gallery* (1856), where he found the somber landscape too much oppressed by Poussin's idealism but the guardian dragon a masterpiece of naturalistic grotesque. Now, surprisingly, he takes the painting up again and devotes a chapter to it, subjecting it to a more complete interpretation, as opposed to technical analysis, than he has attempted thus far with any other Turner. This very fact invites us to follow him rather closely.

He begins with a few details that show the tendency of Turner's mind as it reveals itself in his early work. The first verses he ever attached to a picture, we learn, are from *Paradise Lost.*

> Ye mists and exhalations, that now rise
> From hill or steaming lake, dusky or gray,
> Till the sun paints your fleecy skirts with gold,
> In honour to the world's great Author rise.[42]

They are prophetic of his whole career; "at once his mind was set, so far as natural scenes were concerned, on rendering atmospheric effect;—and so far as emotion was to be expressed, how consistently it was melancholy."[43]

Yet the Garden of the Hesperides would seem to be a happy and hopeful subject but for the dragon's presence there, which, as Ruskin reads it, is the focal point of Turner's vision. In the Greek myth, Gaea had presented the golden apples of love and fertility to Zeus and Hera as a wedding gift. These apples grew on a tree located in a garden in a western island paradise under the sunset where they were guarded by the Hesperides and the talking dragon, Ladon. It was one of these apples, inscribed To the Fairest!, that Eris (Discord) in a fit of pique because she had not been invited to the nuptial festivities for Peleus and Thetis, tossed at the feet of Hera, Athena, and Aphrodite. Thus this dangerous fruit became the primordial cause of the Trojan war. Later Hercules, as his eleventh labor, killed the dragon, Ladon, and carried off the Hesperidian apples.

Turner had depicted this "ghastly sentinel" as if emergent from the cliffs themselves in the upper background and with such grotesque precision as to redeem the whole traditionalistic picture for Ruskin when he reviewed it in 1856. But now he regards it as the major picture of Turner's first period and, more important, "our English painter's first great *religious* picture; and exponent of our English faith."[44] For these reasons he will "analyze it completely."[45]

Although it is the dragon in the distance that most (see pp. 411-12) interests him,[46] he begins with an explanation of the Hesperides in their natural and moral meaning. As "natural types" they were simply representative of "the soft western winds and sunshine," winds that favored vegetation; while the dragon, as a physical type, represented the deadly "Sahara wind or Simoom." However, their physical meaning, in both the Greek mind and Turner's, was entirely subordinate to their "moral significance." In this, their principle meaning, the Hesperides were solar figures; they were "not daughters of Atlas [high western mountains], nor connected with the winds of the west, but with its

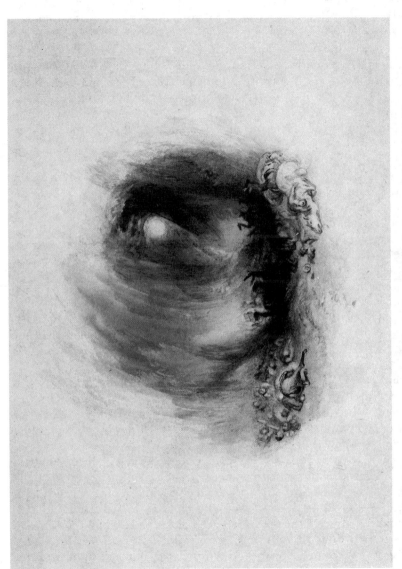

J. M. W. Turner, *The Simoon*. Watercolor, c. 1831. Courtesy of the British Museum.

splendour. They are properly the nymphs of sunset, and are daughters of night."[47] Their many sisters and brothers, children of night, are named by Hesiod. " 'The night begat Doom'; that is to say the doom of unforeseen accident—doom essentially of darkness."[48] They are related also to death, sleep, dreams, censure, sorrow, and other types of our existential boundaries, especially the Fates. The point is that in Hesiod's account these nymphs and their apples are placed "as light in the midst of cloud;—between Censure, and Sorrow,—and the Destinies."[49] Their names, as Ruskin has them, are "Aeglé,—Brightness; Erytheia,— Blushing; Hestia—the (spirit of the) Hearth; Arethusa,—the Ministering."[50]

Into their glowing care the golden apples were given. But this fruit, Ruskin continues, has its own particular meaning. It was given by the earth mother Gaea to Juno, who symbolizes "female power," not the power of love in marriage, but power over the household, for good or evil. Therefore, the apples are the wealth of the earth given to the housewife. But they are earth-wealth watched over by two guardians: as the source of household peace and plenty, life-wealth, they are watched over by the glowing Hesperides; but as deadly wealth, "the source of household sorrow and desolation," they are guarded by the Nereid dragon.[51]

Having explained the Hesperides and their charge, Ruskin proceeds to sketch the lineage of Ladon. The Gorgons, like their sisters the Graiae, were descended from Nereus by way of Phorcys and Ceto. He has already examined their physical meaning ("soft rain-clouds" and "true storm-clouds") earlier in the chapter "The Angel of the Sea." Now this Hesperides dragon is related to them, being the youngest child of Nereus. But "the children of Nereus receive gradually more and more terror and power, as they are later born, till this last of the Nereids unites horror and power at their utmost."[52]

Ruskin devotes considerable space to the meanings of these Nereids as they descend with increasing malevolence of storm power from old Nereus, the calm and gentle sea. We take up with the physical and moral meanings of Phorcys and Ceto, who represent respectively the land-devouring grasp of the sea and its deep places and begat the Graiae and Gorgons, clouds of rain and storm, and, lastly, "The Hesperides' Dragon—Volcanic or earth-storm, associated, in conception, with the Simoom and fiery African winds."[53] And then in a typical piece of quasi-etymological de-allegorization he gives us the moral-spiritual significance of the storm-born monster's lineage.

> Covetousness, or malignity (Phorcys), and Secretness (Ceto), beget, first, the darkening passions, whose hair is always gray; then the stormy and merciless passions, brazen-winged (the Gorgons), of whom the dominant, Medusa, is ice-cold, turning all who look on her to stone. And, lastly, the consuming (poisonous and volcanic) passions—the 'flame-backed dragon,' uniting the powers of poison, and instant destruction.[54]

In books of genesis other than Hesiod's, Ruskin reminds us, giving his image both archetypal authority and resonance, we have heard of a dragon's being busy about an apple tree. Considering that this dragon was, in the Greek mind, descended from the sea, the reader may wish to see a new truth in the biblical verse, "Thou breakest the heads of the dragons in the waters."[55]

Further, in a tradition later than Hesiod, we learn that Ladon was a child of Typhon and Echidna. Typhon represents "volcanic storm and the evil spirit of Tumult"; while Echidna, the adder, descended from Medusa, is "half-maiden, half-serpent" and therefore signifies "the spirit of all the fatallest evil, veiled in gentleness: or, in one word, treachery;—having dominion over many gentle things;—and chiefly over a kiss, given, indeed, in another garden than that of The Hesperides, yet in relation to keeping of treasure also."[56] Again Ruskin attempts to bring Greek and Christian traditions together for greater force.

Echidna, the woman-serpent, or treachery, had a brother in Hesiod's version, the dragon Geryon, who appears in *The Inferno* as the symbol of fraud. And just as Hercules slew Ladon, he also dispatched Geryon in a parallel solar episode.

> We find next that Geryon lived in the island of Erytheia (blushing), only another kind of blushing than that of the Hesperid Erytheia. But it is on, also, a western island, and Geryon kept red oxen in it (said to be near the red setting sun); Hercules kills him, as he does the Hesperian dragon: but in order to be able to reach him, a golden boat is given to Hercules by the Sun, to cross the sea in.[57]

The parallel shows both sea-born monsters guarding wealth in sunset paradises until slain by Hercules as solar hero. They are close enough to enable Ruskin to fuse the two symbols in a sweeping paragraph in which the "complete idea of the Hesperian dragon" archetype emerges from five related accounts.

> The Hesperian dragon . . . is, in fine, the '*Pluto il gran nemico*' of Dante; the demon of all evil passions connected with covetousness; that is to say, essentially of fraud, rage, and gloom. Regarded as the demon of Fraud, he is said to be descended from the viper Echidna, full of deadly cunning, in whirl on whirl; as the demon of consuming Rage from

Phorcys; as the demon of Gloom, from Ceto;—in his watching and melancholy, he is sleepless (compare the Micyllus dialogue of Lucian); breathing whirlwind and fire, he is the destroyer, descended from Typhon as well as Phorcys; having, moreover, with all these, the irresistable strength of his ancestral sea.[58]

Such, then, is the treasure-guarding Nereid in the mythic tradition, as Ruskin interprets it. It is now a question of how truly Turner's apocalyptic imagination in landscape has seen these archetypal features. In his picture, the monster, seen cresting the distant cliff, Ruskin thinks may be three-quarters of a mile in length, while the image itself measures twenty inches. To give his readers some sense of the creature's grotesque power, he provides a reduced copy, etched by himself, in which the dragon, the compressed irregularity of its back-plates emphasized, clasps its cliff in smoky isolation. He entitled his copy *"Quivi Trovammo"* after Dante's *"Quivi Trovammo Pluto il gran nemico."* (The etching was used again in 1871 his *Lectures on Landscape*, delivered that year.) It is "nearly the most wonderful" thing Turner did in his time.

Ruskin must now consider how well this visible myth, his own now as well as Turner's, represents the monster of the Greek mythic tradition he has been interpreting. He is really, of course, comparing his impressions of one with his impressions of the other; however, we are not concerned with the validity of his interpretation but with the use of it, that is, with the way it is incorporated into the larger body of his thought. Not surprisingly, then, he finds that, though Turner may not have known much of the Hesperid tradition, he "knew who the Dragon was," and his image fits the myths "down to the minutest details."

There is, first, the Dragon's descent from Medusa and Typhon, indicated in the serpent-clouds floating from its head (compare my sketch of the Medusa-cloud . . .); then note the grovelling and ponderous body, ending in a serpent, of which we do not see the end. He drags the weight of it forward by his claws, not being able to lift himself from the ground ("Mammon, the least erected spirit that fell"); then the grip of the claws themselves as if they would clutch (rather than tear) the rock itself into pieces; but chiefly, the designing of the body. Remember, one of the essential characters of the creature, as descended from Medusa, is its coldness and petrifying power; this, in the demon of covetousness, must exist to the utmost; breathing fire, he is yet himself of ice. Now, if I were merely to draw this dragon, as white, instead of dark, and take his claws away, his body would become a representation of a great glacier . . . Breaking over a rocky brow so like the truth . . . this dragon's shoulders would be, if they were thrown out in light; there being only this difference, that they have the form, but not the fragility of the ice; they are at once ice and iron.[59]

(Plate IV) J. M. W. Turner. *Apollo and Python*. Courtesy of the Tate Gallery, London.

(Plate III) J. M. W. Turner. *Ulysses Deriding Polyphemus—Homer's Odyssey.* Reproduced by courtesy of the Trustees, the National Gallery, London.